MODERN HUMANITIES RESEARCH ASSOCIATION

TEXTS AND DISSERTATIONS
(formerly Dissertation Series)

VOLUME 15

Editor
D. J. A. ROSS
(French)

Jean Brisebarre: 'Li Restor du Paon'

JEAN BRISEBARRE:

'LI RESTOR DU PAON'

ENID DONKIN

LONDON
THE MODERN HUMANITIES RESEARCH ASSOCIATION
1980

Published by

The Modern Humanities Research Association

Honorary Treasurer, MHRA

KING'S COLLEGE, STRAND
LONDON WC2R 2LS
ENGLAND

ISBN 0 900547 66 9

Printed in England by
W. S. MANEY & SON LIMITED
HUDSON ROAD LEEDS

CONTENTS

ABBREVIATIONS

Works of reference

Du Cange	*Glossarium mediae et infimae latinitatis*
Foulet	L. Foulet, *Petite syntaxe de l'ancien français*
Gf.	F. Godefroy, *Dictionnaire de l'ancienne langue française*
Gossen	C. T. Gossen, *Petite grammaire de l'ancien picard*
H.L.F.	A. Thomas, *Histoire littéraire de la France*
La Curne	La Curne de Sainte-Palaye, *Dictionnaire de l'ancien langage français*
Le Roux de Lincy	*Le Livre des proverbes français et recherches historiques*
Morawski or Mor. Diz	J. Morawski, *Les Diz et proverbes des sages*
Morawski or Mor. Prov.	J. Morawski, *Proverbes français antérieurs au XVe siècle*
Nyrop	K. R. Nyrop, *Grammaire historique de la langue française*
Pat. Lat.	J. P. Migne, *Patrologia Latina*
Pope	M. K. Pope, *From Latin to Modern French*
T−L.	Tobler-Lommatsch, *Altfranzösisches Wörterbuch*
von Wartburg	*Französisches Etymologisches Wörterbuch*

Literary Texts

Erec	*Erec et Enide*, Chrestien de Troyes
Fuerre	*Le Roman du Fuerre de Gadres*, Branch II of the *Roman d'Alexandre*
M.F.R.A.	*The Medieval French 'Roman d'Alexandre'*, general title of the Princeton edition of the *Roman*
Parfait	*Le Parfait du Paon*, Jehan de le Mote
Prise	*La Prise de Defur*
RAlix	The *Roman d'Alexandre* of Alexandre de Paris published in *M.F.R.A.*, Vol. II
Restor	*Li Restor du Paon*, J [ehan] Brisebare
Roman	*The Roman d'Alexandre*
Tristran	*The Romance of Tristran*, Beroul
Venjance	*La Venjance Alixandre*, Jehan le Nevelon
Voeux	*Les Voeux du Paon*, Jacques de Longuyon
Vulgate	*Biblia Sacra Vulgatae Editionis*

INTRODUCTION

The 'Roman d'Alexandre'

The *Restor du Paon* was composed as a supplement to the *Voeux du Paon* which itself is a supplement to the *Roman d'Alexandre*. The complex history of the development of the *Roman*, from the Alexander fragment of Alberic written at the beginning of the twelfth century to the vulgate version compiled and expanded by Alexandre de Paris about 1185, does not concern us here. An account of this development and of the sources of the Alexander material used by medieval writers is given by G. Cary in his survey of the posthumous reputation of Alexander the Great.[1] A brief history of the *Roman* is also given by D. J. A. Ross in his guide to medieval illustrated Alexander literature.[2] The history of the various components of the version of Alexandre de Paris is discussed in the introduction to volume II of the edition of the *Roman* published by a group of scholars at Princeton under the general title *The Medieval French 'Roman d'Alexandre'*.[3]

The version of Alexandre de Paris consists of four branches of which the following are the principal incidents:

Branch I   Youth and education of Alexander. His early conquests including the defeat of Nicholas. Campaign against Darius. Siege of Tyre.

Branch II   Siege and capture of Tyre with interpolated 'Foraging of Gadres'. Defeat of Darius at the Pres de Paile.

Branch III   Death of Darius. Alexander's descent into the sea. First and second defeats of Porus. Alexander and Queen Candace. His ascent into the air. Capture of Babylon. Submission of the Amazons. Treacherous plot of Antipater and Divinus Pater.

Branch IV   Alexander poisoned. Division of his empire. Laments of his peers and of Roxana.

The *Roman* was gradually augmented by the following sequels and interpolations, chiefly works of fiction:

i.   Two poems on the vengeance enacted upon Alexander's murderers, written shortly after the compilation of the Alexandre de Paris poem: *La Venjance Alixandre* by Jean le Nevelon[4] and *Le Vengement Alixandre* by Gui de Cambrai, written before 1191.[5]

ii.   The *Prise de Defur*. This is the Duc Melcis episode interpolated into the body of the poem, composed c.1250 by a Picard.[6]

iii.   The *Voyage au Paradis terrestre*, a thirteenth century French version of the *Iter ad Paradisum*, a Latin prose version dated after 1100 of Alexander's journey up the Ganges in search of the Earthly Paradise.[7]

iv.   The *Voeux du Paon* by Jacques de Longuyon c.1312.[8]

v.   The *Restor du Paon* by Jean Brisebare, before 1338.[9]

vi.   The *Parfait du Paon* by Jean de le Mote, 1340.[10]

The Peacock Cycle

The last three poems form the Peacock Cycle. The *Voeux du Paon*, although an independent poem, has its starting point in the *Roman*. It describes further adventures of Alexander and his followers when they are proceeding to Babylon after the capture of Defur narrated in the *Prise de Defur*. Alexander goes to the aid of Cassamus du Larris whose two nephews Gadifer and Betis and his niece Fesonas are being besieged in Epheson by King Clarus of India who intends to dispossess them and marry Fesonas. During a truce ceremonial vows are made over the body of a peacock by nine knights and three ladies. The knights' vows to perform feats of valour are fulfilled in the ensuing battle and two of the ladies subsequently marry to implement their own vows. The *Voeux* ends with a triple marriage ceremony and finally Alexander prepares once more to depart for Babylon.

Just as the *Voeux* interrupts the action of the *Prise de Defur* so does the *Restor* that of the *Voeux*. The scene is Epheson after the siege and Alexander with his followers are assembled for the festivities and marriages. Brisebare claims that Edea's vow, to restore the peacock in gold, and two marriages were omitted. He describes these and also inserts an account of the early life of Emenidus. There follows a lengthy debate on the respective merits of the twelve vows and finally the poem joins the *Voeux* again. After more feasting Alexander and his knights depart for Babylon.

The final poem in the cycle, the *Parfait du Paon*, forms an addition and conclusion to the series for the *Voeux* and the *Restor* are, according to its author Jean de le Mote, incomplete:

> *Parfait* 14   Ainsi firent cil doy mouvement et moillon
> Mes il en ont lessié le plus meillor coron.

The *Parfait* begins where the *Voeux* and the *Restor* end, that is with Alexander's departure for Babylon. After journeying six days from Epheson he arrives at Melide the city of Melidus, brother of the Clarvus who was killed at the siege of Epheson. Melidus and his son Buciforas have sworn to avenge Clarvus and Alexander declares that he will take the city. Porrus, Marcien and the Baudrain are sent for from their several lands and on the way they pick up Gadifer and Betis from Epheson. They all agree to fight against Alexander again except Gadifer with the result that he and his brother Betis are on opposite sides, but they intend to avoid each other in the battle. Gadifer has brought Edea's golden peacock with him, and as Alexander and his knights are being entertained by their enemy Melidus within the city even more outrageous vows are made. In the ensuing battle there are few survivors: the five bridegrooms from the *Voeux* and the *Restor* are killed and their brides die of grief. Melidus and Buciforas are also killed and Deromadaire, one of Melidus's four daughters, commits suicide. After the carnage the dead are buried and Alexander regrets his vow. He remains fifteen days at Melide and marries off his three remaining knights, Emenidus, Tholomer and Dan Clin, who had been held as prisoners during the fighting, to the three surviving daughters of Melidus. He then departs for Babylon.

The *Parfait* is clearly an imitation of the *Voeux* and the *Restor* but it deservedly never became as popular as the earlier works. Perhaps the potential audience had no taste for such wholesale slaughter.

NOTES

1. G. Cary, *The Mediaeval Alexander* (Cambridge, 1956), pp. 9-74.
2. D. J. A. Ross, *Alexander Historiatus*, Warburg Institute, (London, 1963), pp. 9-12.
3. The following volumes have already been published at Princeton in the Elliott Monographs series:
    Vol. I   M. S. La Du *Text of the Arsenal and Venice Versions* E. M. 36 (1937).
    Vol. II   E. C. Armstrong, D. L. Buffum, B. Edwards, L. F. H. Lowe, *Version of Alexandre de Paris: Text,* E. M. 37 (1937).
    Vol. III   A. Foulet, *Version of Alexandre de Paris: Variants and Notes to Branch I,* E. M. 38 (1942).
    Vol. IV   E. C. Armstrong and A. Foulet, *Le Roman du Fuerre de Gadres. Texte d'Eustache,* E. M. 39 (1942).
    Vol. V   F. B. Agard, *Version of Alexandre de Paris. Variants and Notes to Branch II,* E. M. 40 (1942).
    Vol. VI   A. Foulet, *Version of Alexandre de Paris. Notes and Variants to Branch III,* E. M. 42, (1976).
    Vol. VII   A. Foulet and B. Edwards, *Version of Alexandre de Paris. Variants and Notes to Branch IV,* E. M. 41, (1955).
4. E. B. Ham, *Jehan le Nevelon: La Venjance Alixandre,* E. M. 27, (Princeton, 1931).
5. B. Edwards, *Gui de Cambrai: Le Vengement Alixandre,* E. M. 23, (Princeton, 1928).
6. Lawton P. G. Peckham and Milan S. La Du, *La Prise de Defur and Le Voyage d'Alexandre au Paradis terrestre,* E. M. 35, (Princeton, 1935), pp. 1-73.
7. Ibid. pp. 73-90.
8. a.   R. L. Graeme Ritchie in *The Buik of Alexander,* Scottish Text Society, New Series, 4 vols. (Edinburgh and London, 1921-29).
    b.   Brother Camillus Casey, O. S. F. '*Les Voeux du Paon* by Jacques de Longuyon. An edition of the mss. of the P redaction' (unpublished Ph. D. dissertation, University of Columbia, 1956).
9. R. J. Carey, *Jean le Court dit Brisebare. Le Restor du Paon* (Geneva, 1966).
10. a. V. Hands, '*Le Parfait du Paon.* A fourteenth century poem by Jehan de le Mote' (unpublished Ph. D. thesis, University of London, 1957).
    b.   R. J. Carey, *Le Parfait du Paon,* Studies in Language and Literature, 118, (University of North Carolina, 1972).

DATE AND AUTHOR

Date

The *Restor du Paon* was composed before 1338, the date of P the earliest known manuscript containing it. The date occurs in the second of five colophons (fo. 208r) which reads:

> Chi define li romans du boin roi Alixandre.
> Et les Veus du Pavon. Les accomplissemens.
> Le Restor du Pavon. et le pris. qui fu
> parescript le .xviiie. jor de decembre l'an M.CCC.XXXVIII.

It must post-date the *Voeux du Paon* to which it is a supplement but a precise date for that work has not been established. According to a colophon in W the *Voeux* was composed at the command of Thibaud de Bar, Bishop of Liège, who was killed at Rome on May 29th 1312, so that Jacques de Longuyon must have written it in or before that year if we are to believe W. At any rate the work was in being in 1313 as a copy of it was bought in that year from Thomas de Maubeuge, a Paris bookseller, for Mahaut Comtesse d'Artois.[1]

Antoine Thomas considered that the *Restor* was a work of Brisebare's youth but gives no evidence to support this view (*H.L.F.* xxxvi, 38). The only dated work we have is his *Escole de Foy* (B.N.ms.fr.576) which is preceded by the words, 'Apres s'ensieut l'escole de foy que fist J. Brisebare, L'an M.CCC.XXVII' (fol.93r.col.I), but whether the *Restor* preceded or followed this work is a matter of conjecture. Brisebare was well enough known as a rhymester as early as 1319, as he was employed in that year to provide rhymes for Queen Jeanne de Bourgogne, but whether his fame rested on the *Restor* or on other works we cannot say. We know that he wrote his *Tresor Nostre Dame:*

> Pour venir de pechié au cor
> Et pour des biens faire restor
> Que j'ay perdus par ma folie.
> (B.N.ms.fr.576,fo.114r).

This may be a mere introductory formula, but if we accept that the work was indeed written to atone for a misspent youth one would expect his early work to reflect that youthful way of life. The internal evidence of the *Restor* however suggests only an experienced, older, pious man. The arguments expressed in Part II are reasoned, even ponderous. In Part I moral examples are introduced, for example

David I 319-23 and the woman of Canaan I 324-34; prayers are said for the dead I 96-97 and the 'Te Deum laudamus' is sung II 1281. Indeed the whole of the Emenidus episode, with its theme of redemption after turning from a life of sin, may have attracted an author whose own life had perhaps taken such a turn. He himself could then have taken comfort from the words:

> I 311   Car tout cil qui folie font par temptatïon
> Ne sont pas en la fin mis a perditïon
> Ains les amende diex et si lor fait pardon,
> Et ou plus a de visce et de corruptïon
> La met diex plus de grace et de devotïon.

Also I 337-38, 'Car li maus ne fait tant, ne la confusïon Que li perseverers en la maleïchon'. But whether or not Brisebare connected his own case consciously or sub-consciously with that of Emenidus these lines reflect the attitude of the believer, even of the zealous convert, rather than that of the young man who is still enjoying his 'folie'. Further, there is an interesting portrait of the 'roi des menestreus' in the *Restor* (II 126-33). This man is depicted as experienced, old, white-bearded and pale-faced and the daily activities of his profession are described with some insight. We cannot be sure that this is a self-portrait but it certainly shows some inside knowledge of the way of life of the elderly, privileged fool. I incline to the view that the *Restor* was composed late rather than early, perhaps c.1330, but because of the lack of hard evidence we must continue to date it before 1338 and after the composition of the *Voeux*.

The Author

Brisebare or le Court? The Author is described as Jean le Court dit Brisebare in *H.L.F.* xxxvi 35-66, and this name has been accepted without comment by R. J. Carey in his edition of the *Restor* (see p. 3 note 9).

The name Brisebare occurs as a signature in three works:

1. *Le Tresor Nostre Dame* (B.N. ms. fr.576, fo.114r.)

> 4   Jou Brisebare aÿ tres or
> Mis paine a rimer le tresor
> Le benoite vierge Marie.

2. *Le Dit de l'Evesque et de Droit* (Copenhagen, ms. ancien fonds 2061, fols. 154-61, last five lines):

> Enfin quant vint au departir
> Me connut que songiet l'avoit
> Brisebare, et songiet soit.
> Saciés que plus avant n'en sai
> Pour tant le renc que l'akatai.

3. *Li Restor du Paon*

> I 10   Mais je, qui només sui Brisebare a le fois,
> L'i vuel metre et enter anchois que past li mois.

The words 'a le fois' in line I 10 suggest that the name may not be his family name, but it is certainly the one he uses when he signs his work.

The author of the *Restor* is called Brisebare in the *Parfait* lines 12-13: 'Et Brisebarre aprés, qui Diex face pardon, Y enta le Restor par sa discretion'.

The name also occurs in contemporary and later medieval documents:

1. In a record for payment for supplying verses for Queen Jeanne de Bourgogne on the occasion of the laying of the foundation stone of the chapel of the Hôpital Saint-Jacques, rue St.-Denis, 18 February 1319: 'A Brisebarre, pour trouver les rimes et les dis de la roine et de plusieurs autres xxvis. viiid.[2]

2. In the *Regles de la Seconde Rettorique* composed between 1411 and 1432 (*H.L.F.* xxxvi, 35): 'Ou temps du dit Machault fut Brisebarre de Douay qui fist le livre de *l'Escolle de Foy* et *le Tresor Nostre Dame*'.

Two manuscripts containing his works name the author as Brisebare:

1. B.N.ms.fr.576 contains two poems by Brisebare, *l'Escole de Foy* and *le Tresor Nostre Dame* and the relevant lines are on fo.93r.col.I, quoted above, p. 4, and fo.113v. last line: 'Chi aprés s'ensiut le Tresor Nostre Dame que fist le dit Brisebare'.

2. Charleville ms.100. Three poems have the heading, fo. 121v., read by A. Salmon as 'Brisebarre le Court a Douay l'an V'.[3]

The name Brisebare/-barre was therefore the name the author used himself in his signed works; it was the name used by his contemporaries and near contemporaries; he was even paid under that name. The adoption now of the name le Court can only be justified if there is incontestable evidence in its favour. The opposite is the case. The source of the name seems to be Salmon's reading of the Charleville manuscript but some doubt about this was expressed by G. Paris in a review of Salmon's article. He comments:

En tête de ces pièces M. Salmon a lu: Brisebarre le Court a Douay l'an V, et il appelle en conséquence le poète Jean Brisebarre le Court; mais il faudrait *de Douai* et en outre l'an V ne se comprend pas; je suppose qu'il y a dans le ms. *les fist* (ou *le fist, la fist*) a Douay. L'an V peut désigner, comme le pense M.S., l'an 1355, bien que la désignation soit singulière. (Brisebarre a du composer vers 1330 le *Restor du Paon*).[4]

Although, as G. Paris says, *de Douai* would be preferable, the reading is in fact very clearly *a Douay*; nor do the desired words *les fist* (or *le fist* or *la fist*) occur. In addition there is in my view considerable doubt about the reading *le Court*. The final letter is not a t and a possible reading is *le couil* or *le conil*. Or it may be that the writing conceals an unidentifiable abbreviation.

The evidence for Brisebare is overwhelming and that for le Court extremely tenuous and I propose therefore to call the author of the *Restor* Brisebare/-barre.

Brisebare's Life and Works

About this man who called himself Brisebare little further is known. Jean de le Mote (*Parfait* 1.12) indicates by the formula 'qui Diex face pardon' that Brisebare was dead at that time, and fortunately the *Parfait* is dated by its author (1.3915): 'L'an mil .iii.c. xl. volt ceste branche faire'. Brisebare therefore must have died in or before 1340 and the *Restor* was written before 1338, the date of ms.P. One other work is dated, the *Escole de Foy*, 1327. The date on the Charleville ms.100 gives rise to speculation. The words 'l'an V' in the heading (fo.121v.) were interpreted by A. Salmon as meaning 1355, presumably because the manuscript itself was copied in 1357. This cannot refer to Brisebare who died before 1340. As we have seen from his review G. Paris also doubted this interpretation. If 'l'an V' refers to any date in the fourteenth century, the only other unambiguous date from the point of view of a person writing in in 1357 is 1305. The poems, if they are Brisebare's, would therefore be early works.

We know that Brisebare was sufficiently well-esteemed by 1319 to be employed as a composer of verses by the court of France. The queen was on that occasion accompanied by her mother Mahault, Countess of Artois and Burgundy and the entrance to the chapel was embellished with a statue of Saint Jacques on each side of which were sculpted portraits of the queen and of the principal nobles who had contributed to its construction. Each portrait had an inscription in verse and it was for composing some of these that Brisebare was employed. The chapel of Saint-Jacques-l'Hospitalier stood at the corner of the rue Saint-Jacques-l'Hôpital and of the rue du Cygne but was demolished in the disturbances of 1808 and nothing remains of the portraits or of their accompanying verses.

One other indication of the period of Brisebare's working life is given in the *Regles de la Seconde Rettorique* quoted above (p. 6). '*Ou temps du dit Machault fut Brisebarre de Douay*'. Guillaume de Machault lived from c.1300 to c.1375 and his works are attested from 1324, but this is too long a period to give a precise floruit for Brisebare.

This same passage continues by listing Brisebare's works and commenting on them and their author as follows:

(Brisebarre . . .) qui fist le livre de *l'Escolle de Foy* et le *Tresor Nostre Dame*, et se fist le serventoys de

> S'Amours n'estoit plus poissant que Nature
> No foy seroit legiere a condempner,

et plusieurs autres livres, qui bien font a recommander et a prisier, car ses fais
furent bons, et n'estoit point clers, ne ne savoit lire n'escripre.

The last words of this statement are tantalizingly laconic. It is possible that '*n'estoit
point clers*' merely means that Brisebare was not in holy orders but it is difficult to
accept that he could neither read nor write. Even the alternative *vespere* for
'*n'escripre*' suggested by A. Thomas (H.L.F. xxxvi, 35) is no easier to accept.
Brisebare's works show such a wide knowledge of the Scriptures and of contemporary
theology and law that it seems highly probable that he had at least some schooling.
In addition, his use of syntax is in its subtlety that of a literate scholar rather than
that of an unlettered rustic. Furthermore, in *l'Escole de Foy* he shows some knowledge of school methods, from the teaching of the alphabet to little children
through games to the study of grammar and logic by advanced students.

It seems then that Brisebare could both read and write and I think one must
treat with scepticism the statement in the *Regles de la Seconde Rettorique*,
especially as the *Regles* were composed at least seventy and possibly a hundred
years after his death.

We have already noted Brisebare's method of making a game out of learning to
interest very young children. There is further evidence that he had some knowledge
of the psychology of children in *l'Escole de Foy* for he is aware of the importance
of imagination in their play. The stick the little boy bestrides is his horse and the
dolls the little girl fashions from a few rags are her children:

fo.100r,col.1

> On voit un petit valeton
> Lonc temps chevauchier .i. baston
> Et dist que c'est ses palefrois.
> Une fillette revoit on
> De drapieus faire .i. enfanchon
> Et quant elle en a .ii. ou troys
> Li uns est Conte de Valoys
> A son dit, et li autres roys
> Et li tiers dame de Digon.
> Tant que d'enfance tient les ploys
> Plus grant conte feroit d'un poys
> Que de le conte d'Alenchon.

This is accurate observation but we cannot tell whether he gained his insight from
observing his own children or those of a relative or, perhaps more likely, those of
an employer. It may even have been for such children that he devised his puzzle
method of teaching the alphabet.

Most of Brisebare's literary work is that of a pious man particularly the *Escole
de Foy* and the *Tresor Nostre Dame*. The former, being an attempt at proselytizing,
is by its nature a series of presentations of argument and counter-argument which
allow Brisebare to indulge an apparent penchant for debate which is also evident in
other works, for example in Part II of the *Restor* and in the *Dit de l'evesque et de*

Droit. The latter poem, in B.N.ms.fr.nouv.acq.10056, fols.1-29, as well as in the Copenhagen manuscript (anc. fonds 2061) fols.154-61, is a long work (3740 lines) in octosyllabic rhymed couplets and is an allegory satirizing the clergy and the law. It may be the work of a young man shocked at the behaviour of some of the clergy or that of a disillusioned older man. A reference to the condemnation of the Templars (fo. 13r.col.II, lines 14-21 in the Paris manuscript) places it after the date of the suppression of the Order by Pope Clement V in 1312. The motive for the work may have been to criticize the misconduct of the clergy and to bring about some amendment of morals, but it probably seemed advisable to the author to present it in the form of a dream as we learn from the last five lines quoted above (p. 5). That is the ending in the Copenhagen manuscript. The Paris manuscript omits the name Brisebare, possibly a further precaution against unpleasant consequences. In the Paris ms. the antepenultimate line reads: 'S'il me dist voires, songes soit'.

The *Tresor Nostre Dame* which follows the *Escole de Foy* in B.N.ms.fr.576 (*Escole* fols.93-113v., *Tresor* fols.113v.-120v.) is a long poem in praise of the Virgin Mary. It is in fact a life of Jesus from the Annunciation and birth to the Crucifixion and shows great familiarity with the Gospels as well as with the Old Testament prophecies. Both poems have the same form, stanzas of twelve octosyllabic lines with the rhyme system aabaabbbabba. The *Escole* has 261 stanzas, the *Tresor* 87.

Four shorter poems in honour of the Virgin complete the number of Brisebare's pious works which have survived. They are the 'Serventois de Nostre Dame' in B.N.ms.fr.1543 fo.99r. and the three poems in the Charleville ms.100,fols.121r-122r. The 'Serventois de Nostre Dame' is unpublished. The other three poems, published by A. Salmon, op.cit.p.213, are imitations of love poems whose first line has been preserved. As G. Paris says, loc.cit.p.104, 'Ils sont écrits avec simplicité et non sans une certaine grace'.

NOTES

1. A. Thomas, *Histoire littéraire de la France* (Paris, 1927), XXXVI, 3.
2. H. L. Bordier and L. Brièle, *Les Archives hospitalières de Paris* (Paris, 1877), Part II, p. 67.
3. *Mélanges de Philologie romane dédiés à Carl Wahlund* (Mâcon, 1896), p. 213.
4. G. Paris, 'Trois poèmes de Jean Brisebare le Court, de Douai', *Romania*, 26 (1896), 104-05.

THE MANUSCRIPTS

N1

London, B. L. Additional 16888. Parchment, mid C.14. 240 x 160mm. 161 folios.
28-30 lines to a page. A-N8; O4, P-R8, S9, T-U8, X4.
Two miniatures, 1r. and 142r. Each work begins with an illuminated initial and
fo.1r. has a border of ivy leaves, green and gold, with six medallions, red, green and
gold. The remaining initials are blue or red, not alternating regularly and not always
at the beginning of a laisse.

Contents: *Voeux*   1r.-141r.
            Restor   142r.-161vo.
Bound yellow calf, gilt tooling. Title *Roman du Paon* on spine.

1r. The rubric in red: 'C'est li livres des veus du pavon et des acomplissemens
comment chascuns voua et acompli'.

Incipit: Aprés ce qu'Alixandre ot Dedefur conquis
                    Et a force d'espee occis le roy Melchis

141r. Explicit: Car puis que li vrais diex le siecle commensa
                    Tel prince ne naqui ne jamés ne naitra.
                    Explicit des vouz du paon.

142r. Incipit: Quant Porrus li yndois et tuit si compaignon
                    Orrent par reverance en grant devocion.

161vo. Explicit: Et comme Amenidus sa niece maria
                    A jone Godiffer quant a luy s'acorda
                    Explicit du paon bien ait qui le lira.

N2

Paris, B.N. ms.fr.1554. Parchment, C.14.245 x 165 mm. 160 folios. 30 lines to a
page. A-U8.
No miniatures. Initials alternately blue and red.
Contents: *Voeux*   2r.-139r.
            Restor   139vo.-160vo.

Bound yellow calf, gilt and blind tooling. On the spine: *Les Veus dou Paon. Le Mariage des Puceles*.

2r. In red, 'Ci commencent les veus dou paon et les accomplissemens et le mariage des puceles et le restor dou paon'. In brown ink, written small, 'C'est une partie du *Roman d'Alixandre*'.

Incipit:

> Aprés ce qu'Alixandres ot Dedefur conquis
> Et a force d'espee occis le duc Melchis.

139r. Explicit:

> Car puis que li vrais diex le siecle commença
> Tel princes ne nasqui ne jamais ne nestra.
> Ci fenist ma matiere que ci plus n'en i a,
> Bien ait qui l'a ouie et qui escripte l'a.
> Expliciunt les veus du paon.

139vo. Rubric in red: 'Ci coumence le restour dou paon. Coument Edeas le restoura de fin or'.

Incipit:

> Quant Porus li yndois et tout si compaignon
> Orent par reverence en grant devocion.

160vo. Explicit:

> Et com Emenidus sa niece maria
> Au jene Gaudifer quant a luy s'acorda
> Explicit du paon bien ait que le lira.

N5

Paris, B.N.ms.fr.25521. Parchment, C.14. 205 x 135mm. 172 folios. 28 lines to a page. A-X8Y4.
Six miniatures, five in the *Voeux* 1r.,29vo.,49vo.,70r.,124r., and one in the *Restor*, 151r. Initials red or blue, not always alternating.
Contents: *Voeux*   1r.-151r.
           Restor   151r.-172vo.
Bound red morocco, gilt tooling. On the spine: '*Roman d'Alexandre*. MSS du 14. siecle. Avec Miniat. en vers sur velin'.

1r. Incipit:

> Aprés ce qu'Alixandre ot Dedefur conquis
> Et a force d'espee occis le duc Melchis.

151r. Explicit:

> Car puis que li vrai diex le siecle commença
> Tel prince ne nasqui ne jamés ne nestra.
> Explicit du paon les veuz qu'on y voua.

151r. Incipit (beneath a miniature):

> Quant Porrus li yndois et tuit si compaignon
> Orent par reverence en grant devocion.

172vo. Explicit:

> Et Emenidus sa niece maria
> Au jone Gadifer quant a lui s'acorda.
> Explicit le restor du paon.

N6

Paris, B.N.ms.fr.24386. Parchment, C.14. 268 x 180mm. 183 folios. 30 lines to a page. A-R8S4T-Z8a4 (wanting fourth leaf).

Five miniatures, three in the *Voeux* 1r., 66r.,85r., and two in the *Restor* 141r., 164r. Each miniature is accompanied by an illuminated initial, the remaining initials being alternately blue and red.

Contents: *Voeux*   1r.-140r.
            Restor   141r.-183vo.

Bound red morocco, gilt tooling. On the spine: *Li veu du Paon et li mariage*.

1r. Incipit:

> Aprés ce qu'Alixandre ot Dedefur conquis
> Et a force d'espee ocist le duc Melchis.

140r. Explicit:

> Chascun ot bon cheval viste et remuant
> En la cite d'Ephezon furent tout repairant.
> Explicit les veux du paon et l'acomplissement
> et les mariaiges et le restor.

141r. Incipit (beneath a miniature):

> Seigneur, prince et baron et dames et bourgois,
> On dit en un proverbe et si l'acorde drois.

164r. (Explicit (Part I):

> Aiment miex lor avoir a tout le reprovier.
> Que la grasce des bons qui mout puet avancier.

Below this is a miniature showing the peacock on a silver pillar flanked by three courtiers on the left and three ladies on the right. Beneath it, at the foot of the page, the rubric in red, 'Ci commence le restor dou paon'.

164vo. Incipit (Part II):

> Quant Porus li yndois et tout si compaignon
> Eurent par reverence en grant devotion.

183vo. Explicit:

> Et com Aimeniduz sa niece maria
> A jone Gadifer quant a lui s'acorda.
> Explicit du poon bien ait qui lez lira.

In another hand, 'Explicit du paon bien ait qui sesy escrist a. Explicit'.

O

Paris, B.N. ms.fr.1375. Paper, C.15. 285 x 200mm. 554 folios. Single columns of 22-26 lines, from folio 150 onwards written as prose. A-C20D19E-G20H22I-K18 L16M14N-Y16Z10a16b18c-k12l10m18(wanting 18th leaf).

No miniatures. The beginning of each laisse is indicated by a large initial in the same black ink as the text. The beginning of a new branch has a rubric.

Contents: *Roman d'Alexandre*   1r.-314r.
              Prise de Defur   314r.-343r.
              Roman (completed)   343r.-393r.
              Venjance Alixandre   393vo.-431vo.
              Voeux   432r.-537vo.
              Restor   538r.-554vo.

Bound brown calf. Gilt tooling on spine and the title *Li Romans D'Alexandre* and the initials of Louis Philippe.

1r. Incipit:
> La vie d'Alixandre ainsi que l'ay trouvee
> En pluseurs lieux escripte et de bouche comptee.

314r. Explicit (*Roman* Br. III):
> Alixandre le roy ou tout monde apent
> Devoit porter couronne lendemain haultement.

314r. Incipit (*Prise*):
> Alixandre chevauche a la loy d'emperour
> Amazonne a conquise, Ynde et terre majour.

343r. Explicit:
> Tant qu'on dit qu'ilz pecherent tous deux en une nasse,
> Au xve. jour vint cil qui derrier ne lasse.

343r. *Roman* continues:
> Dous en ot maint enfin qui mestier eut d'entraict,
> Sejourna a grant aise sans remposne et sens lait.

393r. Explicit:
> Le roy qui son royaulme vieult a droit gouverner
> Oncques puis qu'il fu mors nulluy ne vit son per.

393vo. Incipit (*Venjance*):
> Seigneurs or faites paix ung petit m'entendez.

431r. Explicit:
> Tous les hommes demeurent de Alior leur sire
> Le tiennent pour seignour le meillour et le pire
> Autre chose n'en scay ne vous en scay plus dire.
>   Explicit la vengeance Alixandre.

431vo.
> Cy finist le livre Alixandre

> Lequel fist maint Royaulme rendre
> Par sa saige (?) et puissance
> Et du monde eut obeissance
> Par trois jours comme puis comprendre
> chevalier . . . (?).

432r. Incipit:
> Aprés ce qu'Alixandre ot desci conquis
> Et a force d'espee occis le duc Melcis.

537vo. Explicit:
> Car depuis que dieu le siecle commança
> Tel prince ne naquit ne jamés ne naistra.
> Si finist le Veuz du paon.

538r. Incipit (beneath the rubric, 'Cy commance l'estor du paon):
> Quant Porus le yndois et tout ses compaignon
> Orent par reverence et en grant devotion.

554vo. Explicit:
> Et comme Emenidus sa niepce maria
> Au jeune Gadifer quant a luy s'acorda.
> Explicit du paon, bien ait qui le lira.

P

Oxford, Bodleian Library, Bodley 264. Parchment. 1338, 418 x 290mm. 274 folios. To folio 208 in double columns of 45 lines. We are concerned here with the French *Roman d'Alixandre* and its additions contained in the first 208 leaves.

This is a beautiful and luxurious manuscript with numerous miniatures and marginal pictures illustrating the text, and illuminated initials. It has been fully described by M. R. James in the introduction to the collotype facsimile published at Oxford in 1933. He notes the loss of four leaves. These were cut out before the volume was foliated, which he thinks may have been in the seventeenth-century. In each case the excised leaf preceded the beginning of a new branch and I think it probable that they contained, or were intended to contain, a full-page picture marking the new branch. They preceded folios 1, 110, 135 and 175 namely the beginning of the *Roman*, of both parts of the *Voeux* and of Part II of the *Restor*. Full-page pictures do occur at the beginning of the *Prise*, 101vo., the *Restor*, 164vo., the *Roman* Br.IV,188vo. and the *Venjance*, 196vo.

Two full-page pictures were added in the fifteenth century. The first, folio 1, showing Nectanebus in his palace, has been described in an article by D. J. A. Ross who considers it to be a confused and altered derivative of a frontispiece found in certain manuscripts of the Old French Prose Alexander.[1] The second, folio 2, depicts scenes from Alexander's life.

Contents: *Roman d'Alixandre*   3r.-100vo.
           Prise de Defur (in part) 101vo-109vo.

Voeux	110r.-163vo.
Restor	164vo.-182vo.
Prise (completed)	182vo.-185r.
Roman (completed)	185r.-195vo.
Venjance	196vo.-208r.

Two other works are bound in at the end of the volume:

i. *The Alliterative Romance of Alexander*, an extract of 1139 lines in English alliterative verse describing Alexander's communication with the Brahmans, 209-215vo.

ii. *Li Livres du graunt Caam*, author Marco Polo, written C.15, 218-271vo.

Five colophons follow the French Alexander poems, 208r.:

1. Chi definent le Romans d'Alixandre, le veu du pavon—les accomplissemens, li Restors et le pris. Explicit expliceat ludere scriptor eat.

2. Chi define li romans du boin roi Alixandre. Et les veus du pavon. Les acomplissemens. Le Restor du Pavon — et le pris — qui fu parescript le .xviiie. jor de decembre l'an M.CCC.XXXVIII.

3. Explicit iste liber—Scriptor sit crimine liber Xpristus scriptorem custodiat ac det honorem.

4. (In gold letters) Che livre fu perfais de le enluminure au .xviiie. jour d'Avryl— Per Jehan de Grise. L'an de grace .M.CCC.XLIIII.

5. Laus tibi sit Christe quoniam liber explicit iste.
   Nomen scriptoris est Thomas plenus amoris.
   Qui ultra querit.

   M. R. James considers that the first three are by the scribe of the manuscript but the last seems to have been added in the fifteenth century.

3r. Incipit:
> Qui vers de riche estoire veult entendre et oïr
> Pour prendre bon example et prouesce cueillir.

100vo. Explicit (*Roman* Br. III):
> Alixandre li rois cui tout li mons apent
> Devoit porter coroune lendemain hautement.

102r. Incipit (*Prise* after full-page picture on 101vo.):
> Alixandres cevauche a loi d'empereor
> Amazone a conquise, Inde et terre major.

109vo. *Prise* breaks off at these lines:
> De .xiiii. roiaumes se fist seignor clamer
> Quatorze rois en fist ains que morust li ber.

110r. Incipit (*Voeux*):
> Aprés ce qu'Alixandres ot Dedefur conquis
> Et a force d'espee occis le duc Melchis.

163vo. Explicit:

> Cascuns ot boin cheval isnel et remuant
> Au palais d'Ephezon s'en repairent atant.
> Chi finent li veu du pavon.

165r. Incipit (*Restor* after full-page picture on 164vo.):

> Seignor, prince et baron et dames et borgois
> On dist en .i. proverbe et si l'aporte drois.

182vo. Explicit:

> Et comme Emenidus sa nieche maria
> Au jouene Gadifer quant a lui s'acorda.
> Explicit du paon, bien ait qui le lira
> Et qui en tous endrois le dit en prisera.
> Du bien doit on bien dire, ch'oïdire piecha.

182vo. *Prise* resumes:

> Au quinzime jor mut li rois et si s'en vait
> Lors destorne sa voie a Tarantie en vait.

185r. Explicit:

> Li prince se herbergent sus l'eue de Faraigne
> Au matin mut li rois qui malvestie ne daigne.

185r. Incipit: (Voyage to Paradise):

> Or en vait li bons rois qui maint en gentillise
> Tout droit vers Babilone ou sa voie a enprise.

188r. Explicit:

> Descendus est li rois cui la mort est prochaine.
> A joie le rechurent, en la cité demaine.

189r. Incipit (*Roman* Br.IV after full-page picture on 188vo.):

> A l'issue de May tout droit en cel termine
> Que li biau tans revient et yvers se decline.

195vo. Explicit:

> Sor l'eue de Tygris la dousime estoras
> En letres de greiois el mur escrit les as.

196r.

> Chi finent les regrés d'Alixandre.

197r. Incipit (*Venjance* after full-page picture on 196vo.):

> Seignor or faites pais un petit m'escoutés.
> Li sens de nul sage homme ne doit estre celés.

208r. Explicit:

> Riens nel porra garir que il nel faice afflire
> Or s'en vont tuit ensamble el regne de Sartire.
> Cist qui cest romans fist n'en volt avant plus dire.
> Chi fenist la vengeance du boin roy Alixandre.

P6

Paris, B.N.ms.fr.20045. Parchment, C.14. 215 x 125mm. 160 folios plus two paper

fly-leaves front and back. 32-33 lines to a page. A-U8
No miniatures. The first initial is an ornamented A in red and black, the remainder
are red and plain.

Contents: *Voeux*   1r.-117r.
              Restor   117r.-159r.

Bound red morocco, gilt tooling on spine and the inscription '1866 J. Weber
Biblioth. Impériale' with the Napoleonic crowned N.

At the top of fo.1 is the signature Philippes Desportes and at the bottom the crest
of Louis de Bruges painted in red, silver, black and gold.

On 159vo. are some Latin verses on the calender and on 160vo. the Ten
Commandments also in Latin.

1r. Incipit:

> Apriés chou k'Alixandres ot de dephur conquis
> Et a force d'espee ocis le duc Melchis.

117r. Explicit:

> Cescuns ot boin cheval et isniel et courant
> El palais de Fezon furent tout repairant.

117r. Incipit:

> Signour prince et baron et dames et bourgoys
> On dist en .i. proverbe et si l'acorde drois

159r. Explicit:

> Et comment Emenidus sa niece maria
> Au jone Gadifer quant a lui s'acorda.
> Explicit du paon bien ait qui le lira
> Et qui en tous endrois le dit em prisera
> Et du bien doit on bien dire c'oï dire pieça
>   Explicit des veus du paon (This is crossed through in red).

P7

New York, Pierpont Morgan Library, G.24, formerly Donaueschingen 168.
Parchment, C.14. 141 folios. 26-31 lines to a page. Folios 1-24 are lost and also a
number of leaves at the end, perhaps two quires of eight containing approximately
410 lines. Folios 112-18 and 123-24 are also lacking. Numerous miniatures but none
illustrates the *Restor*.

Contents: *Voeux*   25r.-134vo.
              Restor   134vo.-173vo.

25r. The fragment begins:

> Jouenes et avenans clerement reluisens
> De belle affaiteüre de beaus contenemens.

134vo. Explicit:

> Lors desarment Porrus ki grant paine soffri

> Cascune des .iii. dames moult biel le conjoï.

134vo. Incipit:

> Signor prince et baron et dames et borgois
> On dist en .i. proverbe et si l'aferme drois.

173vo. Ends incomplete:

> C'est drois mais elles sont legieres a desdire
> Kar nus n'ara le pris par force de maistire.

Q

Paris, B.N.ms.fr.790. Parchment, C.14. 315 x 230mm. 199 folios plus two parchment fly-leaves at the beginning and one at the end. Double columns of 40 lines each. The *Restor* is contained in one quire of eight which was added to the manuscript by Cangé. It has double columns of 39 lines. 34 miniatures illustrate the *Roman* but there are none in the *Restor*.

Contents:
Roman d'Alixandre	1r.-98vo.	
Prise de Defur	99r.-107vo.	
Voeux	107vo.-163r.	
Roman (continued)	163r.-179r.	
Venjance	179r.-191vo.	
Restor	192r.-199vo.	

Bound red morocco, gilt tooling. Title on spine, *Romans d'Alexand*. Pages gilt-edged.

Cangé bought folios 1-191 in 1724 at the sale of the Bibliothèque d'Anet (note on fol.1). He subsequently added the *Restor* as he states on 192r., 'J'ay tiré cette pièce d'un autre MS pour la joindre a ce Roman'.

192r. Incipit under the rubric 'Ci Commence le Restor dou paon':

> Quant Porrus li yndois et tuit si compaignon
> Orrent par reverence et en grant devotion.

199r. Explicit:

> Et com Armenidus sa niece maria
> A jone Gadifer quant a lui s'acorda.
> Explicit du paon bien ait qui les lira.

Q1

Paris, B.N.ms.fr.2166. Parchment, late C.14. 228 x 272mm. 96 folios, single columns of 31 lines. Three miniatures on 1r.,27vo.,64r. Initials red and blue alternating; bound red morocco. The manuscript is a continuation of B.N.ms.fr. 2165 which contains the first three-quarters of the *Voeux*.

Contents:
Voeux (last quarter)	1r.-32vo.	
Restor	32vo.-63vo.	
Le Jugement au roi		

de Boheme (Guillaume
de Machaut)　　　　　64r.-95vo.

1r. Incipit:

Quant Alixandre voit le Baudrain chevauchant
Baniere desploiee les galons sautelant.

32vo. Explicit:

Assez orent plenté de ce ou leurs cuers bee
Car la furent paiez si qu'a chascun aggree.

32vo. Incipit:

Seigneur, roy, prince et conte, chevalier et bourgois,
On dit en .i. proverbe et si l'acorde drois.

63vo. Explicit:

Comment Emenidus sa niece maria
Au jouene Gadifer quant a lui s'acorda,
Et de l'estrif des veus qu'il y acompaigna
S'en dites tous et toutes .i. Ave Maria.
　　　　Explicit du paon les veus et d'Alixandre.

S1

Oxford, Bodleian Library, Douce 165. Parchment, C.14, third quarter. 252 x 164mm.
249 folios. Single columns of 30 lines. Twelve miniatures of which two are in the
Restor. Initials red with pen-flourishing in blue or blue with pen-flourishing in red.

Contents:　*Voeux*　　　　　1r.-138r.
　　　　　　Restor　　　　　138r.-182vo.
　　　　　　Parfait　　　　　183r.-246vo.

1r. Incipit (beneath a miniature and the rubric, 'Ci conmencent les veus du paon et
li accomplissement, Et le mariage des pucelles et le reçtor et le pris'):

Aprés ce qu'Alixandres ot Dedefur conquis
Et a force d'espee occis le duc Melchis.

138r. Explicit:

Car puis que li vrais deux le siecle conmença
Tel prince ne nasqui ne ja més ne nestra.
　　　　Ci fenissent les veus du paon.

138r. Incipit (after the rubric, 'Et aprés conmence le Reçtor du paon' and a
miniature):

Seigneurs, prince et baron et dames et bourgois,
Ont dit en .i. proverbe et si l'acorde drois.

161r. Explicit (end of Part I):

Aiment miex lor avoir a tout lor reprouvier
Que la grace des bons qui moult puet avancier.
　　　　Explixit le Restor du Paon.

161vo. Incipit (after miniature):

> Quant Porrus ly Indois et tuit si compaignon
> Orent par reverence et grant devocion.

182vo. Explicit:

> Et Emenidus sa niece espousa
> Au joenne Gadifer quant a li s'acorda.
> Ici fine mon livre, de matere plus n'a.
> > Explicit le Restour du Paon.

183r. Incipit:

> Seignours, roy, prince et conte, chevalier et baron
> Bourgois, chanoinne, prestre, gent de religion,
> Vous avez bien oy tous les veus du paon.

246vo. ends incomplete, two leaves being lost:

> Et la tierce place a roys Melidus saisie,
> Et Marciens la quarte, ou honneurs fu florie.

S5

Paris, Arsenal 2776. Parchment, C.14. 250 x 170mm. 154 folios plus one parchment flyleaf front and back. One folio between 41 and 42 is not numbered, consequently the last folio is numbered 153 instead of 154. Single columns of 29-33 lines. A-T8U2.

No miniatures, initials red and blue alternating.

Contents: *Voeux*   1r.-134vo.
             Restor   135r.-153r.

Bound green calf, gilt tooling. Title on spine, '*Roman du Voeu du Paon*'. Leaves gilt-edged.

1r. Incipit:

> Aprés ce qu'Alixandres ot de dedus conquis
> Et a force d'espee occis le duc Melchis.

134vo. Explicit:

> Empoisonnez y fu ains que passast l'anee,
> Jamés de tel signour n'iert faite restoree.
> Explicit li veu du paon. Et commence aprés le Restor du Paon.

135r. Incipit:

> Quant Porrus li yndois et tuit si compaingnon
> Orent par reverence o grant devocion.

153r. Explicit:

> Et Emenidus sa nieche maria
> Au jone Gadifer quant a lui s'acorda.
> > Explicit le restor du paon.

S6

Rouen, Bibliothèque Municipale, 0.8. Parchment, C.14.295 x 195mm. 148 folios
plus three paper fly-leaves front and back. Single columns of 33 lines. A-S8T4. A
miniature on folio 1 has been cut away and the leaf repaired with parchment. There
is a space for a miniature and a large initial on 59r. but neither was executed. Large
initials in red and blue.

Contents: *Voeux*   1r.-131r.
            Restor   131r.-148r.

Bound yellow calf with brown tooling. A double rose stamped at each corner of
front and back covers and five on the spine. The title in gold on the spine, *Le
Restor du Paon.*

On 2r. is the heading 'Le Restor du Paon' although this is the second folio of the
Voeux.

1r. Incipit:

> Aprés ce qu'Alixandre ot Dedefurs conq[uis]
> Et a force d'espee occis le duc Melchis.

131r. Explicit:

> Empoisonnés y fut ains que passast l'anee
> Jamés de tel seignour n'iert fete restoree.

131r. Incipit:

> Quant Porus ly yndois et tuit si compaignon
> Orent par reverence o grant devocion.

148r. Explicit:

> Et a Emenidus sa niece maria
> Au jeune Gadifer quant a lui s'acorda.
>   Explicit le Restor du Paon.

S7

Copenhagen, Royal Library, Thott 414. Parchment, C.14. Small folio. Single
columns of 30 lines. 165 folios. Three miniatures, one of which on 144vo.,
illustrates the *Restor*.

Contents: *Voeux*   1 -144vo.
            Restor   145r.-164vo.

144vo. Explicit (*Voeux*):

> Empoysonnés y fu ains que passast l'annee
> Jamais de tel seigneur n'ert faite restoree.
>   Explicit les Veus du paon. Ci aprés
>   commence le Restor du paon.

145. Incipit:

> Quant Porus li yndois et tuit si compaignon
> Orent par reverence o grant devocion.

164vo. Explicit:

> Et Emenidus sa niece maria
> Au joene Gadiffer quant a lui s'acorda.
> Explicit le Retor du paon.
> Finito libro sit laus [et] gloria cristo.amen.
> Elas en ne se pas assés comment bien avist qui se fist.

U

Paris, B.N.ms.fr.12567. Parchment, C.14. 265 x 190mm. 205 folios. Single columns of 30 lines. The third paper fly-leaf is numbered 1, consequently the first parchment leaf is numbered 2. The last leaf, numbered 206, is blank. A-E8 (wanting 5th leaf), F-R8S6 (wanting 4th leaf), T8U10 (wanting 4th leaf), X-Y8, Z-b6c8d4e2. As far as I can ascertain none of the text is lacking so the excised leaves were presumably blank. However a section appears to have been lost between folios 112 and 113. The catch-word on 112, 'les .iiii. filz Clarvus', is not taken up on 113 which begins, 'Mort l'eust si vousist il ne tint s'a lui non'. There is a gap of some 350 lines perhaps indicating a loss of six leaves. Four miniatures on 2r.,60vo.,121r. and 168vo.

Contents: *Fuerre de Gadres*   2r.- 60r.
           Voeux   60vo.-193vo.
           Restor   194r.-205vo.

Bound brown calf, gilt tooling. Title on spine, *Gaires de Gadres*. Initials red. Ornamented initials at the beginning of the *Fuerre* and the *Voeux*.

This manuscript is considered by Professor D. J. A. Ross to have been made, or at least illustrated, in northern Italy.

U is the only manuscript containing the combination *Fuerre, Voeux, Restor*. It is possible that there existed an edition of the *Fuerre* and the *Voeux* celebrating Gadifer the noble enemy who was slain by Emenidus in the *Fuerre* and with whose children Emenidus was finally reconciled after coming to their aid in the siege of Epheson related in the *Voeux*. Other indications of such an edition are the Scottish *Buik of Alexander* which contains a Scottish translation of the *Fuerre* and the *Voeux* (see note 8, p. 3) and the Latin ms. Vatican, Archivio di San Pietro 36 E which contains a Latin version of the *Fuerre* and the *Voeux*[2].

2r. Incipit (under the rubric 'Ci commence le fuerre de Gadres'):

> Devant les murs de Tyr la dedens en la mer
> Le roy de Macedoine fist .i. chastel fermer.

60r. Explicit:

> Qu' Alixandres li nobles qui tant par fu bons rois
> Maria les pucelles a joie et a noblois
> Ainsi com vous orrés, si vous di sans gabois
> En la fin de ce livre qui est bien fet a drois
> Ce fenist li fuerre des Gadres.

60r. Incipit (under the rubric 'Ci commencent les veus du paon Et l'accomplissement et le mariage des pucelles):

> Aprés ce qu'Alixandre ot Dedefur conquis
> Et a force d'espee ocit le du Melchis.

193vo. Explicit:

> Car puis que li vrais deux le siecle commença
> Tel prince ne nasqui ne jamés ne nastra.

194r. Incipit:

> Quant Porus li yndois et tuit si compaingnon
> Orent par reverence en grant devocion.

205vo. Explicit:

> Et com Aymenidus sa niece maria
> Au joenne Gadifer quant a li s'acorda
> Ci fenissent les veus bien ait qui les lira.
> Ci fenissent li fuerre de Gadres. Et les veus du paon. Et le
> restor tout par ordre. Laus tibi sit Christe quum liber explicit iste.

W

Paris, B.N.ms.fr.12565. Parchment, C.14 (after 1340). 270 x 180mm. 297 folios plus two paper fly-leaves front and back. Single columns of 30 lines. A-I8, K4, L-f8, g6, h-o8, p8 (wanting the last leaf). A luxurious manuscript in a clear book-hand adorned with numerous miniatures, ten of which are in the *Restor*. Most initials are gold and blue.

Contents: | *Prise de Defur* | 1r.- 25vo. |
Voeux	26r.-189r.
Restor	189r.-233vo.
Parfait	233vo.-297vo.

Bound brown tree-calf, red morocco on spine, gilt tooling. The Napoleonic initial N with oakleaves repeated five times. Title in gilt, *Les Voeux du Paon*.

This manuscript is the only one of the *Voeux* which has the author's name and the dedication to Tybaut de Bar, and is the only one having the name of the author of the *Parfait*. This is spelled out by the initials of the final lines and the other manuscript containing the *Parfait*, S1, has lost its final leaves.

1r. Incipit:

> Alixandres chevauche a loy d'empereour
> Amazone a conquis, Ynde et Terre Majour.

25vo. Explicit:

> Tant c'on dist qu'il pescierent andoi en une nasse.
> Au. vie. jour mut cil qui d'errer ne lasse.
> > Explicit de Floridas et de Daury son frere.

26r. Incipit:

> Aprés ce qu'Alixandres ot Dedephur conquis
> Et a force d'espee occis le duc Melcis.

189r. Explicit:

> Tant qu'il fu au dessus de tous ses anemis.
> Cil me nonma l'ystoire qui bele est adevis.

189r. Incipit:

> Seignor, prince et baron et dames et bourgois,
> On dist en .i. proverbe et si l'acorde drois.

233 vo. Explicit:

> Et com Emenidus sa niece maria
> Au jone Gadifer quant a lui s'acorda.

233vo. Incipit (below miniature):

> Seignour, roy, prinche et conte, chevalier et baron,
> Bourgois, canoine et prestre, gent de religion.

297vo. Explicit:

> Tous nous couvient finner nus n'en voist au contraire,
> En Dieu est qui tout fist de nous faire et desfaire.
> L'an mil .iii.c.xl. volt ceste branche faire.
> Explichit le parfait il est tans d'a fin traire
> Car biaus canters anoie che ay oÿ retraire.
>   Explichit.

NOTES

1. D. J. A. Ross, 'Nectanebus in his palace', *Journal of the Warburg and Courtauld Institutes*, 15 (1952), 67-87.
2. D. J. A. Ross, 'A new manuscript of the Latin *Fuerre de Gadres*', *Journal of the Warburg and Courtauld Institutes*, 22 (1959), 211-253.

THE MANUSCRIPTS COMPARED

With the following exceptions the manuscripts contain only the *Voeux* and the *Restor*. In S1 and W the final poem of the cycle, the *Parfait*, follows the *Restor*, which dates these two after 1340. W has in addition the *Prise de Defur* which precedes the *Voeux*. U has the *Fuerre de Gadres*, *Voeux* and *Restor*. Three manuscripts contain the *Roman*, O, P and Q. In O the *Voeux* and *Restor* are at the end of the volume, in P both are inserted into the *Roman* and in Q only the *Voeux is* inserted into the *Roman*, the *Restor* having been taken from another manuscript and sewn in at the end. Q1 ends with a poem unconnected with the Alexander cycle, the *Jugement au roi de Boheme* by Guillaume de Machaut.

There are two main redactions of the *Restor*, that containing the whole poem and another, abridged version, sometimes called the *Pris des Veus* containing Part II only. Seven manuscripts have the complete poem of which N6PP6P7 insert the *Restor* before the end of the *Voeux* and incorporate the remaining *Voeux* material in the *Restor*. The three others, Q1S1W, complete the *Voeux* before beginning the *Restor*.

A study of the variant readings of Part I shows that P stands alone very frequently The following are a few examples: I 44 'Qu'il ne vausist pas estre as tors ne as berfrois'. This refers to a specific place, Tyre, where Alexander was engaged in building assault towers. The other mss with 'en tour/-s ne en b.' have missed the allusion and have replaced it with a general term which could be interpreted as 'in safety'. In I 242 'grant ramage' (p7 'gant r.') is replaced by 'gaut sauvage'. It seems that 'grant', perhaps with a superscript r, was misread as 'gaut' and a suitable adjective introduced to replace 'ramage'. P7's reading supports this conjecture. In I 46 'mors getés frois' in P is replaced by 'ocis tous frois' in the rest.

Sometimes words or phrases that were becoming archaic are modernized, e.g. I 112 'voiant le roi' is replaced in the other mss by 'devant le r.'; 'd'abanois' I 99 by 'de soulas'; 'en sacha' I 167 by 'e. traist hors' (p7 'e. a trait'); 'preuc' I 225 by 'pour'. Sometimes a technical word is replaced: I 244 'ne travers ne paiage', a toll for crossing and for entering, appears in the rest as 'ne treü ne p.' (p7 'passage'). In I 135 'oelletés', 'adorned with eyes' referring to the peacock's tail, has the support of N6Q1S1, but is replaced in P6 by 'eslites' and in P7 by 'colorés'. W omits the line.

Sometimes the syntax is simplified e.g. in I 138-41 where the revision has led to a loss of subtlety. Similarly in I 1319-20, 1326-28 and 1334-36 where in each case the variant reading of the other mss has lost some of the meaning expressed in P. These and other passages are also dealt with in the Notes as they occur.

It will be convenient at this point to use the term a-redaction for P and β-redaction for the rest. The β-redaction has two groups of lines which are not in P. The first is:

I 740a	Mais sa clef li ala mout soutiement enbler
b	Et a une pucele fist le cofre aporter
c	A Aymon a Damas et li dist sans guiler
d	C'a son ostel alast le bon duc demander.

This is an abridged version of I 741-7 which are found only in P:

I 741	Mais la pucele sage, qui tant fist a loër,
	Embla les cles son pere sans point de demorer.
	Ens ou trezor entra qui molt fist a loër,
	Et quant elle fu ens soi prist a aviser
745	Avoec une pucele ou molt se pot fïer.
	Le cofre en aporta por les pierres oster
	Et puis fist a Damas le boin Emon mander.
	La pucele i ala qui bien le sot mander.

It seems likely that the passage was confused in the archetype. P has some needless repetition, e.g. the second hemistichs of 741 and 743 which are almost identical and the word 'mander' which occurs at the rhyme in 747 and 748. It may be that 'sans point de demorer' in 742 belongs to the next line and that the original second hemistich of 742 has been lost. However the version in the other tradition omits the actual entry into the treasure-house (I 743) which is necessary. The redactor of this archetype has made a neat four-line précis whereas the redactor of the P tradition seems to have included as much of the material as he could decipher and filled in the gaps with stereotyped phrases. P may therefore be as close as one can now get to the original.

The second passage not in P (nor in W) is I 1123a-h:

I 1122	'Sire,' dist Marciiens, 'sauf le vostre parler . . .'
1123	'Par ma foi,' dist li rois, 'je l'os por voir jurer.'
1123 a	Dont li marchiés se puet aques bien acorder.
b	'Sire,' dist Martïen, 'ne le voel refuser.' (P7 'je ne' for 'ne le')
c	Chose ke vos vuelliés dire ne commander.'
d	'Ne je,' dist Elÿos, 'puis qu'il le veult greer.'
e	'Par ma foy,' dist li rois, 'si devés conquester.
f	Qu'a ma volonté faire et du tout accorder
g	Avez plus gaaignié que ne poez penser
h	Car je le vous cuit bien et richement solder.
I 1124	Frize et toute Hollande vous doins sans dessevrer.'

Of the extra lines N6P7Q1S1 have a, b, d, e. In addition P7 has c and Q1 has f-h. P6, which omits I 1122-23 has only b, d, e of the extra lines. It may be that something has dropped out of P and W at this point, but the extra lines do not sound authentic. None of the knights is described elsewhere as 'li marchiés' and line 1123b partly repeats I 1122 and 1123e repeats I 1123.

Another feature setting off P against the other manuscripts is the number of lines in P which the rest omit. There are fifty such omissions in Part I alone and the question arises whether the lines are scribal additions in P or whether they dropped out of the archetype of all the other mss. Eight of these lines occur at the end of laisses and they fall into three types: they expand a statement contained in the previous line I 249, 686, 1098; they express agreement with the foregoing action I 1065; they comment on the foregoing action I 377-8, 887, 906, 1245. Let us consider the first type. At the end of laisse .viii. the author announces that he is going to break off his main narrative to tell of the youth of Emenidus:

I 246
        Chi lairons de sa nieche et de son marïage:
        Quant tans sera et poins s'i ferons repairage.
        Si vous recorderons d'Aimon le jouene eage,
        De ses fais de ses dis et de son vasselage.

The last line simply explains in more detail what the author is proposing to do. It rounds off the laisse with a promise of what is to come, but on its own it is difficult to say whether or not it is authentic. The two other lines of this type seem designed to impress and amaze. In the first example the Caliph takes his daughter to see his treasure:

I 683
        Et li peres qui ot le cuer tout desirant
        D'acomplir son voloir l'i mena; si vit tant
        D'or que ne le menaissent .xxx. mulet amblant
        De trestous les plus fors qui sont en orïant.

One could easily stop at 'mulet amblant' but the author of the last line seems intent on driving home his point and perhaps forestalling any derisive comment. 'And I don't mean your ordinary mule' he seems to imply. It is, I believe, a line composed with the audience very much in mind, whether it was written in the study or whether it arose spontaneously as a response to an audience reaction. If it were indeed written in the study then it must have been composed by a man with experience of audiences, who could anticipate their responses even when not facing them, that is to say by a performer rather than a scribe. Further, the use of the present tense 'sont' is more acceptable if the line is considered as a direct address to the audience. The final example (I 1098) is similarly designed to impress: a line which gives the pecuniary value of Alexander's gift of Ireland to Porus.

The lines expressing agreement with or a comment on the action can also be more easily ascribed to a performer than to a scribe. For example line I 887 at the end of laisse twenty-one 'Son pooir en fera, si l'i aït Marchus' with its use of the future tense is an assurance that Emenidus will do as he says. These then are the lines occurring at the end of laisses. But the other lines are also similar. They expand a statement or description, e.g.

I 188   Lor més ne lor mangiers, n'est mestiers qu'on vos die;
      Tout ont a lor voloir dains, chers et vin sor lie.

I 298   Se j'avoie en aiue tous les livres Caton,
      Ne de tous les .vii. sages qui furent de renon.

I 727   Si pensa que c'estoit uns biaus dons por doner,
      Nobles et gracieus por son ami parer

In each case the second line is omitted in the other mss. There is also another type which adds an important incident or clarification to the text. For example:

I 764   Quant elle ot pris congié du repairier s'avoie
      A sa dame a Baudas qui atent et coloie
      Que elle revenist par quoi noveles oie.

 767   A tant es la pucele qui demenoit grant joie:
      A sa dame conta comment Aimes s'aloie . . .

Only P has line 767 which described vividly the moment when the lady sets eyes on her maid and the audience too is invited to picture the girl: 'es la pucele.' In the other mss the moment of arrival is omitted and the girl is merely described as setting out on her journey and then relating the news about Emenidus. Another example (I 782-5) describes the robber band examining the treasure-chest to see how it may be opened:

I 782   Mais li uns resgarda aussi qu'a .i. coron
      La clef vit estekier endroit .i. anglechon.
      La fu prise li cles sans point d'arrestison
      A l'ouvrir i trouverent pierres de grant renon.

The line omitted in the other mss is I 784 so that there is an abrupt transition from the discovery of the key to the opened chest. The line is perhaps not essential to the story but it adds more action to the telling of it. One further little scene will perhaps suffice to show the kind of line P has retained which the other mss omit:

I 355   En celle mesestance l'encontrerent larron
      Et il l'ont arresté; n'i fisent lonc sermon
      Et li ont demandé toute sa natïon
      Et Aymes lor conta sa grant abusïon

Lines I 356-7 are omitted in the other tradition and here again, what is omitted is a little scene showing the characters in action.

 A comparison of the manuscripts having Part II shows a similar result. P has similar independent readings and some forty extra lines. These extra lines are of the same kind as those in Part I and seem generally to be addressed to an audience rather than to a reader. If the lines were composed by a performer, as seems likely, can we say whether they were added to the version reproduced by P? Or were they dropped from the other tradition? They do not stand out as alien material either in content or in style. There are many similar lines to be found which the other manuscripts do not omit, or which not all of them omit. If the performer was not Brisebare then he must have been a man who, in Brisebare's life-time (P was complete by 1338) presented the work as his own (I 10 Mais je qui només sui Brisebare a le fois). It seems more reasonable to suppose that Brisebare himself either wrote them in his original version or that he added them to a performing copy. It would be difficult to prove that they are not Brisebare's and as they form an integral part of a manuscript which is reliable in many other ways there seems to be no point in rejecting them.

The manuscripts of Part I deriving from the β-redaction fall into sub-groups: P6P7 have many readings in common, e.g. I 114 'Arabieus' for 'Kenelius'; I 276 'jusques en son' for 'jusqu'au coron'; I 365 'malart' (P 'l'aloe' the rest 'l'anete'); I 663 'courant' for 'errant'; I 667 'Rosette' for 'Rosenés'. They both support P against the rest in I 324-334 (the story of the Woman of Canaan), in I 586 (in which however they have the variant reading 'emblee' for P's 'jetee') and in I 1467-68. P7 has many pointless revisions, e.g. I 48, 50, 62, 67, 104, 106, 111 etc. Indeed it is so heavily and unintelligently revised in some parts that large passages of it seem to be merely a paraphrase of the text presented by the other mss. See for example I 810-40 of which I give the version of P7 in full in the notes. P6 also has some pointless revisions, e.g. I 126, 197, 237, 426, 499, 541, 572 etc., but appears to be less revised than P7. It is not always secure metrically. Both mss omit a number of lines in addition to the fifty lacking in the whole β-redaction. Together they omit I 334, 849 and 1166-7, P7 omits 20 more in company with one or more of the other mss and P6, 12, and independently P7 omits another 52 lines and P6 another 55.

The remaining four Part I mss, N6Q1S1W have many readings in common, e.g. I 130 'et graces et mercis' (PP6P7 '.vc. mille mercis'); I 132 'me faciés' (PP6 vous f., P7 'vos me faites'); I 255 'aquist' for 'conquist'; I 283 'dame Edea for 'bele E.'; I 365 'l'anete' (P 'l'aloe', P6P7 'malart'); I 750 'venist' for 'voloit', etc. They omit the story of the Woman of Canaan (I 324-334) and also lines I 586, 990, 994 (P7 also omits the last). N6 and S1 have a few readings in common which suggest that these four mss. can be further subdivided into two groups. For example I 988 where N6S1 have 'De cortois us, de gas' for 'D.c. dis, d.gais' and I 993 where they read 'orent' for 'i ot', also I 1079; but as Q1W omit the first two lines mentioned there is nothing to compare them with. Q1 and W probably represent versions further revised and modernized of a redaction deriving from this tradition. They both omit a large number of lines in addition to the fifty omitted in common with the others: W 103 and Q1 nearly 200 which includes a block of 127 lines from the *Voeux* (I 971-1098) probably dropped by the redactor as Q1 has the complete *Voeux* before the *Restor* begins. Q1 in particular has many modern forms, for instance it rarely has a flexional s in the masculine nominative singular e.g. I 144 'un maistre', I 145 'sage maistre' (N6 also has both these forms), I 1320 'Petit mal' for 'Petis maus'; it has the form 'tous ceus' for the older 'tuit cil' ('tout cil' in P) I 311, 'dit' for 'dist' I 200, 211, 220 and passim; 'Leurs' for 'lor' I 306 (P has 'les', the rest 'lor'); I 188 'leurs més' (oblique pl). In I 1367 'Eslut donc' replaces the unusual 'Eslisi' of the other mss, and in I 554 'tent' replaces the obsolescent 'hingue'. In I 11 'anchois que past li mois' is replaced in Q1 by 'au mieus que je porrois' perhaps because the redactor felt that a reference to the actual time of the composition was unsuitable so long after the event. The termination of 'porrois' is guaranteed by the rhyme. It is a form that is not found in P although it was beginning to spread in Middle French.

N6 and S1 present less idiosyncratic versions of the common parent. They have few independent readings and the few lines they omit in addition to those omitted by the whole group are probably the result of scribal lapses. N6 is not very meticulous about rhyme e.g. I 108, I 480.

P offers in many ways a difficult text but the difficulties are too often replaced by apparent and even obvious revisions in the other manuscripts. It is the fullest text and is probably the oldest manuscript. It stands out clearly as the best to use as the base manuscript for Part I.

A study of the manuscripts of Part II results in a similar conclusion. P again stands alone in many readings, e.g. II 131 with its plethora of variants but P has the best reading and Q1W omit the line. Again, in II 725, P with 'atievissement' 'lukewarmness' has the only meaningful reading. Other examples occur in II 703, 761, 901-3 etc., and are fully discussed in the general Notes. P sometimes has the support of a few manuscripts for unusual words, e.g. II 99 'puirie' 'offered' is found also in N2P6W but the rest have a variety of readings; in II 112 'arramie' 'pitched battle' has the support of W and also occurs in the *Voeux* but is replaced by different substitutes in the other mss; In II 954 'lire' meaning 'announce' is also in P6S1W but is replaced in the rest by 'dire'.

P again is fuller in Part II than any of the other mss. In addition to the more than forty lines which they all omit, many more lines are dropped both by individual manuscripts and by groups. W omits 47 lines independently and 14 with other mss; Q1 omits as many as 536 of which 76 are with other mss and 460 alone. 448 of these are in a block (II 595-1043) and comprise one complete round of speeches which indicates the redactor's hand. P6 omits 22 lines of which 14 are independent omissions and P7 omits 31 alone plus 12 with other mss, and in addition is lacking some 412 lines at the end. Of the mss having only Part II the group N1OQU plus N6 omits almost 150 lines in common and a varying number independently: N1, 4, N6 1, Q 3, O 99 and U 587. The last, like Q1, omits one complete set of speeches but whereas Q1 presents the first round complete and omits the second, U breaks off the first round at II 397 and takes up the thread again at the appropriate place in the second round (II 880) so that in effect each speaker makes one speech. A second group having only Part II is formed of N5S5S6 and S7. As a group they omit an extra 93 lines and independently N5 omits 5, and S5S6S7 omit 6, 7 and 36 respectively.

Both these groups must derive from a redaction which intentionally abandoned Part I with its description of the making of the peacock as they all have an additional passage describing it (II 1234a-k). N6 and S1 also have these lines although they do not need them as they have the description in Part I. The variants to these lines, given in the general notes, show that the manuscripts were already being copied from two separate redactions. The group N1N6OQU also has in common II 1249a-c, 1166a and 1183a. Q1 has the last two. In addition they omit a number of lines, including II 1136-41 which Q1 also omits. In II 1149 the group plus Q1 refer to the eagle as 'L'aigle d'or', whereas it was really a live eagle. This is confirmed in II 1209-10, found in all the manuscripts.

S1 is curious in that it omits lines in common with the group N1N6OQU up to II 814 from which point it has most of the lines they omit. Yet it transposes with them lines II 4 and 5 and II 111 and 112, and combines as they do II 521-22. What is more, it has line II 583 following II 579 in common with them and additional lines II 1234-a-k mentioned in the previous paragraph.

N2, which has only Part II, shows no signs of editing to compensate for the lack of Part I and is probably a copy of the second half of a version having the complete poem. It does not belong to either of the main groups of Part II and perhaps derives from the β-redaction at a stage before the various groups developed their individual characteristics.

In his edition of the *Restor* based on W (see note 9, p. 3) Carey acknowledges that many lines are omitted in W which he has supplied, usually from P, (op. cit. p. 38) but he does not state the number. In my estimate this is 208 and as the number of lines in P is 2826 and the number in Dr. Carey's edition, including the lines borrowed from P, is 2691 there are still 135 lacking, not all of which can be dismissed as 'éditorial'. The choice of W as the base manuscript is discussed by D. J. A. Ross in his review of Carey's edition.[1] Ritchie had used that manuscript for his edition of John Barbour's *Buik of Alexander* as he considered the version of the *Voeux* it contained to be closest to the French original used by Barbour for his Scottish translation. Ritchie, vol. I, xlvii-xlviii, thought that it had 'every appearance of being a replica of the author's copy', but this does not mean that its version of the *Restor* is equally authentic as Carey postulates p. 20. Nor does the fact that W has an amplified termination of the *Voeux* recommend it as a suitable base manuscript for an edition of the *Restor*. In my view the extra laisses at the end of the *Voeux*, found only in W, were not known to Brisebare and therefore they do not help in disentangling the end of the *Voeux* from the beginning of the *Restor*. Finally, Dr. Carey claims that the readings of W compared with the other manuscripts are 'les plus sobres'. Unfortunately W shares with all the β-mss the disadvantage of deriving from a heavily revised ancestor. Furthermore, it has the additional demerit of independently omitting obscure readings and archaisms. Its sobriety stems in fact mainly from this avoidance of the problems of a difficult text.

P still emerges as the best manuscript to use for both parts of the poem.

It is difficult to produce with any confidence a stemma capable of reflecting accurately the relations of the manuscripts to each other. But it is clear that, to account for the differences between P and the other mss described above, there must have been quite early on a redactor instructed to modernize and simplify the original text. From this redaction must stem all the mss other than P. It may be that it was at this stage also that the lines found only in P were dropped, perhaps to abridge the work. If on the other hand these lines did not form part of the original text, then they were added to the α-tradition, either by Brisebare for a particular performance, or by another jongleur. In either case they do not affect the beginning of the stemma:

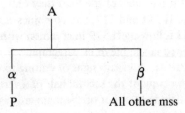

Of the Part I mss P6P7 have a number of readings in common and sometimes support P against the rest, for example with the story of the Woman of Canaan (I 324-334). N6S1 are probably closer to the parent than Q1W which have been further revised and modernized. So for Part I the stemma probably continues as follows,

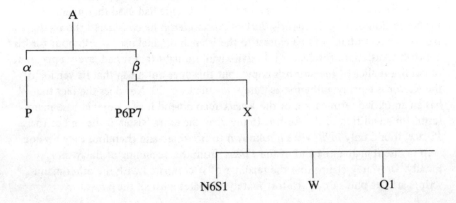

where X represents a revision of the β-redaction separating P6P7 from the rest.

All manuscripts having Part II only belong to the β-tradition, but all of them except N2 follow a redaction devised to exclude the peacock material and the *Enfances Emenidus*. It could be called the *Pris des Veus* as it contains only the debate to decide the prize of honour. The manuscripts following this redaction, to which I have given the siglum Y in the stemma, are N5S5S6S7 and N1OQU. To the second group must be added N6S1 which have Part I also but which follow the *Pris des Veus* redaction for Part II. Both these manuscripts have signs of rupture between the two parts, N6 having a new incipit for the *Restor* to mark the beginning of Part II (fo. 164r. last line) and S1 an explicit for the *Restor* at the end of Part I (fo. 161r.) Q1 also has a number of readings in common with the N1 group although it does not have lines 1233 a-k describing the peacock. N2 seems to be a copy of Part II of an ordinary β-text. The manuscript relations for both parts of the poem may be expressed thus:

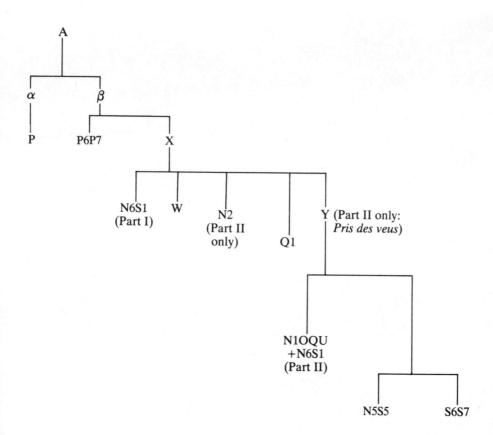

34

NOTES

1. D. J. A. Ross, '*Jean le Court dit Brisebare. Le Restor du Paon* edited by R. J. Carey', *Medium Aevum*, 37, no. 1 (1968), 80-84.

THE *RESTOR* IN RELATION TO THE *VOEUX*

Brisebare's declared aim in composing the *Restor* was to make good an omission in
the Alexander Romance, namely the fulfilment of one of the vows made in the
Veus du Paon, that of Edea to restore the peacock in gold (I 9-11). He grafted his
episode into the *Veus* after the death of Clarus at the siege of Epheson (I 65-67).
It fitted well into the story after Alexander's victory and entry into Epheson and
the *Voeux* proper could then have continued with the marriages, the final feasting
and Alexander's departure for Babylon. However, no sooner had he embarked upon
his *Restor* than Brisebare found he had further matter to insert. First the *Enfances
Emenidus* which he says are not to be found elsewhere in the Alexander cycle
(I 275-78). He intends, therefore, to insert this story into the *Voeux* together with
the new material (I 279-82). Then, in addition to the *Enfances Emenidus* and the
'nuef ouvrage', that is Edea's peacock material, there are two more marriages to add,
those of Eliot and of Lydoine (I 283-93).

The *Enfances Emenidus* and the fulfilling of Edea's vow have logically to
precede the marriages, which means that, having interrupted the *Voeux*, Brisebare
has to return to that work for the three marriages narrated there so that he can add
the two he claims were forgotten. He then completes the narrative of Edea's vow
with a long excursus on the virtues of the peacock, following which gifts symbolizing
the vows are presented to it. Part II consists of a long discussion on the respective
merits of the vows and a prize is awarded for the most worthy. The poem ends with
further feasting and Alexander's leave-taking before departing for Babylon, so that
it returns to the same point as the end of the *Voeux*.

Brisebare's completion of the *Voeux* by inserting his own *Restor* material was
achieved only by recasting some of Jacques de Longuyon's work. This is evident
from the mss which insert the *Restor* into the body of the *Voeux*, namely N6PP6
P7. The redactors of this group were presumably carrying out Brisebare's intention
(*Restor* I 65-67) to insert the work 'aprés la mort Clarus'. They all begin the *Restor*
before the end of the *Voeux* and Brisebare's interweaving of his own work and that
of Jacques de Longuyon replaces the original ending. Indeed, had only these manuscripts survived it would have been impossible to disentangle the contributions of
the two authors. The other manuscripts complete the *Voeux* in various ways before
beginning the *Restor*, consequently those containing Part I of the *Restor*, Q1S1W,
have some of the material twice.

A study of the various endings of the *Voeux* was made by Ritchie in his edition of the *Buik of Alexander* (see note 8, p. 3). He took the last twenty-seven laisses in W, numbering them 1-27 and set the endings of the other manuscripts against them (Ritchie, vol. III, 1v-1xiv). Of these laisses only W has 23-27 which relate events after the departure of Alexander from Epheson, that is, a 'happy end' with the five couples settled in their various territories and producing numerous children.

Laisses 1-22 relate events after the defeat of Clarus at the siege of Epheson up to the preparation for the departure, namely the burial of the dead, the peace terms, the recovery of Porus from his wounds, the marriages and Alexander's farewell. Included in this number are laisses found only in W: 9-12 describing the sending of two knights to Arcade to bring Lidoine to Epheson, laisse 15 which relates the welcome Lidoine receives at Epheson, the end of laisse 19 (11.8578-88) the marriage of Gadifer and Lidoine, and laisse 20, the marriage of Marcien and Eliot. Laisse 9 is also found in P2 which ends at that point incomplete. This ending, excluding the extra material of W and P2 is that of P1P3P4QQ1S5S6S7.

Other groups have an abbreviated ending. Some have only the first two of Ritchie's final laisses: MN2N3N4P5RSS3S4S8S9S10; N5 has laisses 1-7, and NN1OS1U have 1, 2, 4-7. But all these mss end with a summary of laisses 8-22 contained in two laisses in -a and -us respectively called 7a and 7b by Ritchie (vol. III, 1viii).[1] Of these N5 omits 7a. S6 and S7, which have the longer ending, also have the summary in 7a, 7b, which they insert after laisse 2.

Of the manuscripts which insert the *Restor* into the *Voeux* N6PP6 copy the *Voeux* to the end of Ritchie's laisse 7 (the burial of the dead) and have an explicit at this point. P7 copies the *Voeux* only to Ritchie's laisse 2 and then begins the *Restor*, but incorporates 7a after *Restor* I 68. In these manuscripts the feasting and all the marriages are interwoven with *Restor* matter. All the other manuscripts, apart from W, whether they have the longer or the shorter version describe only three marriages before Alexander's departure for Babylon. If the extra material in W was there originally it is strange that all the other scribes should have elected to omit it. It also seems probable that a version without the last two marriages existed at one time or Brisebare would not have felt it necessary to supply them, as he says in *Restor* I 283-93. It seems likely that Jacques de Longuyon considered the marriage of Lidoine and Gadifer to be outside the scope of his narrative of the vows made at Epheson. Lidoine lived in Arcade, apparently a distant land, and the author wanted to get Alexander on his way to Babylon without further delay. The marriage of Marcien and Eliot also has no connection with the vows and seems to be an afterthought. If so it may be that an audience, or the author's patron, urged him to include these two marriages and that they have survivied only in W. The final laisses found only in W (23-27), also seem to have been added later as Ritchie suggests (vol. III, 1xvii). Presenting as they do scenes of tranquil domesticity they are out of key with the epic quality of the vows and the battle scenes.[2]

Given that it was necessary to interrupt the *Voeux* at some point in order to introduce the *Restor*, the position of it in N6PP6 seems to be the right one. It is the most logical as all the protagonists are back in Epheson, the war is over and Edea is able to send for goldsmiths. Moreover, the second laisse of the *Restor* (I 68-88) is almost identical with Ritchie's laisse 8 of the final laisses of the *Voeux* (W 8256-77) so that it follows closely after laisse 7 with which these manuscripts end the *Voeux* and the proper sequence of events is maintained. Brisebare has simply broken into the narrative of the *Voeux* to announce his intention of introducing new material (*Restor* I 1-67). He then returns to the *Voeux* for the triumphal entry into Epheson (*Restor* I 69-88, *Voeux* in W 8256-8277) introducing this passage with a link line (*Restor* I 68): 'En aprés tous ces fais chi devant contenus'.

With the company now assembled in Epheson the scene is set for the making of Edea's peacock and the mission to fetch Lidoine. This narrative, plus the probably interpolated *Enfances Emenidus*, occupies laisses I iii to xxiv of the *Restor* (I 98-953) and is Brisebare's own invention. We return to the *Voeux* for the marriages (*Restor* laisses I xxv to xxviii, I 954-1096 = *Voeux* W 13, part of 14, 16, 17 of the final laisses, 11.8361-8411 and 8470-8537). The version of the *Restor* includes an invention of Brisebare's, the proposal of marriage made by Marcien to Eliot (I 956-72), but the rest of this part corresponds almost word for word with the *Voeux*. The *Restor* now leaves the *Voeux* for the two additional marriages, Edea's discourse on the peacock and the adoration of the peacock, all of which is Brisebare's work. Part II of the *Restor*, the debate, is entirely original and we do not return to the *Voeux* again until the final laisse, where Alexander takes leave of his men and departs for Babylon. This corresponds in content, but not in form, with laisse 22 of Ritchie's final laisses. It will be noted that the manuscripts which break away from the *Voeux* before its proper conclusion do in fact contain most of the material of the longer ending, but this is embedded in the *Restor* narrative and is to a certain extent reworked.

It is probably this interweaving of passages from the *Voeux* and the *Restor* which led A. Thomas (H.L.F. xxxvi, 42) to accuse Brisebare of plagiarism: 'Il nous est bien difficile de prendre un vif intérêt au sujet propre du *Restor du Paon* où Brisebare se traîne sur les données de Jacques de Longuyon, le plagiant parfois littéralement, sans faire preuve du même talent poétique'. I have attempted elsewhere to refute this accusation.[3] It seems to me that Brisebare's intention was not to take over the *Voeux* material and publish it as his own but to graft in his new matter ('enter' is the word he uses, *Restor* I 11, 67 and II 1334) in such a way that the events occured in their proper order. This has led to problems of copying which have been solved successfully I believe by N6PP6 and partially by P7. The other manuscripts which contain the whole of the *Restor*, Q1S1W, have a complete version of the *Voeux* also and consequently include some of the material twice. Finally, it appears from Brisebare's explicit that he himself considered his work to be merely an addition to the *Voeux* and not a separate work with the title *Le Restor du Paon* as it later became. This is the end, he says, of the vows of the peacock (not of the 'restor') II 1329, and he connects this work with the Alexander

Romance, II 1331, apportioning credit fairly between the authors of the *Roman* and of the *Voeux* and himself. His final explicit, II 1340, also refers to the peacock matter and not to the 'restor'.

From the evidence it seems most probable that the *Voeux* originally ended with the departure of Alexander for Babylon having celebrated only three marriages. This is the ending of all the manuscripts which do not contain the *Restor* and, accepting Ritchie's view that laisses 23-27 in W are a later addition, it is the ending of the manuscripts which do contain the *Restor* except for N6PP6P7, and this group incorporates the same ending of the *Voeux* into the *Restor*. It is more likely that the longer version (Ritchie's laisses 1-22) is the original one and was epitomized in laisses 7a, 7b, than that the shorter version should have been expanded. Moreover, if Jacques de Longuyon himself contributed the extra Lidoine material and Eliot's marriage found in W, he must have considered the longer version to be the correct one, as this material is interpolated in the later laisses. It is interesting to note that of the two manuscripts containing the *Parfait*, S1 and W, the latter has the extended 'happy end' to the *Voeux*. Thus the owners of this manuscript would have the choice of two different fates for the personages, a long life of domestic bliss or a speedy and violent death.

NOTES

1. The text of these laisses is given in Ritchie, Vol. IV, 432-32a footnote (7a) and Vol. III, xcvii, Extract V2 (7b).

2. A new edition of the *Veus du Paon* based on Q1, prepared by Fr. C. Casey, contains useful appendices printing in full the laisses additional to Q1. Ritchie's numbering of the final laisses in W corresponds to Casey's edition as follows:

Ritchie	Casey
W 1-3, 3a, 4-7	Q1 278-85
7a, 7b	279a, b
8	286
9-12	286a-d
13-14	287-88
15	288a
16-19	289-92
20	292a
21-22	293-94

I am grateful to Fr. Casey for his kindness in allowing me to see a copy of his work prior to publication.

3. Enid Donkin, 'Le "Plagiat" de Jean Brisebare', *Romania*, 86 (1965), 395-404.

DIVISION OF THE *RESTOR* INTO TWO PARTS

In four of the seven manuscripts containing the whole poem, P6P7Q1W, the line 'Quant Porus li Indoys et tout si compaignon' follows I 1484 'Si que a tous jours mais vous i poés fiier' without a break. The redactors have seen no need to divide the poem. However, the other three manuscripts show some signs of editorial division. N6 has a miniature at the end of the first part depicting a peacock on a pillar (164r.) and underneath it the words 'Ci commence le restor dou paon'. The second part then begins overleaf at the top of 164vo. S1 has at the end of Part I the words 'Explixit le restor du paon' (161r.) and a similar explicit, 'Explicit le Restour du paon' (182vo.) at the end of Part II. P has no explicit at the end of the first part, but Part II begins on a new leaf (175r.) with the decorative treatment reserved in that manuscript for the beginning of a new branch; that is, a large initial, a full border of foliage and birds and a picture extending across the whole lower margin, in this case of musicians and dancers. The beginning of a new branch is usually preceded by a full-page illustration in P but a leaf has been lost at this place and it is likely that it contained, or was intended to contain, such an illustration.

The nine manuscripts containing only the second part of the poem, N1N2N5 OQS5S6S7U, begin with the line 'Quant Porus li Indoys et tout si compaignon' and it seems that a division here would be convenient, if only to avoid the absurdity of numbering their first line 1485. It would be justifiable if the subject matter offered a suitable pause or change at the same point. And indeed, the first part is concerned with the fulfilment of one vow and the second part with the relative merits of all the vows. The first part is narrative, the second part a discussion. The first part could be entitled the *Restor du Paon* and the second part the *Pris des Veus*. They are in fact two parts of one whole which is unified and welded into the original narrative of the *Veus du Paon* by the use of the background of Epheson, the same personages and the marriage festivities presided over by Alexander. I have therefore divided the poem for this edition into two parts, I 1-1484 and II 1-1342, which correspond to the natural demarcation of the contents.

VERSIFICATION

The poem is written in alexandrines in monorhymed laisses of varying length in true rhyme. The following rhymes are used.

-a	I xiv, xx, xxvi. II xxi, xxxi.
-age	I viii, xxii.
-ains	II xii.
-aire	II xvi.
-ais	II xxii.
-ance	I xxxiv.
-ans	I xxviii, xxxiii.
-ant	I xv. II xx, xxviii.
-as	I xxix.
-é	I vii, x, xxv. II xi.
-ee	I xiii, xxiv, xxxii. II xxvii.
-ele	II x.
-endre	II vi.
-ent	II xviii.
-er	I xvii, xxx. II iv.
-és	I xxiii.
-eus	II xvii.
-ie	I vi, xii. II ii.
-ier	I xxxvi. II xiv, xxix.
-iés	II ix.
-ire	II xxiii.
-is	I iv, xvi, xxxv. II v, xxvi.
-ite	II iii.
-iue	II xix.
-ius	I iii.
-oie	I v, xviii. II xiii.
-ois	I i. II viii, xv.
-oit	I xi. II vii.
-on	I ix, xix, xxvii. II i.
-ue	II xxv.
-us	I ii, xxi, xxxi. II xxiv, xxx.

Rhyme words are seldom repeated within a laisse and where they are, one of the lines is often suspect. For example in I ix, a laisse of 129 lines, only two rhyme words occur more than once with the same meaning: *renon* in I 299, 309, 377 and *traïson* in I 321, 344; but I 299, 377 are found only in P and may have been added by a performer or a scribe. Identical rhymes occur elsewhere but not frequently and only twice in consecutive lines: *prisonnier* in I 1444, 1445 and *va* II 852, 853. Here again only P has both lines in each instance. Occasionally such rhymes are separated only by one or two lines, e.g. *reclamee* I 549, 551 (I 551 in P only), *creüs* I 1157, 1159, *fais* II 888, 891. However, in I xx in -a the third person singular present of *avoir* is used at the rhyme as an auxiliary in seven lines, nor can it be said in mitigation that the main verb varies for in five cases it is *faire* I 842, 843, 845, 849, 854.

Words identical in form but different in meaning are occasionally found in the same laisse, e.g. *lie* I 189, 195 (I 189 only in P); *trouvee* I 526, 546; *pris* I 706, 712; *soie* I 760, 771; *mestier* II 579, 580; *nois* II 606, 617; *cois* II 615, 624; *teus* II 651, 654; *venus* II 974, 976; *jus* II 962, 978, 1000 (II 1000 only in P).

Simple and compound words are also used at the rhyme, e.g. *ploie* I 172, *sousploie* I 176, *emploie* I 184; *laissie* I 465, *entrelaissie* I 481; *apele* II 404, *rapiele* II 413; *dire* II 924, *contredire* II 926, *redire* II 927, *mesdire* II 937.

Proper names appear in various forms to suit the rhyme e.g. Elias for Eliot I 1110, Gadifer for Gadifer II 585, Betus for Betis I 1172, Ydorie for Ydorus I 194. The adjectival form *macedonus* for *macedonois* is found in I 69, I 1154 and a form Dame Phesonois at the rhyme in I 49. The latter may be adjectival but it is more probably a variant of Phesonas. Most of these forms are in the *Voeux* and the *Fuerre de Gadres* and similar deformations occur in the other Alexander poems so Brisebare was simply following the tradition. Other words are deformed at the rhyme but less frequently. I have found *soustais* II 898 perhaps for *soutis, servitier* I 1361 for *serviteur, secree* II 1103 for *secroie, biois* I 20 for *biais, rebois* II 625 perhaps for *rebors, enfouois* I 4 for *enfouis*, and *eskais* II 916 which is not in the dictionaries and may also be a deformation for the rhyme.

Enjambement

Enjambement in early epics in alexandrines was rare. A study of Brisebare's practice shows that, in spite of an occasional use of epic formulas, he felt free enough also to use enjambement. Some results of a sentence continuing over the rhyme are:

i.   past participle separated from its auxiliary: I 66, 67; 322, 323; 942, 943.

ii. subject separated from verb: I 47,48; 70,71; 83,84; 190,191; 212,213; 214, 215; 1174,1175; 1186,1187; 1319,1320; 1388,1389; II 400,401; 598,599; 857,858.

iii. verb separated from its object: I 225,226; 435,436; 465,466; 565,566; 651,652; II 36,37; 42, 43; 421,422; 432,433; 646,647; 741,742; 809,810; 896,897; 1271,1272; 1334,1335.

iv. auxiliary separated from infinitive: I 364,365.

v. miscellaneous: I 36,37; 335,336; 361,362; 419,420; 537,538; 683,684; 684,685; 1257,1258; II 422,423; 526,527.

Enjambement of the caesura also occurs. In the following cases a medial pause would separate:

i. subject and verb: I 58, 213, 245, 311; II 1258.

ii. noun and complement: I 67; II 42, 146, 1296.

iii. verb and object: I 41, 166, 180, 311, 683, 716; II 599.

iv. auxiliary and infinitive: I 177; II 562.

v. auxiliary and past participle: I 207, 215, 216, 376, 522; II 375, 376, 377, 455.

Some of these do not admit of even the slightest pause after the sixth syllable:

I 716 Sa clef en s'aumosniere prist, s'ala defremer

II 146 'Seignor,' ce dist li rois des hiraus 'c'est tout cler'

Also I 177, 180, 207, 212-13, 215, 216, 522; II 42, 377, 455, 562, 1296.

It is not certain how such lines should be treated. G. Lote considers three schools of thought in his *Histoire du vers français*[1] . First that of Tobler who believed that lines in which a pause would interrupt the sense have no caesura. Second that of Gaston Paris who supposed that the caesura was mobile; and third that of Leon Gautier in whose view the caesura did not shift and in the alexandrine there would always be a stress on the sixth syllable. Lote himself subscribes to the third school, drawing support from the oldest treatises which prescribed only one caesura, and from music. The theory is that the caesura is always in the same place and this makes a logical division where possible. Where this is not possible the break occurs all the same and logic is sacrificed to the rules of prosody. It is left to the skill of the performer to include the pause and at the same time to carry over the meaning.

Enjambement of the line is not considered so flagrant when the sense continues to the end of the next line, nor when it reaches the caesura. However, it is considered audacious when it overflows the rhyme by two or three syllables, and pernicious when it goes beyond the caesura without reaching the end of the line as another enjambement almost always follows (Lote, vol. I, 247-64). In our text most examples of enjambement reach either the caesura or the end of the next line, but a considerable number fall into the 'audacious' category, e.g. I 212-13, 465-66, 1257-58; II 400-01, 809-10 etc.

Hiatus

Hiatus of e where elision was not compulsory was freely admitted in O.F. Brisebare takes full advantage of this, using elision or hiatus as suited the metre. Hiatus occurs with *ne avoirs* I 4, *ne i* I 244, *je ai* I 279, *je en* I 1157, *que avoir* I 165, *que il/elle* I 215, 473, 538, 822, 971, 1324, 1326, 1349, 1440, 1463, *que on* II 26, 500. It occurs in ms. P only with *que a* I 1484, *que el* II 277, *que on* I 1445 and *que il* I 1464.

Hiatus was not normally permissible with *ne* from *non* and only P has *ne i* in I 244.

With words of more than one syllable the position is less clear. A. Tobler thought that elision of e should be considered the rule, hiatus being an occasional procedure in certain circumstances but it is not certain what these circumstances were. He quotes Mall who in his introduction to the *Comput* of Ph.de Thaon suggests that it was used where more than one consonant preceded the final e, e.g. *Entre icel saint jurn* 2223, but Tobler was not convinced[2]. The examples of hiatus in the *Restor* (ms. P) show that the final e is preceded usually not by two different consonants but by a double consonant or by l or r; *elle ot* I 817, *elle i* I 934, *s'orfavresse estoie* I 161, *chiere enbronchie* II 88, *faire un* II 699, *guerre esmue* II 1034, *menchoinne isnele* II 429. In the single example of a group of different consonants preceding final e the last of these is r as it is in the example quoted by Tobler: *moustre a* I 143. Most of the other manuscripts avoid the hiatus in these cases. All do so in the two instances with *elle* and in I 161 by inserting a glide e between the v and r of *orfavresse*. It is possible that P inadvertently omitted this e. The hiatus could also have been shifted back to *se*, but this was not done and it is arguable that Brisebare intended the pause to be where it occurs in P particularly as this position softens the sibilant repetition of ess. Only P6 W support P in II 88 and there is no support from the other manuscripts for the remaining examples. P may be wrong but as there is no agreement in the variants it seems that individual attempts have been made to avoid the hiatus and I have not considered it appropriate to alter P.

NOTES

1. G. Lote, *Histoire du vers français*, 3 vols (Paris, 1949-55), I, 237-45.
2. A Tobler, *Vom französischen Versbau* (Leipzig, 1903), p. 64.

LANGUAGE

Phonology

A study based on the rhyme words shows that the author used both Francien and Picard forms. For instance, the laisse in -endre (II 275-92) has words with the glide consonant d (not normally found in Picard texts) rhyming with words where the d is organic, e.g. *engendre* II 285, *mendre* II 280, *cendre* II 287 rhyme with *entendre* II 275, 290, *aprendre* II 288, *vendre* II 283. The laisses in -ains,-anche-ance, -ans,-ant have rhymes deriving from tonic e and a followed by a nasal consonant, e.g. *plenus>plains* II 464, *planus>plains* II 480, *minus>mains* II 470, *manus> mains* II 481, *commanche* I 1282, *senefianche* I 1249, *ensciant* II 812, *enfant* II 801. This is also found in Francien works of this date but the consistent spelling in *a* suggests a Picard text. The laisse in -ent shows the normal Francien development of tonic e plus nasal and includes the spelling in -ent of some of the words in -ant in the laisses mentioned above, e.g. *orient* II 736, *enscient* II 697, 712. The laisses in -is also show normal Francien development whereas laisses in -ie, -iue, -ius include many Picard forms. The following are the main Picard elements which can be attributed to the author:

i. Past participles in -ie (Francien -iee). This occurs consistently, e.g. *estekie* I 485, *laissie* I 465 rhyming with *mie* I 473, *vie* I 493.

ii. Forms in -ius, -iue. These evolved in several ways:
   a. By reduction of Francien -ieu, e.g. *lius* I 109, *gius* I 99, *chius* I 105, *liue* II 772, *giue* II 771, (Pope § **546 and §1320, vi).[1]
   b. -ivum>-iu instead of -if, e.g. *pensius* I 102, *ententius* I 115. A feminine in -iue was perhaps formed on the masculine in -iu, e.g. *pensiue* II 767, *ententiue* II 768, (Gossen § 21).[2]
   c. -ilis>-ius instead of -is, e.g. *sotius* I 107, *seignorius* I 108, *ostius* I 116, (Gossen §20 and Pope § 1320, xix).
   d. The reduction of -uee to -ue, only in *gliue*<*glu+ata? (Pope §1320, v).
   e. *eslius* I 103 may be the result of the influence of Picard strong perfects such as *biut* (Pope §1056**). The form *esleüs* occurs I 81, II 984, 1297 also at the rhyme.

Some of the words in -ius in laisse I iii occur again in the laisses in -is showing the normal Francien development, e.g. *gentis* I 158, *soutis* I 700, *poëstis* II

217, *seignoris* II 229, *ententis* II 265 etc.

iii. The loss of atonic e in hiatus before a vowel in *esmue* II 1030, 1034 (Pope §1320,x). However the e is maintained where it is needed for the metre, e.g. *creüe* II 1010, *meüs* II 1307. but *esmus* I 862 and *mus* I 878.

iv. The absence of diphthongization of tonic free open o and e when followed by a palatal sound in e.g. *proie* I 170, 770, II 519, *noie* II 539, *apoie* II 546, *anoit* I 451 (Pope §1321, i and §1322, x considers this an eastern and north-eastern phenomenon).

v. Words in -anche-ance from -antia rhyming with derivatives of -anca, e.g. *senefianche* I 1249, *sustance* I 1252, *plaisanche* I 1260 rhyming with *franche* I 1246, *brance* I 1268 (Gossen §§38,41).

vi. The reduction of ts to s in rhymes such as *fais<factos* II 890 and *mais<magis* II 880; *vois<vocem* I 14, *dois<digitos* I 55 and *trois<tres* I 31. Gossen §40 notes that from the middle of the thirteenth century and particularly in the fourteenth the influence of the Francien spelling -z in such words spread to the Picard region. However this influence was less strong in the northern part. In ms. P the symbol z is found only in intervocalic position where it appears to be an alternative for a voiced s, e.g. *Ephezon* II 1284, *Epheson* II 752.

Morphology

The main characteristic is the preservation of older forms of nouns and verbs. The two-case declension system is maintained throughout P in nouns, adjectives and articles by the author and the scribe. The forms at the rhyme, which can be ascribed to the author, are nominative singular masculine *senés* I 921, *reposés* I 914, *jolis* I 1325 etc. and nominative plural *asorté* I 959, *fondé* I 964, *parchonnier* I 1374 etc. Substantives deriving from Latin nouns ending in -er in the nominative singular have an analogical s, e.g. *freres* II 1258, *peres* I 323,1137, *orfevres* II 299, *maistres* I 144, nominative plural *maistre* I 187. In most cases the form does not affect the metre although it does so in I 1137 and I 187.

Feminine nouns and adjectives having a flexional s in the nominative singular in O.F. have retained this form in P, e.g. *biautés* I 923 but *biauté*, oblique singular, I 221, both of these occurring at the rhyme. Among examples affecting the metre are *loyaus* II 412, nominative singular, and *mortel* I 344, oblique singular. A few adjectives of this latter type occur with an analogical feminine form, e.g. *crueuse* II 755, *verde* II 901, *fole* I 1051. *Grans, fors, tel, quel* have either the etymological or the analogical form as suits the metre, e.g.:

Nom.sing.   *grans* I 475, 1029, 1096 (rhyme), 1182, II 1010, 1015. *grande* II 418. *fors* II 308, 541. *tele* II 921.

Obl. sing.   *grant* I 72, 77, 185 . . . (55 times). *grande* I 279, 780,854 . . . (8 times). *forte* I 1265. *tel* I 371, 787, II 646, 795. *tele* I 584,1035, II 313. *quel* I 301,597. *quele* I 902.

Nom.pl.   *teles* I 893.

Obl. pl.   *grans* I 1057,1214, II 170,676. *quels* I 425. *ques* I 287. *queles* I 1330.

The feminine definite article has normal Francien as well as Picard forms, sometimes both in the same line: I 190 *la bele Edea, li blonde, l'escavie.* The relative frequency is:

Nom. sing.	*la*	78	*li* 28		l'	11
Obl.sing.	*la*	134	*le* 12		l'	41

Verbal forms generally show the normal development but in the imperfect indicative and conditional, only the etymological termination of the first person singular is found. This is guaranteed by the rhyme in the laisses in -oie and must be the author's usage, e.g. *trouvoie* II 509, *desobeïssoie* II 549, *voloie* II 542, *cesseroie* I 163, *prendroie* I 761.

In the past definite third person singular there is no final t in the weak perfects of the i- and u- type, although this had begun to be reintroduced in the early thirteenth century (Pope § 998). The only exception is *morut* I 272, II 1220, but in neither case is this at the rhyme.

Apart from these conservative tendencies the main dialectal forms attributable to the author are:

i.   a.   The possessive pronoun forms *miue* II 773 and *siue* II 775 at the rhyme, but *moie* II 235, 266, 346 and *soie* I 500 (Gossen § 69, Pope § 1320, xxv).

    b.   Picard *nos, no* and Francien *nostres, nostre* are found in almost equal proportions, e.g. *no dieu* I 90, *nostre droit avoé* I 226, *nos maus* I 1111, *nostres rois* II 195 (Gossen § 68, Pope § 1320, xxv).

ii.   Future and conditional forms with an interconsonantal vocalic glide in some cases, presumably where an extra syllable was required, e.g. *avera* I 1175, etc., but *avra* I 433 etc. *Devoir* has only the form *deveroit* II 485, 783, whereas *savoir* has the v eliminated in each case, e.g. *saroie* I 183 etc. Also *prendera* II 867 but *prendroie* I 761, *vivera* I 635 but *vivra* II 867, *isterai* II 169 (Gossen § 74, Pope § 1320, xiii).

iii.   The form in -iesmes of the first person plural imperfect indicative is found once in *veuliesmes* II 194. As three syllables are required the form must be the author's (Gossen § 79, Pope § 919** and § 1320, xxvii).

iv.   The second person plural termination in -es is used except in *orrois* II 334, *escondirois* II 346, both future, and *debatois* II 621, present indicative, (Pope § 896). All these are at the rhyme.

Syntax

Only one usage presents itself as peculiarly Picard and it occurs only once in *Fai me .i. message au roi* II 975. As the necessary elision can be made with *me* but not with *moi* it can be ascribed to the author (Gossen § 81).

Language of the scribe

The following are considered to be Picard traits:

i. Close e develops like open e before 1 plus consonant to -aus instead of -eus. The personal pronoun forms *yaus* and *aus* are found nine times each and *euls* once in I 1016. The demonstrative plural is found once in the Francien form *ceuls* I 1462, once in the form *ciaus* I 807 and five times as *ceaus*. Also *solaus* I 711, II 643,1254.

ii. Reduction of -ieu to -iu, e.g. *mius* I 345 (used substantivally) but *miex* in all cases when used as an adverb; *ius* I 1281 but *iex* in all other instances. Forms deriving from -ocu are generally spelt -iu, e.g. *liu* in eight cases but *lieu* in II 393,1250; *fus* II 415; *jus* I 89 and passim, *gius* II 771, *ju* II 123,247, *giu* I 1317. *Diex, dieu* occur 45 times but the reduced forms are found also: *dius* (nom. sing.) I 104 at rhyme, *diu* (obl. sing.) I 1160, II 956,1056,1075, *diu* (nom. pl.) II 176,182,438, 1215,1218, *dius* (obl.pl.) I 98 at rhyme, II 820.

iii. Close e plus nasal becomes -ain-, e.g. *chaint* I 1433, *mains* (from *minus*) I 543 and passim, *painte* I 466, *paindre* I 1423.

iv. Reduction of final ts to s, e.g. *fais* I 249 and passim, *dis* I 249 and passim, *grans* I 475 and passim.

v. Frequent metathesis of r, e.g. *fremés* I 910, *bregier* II 562, *esprivier* I 688, *afrumant* II 821, *affremer* II 7, *mousterrai* II 778.

vi. The development of o followed by a nasal to u is not peculiar to Picard, but Gossen (§28) found forms in -ou- particularly frequent in the texts he studied. In fact the rhymes showed that o before n was so close and so denasalized that the sound could be confused with ou. Forms in ms. P such as *mostrant* I 1289, *couvient* II 191, 593,631 and passim are examples of this phenomenon, in fact the scribe uses the symbol for *con* to represent *cou* in *plus c'outrecuidiers* II 390. Other graphies demonstrating the tendency but without indicating the degree of nasalisation are *courounee* II 1135, *avirounee* II 1128, *pumier* I 370,1439, *oumage* I 240 etc.

vii. *Verb forms*

    a. Picard *eut* for *ot* from *habuit* occurs I 303,304,342 and passim, but it is far outnumbered by the Francien form, (Gossen § 72).

b. The first person singular of the present and past definite tenses in -c(h), e.g. *loch* II 1012, *cuich* II 185, *asench* II 1051, *renc* I 130, *siuc* II 648, *och* I 832, Francien *oi* from *habui*, (Gossen § 75).

c. The present subjunctive in -che, e.g. *plache* II 81, *faiche* II 251, *faice* II 687, *faichiés* I 202 *fachiés* I 132,389 (Gossen § 80).

Among traits found in neighbouring dialects as well as in Picard are:

Walloon

i. Vocalization of preconsonantal 1, e.g. *fiex* I 340,393,460, *gentiex* II 155, 899, *prius* (peril+s) I 561, II 161. The form *prius* also shows the Picard reduction of unstressed vowel which is found also in the oblique singular *pril* I 558, although in I 593 and II 852 the full form *peril* is found.

ii. -ivu becoming -iu, -ieu, e.g. *hastiex* II 260 and the feminine *caitiue* I 821 perhaps formed on the masculine.

iii. Unstressed possessive adjectives show normal Francien development except *sen* for *son* II 1181 and *se* for *sa* I 320,1321,II 889.

Walloon and Lorrain

i. The palatalization of countertonic e to i before n and 1 *mouillés* and of intertonic e before s,z, e.g. *engignier* II 567, *pignon* I 369, *mignier* I 1469. *millors* I 720, *millor* I 1326; *orison* II 1277, *demorison* I 1046, *caplison* I 263, *cognissans* I 1081, *cognissance* I 1288, *cognissiés* II 105.

Francien forms are also found. For example *seignor* occurs only in that form, and *mangier* occurs in I 1153,1362, II 1286,1291,1294. It may be that the form *mignier*, which Gossen § 34 claims to have found only in texts from Douai, Lille and Saint-Quentin, is that of the author and was introduced for the sake of the pun with *mignes*. The form *meillor* occurs except in the two instances cited above and *conseilla* II 845 also has the Francien form.

ii. The retention of final t unsupported, e.g. *piet* I 1329 and passim; *gret* II 527,702 but otherwise *gré; pechiet* II 321,324 etc.

iii. The retention of Germanic initial w, e.g. *waucrant* II 1223, *awardee* I 1187. But the sound is usually represented as in Francien, e.g. *gaignars* II 967, *gaitierent* I 774, *garandir* II 193, *garant* II 240,824, *guerredons* I 149,773, 1057, *guiïe* I 517, *guise* I 1438, II 609.

iv. The absence of an interconsonantal glide in the groups n'r, l'r, e.g. *engenre* II 889, *menre* I 167, *semonra* I 432, *tolroit* II 314, *tauroit* II 42 etc. In no case is the glide consonant found except where the scribe was constrained to use it in the laisse in -endre. On the other hand the glide consonant b is found in most cases in the group m'I, e.g. *assembla* I 1026, *samblant* I 677, *assemblee* I 1029. Exceptions: *descanlé* (for *dessemblé*) I 958, *humle* II 776, also *humeles* I 118 and *humelment* I 1230 where a vowel separates the two consonants.

v.　The tonic form *mi* of the personal pronoun in II 154, 529,540 but *moi* in twelve other instances.

vi.　The third person plural of the past definite in -isent, e.g. *disent* I 90, *assisent* I 87, *prisent* I 397, *fisent* I 53 and passim. I have found only one exception, *firent* II 150.

vii.　Imperfect subjunctive with intervocalic s preserved, e.g. *fesist* I 305 and passim, *vausist* I 44, *vausisse* II 199 and the analogical *offresist* I 1461.

viii.　The frequent breaking of tonic open e blocked and free, e.g. *rapiele* II 413, *turiele* II 425, *affiert* I 300 and passim, *desiert* I 1349, *aouviers* I 700, *iestre* II 373.

Walloon, Lorrain and Norman

i.　The reduction of -iee to -ie. Found mainly in past participles feminine of the first conjugation this is the only form of such participles in the *Restor*, e.g. *solatiie* I 947, *priie* II 522, *baignie* II 1145.

ii.　The development of open o followed by l blocked to au, e.g. *faus* I 653, *caupee* I 582, *decauper* II 158, *saudoiier* I 1422, *vautie* II 108, *vausisse* II 199, *tauroit* II 42, *retaurai* II 1077, but *tolroit* II 314, *tolra* II 872 etc.

Norman

i.　The development of l plus yod final to l, e.g. *oel* II 289, *eul* I 1290, *vuel* I ll and passim, *voel* II 73 and passim, *veul* I 1110 and passim. The forms *oelletés* I 135 and *voellans* I 1068 may also show this phenomenon but we do not know the phonetic value of the group -ll-.

NOTES

1.　M. K. Pope, *From Latin to Modern French*, (Manchester, 1952)
2.　C.T. Gossen, *Petite grammaire de l'ancien picard*, (Paris, 1951)

INTEREST AND LITERARY MERIT OF THE *RESTOR DU PAON*

There are two major contributions to the peacock cycle contained in the *Restor*.
First, the making good of a genuine omission in the earlier poem, the *Voeux du
Paon*, by the interpolation of an account of the fulfilling of Edea's vow to restore
the peacock in gold; and second, the recapitulation of the deeds of valour
performed in fulfilment of the vows, presented in the form of a debate to determine their relative merits and to award a prize of honour. The first is necessary to
complete the *Voeux* story and the second is the only known example of a *débat*
of this nature and seems to be an imitation of the proceedings at the literary
contests held at the *Puys* of north-eastern France which were popular from the
twelfth century until well into the fifteenth.

In addition there are two stories of unusual interest: an account of the early
life of Emenidus incorporating an Arabian Nights tale of a villainous magician and
the Caliph of Baghdad's daughter (I 250-905), and a brief reference to the story
of Basin the Enchanter and Charlemagne (I 624-46).

The first of these tales appears to be the sole example in French of this strange
oriental adventure. It was published under the title 'une histoire de brigands' by
G. Bonnier. He considered this tale of a gallant robber rescuing a damsel in distress
to be the most interesting part of the *Restor* and suggested that it was an invention
of Brisebare's.[1] Brisebare himself gives no clue to the source of his story although
he does say it is not to be found in the Alexander poems (I 275-78). However, the
local colour, especially in I 524-42, suggests an authentic oriental background and
its source may still be found.

The Emenidus story stands out from the rest of the work in subject matter and
treatment and shows indications of being a later addition to the poem:

i.   It is preceded by a second address to the audience (I 250-51) and may have
been composed for a nobleman and presented privately as a separate work.

ii.   The new address is followed by a second summary of the previous exploits of
Alexander. Although the two summaries contain different information it
would have been more satisfactory artistically to include all the information
at the beginning of the work. One can imagine the hearty concurrence of the
audience at the words 'Assés l'avés oï' (I 252) if they were expected to listen
to a second summary after an interval of less than two hundred lines.

iii.   The subject matter is not mentioned in the poet's declaration of intentions (I 9-11 and I 65-67), nor does it appear at the end of the poem where he summarizes what he has done (II 1334-39).

iv.   The subject matter, a swift narrative of adventure, has nothing to do with the peacock and is unlike the rest of the poem which contains little action and is mainly an exercise in disputation together with a long exposition of the peacock's virtues.

On the other hand in none of the manuscripts of Part I is the *Enfances Emenidus* omitted. This could indicate that the episode is not an interpolation and always formed part of the poem. However, the episode could also be an interpolation that was by chance copied into all the manuscripts that have survived. It was perhaps written very soon after the composition of the original poem and before the archetype of the surviving copies was made.

If it is an interpolation it has been introduced very neatly into the poem. The last laisse before this story (viii I 230-49) and the final laisse of the story (xxii I 888-906) both have the same rhyme in -age. If one omits the end of laisse viii and the beginning of laisse xxii (I 242-49 and I 888-96) the remaining lines could form one laisse: Emenidus takes leave of Alexander and rides quickly to Archade to fetch his niece. This journey is a suitable point to interrupt the narrative. The author had merely to add I 242-45 to bring Emenidus into a great wooded tract where he could be left riding and then explain that he proposed to introduce this story (I 246-49). The *Enfances Emenidus* end at I 896, which is a repetition of the content of I 241 and it is probable that I 897-901 completed the laisse begun at I 230 in the original version. Lines I 902-06 were probably added to link the new material to the rest of the work and also to remind the audience why Emenidus has undertaken this journey. Without this interruption of some 660 lines it would not have been necessary to repeat the explanation given in I 217-25.

Finally, if the Emenidus story is an interpolation was Brisebare its author? Clearly the author of the 'nuef ouvrage', namely the restoration of the peacock (282-88) and the two marriages (I 289-92), is Brisebare for he has given his name in I 10. Then who is the 'je' in I 279-80 who wants to relate the history of Emenidus and add it to the *Voeux* with the 'nuef ouvrage' at the end? The author of the *Enfances Emenidus* goes on to say that the poet of the *Voeux* would have made a better job of this new work 'Que faire ne porroie selonc m'entention/Se j'avoie en aiue tous les livres Caton' (I 297-98). The person speaking here must be the author of the new work, Brisebare, but the 'je' here must be the same person as the 'je' in I 280. Therefore the author of the 'nuef ouvrage' and of the *Enfances Emenidus* are one and the same person, namely Brisebare.

I believe, therefore, that Brisebare interpolated the Emenidus story into his own work, but whether it was written for a patron is not certain. Brisebare merely states that he himself wants it to appear in the *Voeux* because of his affection for

Emenidus (I 279-82). He may simply have come across this romantic tale and thought to embellish his work with it. It does not occur in the known Alexander poems although there is a laconic reference to the early life of Emenidus in Br. IV (*M.F.R.A.* vol. II). The knights are expressing their grief at the death of Alexander.

721   Aprés Cliçon le conte, le grant duel renovele
                Emenidus, li fieus l'amiraut de Tudele,
                Qui por l'amor avoir de la noble pucele
                Combati au gaiant es plaines de Castele
                Tant que le cuer li traist par desous la mamele.

In his *Notes and Variants to Branch IV* (*M.F.R.A.* vol. VII) A. Foulet merely states p.112, that 'this romantic history of Emenidus' parentage and fight against a giant appears to be a fanciful invention of the author of the stanza'.

The second story, although only a brief summary of Charlemagne's adventure with Basin the thief, is valuable evidence pointing to the existence at one time of a French version of this epic. Versions of the story exist in other languages, see I 624-46 notes. In the *Restor* Charlemagne at the command of an angel accompanies Basin the Enchanter on one of his thieving expeditions. Using his magic arts Basin enters the house of one of Charlemagne's knights whose wife happens to be Charles's cousin. Basin arrives in time to overhear the husband disclosing to his wife a plot to murder Charles. The wife declares that she will warn the king and the traitor strikes her in the face so that it bleeds. Basin steps forward, invisible, catches the blood in his glove and takes it to Charles whom he informs of the plot. The king is therefore able to ward off the attempted assassination. Another brief reference to the story in French is found in *Renaud de Montauban* but this concentrates on the seizing of the conspirators and does not include the episode of the traitor striking his wife and Basin catching the blood.[2]

Because of the way the new additions are inserted into the *Voeux* a study of the composition of the *Restor* as a whole would be unrewarding. The interest lies rather in the skilful way in which the author has woven the various components of his poem into each other and into the *Voeux*. This is particularly apparent in Part I, for the beginning and end of the peacock story are widely separated by other material, yet the author does not allow his audience to forget the peacock during the intervening laisses as is shown in the following analysis.

The Peacock Material

After an introductory laisse summarizing the *Roman d'Alixandre* and the *Voeux du Paon* (I 1-67) Brisebare sets the scene in Epheson after the raising of the siege with an assembly of knights and ladies in the Chamber of Venus (I 68-97). Practically the whole of this scene is taken from the *Voeux*.

During the ensuing festivities Edea sends for goldsmiths, gives them instructions and they set to work (I 98-156). The goldsmiths are left working and recede into the background as attention focuses on the lovers (I 157-206) but their presence is not forgotten for they are given money (I 166-70) and I 181-84) and they are depicted at work again (I 185-86) and being served with food by Edea (I 187-91). They finally fade out as interest turns to Emenidus. He has promised his niece Lidoine to Gadifer and so must go to his land of Arcade to fetch her (I 192-245). This part was also, according to Brisebare, omitted from the *Voeux*.

This journey of Emenidus is used then as a pretext to insert the *Enfances Emenidus* (I 246-896).

Following such a long digression Brisebare has to remind his audience of the purpose of Emenidus's journey (I 897-906). He also needs to remind them of the peacock, so he works it in after Lidoine's arrival at Epheson (I 907-40), for she must be taken to the workshop to see it (I 941-53).

The marriages and further feasting are now dovetailed into the narrative (I 954-1185). This section comprises laisses from the *Voeux* plus additional material by Brisebare. Finally the scene is set for the presentation of the peacock (I 1186-1206), Edea's panegyric (I 1207-1336) and the adoration (I 1337-1464). Part I ends with more festivities (I 1465-75).

The Enfances Emenidus

In contrast to the peacock story the *Enfances Emenidus* is a swift, vigorous, well-structured tale with no extraneous matter interpolated. It is told with economy in just over five hundred lines. There are several episodes but every element is necessary for the development of the plot leading up to the final meeting of Alexander and Emenidus at a point in the latter's career when he is at last worthy of becoming Alexander's liege man.

The author has set himself the problem of bringing together Alexander, a king's son, and Emenidus, a nobleman's son turned thief. The two are at first widely separated by their condition and by physical distance. The story begins with Emenidus at Capharnaon, the victim of a series of catastrophes but lucky nevertheless. His father's land is devastated but Emenidus escapes and is adopted by a gang of thieves. Their kindly treatment of him and his eventual promotion to be their leader is overshadowed by his secret dissatisfaction with their way of life. Their headquarters is at Damascus.

The Alexander strand is taken up. He is still a youth in Macedonia. Thwarted in his desire to marry the daughter of the Caliph of Baghdad he sends a robber-magician to abduct her.

By chance the two strands of the story come together for Emenidus is temporarily in Baghdad in order to carry out a wager. (Damascus and Baghdad are close together in Brisebare's geography). Emenidus recognizes the robber for what he is by his demeanour, (thus demonstrating that good can be derived from the evil of a robber's life for Emenidus's experience makes it possible for him to rescue the Caliph's daughter.)

After the first climax with the slaying of Alexander's magician and the rescue of Rosenés the chances of Emenidus ever becoming Alexander's liege man seem even more remote. There is a pause in the narrative and Brisebare tells the story of Charlemagne and Basin thus emphasizing that everything that has happened is providential.

The narrative is resumed slowly with Rosenés pondering how she may reward Emenidus secretly and there is a long description of the Caliph's treasure. However, the second crisis is rapidly reached after Rosenés steals her father's jewels and sends them to Emenidus. It is this gift which makes it possible for Emenidus's robbers to disband and lead independent, respectable lives elsewhere. Thus Emenidus is free of the encumbrance of a gang of thieves. It also leads to his downfall for it is while he is attempting to sell his share of the jewels that he is arrested. His trial, condemnation and finally his rescue by Rosenés's confession follow in quick succession and he is raised to the rank of seneschal.

With Emenidus in an honourable position it is time to take up the Alexander strand again. When the would-be abductor of Rosenés fails to return Alexander declares war on the Caliph and marches to Baghdad. Here it is that he sees Emenidus for the first time fighting in the Caliph's army. Enthralled by his prowess he persuades Emenidus to become his liege man and gives him the land of Arcade.

The 'Pris des Veus'

The account of the *débat* in Part II differs in style both from the slow unfolding of the peacock material and from the racy narrative of the *Enfances Emenidus*. The medieval audience may have been eager to hear yet again of the exploits undertaken at Epheson but it is probable that the main interest for them lay in the skill with which the relative merits of each vow are put forward. (See II 146-1043 note). The arguments are presented competently in terms of the rules of chivalry and courtly love. But it is a contest that no one wins and the issue is finally decided by a lottery.

Although it is the worth of vows and not of *chants royaux* that is being considered the debate takes place in a framework that has certain similarities with what is known of the procedure of the literary contests held at the *Puys* that were held on public holidays at various towns in north-eastern France. These points of resemblance are briefly as follows:

The Judges

In a study of the works of Adan de le Hale, H. Guy notes that at Arras the judges at *Puys* were called 'entendeurs', 'la noble compagnie', 'la gent jolie', or simply 'la gent'.[3] In the *Restor* Alexander talks not of 'entendeurs' but of 'auditeurs': 'De premiers deuissons avoir auditeurs pris/Par quoi li jugemens fust au cler esclarchis' (II 1047-48). Earlier, after first proposing that a debate be held, he had taken a few of his guests into the *Chambre Venus* and, looking round the group, had said, 'chi n'a fors compaignie' (II 64). This is a strange pronouncement taking 'compaignie' in its usual sense, 'there is nothing but companionship here'. But if we take 'compaignie' to mean a panel of judges in terms of a literary contest the words become more meaningful: 'there are only judges here', (i.e. we are all judges). He then says that they are all equal: 'Vous i valés que rois, je n'i vail que mesnie' (II 68). Later, the same people are called 'toute celle gent' (II 92), and when Eliot appeals to the judges she calls them 'gent de bien' (II 1008).

Of course, all these words have their usual everyday meanings and it is not easy to determine whether Brisebare is using them in a technical way or not, but it could be that at least the words 'auditeurs' and 'compaignie' are so meant.

Flattery of the Judges

H. Guy records that attempts were made to influence the judges by flattery (op. cit.pp.XLVIII-XLIX). A similar appeal is made by Eliot:

II 1006	Voirs est que cascuns sos essauche sa machue
	Mais vous n'estes pas teus comment que je m'en jue.
	Ains estes gent de bien et d'ounor parvenue,
	De grant scïence plaine et partout cogneüe,
1010	Et tant seroit en vous plus grans blasmes creüe
	Si gens de si grant bien se trouvoit decheüe.

Poets would also beg for indulgence, for example in the following lines quoted by Guy (op.cit.p.XLIX n.4):

> Jugeur, si j'ai mesparlé
> Ne m'en voeillés escharnir.

In contrast the 'rois des menestreus' in the *Restor*, a veteran of the game, scorns such practice and appears to care little for anyone's opinion:

> Se la chose ai mal dite
> Repris soie a vo gré, ja n'en ruis prendre arbite. II 144-5

The Prize

At the *Puys* the prize was the title of 'roi' and a crown. The latter was given by the reigning 'Prince' or president of the *Puy* and was usually of silver. Others taking part received a chaplet of leaves (Guy op.cit.p.XXXIX and LI).

In the *Restor* the prize is chosen by Marcien who considers the respective merits of a sparrow-hawk (II 1108), a chaplet of leaves (II 1111), a crown of gold (II 1126) and an eagle (II 1135). The first two are rejected in favour of an eagle wearing a crown of gold.

Not only the debate but the whole poem seems to reflect the atmosphere of the *Puys*, partly perhaps because of the general air of festivity and holiday, but partly also in more specific ways. The programme of events varied in the different towns as is shown in the following lines quoted by Guy (op.cit.p.XLI):

> Va t'en aux festes de Tournay,
> A celles d'Arras et de Lille,
> D'Amiens, de Douay, de Cambray,
> De Valenciennes, d'Abbeville;
> La verras tu manieres mille
> De servir le prince des sos,
> Dedens les sales et par vile,
> En plein midy et a falos.

The festivities usually included a Mystery play, a literary contest and a series of jeux-partis which of course are not part of the celebrations at Epheson. But these do take place 'dedens les sales et par vile, en plein midy et a falos'. The feasting takes place in the Great Hall (II 55) and the debate in the *Chambre Venus* (II 57), but the procession in search of an eagle winds through the streets:

II 1148   Lors se leva li rois, si s'est sa gens levee,
           D'ostel en ostel ont une aigle demandee.
           A un ostel en vinrent s'en ont une trouvee.

The crowd then proceeds towards the *feste* followed by a group of minstrels playing and singing (II 1153-58). And all this merrymaking certainly took place by day and by night: 'Molt i ot grant deduit jusques a l'anuitier/Et la nuit toute nuit jusques a l'esclarier' (II 1243-44).

Two of the rules to which the *Prince du Pui* of Arras was committed were that he should on the following day hold a service for the dead and give a 'disner solempnel' at the time of the festivities (Guy, op.cit.p.XXXIX). In the *Restor* the 'service des morts' is ordered by Alexander (II 1271-72) to take place on the next day 'Lues que li solaus fu levés et apparus' (II 1254). There is also a dinner given by Emenidus (II 1286-95) but, as we have noted, the whole background of the *Restor* is one of continuous feasting.

Finally, it seems not unlikely, considering the way in which Brisebare addresses his audience, that the poem itself was presented as part of the entertainment at just such a *Puy* as it is imitating. The opening line, 'Seignor, prince et baron et dames et borgois' suggests that the author was addressing an open session at which the 'borgois' were present as well as the nobles. For the *Enfances Emenidus* we find that the audience has changed: 'Seignor et damoiseles, cevalier et baron,/Clerc et gent seculiere et de religion' (I 250). The 'borgois' are not included and one is tempted to conclude that this lively story was perhaps offered at a private session.

Style

The *Restor* is Brisebare's only venture into epic romance with its archaic form of monorhymed laisses in alexandrines. It was naturally necessary to imitate the style of the earlier works of the cycle so that the new matter would blend in with the old without too obvious signs of patching. It is a form that Brisebare was able to adopt with great facility.

Thus, descriptions of people and places are conventional. Knights are 'preus' nobles et sotius' (I 107), 'grans et corsus' (I 866), 'jouene au cler visage' (I 904). They have 'le cuer cortois et sage' (I 230,888) or 'cuer de lyon' (I 253 and passim), or they may have 'la chiere molt lie' (I 501). Ladies are described as 'li gaie et li rians' (I 1207), 'la noble la gentius' (I 101), or 'Blonde et vaire et rians, blance et encoulouree' (I 527), etc. Most of them are praiseworthy and beautiful e.g. 'ou tant a de biauté' (Rosenés I 391, Lidoine I 221), 'qui tant/molt fait a loër' (Elyot I 1117, Lidoine I 1128, Rosenés I 741). Geographical locations are simply 'bien seans' (Ireland I 1097), 'longe et large' (Arcade I 239), at most their amenities are listed, as in the description of Emenidus's stronghold: 'Nobles estoit et biaus et ricement fremés/D'yaues et de montaignes, de mares et de prés' (I 910-11). Even meals are described in stereotyped phrases: 'Lor mes ne lor mangiers n'est mestiers qu'on vous die/Tout ont a lor voloir dains, chers et vin sor lie' (I 188-89).

There are two exceptions however. The portrait of the 'roi des menestreus' has real life. He is depicted as an elderly, world-weary minstrel, his face pale and trouble-worn, whose profession has involved him in the playing of many roles. He even used his position as a privileged fool to taunt members of the household (II 126-33). Yet he was also something of a herald, for he was well-versed in the rules of jousting and tourneying (II 103-23 and II 136-38). However, he has the pride of an independent and respected man for he speaks as he thinks fit and is indifferent to the possibility of reproof (II 144-45). Nor is he afraid of rebuking the knights for their lack of perception during the debate (II 559-94). It seems that such a realistic portrayal must derive from first-hand knowledge: could it perhaps be a self-portrait?

The second description showing some originality is not of a person but of the Caliph's treasure (I 687-714). Here Brisebare describes a panorama worked in gold depicting various hunting activities. The fashioning is so realistic that everything seems to be in movement. Birds of prey and their victims appear to be flying through the air; partridges seem to be entering snares while dogs in the background are raging to get at the birds. The branches of the trees are laden with small birds apparently singing so lustily that they make the very leaves tremble. Deer and boar and huntsmen are also portrayed. There was also a sort of *mappa mundi* in gold with hell and the earthly paradise and the waters between, and above a sky of azure with the sun, moon and stars represented by jewels. These too seem to be objects with which Brisebare himself was familiar.

Apart from these two examples the descriptions in the *Restor* are mainly stereotyped, but Brisebare has a talent for presenting his characters in a lively way without actually describing them. This is usually done by showing them in action: in the case of the goldsmiths they are merely being talked to, but by the time Edea has finished giving her instructions we see a group of real people. It is through Edea's speech in which she tries to allay their suspicions that we can imagine a disgruntled, muttering crowd, perhaps eyeing each other appraisingly, wondering why so many have been sent for. Some may be offended in their professional pride, others may be aggrieved because they see the financial reward dwindling if it has to be shared. But Edea explains her reasons (I 137-48) and assures them that they will receive good payment (I 149-51) and finally they agree to do what she asks (I 152).

Another character is presented vividly in two lines. Emenidus visits a jeweler to sell his jewels and falls into the trap set by the Caliph. But instead of simply recording the arrest Brisebare evokes in a few words a picture of the jeweler, probably physically incapable of tackling Emenidus single-handed, but smooth-tongued and able to beguile him with plausible talk until the Caliph's men arrive:

I 800   A un lapidier vint, ses pierres aporta.
          Entrues que ciex de lobes le tint et herlusa
          Errannment au Califfe par .i. mes le noncha.

The Caliph too, though not described physically, is presented, not without humour, as a person of flesh and blood. He is a somewhat wily and secretive man. In his view Alexander was not a good enough match for his daughter but he concealed his thoughts from Philip's ambassadors (I 404-05) and excused his refusal in diplomatic speech (I 409-16). However, he is no match for his daughter who pretends to be ill to make him show her his treasure (I 679-82). Although she can hoodwink him he is wary enough not to give her the keys to the treasure-house, but not wise enough to see that she will not let the matter drop (I 730-40) and so this young girl 'qui tant fist a loër' steals his keys (I 741-2). He is far-seeing enough to realize that he can trap the jewel-thief when he tries to sell the jewels instead of wasting time hunting him out (I 795-7), and when Emenidus is brought before him he behaves like an autocratic ruler by making a summary judgement and condemning him to death (I 811-15). But his daughter is able to soften his heart for he believes without question her extraordinary story (which happens to be true this time) and is soon joyful again and heaping rewards upon Emenidus.

Brisebare's presentation of lively scenes is often achieved by a skilful manipulation of tenses. This ability to present characters and scenes vividly is the author's strong point and raises the work above the dull imitation of epic style that it could so easily have become. For the poem is not without line-fillers, some of which may be traditional epic formulas. For example: 'c'est tout cler' (I 1137 and passim), 'n'est mestiers qu'on vous die' (I 188), 'que vous diroie je? ' (I 1458). Sometimes words with similar or opposite meanings are linked by *et* to fill a hemistich: 'conquis et achievé' (I 215), 'promis et presenté' (I 216), 'sans rente et sans treuage' (I 241), 'par cler et par ombrage' (I 243). Characters swear by any gods that suit the rhyme: 'par les diex de Tudele' (II 402), '. . . de Chaldee' (I 568), '. . . d'Aumarie' (I 477), '. . . d'Abilant' (II 820), etc. Occasionally Brisebare imitates epic style by stringing together epic formulas, particularly in passages describing fighting. In the following, where Emenidus challenges the robber magician, practically every hemistich is a formula:

I 565
        Un boukeler d'achier qui pendoit a s'espee
        Prist, et l'espee traist. Quant il l'ot entesee
        Vers le larron ala, se li fist deffiee.
        'Lerres,' ce dist li dus, 'par les diex de Chaldee
        La pucele lairés car mar l'avés emblee.
        N'onques mais n'achatastes si crueuse vespree.'

It will be noted that here the rigidity of the alexandrine is softened by the enjambement of I 565. The fight between Emenidus and the enchanter is similarly made up of formulas (I 574-80) as is the account of Emenidus's exploits in the battle between the forces of Alexander and those of the Caliph (I 870-74).

A few similes and metaphors are found. Some are simple comparisons with everyday things, from the viewpoint of a fourteenth century audience, e.g. 'dous que mius' (I 119), 'si c'oiziaus pris a gliue' (II 752), and the Baudrain takes Alexander's sword from his hands 'aussi briement que s'il fuissent de cire' (II 947). Some have a pastoral flavour: 'Nous jugons ensement que brebis qui aignele/Ce qu'on voit par dehors', (II 421-22), 'Car aussi c'uns clos leus va vers la bergerie/ Traversa de Baudas la plus maistre cauchie' (I 495-96), 'Car d'ounor est floris et feullis comme rains' (II 487). Other comparisons are with pursuits perhaps more familiar to a courtly audience: 'Et ele vous regete uns iex plus pleins de las/Que ne soit escremie ne li jus des escas' (I 1113-14), 'Que de joie fu si garnie et assazee/Que s'en lait fust baignie et de miel arousee' (II 1144-45). In one example the 'roi des menestreus' describes the knights as they go into battle in rather high-flown terms:

II 564
        Angelot empenné samblés au desrengier
        Et joint esmerillon as lanches abaissier
        Ou sauvage lÿon as escus embrachier.

Finally, Brisebare lends weight to some of his arguments by invoking the popular wisdom contained in proverbs. Many of them are noted in the collections of Morawski and Le Roux de Lincy although these are frequently expressed in different words. A list is appended at the end of this work.

NOTES

1. G. Bonnier, 'Une histoire de brigands', *Otia Merseiana*, 3(1903), 23-45.
2. *Renaud de Montauban*, edited by H. Michelant (Stuttgart, 1862), pp.266-67.
3. Henri Guy, *Adan de le Hale* (Paris, 1898), pp.XLV and XLVIII-L.

TREATMENT OF THE TEXT

All additions to the text are enclosed in [ ] and exclusions in ( ). These alterations, except for the correction of obvious errors, are discussed in the general notes.

The acute accent distinguishes tonic e from atonic e when final or followed by s
in polysyllabic words, in such monosyllables as 'griés', 'piés' (but 'grief', 'piet')
and to distinguish words such as 'lés' (<*latus*) from their homonyms. The cedilla
and trema are added to indicate pronunciation. Punctuation is in accordance with
modern practice, and i and u are distinguished from j and v.

TEXT OF *LI RESTOR DU PAON*, PART I

.i.

fo. 165r. 1   Seignor, prince et baron et dames et borgois,
                On dist en .i. proverbe, et si l'aporte drois,
                Q'uiseuse est molt nuiseuse; et se dist li Englois
                Que pau vaut sens repus ne avoirs enfouois,
           5   Dont ciex qui set les biens ne doit pas estre cois.
                Et diex qui les biens donne et sans nombre et sans pois
                M'a donné par sa grace engien -s'est biaus envois-
                De rimer les grans fais des contes et des rois.
                Or (e) faut en Alixandre encore .i. molt biaus plois,
           10   Mais je, qui només sui Brisebare a le fois,
                L'i vuel metre et enter anchois que past li mois.
                Bien fu dit qu'Alixandres, li rois macedonois,
                Convoita tout le monde et puis ot a son cois
                Sor terre et air et mer et seignourie et vois
           15   Et des autres serviches et hommages et fois.
                En mer se fist geter en un tonnel voirrois,
                N'i ot autres droimons, barges, sales ne tois
                Que le tonnel de voirre et ces foibles alois.
                La aprist as poissons et joustes et tornois.
           20   Et si se fist en l'air en un cuir de bïois,
                A .iiii. grans griffons fameilleus et destrois
                Porter (par) [por] tout le monde vëoir, ce n'est nus nois.
                Nicolas de Nicole [prist] et (tous) ses Nicholois,
                Surie et Alemaigne, Persans et Aufricois,
           25   Gresse et Inde Major et les Babilonois
                Et la tour de Babel de fin marbre liois,
                Amazone la riche et Rommains et Franchois
                Et toute Femenie ou est grans li cointois.
                La cité prist de Tir et conquist les destrois.
           30   Es vaus de Josaphat es pres et es marois
                Envoia de ses hommes .vii. cens rengiés et trois
                Por forrer le bissal es marés et es bois.

Et dans Emenidus conduisoit les conrois.
La vint li dus Betis o .xxx. mil Gadrois;
35 En sa compaigne estoit Gadifers li cortois.
Entre Griex se ferirent; grans i fu li estrois
De gens et de cevaus, de cheüs et de drois.
La ot Emenidus molt paines et anois.
Par faute de message, dont ce fu grans desrois,
40 Vĕoit ses compaignons morir el sablounois
Et par destreche boire lor sanc et lor esclois.
Col. II D'aler en son message faisoit cascuns rebrois,
Car tous li mains hardis estoit de cuer si rois
Qu'il ne vausist pas estre as tors ne as berfrois.
45 En fin, por nos porpos ataindre sans deffois,
Gadifers du Laris i fu mors getés frois.
Quant Gadifers fu mors rois Clarus li Indois
Assist en Epheson les siens enfans (tout) [tous] trois,
Betis et Gadifer et dame Phesonois.
50 Lor oncles Cassamus ala au roi grejois
Por nonchier de Clarus l'orguel et les buffois
Et li preus Alixandres i mena ses Chaldois.
La fisent .i. poignich et Griu et Barbarois;
Si i fu pris Porus et ses nies li Baudrois.
55 En Ephezon les traist Cassamus par les dois,
Mais il n'i orent buies, cep ne fer espaignois,
Ains estoient as tables assis as plus haus dois.
La ochist .i. paon Porus d'un arc turquois.
Ains miex ne fu parés ne hastiers ne epois,
60 Car mangiés fu a joie et a grans esbanois.
Au mangier fisent veus et penius et narois,
Qui furent acompli sor les destriers norois.
Mais Edea voua, et s'en jura ses lois,
Qu'elle le restorroit d'or fin arrabiois.
65 Et ciex qui le rima, lui cortement es plois,
Oublia ce restor, mais je l'ai a mon cois
Enté aprés la mort Clarus le Mazonois.

.ii.

En aprés tous ces fais chi devant contenus,
En Epheson entra li rois macedonus.
70 Liés estoit et joians de ce qu'estoit vencus

Ses tresgrans anemis, qui ot a non Clarus.
Par devant la grant sale est a piet descendus;
Garchon salent avant, les destriers ont tenus.
Assés ot avoec lui rois et princes et dus.
75 En la sale monta et dans Emenidus
Et les dames s'en vont en la cambre Venus.
Grant joie demenerent por deduire Porus.
'Comment vous est, biau sire,' ce li dist Edeüs.
'Par ma foi' dist la dame, 'grans biens m'est avenus
80 Voire lonc l'aventure et les maus qu'ai eüs,
Car li dieu m'ont aidié tant que sui esleüs
Avoec la compaignie el mont que j'aime plus.'
En tant com il parloient s'est laiens enbatus
Cassïel li Baudrains et Marciiens ses drus.
85 Et quant Porus les voit, bien les a cogneüs;
S'il eüst le pooir encontre aus fust venus.

fo. 165v. Et chil le saluerent et puis s'assient jus.
Longement fu entr'aus li parlemens tenus
D'(amors) [armes] et de ses fais d'(armes) [amours] et de ses
    jus.
90 Puis disent a Poron, 'Loons no dieu Marcus,
Car cascuns de nous est liges hom devenus
Au fort roi Alixandre, qui nous a retenus,
Et nous a de prison quités et absolus,
Et nos amis, qu'il a et mors et confondus,
95 Avons ensevelis en tres nobles sarcus.
Or prïons por les ames, si n'en dolousons plus,
S'aquerrons joie et pais; il n'est si boins escus.'

.iii.

Molt fu celle compaigne joiouse sor tous dius.
Plenté i ot de feste, d'abanois et de gius.
100 Ciex qui miex le sot faire, le moustre qui miex miex,
Fors la bele Edea, la noble, la gentius,
Car d'une chose estoit li siens cuers molt pensius;
C'est qu'elle se trouvoit entre les plus eslius
C'onques formast nature ne c'onques crëast dius,
105 Qui puissent vivre en terre ne regner en ses chius.
Et entre ceaus avoit amors tout a son kius,
C'est li soudans de Baudres, preus, nobles et sotius.
Du paon li souvint et des veus seignorius

Que cascuns acompli quant tans en fu et lius;
110 Et li siens ert a faire qui ert plus aësius.
Si en jura ses diex, tous les plus poëstius,
Qu'elle l'acomplira voiant le roi des Grius.
Orfevres fist mander moiiens, jouenes et viex,
Grius et Macedonois, Caldains et Kenelius.
115 Grant plenté en i vinrent, et du faire ententius,
Raëmplis de science, garnis de boins ostius.
Et celle en qui n'estoit felonnie n'orguius,
Les rechut par uns mos si humeles et si pius,
Que ses plus lais parlers lor sambloit dous que mius.

.iv.

120 Quant la bele Edea ot les maistres coisis,
Hounestement les a rechus et conjoïs.
Encontre aus se leva, par les mains les a pris,
Dalés li les assist sor .ii. riches tapis.
Bel et cortoisement les a a raison mis.
125 'Seignor, li dieu des Griex, Jupiter et Venis,
Vous doint joie et hounor, grace et plenté d'amis
Sans terme et sans mesure adés a vo devis.
Mes messages vous ai envoiiés et tramis,
Et cascuns de vous s'est a mon mant obeïs.
130 Por itant vous en renc .v. cens mille merchis.
Or vous dirai porquoi vous tramis mes escris.
Col. II Je vuel que vous fachiés, quant vous i serés mis,
Un paon qui soit d'or entailliés et massis,
De pierres precïeuses, jagonses et rubis,
135 Vuel qu'il soit oelletés et signés et polis;
Sor .i. piler d'or fin jolis sera assis.
Et se mandé vous ai, cha .v. cha .vii. cha dis,
N'esse mie por chose que mes cors ne soit fis
Que cascuns ne soit bien de science garnis,
140 Mais por ce qu'on l'eüst bien parfait et empris,
Et por ce que li oevre en soit de plus haut pris,
Et qu'entre pluseurs sages truev'on pluseurs avis,
Et diex moustre a l'un ce qu'autres n'a apris.
Ce que ne voit uns maistres voit bien .i. aprentis;
145 Et por ce ne vaut mie uns sages maistres pis
Se il prent en autrui ce qu'on a en lui pris.

Si vous pri qu'eslongiés de vos cuers tous estris
Et qu'en vous ne norrisse envie ne despis,
Car ja vos guerredons n'en ferai plus petis,
150   Ains sera a cascun aussi tres bien meris
Que se de l'un de vous fust parfais et furnis.'
De quanques lor pria fu d'yaus fais li ostris.
Le vin a demandé, et quant les ot servis,
En ses cambres les maine, si les a bien garnis
155   Du plus fin or d'Arrabe qui soit ens ou paiis.
Lor harnas apresterent, a l'oevre se sont mis.
Ens en lor forge entrerent Gadifers et Betis
Et li soudans de Baudres, Cassïel li gentis.
Quant Edea les vit pris les a et sasis.

.v.

160   'Seignor,' dist Edea, 'se Marcus me doint joie,
Vous paieriés le vin s'orfavresse estoie.
Ou vous tenriés prison, se l'otroi en avoie
Des maistres de nostre oevre, ja ne m'en cesseroie.'
'Bele,' dist li Baudrains, 'le vin bien paieroie,
165   Mais j'aim miex vo prison que avoir camp ne voie.'
Et Gadifers ouvri s'aumosniere de soie.
.ii. besans en sacha sans la menre monnoie,
Si lor jeta et dist, 'a vo prison m'aloie,
Seignor, je ne vuel pas que por tant quites soie.'
170   Betis refist autel, n'atent pas qu'on l'en proie,
Et Edea sousrist et a la fois rougoie.
Qui dont veïst comment le Baudrain tient et ploie
Il n'est nus si enfruns qui n'en demenast joie.
Et li Baudrains qui sot en amors mainte voie,
175   Por son desir acroistre i met dangier et broie.
A le fois li eschape, puis se faint et sousploie
fo. 166r.   Par quoi elle le puist prendre comme sa proie
Quant assés ont jué, sor le jonc qui verdoie
S'asisent en parlant d'amors qui les mestroie,
180   Car il fait boin laissier le ju ains qu'il anoie.
Puis prist a l'aumosniere qui tint a sa coroie
Dis mars de fin argent; as mestres les envoie.
Miex fu remerchiiés que dire nel saroie
Car qui as sages donne, molt bien son don emploie.

.vi.

185 Riches fu li ouvrages et de grant seignorie,
Molt se penoit cascuns de mostrer sa mestrie,
Et bien furent servi li maistre et lor maisnie.
Lor mes ne lor mangiers, n'est mestiers qu'on vos die;
Tout ont a lor voloir dains, chers et vin sor lie,
190 Car la bele Edea, li blonde, l'escavie,
Les servoit et de miex qu'elle ne fust servie.
Li dus Aimes oï celle martellerie,
Caulus et Aristés (et) Marciiens de Perssie
Et la bele Elïos, Fezone et Ydorie.
195 Vers la forge s'en vont cantant a chiere lie.
Quant Edea les voit, a haute vois escrie,
'Se ne fussiés les plus, par les diex d'Aumarie,
Vous païssiés le droit de nostre orfaverie,
Ne ja por bien paiier n'en eschapissiés mie.'
200 'Bele,' ce dist li dus, 'sans point de felonie
Nous rendrons a vous pris et sans faire partie,
Mais que vous faichiés tant par vostre cortoisie
Que vous nous recreés, et sor prison brisie.
Se prions le Baudrain de nostre plegerie,
205 Ne voi que nus i puist faire plus grant aiie.'
'Sire,' dist la pucele, 'mes cuers le vous otrie.'

.vii.

Quant li dus Aimes ot assés ris et jué,
Betis en apela et Gadifer l'ainsné,
Et Marciien de Persse, Caulus et Aristé,
210 Dames et damoiseles et tout l'autre barné.
'Seignor,' dist li dus Aimes, 'veés la verité
Que la guerre por quoi sommes chi assamblé
Est finee, no dieu en soient aouré.
Or apartient que cil qui ne sont marié
215 Aient ce que il ont conquis et achievé,
Ou ce que on lor a promis et presenté;
Et moi et Gadifer nous sommes (achievé) [acordé]
De la mort de son pere que diex ait pieté.
Par devant ses amis ai le fait amendé,
220 Et il le m'a par tant, si qu'il dist, pardonné.

Ma nieche li promis, ou tant a de biauté,
Col. II   Et bele terre et rice par molt grant amisté,
Betanie la large ou tant a de bonté.
Or ne voel pas qu'il cuide que je l'aie gabé,
225   S'irai preuc ma cousine. S'avoie demandé
Congiet a Alixandre, nostre droit avoé,
Car ce et el voel faire et laissier par son gré.'
'Sire,' dist Gadifers, 'ce vient de volenté.
Bien me plest et soufist ce qu'avés devisé.'

.viii.

230   Molt ot Emenidus le cuer cortois et sage.
Congiet prist as orfevres et a tout le barnage,
Et molt bien lor paia le droit de lor usage.
Querre ala Alixandre par tout son herbergage:
En la cambre Venus ens el plus maistre estage
235   Le trouva. Si li dist en riant son corage,
Et il li otrïa et loa le voiage.
Li dus Aimes monta et cil de son maisnage.
Tant cevaucha par plains, par prés et par bosscage
Qu'il entra en Archade, qui est et longe et large,
240   Que li rois Alixandres, qui en avoit l'oumage,
Li donna quitement sans rente et sans treuage.
Par .i. matin entra dedens .i. grant ramage.
Bien pooit cevauchier par cler et par ombrage,
Car il ne i donnoit ne travers ne paiage,
245   Ne chose nulle qui tornast a [son] damage.
Chi lairons de sa nieche et de son mariage:
Quant tans sera et poins s'i ferons repairage.
Si vous recorderons d'Aimon le jouene eage,
De ses fais, de ses dis et de son vasselage.

.ix.

250   Seignor et damoiseles, cevalier et baron,
Clerc et gent seculiere et de religïon,
Assés l'avés oï, et nous le repeton,
Comment rois Alixandres, qui ot cuer de lyon,
Prist et mist tout le monde en sa subjectïon,
255   Et comment il conquist les pers de sa maison.

Si doi cousin estoient par generatïon
Danclins et Tholomers, cil noble compaignon.
En Inde ala conquerre le riche roi Poron.
Et Porus son neveu, le fil au viel Claron,
260 Le jouene Gadifer, Martiien et Beton,
Conquist a Ephezon, et le preu Cassïon.
Dauris et (Philotas) [Floridas] prist devant le doignon
De Defur la cité par fiere caplison.
Graciiens l'i mena et la devint ses hon
265 De la terre qui fu son pere et son taion.
Caulus et Arristé prist en autre roion,

Perdicas et Lÿone, Licanor et (Cliton) [Sanson],
Antigonus de Gresce et dant Anthiocon,
Le noble Filotas et le preu Festïon,
270 Et Divinus Pater et de Monflor Pieron,
Et dant Antipater, qui brassa le puison
Dont li boins rois morut par grant deceptïon.
Ensi cueilli les boins par mainte regïon
Et les mauvais metoit en fin sans raënchon.
275 Mais on n'en list, ne cante ne ne fait mentïon
Ens es fais d'Alixandre du chief jusqu'au coron,
Quant, ne comfaitement, ne par quele occoison,
Li fors rois Alixandres conquist le duc Aimon.
Mais je ai au boin duc si grande affectïon.
280 Que je vuel que on truist ens es *Veus du Paon*
Comment Emenidus fist au roi de lui don,
Avec le nuef ouvrage en la conclusïon,
Comment bele Edea, qui ot cuer net et bon,
Le paon restora de fin or sains laiton,
285 Et le fist eslever sor un noble perron
Por metre les hardis en memoratïon
Ques treshautes proëches qu'on fist en s'occoison,
Par quoi proëche eüst en aus mieudre cruchon;
Et du haut mariage et de l'assamblison
290 De la bele Elïot et du preu Martïon,
Du jouene Gadifer du castel d'Ephezon,
Et de la nieche au duc, qu'on dist Emenidon,
Que ciex entroublia qui les veus fist en son
Qui ne furent pas fait d'engien de camïon.
295 Car s'avisés en fust par aucune raison
Cest oevre eüst miex mise a execution,
Que faire ne porroie selonc m'ententïon

Se j'avoie en aiue tous les livres (T) [C] aton,
Ne de tous les .vii. sages qui furent de renon.
300 Or affiert bien qu'on sache sans nulle soupechon
De quel gent li dus fu et de quel natïon,
Quels il fu, dont il vint et sa conditïon.
Povre commencement eut li dus, ce dist on,
Et s'eut tres boine fin et s'eut tres boin moillon.
305 Car qui des boins del monde fesist disputison,
Et fesist sor les fais examinatïon,
S'en portast il le pris sans (similatïon) [simulatïon]
De son commencement ferai declarison,
Non pas por abaissier sa grace et son renon,
310 Mais por metre son bien en apparissïon.
Car tout cil qui folie font par temptatïon
Col. II Ne sont pas en la fin mis a perditïon.
Ains les amende diex et si lor fait pardon,
Et (leur) [ou] plus a de visce et de corruptïon,
315 La met diex plus de grace et de devotïon.
Car quant li (maisons) [madres] brise, a remetre en fachon,
Vaut miex que quant il fu sains sans comparison.
Teus est ciex qui de dieu a l'inspiratïon.
Ce s'apert a David, le pere Salemon,
320 Qui nombrer vuet son pule par se presomptïon,
Et si fist homicide, luxure et traïson,
Et puis par sa bonté fu en mainte lechon
Peres de dieu nommés par figaratïon.
Ens ou Saint Euuagille de dieu nostre patron
325 Disoit li Chananee, qui fu de Chananon,
'Jhesus, fiex de David par incarnatïon,
Aiïés de moi pité, Sire, et compassïon,
Et se dignes je sui par indignatïon
D'avoir le pain benoit, que ont (nostre) [vostre] enfanchon,
330 Si faites de moi, Sire, ensi que du kiegnon,
Qui des mies de tables prent la refectïon.
Car ja si pau n'avrai de vo beneïchon,
Que ce ne soit assés por ma sauvatïon
Par la grace des diex (et de no) [de nostre] regïon.'
335 A l'ounor del duc fai ceste narratïon
Son fait qui mue en bien sa conversatïon.
Car li maus ne fait tant, ne la confusïon,
Que li perseverers en la maleïchon.
Molt fu Emenidus de noble extractïon,

340 Fiex d'un rice home, duc, qu'on apele Blaton.
Aspremont maintenoit ou mainent li grifon.
Si eut guerre a .i. roi molt crueus et felon,
Qui tenoit les desers d'outre Capharnaon,
Ciex qui occist son pere par mortel traïson,
345 Le mius de son lignage et de sa gent fuison.
Mais d'Aimon ne vaut faire malvaise occisïon,
Por ce que le veoit petitet valeton.
Mais si gasta la terre entor et environ,
Qu'on n'i refist ains plus nulle habitatïon
350 Par defaute de gent. S'i norrirent dragon,
Lÿon, ours et serpent, lupart, escorpïon,
Qui d'enfans et de femes fisent devorison.
Et Aymes s'enfuï faisant grant plorison.
Onques n'i espargna ne haie ne buisson.
355 En celle mesestance l'encontrerent larron,
Et il l'ont aresté; n'i fisent lonc sermon,

fo. 167r.   Et li ont demandé toute sa natïon,
Et Aymes lor conta sa grant abusïon.
Avec aus le retinrent, s'en fisent lor garchon,
360 Et puis se prouva si en celle robison
Qu'il en fisent lor maistre, s'avoit double parchon
De quanques conqueroient. En celle opinïon
En la cit de Damas fisent lor mansïon.
Mais comment que la fust, miex amast .i. faucon
365 Jeter aprés l'aloe et l'ostoir au hairon,
Qu'il n'eüst a tolir un moine son plichon.
Et puis fu il si preus, que haubers ne blason,
Espees et espiels, hyaumes et espouron,
Ceval et palefroi, banieres et pignon,
370 Pumier, fraisne et sapin et lances et tronchon
Furent par ses fais mis en tel perfectïon,
Que se toutes ces choses, sans nulle mesprison,
Peüssent par nature avoir parole et (non) [ton],
Aourer le deüssent, aprés no dieu Jheson,
375 Et par grant reverence faire inclinatïon;
Car diex estoit en armes apelés par droit non.
On ne parloit en terre fors que de son renon,
De ses fais, de ses dis, qu'il (faison) [faisoit] a bandon.

.x.

Seignors, a icel tamps que vous ai devisé,
380 Avoit en Macedone, la noble royauté,
Un roi qu'on apeloit (Philippon) [Philippe] en verité.
Col. II Et ciex rois ot un fil a sa feme engenré,
Qu'on avoit Alixandre par son droit non nommé.
N'avoit mie .x. ans et s'iert de jouene aé,
385 Et si convoitoit ja qu'on l'eüst marié.
Un jor vint a son pere, com l'ot araisonné,
'Sire,' dist Alixandres, 'entendés mon pensé.
Je vaurrai feme avoir se il vous vient a gré.
Si voel que vous fachiés ce que j'ai entesé.
390 Mandés nostre Caliphe de Baudas la cité
Qu'il vous envoit sa fille ou tant a de biauté,
Car je en vorrai faire m'espouse en carité.'
'Biax fiex,' ce dist li rois, 'a vostre volenté,
Puis qu'il vous plest ensi, ja nen ert trestorné.'
395 Il fist .i. brief escrire, et quant l'ot seellé
Deus barons le kierka ou molt ot de bonté.
A tant prisent congiet. Quant il furent monté
Tant errerent par bos et par camp et par pré
Qu'il vinrent a Baudas droit a .i. avespré.
400 Bien furent du Caliphe recheü et festé.
Il fist les tables metre, et quant orent soupé,
Lor brief li donnerent, et quant il (l'ont) [l'ot] quassé,
Et il ot bien l'escrit porliut et resgardé,
Si pensa en son cuer, tout ne l'ait il moustré,
405 Qu'il tendoit por sa fille a plus grant dignité,
Car li rois Alixandres, ou tant ot de fierté,
N'estoit mie a che point de tele auctorité,
Que il a puissedi par sa proëche esté.
'Seignor,' dist li Califes, 'vous soiiés bien trouvé.
410 Je voi auques que c'est, que li rois m'a mandé.
Je tieng cest mandement a molt grant amisté.
Mais tant li dirés vous, quant serés retorné,
Qu'il ne le tiegne pas a duel ne a viuté,
Que l'estat de ma fille j'ai bien considéré,
415 S'est de trop jouene eage, bien i ai resgardé,
Por metre en mariage, ce me samble en non Dé.'
Et cil li respondirent, qui molt erent sené,
'Sire, ce poise nous, par nostre loyauté.'

A lui prisent congié, se l'ont remerchié
420   De sa grant cortoisie. Quant orent reposé,
Si murent au matin, lues qu'il fu adjorné,
Jusqu'au roi Pheilippon ne se sont arresté.
Quant furent d'Alixandre recheü et festé
Errant lor demanda par tres grant amisté,
425   'Quels nouveles,' fait il, 'or ne me soit celé.'
Et il li respondirent, 'S'avons no tans gasté.

fo. 167v.   Car il nous dist ensi, en boine loyauté,
Que sa fille est trop jouene, ce nous a il moustré,
Quel que soit par ce tour se tient a excusé.'
430   Quant Alixandres l'ot d'aïr a tressüé.
Si en jura ses diex qui ont grant poësté
Qu'il semonra ses os et son grant parenté,
Si l'avra, vuelle ou non, se il l'avoit juré.

.xi.

Molt par ot Alixandres le cuer triste et (marit) [destroit]
435   De ce que li Califes (li avoit escondit) [escondit li avoit]
Sa fille qu'entresait a feme avoir vorroit.
Phelippes li siens peres molt bel le confortoit
Mais li confortemens poi ou nient li valoit.
Ains juroit Alixandres les diex ou il creoit
440   Que tout son grant linage et ses os semonroit
Et esforchiement sour le Calife iroit
Et lui et sa grant terre a force essilleroit.
En ce point en la court uns lerres repairoit
Qui par enchantement le pule souduisoit
445   Que nus (nus) encontre lui garder ne se pooit
Qu'il ne fust enchantés par les ars qu'il savoit.
Quant il vit Alixandre qu'ensi se dementoit
Vers le pere se traist qui molt souples estoit.
'Sire,' ce dist li lerres, 'qui croire me vorroit
450   Ja broigne ne haubert vestir n'en convenroit,
Car je feroie bien a cui qu'il en anoit
Qu'Alixandres vos fiex la damoisele avroit.'
Phelippes respondi que molt bien li plaisoit,
Et Alixandres dist que s'ensi le faisoit,
455   Que si cortoisement en fin paiiés seroit
Col. II   Que jamais par raison disete n'averoit.

.xii.

Quant li lerres, qui ot le cuer plain de boisdie,
Ot la besoigne emprise et enconvenenchie,
Il demanda congiet et li rois li otrie,
460   Et ses fiex Alixandres et la chevalerie.
En ce point que li lerres ot sa voie acoillie
Estoit Emenidus et sa grant compaignie
En la cit de Damas en une braderie.
La estoit lor repaires et lor herbergerie.
465   Aprés souper estoit, s'orent droite laissie
La table, qui estoit painte et entaillie,
Couverte de hanas et de boin vin sor lie.
Por lui solaciier cascuns chante et versie.
'Seignor,' ce dist li dus, 'or faisons gaigerie.
470   La nuis est tenebreuse, hideuse et obscurchie.
Por combien irés vous cascuns sans compaignie
En la cave a Baudas qui tant est resoignie? '
Et il li respondirent que il n'iroient mie
Por trestout l'or d'Arrabe, de Gresse et de Perssie.
475   'Par foi,' ce dist li dus, 'c'est grans couarderie.
Se cascuns me vuet d'or doner une puingnie,
G'irai encor anuit, par les diex d'Aumarie,
Ou autant en donrai cascun en sa partie.'
Et il li otroiierent, mais qu'il lor senefie
480   Comment li verités lor iert certefiïe,
Comment celle voie ert faite ou entrelaiissie.
Et Aymes respondi, sans point de felonnie,
'En ma main porterai une perce aguisie.
Se demain a plain jor a nonne ou a complie
485   Vous l'i poés trouver gisant ou estekie,
Bien avrai envers vous ma gagure aquitie.'
Bien lor plot et quant ot la mise fianchie,
Erranment prist congiet si vint a chiere lie.
Li lerres Alixandre qui ot non Faus s'i fie
490   Estoit pardevant lui sans faire joquerie,
Car forment se hastoit d'acomplir la folie.
Et li dus ot molt tost sa maniere coisie
Et molt bien recognut qu'il estoit de lor vie
En passer coiement a l'alure quatie,
495   Car aussi c'uns clos leus va vers la bergerie,
Traversa de Baudas la plus maistre cauchie

Et tant fist qu'il vint droit a la mananderie
Ou la fille au Califfe avoit esté norrie.
Car por ce qu'estoit veves et sa feme ert fenie
500   L'ot une soie antain par fianche kierkie.
fo. 168r.   Et Aymes le sivoit a la chiere molt lie,
Si que toute sa mise avoit entreoubliie,
Car esprouver voloit le tour de sa maistrie.
Une eschiele de soie a li lerres sachie,
505   Qui a gravais d'achier estoit entrelachie.
Et quant sor le maison l'ot li lerres lanchie
En la maison entra. Quant il l'ot despechie
Si enchanta la dame et toute la maisnie,
Et puis ala au lit ou la bele ert couchie,
510   De qui rois Alixandres voloit faire s'amie.
Enranment le vesti et quant il l'ot vestie,
En ses bras l'embracha et quant l'ot enbrachie,
La maison deffruma, s'issi a la cauchie.
Quant li lerres le vit en biauté adrechie,
515   Si pensa que premiers avroit sa drüerie.
Por plus paisiulement acomplir sa veulie
En la cave a Baudas l'a menee et guiïe,
Por ce qu'on n'en oïst ne cri ne hüerie.
Et Aymes de rechief a la dame sivie,
520   Et juroit que se chius li faisoit vilonnie
Que le chief li taurroit a l'espee forbie.

.xiii.

Quant li fors lerres ot la pucele reubee,
En la cave a Baudas l'a conduite et menee.
C'estoit une cisterne hideuse et redoutee.
525   De malvais espris plaine et de gent poi hantee.
La pucele esgarda, et quant il l'ot trouvee
Blonde et vaire et rians, blance et encoulouree,
Col. II   Molt fu sa volentés de folie embrasee.
La pucele embracha, et quant l'ot enversee,
530   Por par plus grant delit faire sa destinee,
Deffist l'enchantement dont il l'ot enchantee.
Et quant elle perchut qu'elle ert si malmenee
Elle pria merchi car molt fu effraee.
Et li lerres juroit son sanc et sa coree

535 Que de li averoit sa volonté outree.
Et celle souspiroit qui molt fu espantee,
Et bien se maintenoit com feme entalentee
De garder s'ounesté que elle avoit gardee
Por venir a l'ounor a quoi ert ordenee.

540 En ses dras se tenoit si close et enfremee
Qu'en ses dras ne trouvoit li lerres nulle entree,
Ains sambloit qu'elle i fust cousue et chimentee.
Mais por ce ne fu pas de lui mains tormentee,
Ains fu molt du larron froissie et degetee;

545 Et li leres n'en pot point faire sa pensee.
Quant elle vit qu'en lui n'estoit pités trouvee,
Et qu'elle afeblissoit, quar molt estoit lassee,
Sa devotïon a par grant desir tournee
A Venus la diuesse, et si l'a reclamee

550 Qui ou paiis estoit de molt grant renommee
Et de molt grant afaire et souvent reclamee.
'Dame', dist la pucele, 'qui savés ma pensee,
Et que de foliier ne sui entalentee,
Mais a toute honesté li miens cuers hingue et bee,

555 Ne consentés qu'ensi soie chi vïolee.
Dame, si voirement que sui a vous donee,
Par mon contrepois d'or si tost que je fui nee
Voelliés que de ce pril soie anuit delivree.'
Puis dist, 'Ne vous anoit, france dame honneree,

560 Se ceste oblatïon je vous ai reprouvee.
Pr(r)ius et necessités, dont je sui apressee,
Font qu'en priant me sui vers vous desmesuree.'
A ces mos oï Aymes ses plains et sa criee.
De courre s'esforcha, s'aleüre a hastee.

565 Un boukeler d'achier qui pendoit a s'espee
Prist, et l'espee traist. Quant il l'ot entesee,
Vers le larron ala, se li fist deffiee.
'Lerres,' ce dist li dus, 'par les diex de Chaldee,
La pucele lairés car mar l'avés emblee.

570 N'onques mais n'achatastes si crueuse vespree.'
Et chiex li respondi, qui la chiere ot enflee,
Qu'a cui qu'il en anoit, a lui seroit privee.

fo. 168v.   Et puis si l'enmenroit a qui qu'il desagree.
Il tenoit en sa main une hace acheree,

575 Et a senestre avoit une targe nervee,
Et Aymes feri sus, et si l'a assenee

Qu'en .ii. moitiés l'i a fendue et tronchonnee.
Et chiex se deffendoit, fiere fu la mellee,
Grans cops donnent l'un l'autre, sans point de demoree.
580   Bien i fu de cascun la prouesche moustree.
Briement a la (a) fin [fu] la chose (fu) si menee
Que li lerres au roi ot la teste caupee.
L'ame de lui emportent li dyable a volee.
La pucele en fu lie quant [vi] tele colee.
585   Adonques fu la bele rescousse et remenee
En la maison de quoi li lerre[s] l'ot jetee.
Mais mainte parole ot cele nuit reversee
Car li dus l'acola, et quant l'ot acolee,
De l'angoisse qu'elle ot soufferte et enduree
590   En ses bras se pasma, et quant fu relevee
Li dus le conforta par parole avisee.
'Sire,' dist la pucele, 'vous m'avés destornee
De honte et de peril, c'est verités prouvee.
S'en avés m'amistié a tous jors conquestee,
595   Et si je puis, bien ert la paine restoree.
Mais encore sui pau de vous asseüree,
Car ne sai a quel fin vostre entente est tornee.
Se vous pri, quant vostre oeuvre a bele et bone entree,
Que bien soit maintenue et bien continue[e].'
600   Et Aymes respondi com persoune senee,
'Dame, sor ce point est m'ententïons fondee.'

.xiv.

Col. II Ainsi Emenidus la bele asseüra.
En son conduit se mist et il le remena
En la maison de quoi li lerres le jeta.
605   Mais en cel repairier elle li demanda
De quoi il se melloit; et il li devisa
Que lerres et reuberes avoit esté piecha,
Et qu'a Damas manoit, et l'ostel li nomma,
Et elle le retint et molt bien l'(entierna) [entierva],
610   Au departir cascuns tenrement souspira.
Elle entra en l'ostel et si le refrema,
Et si priveement en son lit recoucha
Qu'onques puissedi nus garde ne s'en donna.
Et Aymes s'en parti et si se ravisa

615 Que por l'amor la dame sa mise entroublia.
En la cave s'en vint, le pel i esteka,
Quant il l'ot estekiet tant fist et tant erra
Qu'a Damas s'en revint, ses compaignons trouva.
Sa besoigne lor dist, mais point ne lor conta
620 L'aventure de quoi eürs l'aventura,
Mais por l'ounor la dame l'aventure cela.
Et bien samble que diex par raison ordena
Qu'Aymes devenist lerres et qu'a ce s'acorda.
Maufais por pis abatre est loés grant tans a.
625 Et ne treuv'on que diex par son angle manda
Au fort roi Charlemaine, et se li commanda
Que il alast embler? Et li rois i ala

fo. 169r.   A Basin l'enchanteur, par nuit s'acompaigna,
Qui par enchantement en la maison entra
630 D'un riche traïtour, s'oï et escouta
Que li lerres disoit, 'Ma dame, entendés cha:
Je voel que secrés soit ce que vous orrés ja.'
Et li dame a celer errant li otria.
'Dame,' dist li traïters, 'Karles mordris sera
635 A ceste Pentecouste que plus ne vivera.
Bien le sai car je fui ou on le devisa.'
Quant la dame l'oï, d'angoisse tressua,
Car c'estoit ses cousins et si le maria.
'Certes,' ce dist la dame, 'li boins rois le savra.'
640 Quant li traïtres l'ot si grant cop li donna
Par mi le nes que tout le vis ensanglenta.
Bazins passa avant et si s'agenoilla,
Si rechut en son gant le sanc qu'elle sanna.
Et puis vint a Karlon et le fait li conta,
645 Et Karles s'en retraist et dieu en merchia,
Et bien contre ce fait puissedi se garda.
Ensi Emenidus son seignor destorna
D'anui par le larchin de quoi il se mella.
Car ce fust grans meschiés, par dieu qui tout crea,
650 Se li rois Alixandres, qui diex tant hounera,
Eüst le remanant du larron qui embla
Rosenés que puis prist a feme et espousa.
Et de tant fu il faus et molt s'outrecuida
Quant onques en larron telement se fia
655 Que s'ounor et sa vie querre l'i envoia.

.xv.

Molt ot Emenidus le cuer liet et joiant
De ce que sa besoigne ert en boin convenant.
A ses compaignons vint, si les trouva gisant.
Errant les salua, si lor dist en riant
660   Qu'en la cave laissa le grant pel estekant.
Et il se descouchierent, molt se vont merveillant,
Et quant vint au matin aprés soleil levant
En Baudas en alerent que miex miex tout errant.
Si virent en la cave estekier le perchant,
665   La debte li cognurent a rendre a son commant.
Chi vous entrelaisson d'Emenidon, a tant
De Rosenés dirons, au gent cors avenant,
Qui molt vise en son cuer, et va souvent pensant
Qu'elle porra donner (a) Emon le combatant
670   Car elle n'avoit nul joiiel si souffissant
Qui samblaissent por lui ne boin ne assés grant.
Si pensa qu'elle iroit le sien pere assaiant
Col. II   S'il avoit riens de boin qu'au cuer li fust plaisant.
Puis s'en vint a la court par .i. jour deduisant,
675   Tout li fisent hounor, li sage et ignorant.
Quant ses peres le vit si le va enbrachant,
Si redist li Califes, 'Dites moi vo samblant.
Quels besoins vous amaine? ' Elle li dist errant,
'Sire, malade sui, se me vois deduisant,
680   Trop m'anoie a l'ostel, si ai le cuer pesant.
Molt volentiers verroie et derriere et devant
Vo trezor qui est plains d'or et d'argent luisant.'
Et li peres qui ot le cuer tout desirant
D'acomplir son voloir l'i mena; si vit tant
685   D'or que ne le menaissent .xxx. mulet amblant
De trestous les plus fors qui sont en oriant.

.xvi.

Molt estoit cil trezors de tous bien[s] raëmplis.
Espriviers et faucons et mallars et pertris
I avoit de fin or si proprement assis
690   Qu'il sambloit que cascuns volast en l'air tout vis,
Et que li mallars fust por le faucon quatis.

Et sambloit a cascun qui les veoit avis
Que les pertris entraissent dedens le rois toudis.
Et s'avoit par derriere des chiens grans et petis,
695   Et bien sambloit que fussent de pertrisier apris
Et des pertris aherdre engrés et engramis.
Et si estoit li lande et li gaus d'or foillis
Cargiés de louseignols, d'aloes, de mauvis,
Les cols tous estendus et estierkis les pis,
fo. 169v. 700   Et le[s] biés aouviers par engien[s] si soutis
Qu'il faisoient trambler les rainsiaus d'or folis,
Et sambloit proprement qu'il getaissent lor cris.
Et si avoit les chers de courre amanevis,
Les dains et les sainglers et noirs et blans et bis
705   Iriés et escumans, felons et agregis;
Et les veneurs qui orent de[s] chers et des pors pris.
Et si estoit li mondes d'or portrais et massis,
Infers et d'autre part terrestres paradis,
Et li mers et les eues de quoi il est partis.
710   Et s'estoit par deseure li chiels fais d'asur bis.
D'une escarboucle estoit li solaus resplendis,
Et la lune i estoit d'un saphir de haut pris.
Les menues estoilles estoient de rubis.
Li resgarders passoit tous terrïens delis.

.xvii.

715   Molt sot bien li Califfes sa fille rescreer.
Sa clef en s'aumosniere prist, s'ala defremer
Un forgier, s'en sacha .i. cofre biel et cler.
'Fille,' fait il, 'tout ce que poés esgarder
Ne vaut riens envers ce que je vous voel mostrer.
720   Car ci dedens a pierres, les millors c'est tout cler,
Qui soient tant que ciex et terre puet durer.
Et miex valent en pris (et) [par] les diex de la mer,
Que toute ma grant terre qui les vauroit esmer.'
Le cofre desfrema, si prist a deviser
725   La force et la vertu qu'elles ont en ouvrer.
Quant Rosenés oï les pierres tant loër,
Si pensa que c'estoit uns biaus dons por doner,
Nobles et gracïeus por son ami parer.
Et li boins dus estoit adiés en son penser.

730 'Peres,' dist la pucelle, '.i. don vous voel rouver
Que les clés du trezor me cargiés a garder.
A le fois i venrai por mon cors deporter.'
'Fille', dist li Califes, 'ne fait [pas] a greer,
Mais rouvés autre chose si porrés assener.'

735 'Peres,' dist la pucelle, 'tant me soliés amer
Que ne me vausissiés nulle chose veer.'
'Fille,' dist li Califes, 'ne vous devés douter.
Je vous aim, mais a moi doi plus de foi porter.'
A tant entrelaissierent andoi ce plet ester,

740 Car il cuida tres bien (qu'elle) [le] deüst oublïer.
Mais la pucele sage, qui tant fist a loër,
Embla les cles son pere sans point de demorer.
Ens ou trezor entra qui molt fist a loër,
Et quant elle fu ens soi prist a aviser

Col. II 745 Avoec une pucele ou molt se pot fïer.
Le cofre en aporta por les pierres oster
Et puis fist a Damas le boin Emon mander.
La pucele i ala qui bien le sot (mander) [trouver].
Et lues qu'Emenidus le vit laiens entrer,

750 Pensa en son maintien c'a lui voloit parler.
Bien l'ala rechevoir et tres bien (ormerer) [ounerer.]

.xviii.

Quant la pucele fu en l'ostel qu'en diroie?
Li dus Emes se mist erranment a la voie.
'Sire,' dist la pucele, 'mais qu'il ne vous anoie,

755 Avés vous a non Emes? ' Et il li dist, 'Bele, oie.'
'Sire,' dist la pucele, 'ma dame a vous m'envoie
De Baudas (en) [et] ce cofre, ne sai se c'est monoie,
Vous presente [et] s'amor que je miex ameroie.'
Et li dus le rechut et si en fist grant joie

760 Et puis li presenta joiaus d'or et de soie.
Mais elle respondi, 'Por riens ne les prendroie.'
'Bele,' dist li dus Aimes, 'tous li miens cuers s'otroie
A ma dame servir de quanques je porroie.'
Quant elle ot pris congié du repairier s'avoie

765 A sa dame a Baudas qui atent et coloie
Que elle revenist par quoi novele[s] oie.
A tant es la pucele qui demenoit grant joie.

A sa dame conta comment Aimes s'aloie
A faire son service a qui qu'il en anoie.
770 'Bele,' dist Rosenés, 'par les diex que on proie,
Il appartient molt bien que cortoise a lui soie,

Que l'ounor qu'il me fist restor(er)er ne porroie.'

.xix.

Molt ot Emenidus noble et bel guerredon,
Mais molt bien le gaitierent trestout si compaignon,
775 Et li disent, 'Qu'est che par desous vo gieron?
Nous i vaurrons avoir cascuns de nous parchon.'
Et il lor respondi, 'Par nostre dieu Marcon
Ja ne vous en ferai fraude ne traïson.'
Le cofre lor moustra et mist en abandon,
780 Mais du brisier estoient en grande souspechon,
Por ce que le veoient de si bele faichon.
Mais li uns resgarda aussi qu'a .i. coron
La clef vit estekier endroit .i. anglechon.
La fu prise li clés sans point d'arrestison,
785 A l'ouvrir i trouverent pierres de grant renon.
Entreaus les departirent sans noise et sans tenchon.
Et quant virent qu'il orent gaaigniet tel fuison,
Si se retraist cascuns droit a sa natïon,
N'il n'orent onques puis voloir d'estre larron.
790 Et Aimes a Damas remest a sa maison
Tous seus, que il n'i ot ne per ne compaignon.

.xx.

Aynsi Emenidus la tous seus demora.
Un poi de tans aprés li Califfes ala
A son trezor: son coffre demanevet trouva.

Par toute sa grant terre as lapidiers manda
Que s'on aportoit pierres a vendre cha ne la
Qu'en les prenge, et celui qui les aportera.
En ce point Emenidus une fois s'apensa
Que por avoir argent ses pierres vendera.
800 A un lapidier vint, ses pierres aporta.
Entrues que ciex de lobes le tint et herlusa

Erranment au Calife par .i. mes le noncha.
Et si tost qu'il le sot ses gens i envoia.
Quant il i sont venu cascuns cogneüt l'a
805 Et ont mis main a lui, n'en vous mentirai ja.
Que vous diroie, on prist Aymon et enmena
Par devant le Calife o tous ciaus qui sont la.
Aymes fu molt honteus quant on si l'enmena.
Le Calife salue errant qu'il l'avisa.
810 Li sires li respont que gaires ne l'ama.
Li Califes des pierres erranment l'aprocha
Mais por l'amor la dame onques ne s'escusa
Mais tout de chief en chief la chose devisa.
Et por ce que son fait ne cognut ne nia
815 Li Califfes a pendre erranment le juga.
Et quant Rosenés vit qu'a Aimon ensi va
De meschief qu'elle ot d'angoisse tressua,
Et de la grant dolor que a son cuer en a
Quatre fois s'est pasmee, pres que ne devia.
820 Et quant fu relevee molt de fois souspira
Et dist, 'Lasse caitiue, cis homs por moi morra.'
Elle s'avise et dist que elle s'en ira
Droitement a son pere, le fait li contera.
Elle li vint devant et si s'agenoilla.
825 'Sire,' dist la pucele, 'por dieu entendés cha.
fo. 170v. Je sui toute certaine cis homs a tort moura.
S'il vous plest je dirai comment la chose va.
Sachiés certainement, je n'en mentirai ja,
Uns lerres avant hier dedens mon lit m'enbla,
830 Et par son grant malice me ravi et porta
En la hideuse cave, illuecques m'esconsa.
De nullui n'och aïwe, fors de cel home la.
Ensi qu'il m'enportoit ce larron encontra,
Belement me sivi jusc'au liu ou ala.
835 Adont me souscouru et si me ramena.
Por celle cortoisie qu'il me fist adont la
De ce si m'avisai, si com vous dirai ja,
D'un joiiel a donner, car bien deservi l'a.
Les pierres vous emblai et de moi il les a.
840 Sachiés le vraiement que autrement ne va.'
Quant li peres l'oï forment s'esmerveilla,
'(Sire) [Fille],' dist li Califes, 'grant damage fait m'a
Mais encore ain ge mieux l'ounor que fait vous a —

Son cors ne son lignage jamais ne mescherra
845 Se je puis esploitier de ce que fait en a,
Quant por vo cors garder sa vie aventura—
Que toute ma grant perte, bien ait qui l'engenra.'
Joians fu li Califes, le fait li pardonna,
Et por la grant hounor qu'a sa fille fait a
850 Dist en sa boine foi que il li merira.
Senescal de sa terre le fist et molt l'ama,
Tous les jors de sa vie grant honnor li porta.
Bien li samble en son cuer ja ne deservira
La grande loyauté qu'a sa fille faite a.
855 Du Calife lairons tant que poins en sera,
Si dirons d'Alixandre comment il esploita.

.xxi.

Molt fu rois Alixandres dolans et irascus,
Et Phelippes ses peres li anchiiens kenus.
Quant il ot atendu .iii. semaines ou plus
860 Et il vit que ses lerres n'estoit point revenus
Si pensa qu'il estoit occhis et retenus.
Ses homes fist mander, quant il les ot esmus,
Sor le Calife ala iriés et fourmeüs,
Sa terre li gasta par armes et par fus.
865 Li Califes vint outre o toutes ses vertus,
Aymon fist cevalier qui ert grans et corssus,
Et si bien se prouvoit et estoit si cremus
Qu'a s'enseigne porter fu sor tous esleüs.
Et Aymes l'enkierka qui n'iert mie esperdus.
870 Tant i trencha de hyaumes, tant i percha d'escus,
Col. II Et tant trencha de bras et de chiés et de (lius) [bus],
Et tant fist de destriers et de chevaus grenus
Estrahiiers par les chans et de seignors cheüs
Qu'Alixandres li preus en estoit tout confus.
875 Non preucques et son [cuer] ert de grace enquenus
Que par grant amisté le sivoit sus et jus,
Et li prioit adiés que devenist ses drus;
Et a la fois faisoit aussi que s'il fust mus,
Et puis si respondoit, quant tant s'estoit tenus,
880 Que de lui ne fust plus tels parlemens tenus.
Jusqu'adont que ses sires seroit mors ou vaincus,

Ne seroit de sa guerre retenir recreüs.
Mais tant li disoit il, que par son dieu Marcus
S'a cest haut mariage pooit avenir nus,
885   Il feroit qu'Alixandres en seroit revestus
Se ses boins parlemens pooit estre entendus.
Son pooir en fera, si l'i aït Marchus.

.xxii.

Molt ot Emenidus le cuer cortois et sage.
Briement, por abregier le gros de nostre ouvrage,
890   Cascune des parties le tenoit a si sage
Que il les acorda et fist le mariage.
Rices furent les noches et de noble barnage,
Teles qu'a Alixandre afferoit par usage.
Enfin quant repairier vaut a son herbergage
895   Le boin duc enmena, si fu de son manage.
Archade li donna qu'il tenoit sans servage,
Et li dus le servi sans visce et sans outrage,
fo. 171r.   Et a conquerre aida tout son grant hiretage,
Et tous ses anemis destruisoit a hontage.
900   Es especïaument sor tout l'autre avantage
Il occist Gadifer qui molt li fist damage.
Por la quele acordance il emprist le voiage
D'aler pruec sa cousine (et) [en] Archade la large
Por doner Gadifer, le jouene au cler visage,
905   Por venir a s'amor et fuïr son haussage.
Bien li samble a ce faire n'i avroit nul outrage.

.xxiii.

Quant Emenidus fu dedens Archade entrés,
De sa terre passa .ii. des mieudres cités,
Puis vint a .i. castiel qui ert auques dalés.
910   Nobles estoit et biaus et ricement fremés
D'yaues et de montaignes, de mares et de prés.
La trouva sa cousine dont molt estoit amés.
Molt fu bien conjoïs et richement fiestés.
Quant ot but et mangiet et il fu reposés
915   Sa cousine conta comment ert accordés

Au jouene Gadifer qui tant est redoutés.
'Nieche,' ce dist li dus, 'se vous le crëantés
A feme vous avra et a marit l'avrés,
Et par tant en sera li meffais pardonnés.

920 Et sachiés que por riens gagier ne le devés,
Car entre les sachans est uns des plus senés,
Entre les honorables est li plus honnerés,
Et entre les plus biaus est li graindre biautés.'
'Sire,' dist la pucele, 'si soit com dit avés.

925 Ja riens ne desvaurai que me commanderés.'
'Cousine,' dist li dus, 'errant vous atornés,
Car lues vorrai mouvoir qu'atornee serés.'

.xxiv.

Col. II Quant la pucele fu richement atornee
Li dus Aimes monta quant elle fu montee

930 Sor .i. ceval norois qui ot la crupe lee,
Plus soëif va l'amblure, c'est verités prouvee,
Et si bien cevauchierent et soir et matinee,
Que d'Efezon coisirent la souveraine entree,
Car forment desiroit qu'elle i fust menee.

935 Quant il vinrent au pont de la grant tour quaree
Li boins dus l'embracha et quant l'ot desmontee
Erranment l'enmena en la sale pavee.
Molt fu bien recheüe et ricement festee
De contes et de dus, c'est verités prouvee.

940 Meïsmes li boins rois l'a forment honnoree.
Quant dame Fezonas qui molt estoit senee,
Et la bele Edeas et Ydorus menee
L'orent dedens la cambre que Venus ot fondee,
Molt fu de riches dras et souvent reparee,

945 Et molt fu richement servie et houneree
De quanqu'on pot de boin desirer par pensee.
Quant fu solatiie et un poi reposee
La cortois(i)e Elïos l'a par la main combree;
Betis et Gadifers qui molt l'orent amee

950 L'ont a l'orfaverie et conduite et menee
Por vëoir du paon la haute oevre eslevee.
En alant li conterent la parole avisee
Par quoi celle oevre fu et conduite et ouvree.

fo. 171v.

Enns en l'orfaverie desous un drap ouvré
955 S'assient doi et doi l'ouvrage on[t] resgardé.
Et la bele Elÿos a Martiien parlé
Et elle le resgarde si a un ris jeté.
'Bele,' dist Marciiens, 'nous somes descanlé,
Et tout lie autre sont, ce m'est vis, asorté.
960 Se m'amors vous plaisoit, sachiés en verité
Que donnee vous ert sans nulle iniquité.'
'Sire,' dist Elÿos, qui ot le cuer sené,
'Vous dites cortoisie et grant humilité,
Et uns sages desclaire, ou maint bien sont fondé,
965 Qu'on doit amer tout ce en quoi [il] a bonté.
Et il apert en vous si grande loyauté
Qu'on tenroit le refus a grande foleté.
Et por tant preng le don et retieng en bonté
Et autretel vous doins(t) car maint ont raconté
970 Que li amoreus tout aiment por estre amé.'
Entrues que il parloient d'amors et d'amisté
Et de sa seignourie et de lor grant bonté
A tant es .i. vallet qui lor a escrié
'Seignor, venés mangier, li rois l'a commandé!'
975 Lors issent de la cambre, el palais sont entré,
Et mainent les puceles, ou molt ot de biauté.
.ii. et .ii. par la voie si sont bien assorté,
Cascuns a sa cascune molt estroit acolé.
Et tout parlant d'amors en sont ensi alé,
980 Tant qu'il vinrent au liu dont je vous ai conté.
Alixandres les voit, grant joie en a mené.
En sorriant a dit, 'Vous soiiés bien trouvé
Tout ensi com vous estes et duit et aüné.'
Par les mains les a pris, s'ont ensamble lavé,
985 A l'assëoir as tables se sont entremellé.
Grant joie et grant [de]duit ont ensamble mené,
Et molt ont grant honor l'un a l'autre porté.
De cortois dis, de gais et de joli pensé,
Furent si bien servi com a lor volenté:
990 Onques gens miex ne furent a trestout lor aé.
Et par devant le roi sont si sergant alé
Qui porterent les mes qu'on li ot presenté
Grues, cignes, marlars i ot a grant plenté,

Et tant des autres mes que ja n'ert raconté.
995 Aprés mangier laverent et puis se sont levé.
Col. II Molt i ot en la sale cel jor ris et gabé,
D'unes choses et d'autres a molt grande plenté.
Ne vous savroie a dire de ce qu'il ont parlé.
Et quant ce vint au soir que il orent soupé
1000 Lors va cascuns couchier tant qu'il fu ajorné
Que li rois se leva o son riche barné.
Que vous diroie je? Tant i ont sejorné
Que Porus fu garis et venus en santé.

.xxvi.

Che fu par .i. matin que li rois main leva,
1005 O lui ses .xii. pers que avec lui mena.
Molt i ot sejorné qu'il ne lor anoia.
Dont vint Porus avant qui o lui amena
Marciien son cousin que molt forment ama,
Et Cassiiens de Baudres les puceles guia
1010 Par devant Alixandre que grant joie mena.
Quant il voient le roi cascuns le salua,
Et enclinent vers terre des iex le sousploia;
Et li rois vint vers aus et molt les honnera.
Dessus .i. drap de soie qu'on lor appareilla
1015 Se sont ensamble assis, mais petit demora.
Gadifers et Betis o euls s'acompaigna.
Et li rois Alixandres tantost lor devisa
Comment cascuns d'yaus .v. s'amie espousera:
'Lors sera boine pais, li uns l'autre amera;
1020 Molt sera grans li sires qui riens vous mesfera;
Se on le puet ataindre grandement l'amendra.
Et se nus vous mesfait, ce que ja n'avenra,
Faites le moi savoir, mes secours i venra.'
Quant li baron l'entendent cascuns l'en mercia.
1025 Tantost par le paiis la nouvele en ala.
Dames et cevaliers assés la assembla.
Erranment Gadifers a sa gent commanda
Qu'on tenge tres et tentes ou la feste sera.

.xxvii.

Molt fu grans l'assemblee ou palais d'Epheson,
1030 Car de tout le paiis entour et environ
I furent assemblé li prince et li baron
Et dames et puceles dont il i ot fuison.
Devant la sale furent tendu li pavillon
Et la tente le roi, mais je croi que nus hom
1035 Ne vit onques si bele ne de tele faichon.
Les cordes sont de soie et d'or fin li passon.
Lors descent Alixandres jus del maistre doignon
O lui les .v. puceles qui li sont au gieron.
S'i fu Porus l'Indois qui ot cuer de lÿon
fo. 172r. 1040 Et li soudans de Baudres qui fu de grant renon,
Et Marciiens de Persse qui bien entent raison,
Gadifers et Betis, Perdicas et Lÿon,
Caulus et Aristés et dans Emenidon,
Dauri et Floridas et le preu Festïon
1045 Et Graciiens de Tyr qui fu cousins Sanson.
Lors parla Alixandres, n'i fist demorison,
Et apela Porus hautement par son non.
En riant li a dit, 'Or rechevés le don
De Fezonas la bele a la gente fachon.
1050 Vous amés li uns l'autre, piecha dit le m'a on,
Et por li fu emprise la fole aatison
Es veus qui furent fait au mangier le paon.
Puis fumes mis a poi a grant destructïon.'
Dont fu Porus honteus si baissa le menton,
1055 En molt grant tans aprés ne dist ne o ne non.
Et quant vint au parler si dist s'ententïon,
'Grans merchis,' dist (li) [il], 'rois chi a gent guerredon,
Mais du fait avenu ne faites mentïon,
Dont aie honte et blasme et tout mi compaignon.'
1060 'Par ma foi,' dist li rois, 'or n'aiiés souspechon
Que je n'ai chose dite qui soit se por bien non.
Car s'au besoi[n] g voloie par nostre dieu Marcon
Por mon cors a garder, porter mon gonfanon,
N'i esliroie je persone se vous non,
1065 Et tout aussi le dient cil de ma regïon.'

.xxviii.

	Ore entent bien Porus et est aperchevans
Col. II	Qu'Alixandres li rois est auques desirans
	De lui porter hounor, d'estre ses bien voellans.
	Doucement li a dit, 'Je sui obeïssans
1070	De faire vo plaisir, tant com serai vivans.
	Mais par trestous les diex en cui je sui creans,
	Se j'estoie aussi preus com vous estes disans,
	Plus conquerroie terre ains le jor de .vii. ans
	Qu'onques encor n'en tint li riches rois Prians.'
1075	'Par ma foi,' dist li rois, 'je n'en sui pas gabans.'
	Puis dist a Fezonas qu'il saisi par les flans,
	'Pucele deboinaire, or soiiés rechevans
	Le cors du plus preudomme qui ains fust a nul tans.
	Il est preus et hardis et bien entremetans,
1080	Avisés en ses fais, n'est pas outrecuidans.
	Molt a por vous fait d'armes; soiiés li cognissans.'
	La pucele fu sage cortoise et avenans,
	Blons ceveus ot et sors plus qu'ors fins reluisans,
	Simple regardeüre et les iex sourrians,
1085	La bouce vermeillete, les dens menus et blans.
	Au roi a dit, 'Biau sire, toute sui desirans
	De vostre voloir faire, je sui en vos commans.
	Je vouai au paon, N'est pas passés li ans,
	Que n'avroie mari se n'en estiés greans.'
1090	'Par mon chief,' dist li rois, 'j'aim molt tes convenans
	Et de ce qu'avés dit ja n'i serés perdans,
	Ains en serés ancui couroune d'or portans.'
	Lors l'espousa Porus, qui molt en fu joians;
	Tantost les courouna Alixandres li frans
1095	De coroune doree d'or fin arrabians.
	Inde Major lor donne ou la ricesce est grans
	Et la terre d'Yrlande, qui tant est bien seans,
	Et la grant revenue qui valoit mil besans.

.xxix.

	Aprés le mariage Porus et Phesonas
1100	Alixandre[s] d'Alier, li fiex Olimpias,
	Maria le Baudrain a la bele Edeas.

Norewegue la terre lor donne sans nul gas,
Puis maria Betis en cel meïsmes pas,
Et la bele Ydorus en qui n'ot villain[s] gas.
1105 Engleterre la large lor dona haut et bas,
Car de biau don doner ne fu ains .i. jor las.
Marciien apela belement par compas
Et la bele Elïot resaisi par les bras.
'Marciien,' dist li rois, 'par les diex de Baudas,
1110 Je veul que vous prendés la cortoise Elias.
Par autre tour ne puet nos maus trere a respas,

fo. 172v.   Car on m'a dit por voir que ne le haés pas,
Et elle vous regete uns iex plus plains de las
Que ne soit escremie ne li jus des escas.

.XXX.

1115 'Martiiens,' dist li rois, 'par les diex de la mer,
Vous molt voel, ce m'est vis, hautement marïer.
Elÿos est tres sage et molt fait a loër,
Et de haute lignie, en li n'a qu'amender.
Et on vous puet molt bien entre les haus conter
1120 Et entre les plus sages que on porroit trouver,
Vous porroit on bien prendre, eslire et essenter.'
'Sire,' dist Marciiens, 'sauf le vostre parler . . . '
'Par ma foi,' dist li rois, 'je l'os por voir jurer.
Frize et toute Hollande vous doins sans dessevrer.'
1125 Aprés fist Gadifer huchier et appeler.
'Gadifer,' dist li rois, 'je vous voel marïer
A toute la plus bele que on porroit trouver,
La nieche au duc Ayme qui tant fait a loër.
Avoecques ly vous doins, sans jamais rapieler,
1130 La terre des Galois et d'Escoche a garder.
(Ydoire) [Lydone],' dist li rois, 'prendés le baceler
Por le pais de vostre oncle et son pere a garder,
Que vos oncles occist a Gadres sor la mer.'
'Sire,' dist la pucele, 'fors est a oublïer
1135 La mort de mon chier frere que tant soliés amer.
C'est Pirus de Monflor qui tant fu preus et ber,

Col. II   Que ses peres occist a Gadres, c'est tout cler.
Mais puis qu'il vuet la mort de son pere oublïer
Por vostre volenté voel mon voloir quasser.'

1140 Li rois l'en merchia puis les fist assambler,
A grant joie les fist icel jor marïer.
Grant feste ot ens es tentes; quant vint au caroler
Li fors rois Alixandres por sa gent rescrïer
Commencha voiant tous premerains a fester.

.xxxi.

1145 Quant li rois Alixandres ot donné a Porus
La bele Phezonas et Betis Ydorus,
Le Baudrain Edeas, Marciien Eleüs,
Et au preu Gadifer la (cortoise Ydorus) [belle Lydonus],
La nieche au viel Aymon qui tant estoit cremus,
1150 Les tables fist couvrir; quant poins en fu venus
Li rois s'ala laver et puis s'assisent jus.
Molt i orent boins mes, deviser nel set nus,
La fu bien li mangiers servis et maintenus.
Signe fist de parler li rois macedonus.
1155 'Seignor,' ce dist li rois, 'je voel estre entendus.
La feste doit durer bien .xv. jors ou plus.
S'en ai fait .xv. pars, se je en sui creüs.
Des .xv. en ai les (.vi.) [.v.] a mon oes retenus,
De vos .v. mariés, cui grans biens est creüs,
1160 Asserrai cascun jor el nom no diu Marchus
Et el nom de celui iere adiés porveüs
Des .iiii. rechevoir de tous les autres drus;
Et des autres .x. jors ai les .v. esleüs
Por nos .v. mariés, ce ne mescroie nus,
1165 Si tenront court pleniere as grans et as menus,
fo.173r. Et les autres .v. jours, dont je me sui tenus,
Avront nos .v. puceles, je m'i sui assentus.
Si verront par .v. jors les festes et les jus,
Mais as .v. jors premiers vaurrai estre tenus,
1170 Et le sizime doins Poron le fil Clarus,
Et le septisme avra la bele Phezonus,
Ydorus le witisme, le nuevisme Betus,
Elÿos le disime, l'onzime Marcïus.
(Je done) [Lydone] le dousime, Gadifer (le) [li] membrus
1175 Le trezime avera, li Baudrains le sourplus
Fera se il li plest et s'amie Edeüs.'
Adont i ot rizee de jouenes (et) de kenus.

'Seignor,' dist Aristés, 'Lÿones et Caulus,
Nos boins rois nous a miex fiestés et repeüs
1180   Que se il eust nos mes doublés de .iiii. lus.'

.xxxii.

Molt i ot ens es tentes grant feste et grant rizee.
Molt bien fu [d]'Alixandre(s) sa grans gens rescr[i]ee
Et par .v. premiers jors conjoïie et festee.
Cascuns des .v. espeus et cascune espousee
1185   Bel et cortoisement acompli sa jornee.
Quant vint a la quinzaine, qu'Edea la senee
Avoit desiranment nuit et jor awardee –
De faire largement est bien entalentee –
Les tables fist couvrir, molt tresbien avisee.
1190   Molt i ot d'escuiers qui servent a volee.
Alixandres s'asist et sa gent honneree
Et molt fu largement servie et assazee,
Car la bele Edea qui molt estoit senee
De table en table aloit dire a grant alenee,
1195   'Seignors, faites le bien, buvés ceste vinee.
Mal ait cui il desplaist, sachiés que molt m'agree.'
Entre .ii. mes quant (vint) [plus] la gens fu enparlee,
Vers la chambre as orfevres est guenchie et tornee,
O li .ii. damoiseles dont molt estoit privee.
1200   La paon fist porter en la tente roee.
Devant le roi des Griex s'est en haut escriee,
'Entendés moi Indois, Grieu et gent de Chaldee.
Je vouai au paon, n'i a pas une anee,
Por la haute proëche qu'en son non fu mostree
1205   Que je le restorroie, si m'en sui aquittee.
Ves en chi le (trezor) [restor] d'oevre bien manouvree.'

.xxxiii.

'Seignor,' dist Edea, li gaie et li rians
Col. II   Veschi une relique, noble et esmerveillans.
Aouree doit estre et d'ommes et d'enfans,
1210   Que boins espoirs i est por les desesperans,
Memoire as oubli[é]s, ricesce as mendians,
Hardemens as couars, raliance as fuians.

Et si sont au pavon les .vii. pierres seans
Par les queles j'enteng les .vii. vertus plus grans
1215   Qui doivent estre en ceaus qu'en amors sont manans.
Et molt bien sont les pierres au paon afferans.
Chis paons senefie les quis et les vivans
Qui sont viande as preus et as bien combatans.
Et nus hom ne fu onques preus ne entreprendans
1220   Se il(n'ait) [n'avoit] amie, ou s'il n'estoit amans,
Ou il n'avoit espoir d'amor en aucun tans.
Premierement i siet el chief li dyamans
Qui fait riches les boins et les preus convoitans.
Ceste aprent qu'amans soit en amor conquerans.
1225   Aprés siet li saphirs qui fait les gens plaisans.
Ceste aprent qu'amans soit en vertu habundans,
Car bontés fait les cuers en amors bien ceans.
La tierce est li rubins qui molt est avenans,
Qui fait simples les cors, si nous est demonstrans
1230   Que cuers d'amant doit estre humelment conversans,
Simples sans doublerie et de fais sans beubans.
Et la pierre esmeraude est aprés ensivans.
Ceste aprent qu'amans soit envoisiés et joians
La chincquisme pierre est escarboucle luisans.
1235   Ceste aprent qu'amans soit en tout si conquerans
Que por enluminer les cuers des resgardans
Si qu'il soit occoisons des biens des vergondans.
Aprés siet li esconse: ceste pierre est croissans
Senefie qu'amans soit (et) secrés et celans
1240   Se des biens d'amors vuet estre oirs et atendans
fo. 173v.   La septisme est jagonse qui molt est confortans,
Qui son seignor destorbe de murmure et d'ahans.
Ceste aprent qu'amans soit paciens et soffrans:
Qui tout sueffre, tout got, riens ne li est grevans.
1245   Ciex qui ert deboinaires, riens ne li ert fallans.

.xxxiv.

'Seignors,' dist Edea, li envoisie et franche,
'Grant chose est du paon, por voir le vous fiance,
Qu'il n'i a riens en lui par toute ma creance
Qui n'ait boine mistere et grant senefianche
1250   En amors et en armes ou mains boins cuers s'avance.
Il est biaus par defors et de noble samblanche

Et par dedens est boins et plains (et) de grant sustance.
Cis poins chi nous aprent et done (soustenance) [souvenance]
Que qui en amors a d'amors la maniance,
1255   Estre doit gracieus dehors sans desplaisance,
Et par dedens le cuer loyaus sans dechevance.
Li keue, cors et ciefs tienent par droite us(u)ance
Ensamble; et s'a le cors auques grant par parance,
Grant keue et petit chief. Tout ce est ramembrance
1260   Que volenté d'ami doit tenir a plaisanche
Et joindre a desirier et croistre en habundance,
Et d'un petit cuidier faire grant esperance.
Boine vie est d'amer qui la a souffissance.
Les plumes et les penes dont il vole et s'eslance
1265   Mostrent que ciex qui a ferme et forte creance
Doit estre viguereus et avoir sa beanche
D'adiés lui eslever entre haute honorance.
Et li ongles de quoi il se tient a la brance
Si fort que il ne chiet por nulle mesestance
1270   Nous mostr(a) [e] que proëce n'ait en lui defalance.
Ains ait sans decaïr ferme parseverance.
Li paonchiel qu'il a par carnel acointance,
Qu'il nourrist et alieue et jete hors d'enfance,
Qui font aprés sa mort de lui (parseverance) [representance],
1275   Senefient que quant li boin font recordance
Des proëces as preus que li mors adevance,
Par le delit qu'il ont en la considerance
(Qu'on convient) [Conchoivent] .i. desir qui lor done hengance
De ces boins resambler par boine acoustumance,
1280   Et par espoir ci ont tout li boin racordance.
Et li keue ou tant a d'ius, par droite ordenance,
Senefie merchi, par qui amans commanche
A amer de fin cuer, loial sans decevance.
Et ce qu'elle est des plumes legiere sans pesance,
1285   Qui debrisent au vent sans nulle contrestance
Col. II   Nous moustre qu'en merchi a poi d'asseüranche:
On le donne et retaut a petit de muanche.
Ce qu'il i a tant d'yex, luisans sans cognissance,
Et qu'il ne voient riens, mostrant sans comparance
1290   Qu'amans ait a merci l'eul par grant desirance.
C'est uns plaisans deduis et une aveulissance.
Mais li (veus) [biens] qui en vient (par aise) [passe] le mesestance,
Car on [en] est loyal et noble en contenanche.'

.XXXV.

'Seignor,' dist Edea, 'de liés et de maris

1295   Doit estre li paons aourés et servis.

Car il est occoisons des fais les plus eslis

Qu'onques fuissent par armes acompli, ce m'est vis.

Et se ce est viande as preus et as hardis

Et as vrais amoureus qui l'amer ont empris

1300   Autre raison i a, s'est drois que le devis:

Li paons vers le keue est nobles et jolis,

Et s'est devers les piés auques lais et despis.

Ensi est de proëces d'amies et d'amis.

Par les piés entent on commencement toudis,

1305   Par le keue le fin, mes cuers en est tous fis.

Car li piés d'un (outrage) [ouvrage] est tous premiers bastis,

Et puis est sor le piet parfais et acomplis,

Et tout soit en bas liu et rudement assis

Li combles c'est li fins, quant haut est agensis.

1310   Ensi est des tournois, des joustes, des poignis.

Il commenchent par paines, par süers et par cris,

Mais a tous les meschiés n'apartient fors qu'oublis,

Car li fins en est joie, hounors et los et pris.

Et d'autre part amors, de quoi j'ai plus apris,

1315   Commenche par cremeur et par durs escondis,

Mais li conclusïons, qui nommee est merchis,

Est plaine de solas et de giu et de ris,

De cortois parlemens et de secrés delis.

Et por ce ne doit estre cachiés n'arriere mis

1320   Petis maus que por estre en grans biens convertis.

Aprés, quant li paons est en se reue mis,

Et il est estendus por estre plus jolis,

En coloiant resgarde haut et bas par avis,

Lues que il voit ses piés s'en est tous amortis.

1325   Ensement fait li preus et li amans jolis

Quant il voit que il est por le millor espris,

De quoi nus hom ne puet estre amés ne joïs

Por riens qu'il sacent faire et en amant toudis.

Dont resgarde son piet, c'est comment il est pris,

1330   Et de queles vertus li siens cuers est garnis.

fo. 174r.   Quant il voit qu'il n'est mie de bien si raëmplis

Qu'il appartiengne a estre de celle dame oïs

S'en devient par ce point honteus et abaubis.

Et se il est en armes en grans los esqueillis
1335 Et il voit que il est en ce point amortis
Que por avoir tel los, s'en est tous asouplis.
Et puis que li paons portrait selonc mes dis
Les amans et les preus, estre (tous) [doit] conjoïs
(Ciex) [Cis chi] qui represente (chi) et les mors et les vis,
1340 Et especïaument celui qui fu rostis
Et qui a si grant joie fu mangiés et repris,
Qui avant hier fu trais de Porus et occhis.
Par quoi je li met sus, poi i vaut li detris,
Qui d'aourer doit estre premiers entalentis.
1345 Et aprés offerront Gadifers et Betis,
Martiiens li courtois et li Baudrains faitis,
Nostre .v. marié(es) as mantiaus d'asur bis
Qui ont servi Amors; or les a si servis
Que elle les desiert et adés a siervis
1350 De ce de quoi Dangiers les avoit asservis.
Car a cascun a fait trouver ce qu'il a quis.
Et aprés offeront tout li autre marchis
Qui ont les veus hautains voés et acomplis.
Et puis rois Alixandres, qui tous nous a conquis.'
1355 A ces mos s'escriierent Macedonois et Gris,
'Molt bien dist Edea, ses cors soit beneïs.
Car elle nous a tous festés et esbaudis.'

.xxxvi.

Molt fu noble la cours, n'i ot que desprisier.
Quant on ot tant servi les napes font sacier,
1360 Les tables descouvrirent sergant et escuier.
Noblement ont servi li vaillant servitier.
Aprés mangier s'alerent li baron redrechier
Et puis vers le paon s'en vont agenoillier;
Col. II Et la bele Edea qui ot grant desirier
1365 D'acroistre le deduit por sa feste essaucier,
Entre les menestreus, qu'on devoit plus prisier,
Eslisi par acort et fist un tresorier
Por le paon garder et l'aport maniier
Et a ses compaignons partir et despicier,
1370 Por ce qu'elle faisoit, a verité jugier,
La grace as menestreus fraindre et amenuisier,

Et qu'on n'entendoit pas au paon festoiier
Vaut on restor de ce qu'il fussent clachonnier
De l'aport, et (de) [que] tout i fussent parchonnier.
1375 Dont commencha cascuns a faire son mestier:
La oïst on vïelles, tromper et grelloiier,
Et orgenes orgener, tamburer et treschier,
Harper et chitoler, baler et pietiier,
Et biaus dis recorder, chanter et versiier
1380 Et enforchiement caroler et treschier
Pardevant le paon, por la gent envoisier.
Il n'i fu menestreus n'i fesist son mestier,
Et trestout s'acordoient si bien sans desvoiier,
Qui la fust a ce point il peüst bien cuidier
1385 Qu'il fust en paradis, qu'on doit tant graciier,
O les gens Jhesu Crist por lui solatiier.
Quant on ot tant festé qu'il fu poins du laissier,
Dessus une grant table assist un oreillier
Edea, et s'ala le paön sus couchier.
1390 Et li baron s'alerent pardevant arrengier
Por offrir au paon et aus humiliier,
Et par grant reverence loër et graciier.
Mais de Porus l'Indois fisent le renc premier,
Li autre marïet restoient par derrier.
fo. 174v. 1395 Ens ou tierch renc estoient li autre cevalier
Qui avoient les veus fais au paon trencier,
Ou quart avec les dames Alixandres d'Alier,
Et ou quint renc sa gent et tout autre princier.
Molt i ot rice offrande et molt fist a proisier,
1400 Car Porus i offri son auferrant courssier
Ens ou nom de celui qu'il toli avant hier
Au rice   duc d'Arcade as lanches abaissier –
Mais il le rachata de mil livres d'or mier.
Et li Baudrains offri son riche branc d'achier
1405 Por celui qu'il ala Alixandre esrachier
En milieu de sa gent en l'estor plus plenier –
De son contrepois d'or le fist contregagier
Du plus fin que on pot trouver ne esligier.
Et li preus Marciiens offri son esprivier
1410 Qui tant ert gens et biaus et tant fist a proisier –
De cent mars de fin or le rala esligier.
Aprés fisent offrir le courtois Gadifer,
Le boin, le preu, le sage, le vaillant cevalier.

Offri le confanon de son confanonnier
1415 Ou nom de l'estandart qu'il ala debrisier
Quant il fu a l'estor au tornoiement fier,
Auquel li rois Clarus se devoit raliier.
Et Caulus i offri son boin hyaume d'achier
Qui tant ert fins et boins, nus nel pot esprisier,
1420 En [s] ou nom de celui qu'il ala deslachier
Au Baudrain Cassiien pour son veu aquitier.
Et li preus Aristés offri un saudoiier
Qu'il eut de fin argent fait paindre et entaillier,
Et couvers de ses armes por le plus renvoisier,
1425 Por ce qu'a Fezonas voua sans fausnoiier
Que il li aideroit son droit a desraisnier,
Ne jamais d'Epheson ne voloit piet vuidier
Jusqu'adont que Clarus poroient paassier,
S'Alixandres ses sires ne l'en voloit cachier,
1430 Por sa grant seignorie l'en peüst bien jeter.
Et Perdicas offri d'or un arbalestrier
Atorné et armé ensi qu'il ert mestier.
Son arc tint en sa main et s'ot chaint le baudrier,
Por ce que il voua les pietons a aidier
1435 En la grosse bataille qui fu des avant hier.
Betis en offri un qui cousta maint denier
Por ce que Perdicas voua acompaignier
Entre .ii. rens a piet a guise de baivier.
Lÿones une lanche i offri de pumier
Col. II 1440 Por ce que il voua, por son veu apointier,
Qu'a l'ost le roi Clarus iroit sans resoignier
Por a son fil l'ainsnet jouster et deffiier,
Por ce que il voloit son boin pris avanchier,
Et Floridas offri aussi c'un prisonnier
1445 Bien fait a la maniere que on fait prisonnier,
Car le Baudrain voua a prendre et a loiier.
Et Phesonas offri un aniel biel et chier
Por ce qu'elle voua sans jamais renonchier,
Et fist un veu si fort, nus nel porroit prisier,
1450 Qu'a nesun mariage ne voloit repairier
Ne a homme vivant ne voloit marïer
S'Alixandres li preus n'estoit a l'alliier.
Et la bele Ydorus offri sans detriier
.ii. aniaus de fin or qu'elle ot fait apairier,
1455 Por ce qu'au paon vaut vouer et fianchier

Qu'a tous jors ameroit son dru de cuer entier,
Sans jamais repentir ne faire prolongier.
Que vous diroie je por l'ouvrage alongier?
Molt i offri cascuns l(on) [ar] gement sans bringier,
1460 Alixandres meïsmes ne s'i vaut desliier
Qu'il n'offresist aussi por l'ounor essauchier
Du paon qui la fu, et de ceuls qu'il ot chier.
Ains offri un saphir que il avoit tant chier,
Que il nel donast mie por d'or plain .i. sestier.
1465 La orent menestrel maint don et bel loiier.
La veïst on les larges, riches dras despoillier,
Donner as menestreus qui fisent lor mestier
De la feste esbaudir, de baler, de treschier.
Et li villain (avuec) [aver] les lessierent mignier
1470 As mignes et as vers par lor outrecuidier,
Qu'il aiment miex l'avoir atout lor reprovier
Que les graces des boins, que molt puet avancier.
Molt i ot grant deduit jusques a l'anuitier,
Et la nuit toute nuit jusques a l'esclairier.
1475 Cascuns se penoit molt de la feste essauchier,
Et la bele Edea, a qui n'ot qu'enseignier.
S'en rala en la cambre ou furent li ouvrier.
Bel et cortoisement les prist a araisnier.
L'ouvrage a resgardé et devant et derrier.
1480 Bien li sist toute l'oevre, a celer nel vous quier.
Cortoisement le fist et largement paiier,
Et li uns por aus tous respondi sans blangier,
'Dame, nous sommes tout vostre sans recouvrier,
1484 Si que a tous jours mais vous i poés fiier.'

                                        (end of Col. II)

TEXT OF *LI RESTOR DU PAON*, PART II

.i.

fo. 175r.

1   Quant Porus li Indoys et tout si compaignon
      Eurent par reverence en grant devotïon
      Loënges et merchis rendues au paon,
      Por le bien qui estoit venus par s'occoison,
5   Et faite de commun offrande de renon
      Samblables a lor veus par repetatïon,
      Por en aus affremer le memoratïon
      Alixandres d'Alier, qui ot cuer de lÿon,
      Apela Elÿot bassement par son non,
10 Marciien le Persant, le riche Anthioton,
      Festïon, Licanor, Tholomer et Cliton,
      Et tous ceaus qui n'avoient part a la vouison.
      A une part les traist, si lor dist a bas ton
      'Seignor,' dist Alixandres, 'entendés ma raison.
15 Toute chose a .iii. tans a prouver par raison:
      L'entree et le moiien, la fin c'est le coron.
      Dont chose empris[e] en bien, quant elle a bon moilon,
      Desire que elle ait boine conclusïon.
      Et hom qui vuet avoir haute perfectïon
20 Trois vertus doit avoir en conversatïon:
      Proëce et hardement et scïence a fuison.
      Hardement en prendant sans hide et sans frachon,
      Proëche pour mener a exsecutïon,
      Sens por faire du bien la declaratïon.
25 Onques mais si biau[s] fais ne vit, je croi, nus hon
      Que on fist por l'oisiel, por Phezone et Poron.
      Par (hautement vouer) [hardement voé] furent, bien le set on,
      Par proëche achievé(r) a noise et a tenchon.
      Huchons a no conseil des menestreus de non
30 S'en dirai, s'en diront cascuns s'ententïon,
      Si assenons le pris sans simulatïon
      Par voie de science et de discretïon.
      S'averons le tierç point de no comparison,

Car labour sans loiier est merchis sans pardon.
35 Li glore du mont est en .ii. poins, ce voit on,
En preus et en hounors. Mais assener doit on
Le proufit as petis, l'ounour au haut baron.
Et se li petis prent as biens refectïon
Li grans prent es hounors peuture et norrechon.
40 Car grans hons sans honnor, plains de confusïon,
Ne vit mie, ains languist, et por mort le cont'on.
Col. II Et hounors est en pris d'armes; dont tauroit on
A haut homme sa vie et sa droite parchon,
Qui en ce sousplanter vorroit sa beneichon
45 Et son pris amenrir, et por tant le doinst on
Si qu'on n'i puist avoir blasme ne reprochon.'
A cest mot commander a fait par un garchon
Li rois a caroler tous ceaus de sa maison.
Molt i ot grant deduit ou chastel d'Epheson.
50 La peuist on oïr mainte note et maint son
Et respondre et chanter mainte boine canchon,
Des gais, des amoreus dont il i ot fuison,
Et especïaument du Baudrain Cassïon,
Phezone et Ydorus et dant Emenidon.

.ii.

55 Quant en la sale fu la feste commenchie,
Des menestreus de non prist li rois en partie:
En la cambre Venus, qui d'or estoit polie,
Les mena li boins rois o sa grant baronnie.
Assize a delés lui sor un drap d'Aumarie
60 Elÿot, qui estoit cortoise et enseignie:
D'autre part Matiien, le seigneur de Persie.
Li autre sont assis sor le jonc qui verdie.
Li rois les resgarda qui d'ounor ne mendie.
'Seignor,' dist li boins rois, 'chi n'a fors compaignie.
65 Cascuns de nous com peu qu'il ait de manandie,
Selonc l'ententïon que nous avons ourdie,
Y doit faire autretant que li rois d'Ermenie.
Vous i valés que rois, je n'i vail que mesnie.
Seés vous tout amont en une riulle onnie,
70 Et en fin de querele, a nostre departie,
Soit cascuns hounorés selonc sa seignorie.
Alons avant au vif en l'oevre qu'est bastie,

Car je voel que cascuns s'ententïon deslie.'
Elÿot resgarda, si dist, 'Dame adrechie,
75   La premeraine vois de vo droit vous otrie.'
'Sire,' dist Elÿos, 'vous dites cortoisie,
Mais sauve vostre pais, il ne m'avenra mie.
Mariee m'avés, de cuer vous en merchie,
S'ai seignor et mari qui ma volenté guie.
80   Mesire(s) est et vous siens tant que serés en vie.
Ja ne plache a nos diex que soie tant hardie
Que de tant desor lui par mon gré m'enhardie,
Ains ert obedïence adiés vers lui paiie,
Et de lui envers vous s'a mon voloir s'otrie.
85   Teus est il, dont il n'est mestiers qu'on l'en castie,
Por metre cuer et cors, terre et hounor et vie.'

fo. 175v.   Martiiens l'esgarda; ne puet müer ne rie,
Sa main devant son vis, sa chiere enbronchie.
Li uns l'autre cloignoit, et en secret pietie,
90   Car si tresbel raisnoit au roi de Mazonie,
Et en tout avoit si sa maniere agensie,
Que toute celle gent qui la ert aünie,
En disoit tresgrant bien, et estoit bien paiie.
'Bele,' dist li fors rois, 'm'entente avés matie.
95   Vostre ententïons est sor si haut bien logie
Que je ne vous os plus prisier que ne mesdie.'
A Martiien l'offri, mais il l'a deguerpie,
Et a cascun d'yaus tous — n'a cel ne l'escondie.
Quant li parole fu porportee et puirie,
100 De cascun escondite et du plus resoignie,
Entre les menestreus fu de cascun baillie
Et par commandement enjointe et rekierkie.
'Seignor,' ce dist li rois, 'a vous est avoiie,
Car le plus i savés et qui miex set miex die.
105 Les armes cognissiés, et la bachelerie
Des jouenes bacelers ou prouesce est fichie.
Quant vassaus a ou poing sa grant hanste enpoignie,
Son hauberc en son dos et sa targe vautie,
Et il est sor les camps a bataille rengie,
110 Armés et enfourchiés ou destrier de Surie,
Et il est bien requis ou il fait l'envaïe,
Ciex qui cevauche entour et voit ce [le] arramie
Doit miex savoir comment sa lance a enploiie,
Com bel cop il rechoit, comment il le renvie,

115   Comment sa gent se part, comment il les ralie,
Que ciex qui sa teste a en son hyaume enbuissie,
Et qui a le cuer plain d'ire et de felonie.
De son pris resgarder de riens ne s'ensounie.
Il est bien, qui le voit, que pas ne l'entroublie,
120   Et por itant vous ai la parole baillie
Que savoir en devés la juste priserie.
Car qui jue as eschés, plus de legier varie
Que ciex qui voit le jú et point ne s'esbanie.'

.iii.

Quaint li fiex Filippon ot sa volenté dite,
125   Li rices rois des Griex qui nul bien ne despite,
Li rois des menestreus qui les autres aquite
Se leva en estant pardessus la carpite.
Par grant aage avoit fache palle et afflite,
Barbe blance et chenue et pas n'estoit petite.
130   L'un jour faisoit le fol et l'endemain l'ermite,
Et comme nains bochus et com contrais habite,
Col. II   Les preus claime coars, l'un wihot, l'autre herite,
Ensi que ses voloirs por plaire li endite.
De parler s'apresta car cascuns l'i encite.
135   'Sire,' dist li varlés, 'par tous les diex d'Egite,
L'ordre des armes ai en mon cuer bien escrite.
De joustes, de tornois, en quoi on se delite,
Ai vut donner le pris d'aucune chose eslite.
Mais de(guerres morteus) [guerre mortel] , qui est en sang
        confite,
140   De quoi la mieudre gent est conquise et adite,
Requise par ireur, par eür desconfite,
Poi en voi donner pris, mais elle est bien descrite
Entre les bien parlans, ou souvent est redite
La proësce des preus. Se la chose ai mal dite
145   Repris soie a vo gré, ja n'en ruis prendre arbite.'

.iv.

'Seignor,' ce dist li rois des hiraus, 'c'est tout cler
Que de guerre[s] morteus voi peu le pris donner,
Mais nus ne doit ces fais a autres comparer:
Ce sont li souverain que on porroit penser.

150 Fine amors et reviaus firent les veus vouer,
Desiriers (de) [et] voloir les fisent achiever,
Et quant il plest as diex qu'en joie puet finer
Nus ne doit le moiien fors qu'en joie conter.
Et por, endroit de mi, le pris miex assener

155 Le doins a Gadifer qui est gentiex et ber.
De boin sang fu estrais quant il osa penser –
Et de boine nature que ce puet aviser –.
Que il iroit tous seus l'estandart decauper –
En toute l'ost n'en ot qui si osast vouer –

160 Au riche roi Clarus, qui le faisoit garder
As plus preus de sa gent por les prius agrever.
Mais il s'i embati et sans contremander
Et a son branc d'achier l'ala jus craventer.
Teus cors ne fu onques fais de baceler

165 Que par son cors peüst une ost desbareter,
Ne l'estandart brisier et la gent desmenbrer,
Et a sa volenté fuïr et reculer.
Et par ceste raison m'i voel je acorder,
Ne ja n'en isterai se je n'och miex rimer.'

170 'Grans merchis,' dist Clitons, 'g'i sai a amender.
Nonporquant le vassal ne voel de riens blasmer,
Ne que nus puist plus haut par proëce monter,
Mais il n'est si biaus fais qu'on ne truist bien son per.
Dont li veus le Baudrain fait bien a relever,

175 Car nus ne puet plus grant, ce m'est avis, vouer.
Quant li diu vuelent tant nostre roi amonter

fo. 176r.
Que il l'ont fait seignor d'air, de terre et de mer,
Et de hautes vertus le vuelent si parer
Que on se puet en lui de proësce mirer,

180 Et de tous autres biens a bien examiner,
Par raison pour son veu tenir a singuler.
Quant fortune et li diu le vuelent si mener,
Et contre lor pooir les fait tant ravaler
Qu'en milieu de sa gent li vint s'espee oster

185 Je ne cuich que nus hom peüst plus haut vouer.
Se Gadifers ala l'estandart desfroër,
Boine raison i a s'on le vuet escouter.
Li estandars ne set ne traire ne parler
Ni son anui fuïr, ne haïr ne amer.

190 Se cil vuelent fuïr qui le veulent tenser
Il couvient l'estandart trebuchier et verser.

Mais se nous qui devons le roi des Griex hourder,
Et son cors garandir et lui avironner,
Par defaute de cuer veuliesmes reculer,
195 S'a nostres rois bien cuer d'un haut home agarder,
Corage d'envaïr et cors pour le mater;
Et de tant fu li veus plus fors a achiever.
Se chi ne fust li rois, qui sor nos doit regner,
Le parler en vaussisse un poi plus demener,
200 Mais devant lui ne voel son haut pris aconter,
Pardevant l'omme doi sa loënge celer,
En derriere nonchier, florir et repeter.
Mais por ce ne fait pas li fais mains a peser,
Mais adont le doit on plus hautement loër,
205 Se la cause couvient reponre et annuler.
Et por tant au Baudrain voel le pris assener,
Et di que de son droit l'en doit sor tous porter.'
'Clitons' dist Marciiens, 'qui vous vuet escouter,
A vos paroles puet bien aprendre a parler.
210 Quant li Baudrains fu teus que por tel fait ouvrer
Dont fu cil souverains qui l'osa enverser,
Et au voloir du roi le fist enprisonner.
Par la grandeur du fait puet on l'autre prover.
Por Floridas le di, qui s'i vaut esprouver.'

.v.

215 'Clitons,' dist Marciiens, 'je sui certains et fis
Que se fortune avoit a un vassal promis
Tout le confort des diex, qui plus sont poëstis,
Et l'eüssent de accort a aidier entrepris,
Ne porroit il par aus monter en plus haut pris
220 Que de tollir l'espee au riche roi des Gris.'
Alixandres rougi si enbroncha le vis.
Col. II 'Marciien,' dist li rois, 'biaus sire, grant merchis.
Vous me loërés tant en florissant vos dis
Que fuïr n'oserai quant serai desconfis.'
225 'Sire,' dist Marciiens, 'de riens n'i a mespris.
Au dit d'un vantëor i avroie pau mis;
Et tant a mon pourpos la je sui revertis:
Se li Baudrains fu teus qu'en parlant vous devis,
Li veus de Floridas fu tant plus seignoris
230 Quant a vous le livra enprisonné et pris.

Li preus qui preu conquiert sans estre mal baillis
Doit pardeseure lui resner et estre assis,
De tant que li fais porte a quoi il soit commis.
Dont n'ert a Floridas li (fais) [pris] pas escondis.
235 De moie part li doins, de qui que soit laidis —
Il me samble tresbien et si est mes avis —
Mais il ne l'eüst pas se Cassamus fust vis,
Car onques plus grans veus ne fu en plet bastis
Que de mon oncle aidier, qui ert ses anemis,
240 Et de vouer qu'il ert par lui a garant mis
(Se) [S'a] meschief le trouvoit entre les Arrabis.
Li cuers qui ce voa ne fu onques falis,
Ne de maise ire plains, mais d'amors si espris
Qu'a paines set haïr ceaus qui li font le pis.
245 Aidier les anemis en morteus fereis,
Es[t] fais deseure fais, hardis outre hardis.
Car ciex qui jue au ju est trop plus que chaitis
Quant on done au ribaut que sor lui a conquis.
Et se plus jue a lui quant il est regarnis
250 Souvent avient qu'enfin se trueve desconfis.
Ensi fist Cassamus, diex li faiche merchis,
Quant il aida Clarus de qui estoit haïs.
Et quant li preudons est de cest siecle fenis
Le plus grant doi aprés eslire, a mon avis.
255 Et por tant de ces veus la huee et le pris
Otroi a Floridas qui d'ounor est floris,
Car je ne le puis miex assener, ce m'est vis.'
'Sire,' dist Tholomers, 'chi estes ses amis.
Je retieng le parler quant en serés partis,
260 Car un poi sui hastiex et si me tais envis.
'Par mon chief,' dist li rois, 'chi affier[t] bien .i. ris.
Reposons nous .i. poi, s'en ert plus fors nos cris.
Si nous huchiés le vin, car trop est alentis,
Si nous rafreschirons, s'iert li parlers plus fis.
265 Je ne puis pas au sens estre si ententis,
Moie soit la couroune, vostre soit li estris.
fo. 176v. Se nos parlers estoit un poi plus rafreschis
Tholomers avroit miex cause d'estre oïs.'
Lors i ot maint vallet en la chambre salis
270 Qui donerent le vin plus froit que marbre bis,

Et lues qu'il orent beut, ont le parler repris.
D'Egipte Tholomers, qui molt estoit pensis,
Nonporquant de parler n'estoit mie abaubis,
Bien en sot la maniere, si com dist li escris.

.vi.

275   'Seignor,' dist Tholomers, 'a verité entendre,
Marciien ne saroie aprendre ne reprendre.
Ains est li plus sachans que el mont puisse prendre;
Mais por ce ne voel pas a tous ses dis descendre,
Tout li sens sont seüt, mais s'aucun(s), par aprendre,
280   (Sent) [Sont] parfait en un point en autre part sont mendre.
Dont nus ne puet les sens tous savoir ne comprendre,
Et por tant, saus tous drois, car a el ne voel tendre,
De pure ententïon, sans ma volenté vendre,
Doins Edea le pris, de droit le puet atendre.
285   Li restors du paon tous les autres engendre:
Quant ert sor son piler colïans que calendre,
Et li boin qui or sont seront müet en cendre,
Cil qui aprés venront i porront molt aprendre,
Car ce qu'on voit a l'oel puet plus .i. cuer resprendre
290   Que ce qu'aucuns vorroit par oïr dire entendre.
Por ce, de son bienfait li voel boin loiier rendre,
Ne biautés d'autre veu ne m'en porroit sosprendre.

.vii.

Quant Tholomers ot dit tout ce que lui plaisoit,
Antigonus parla qui dalés lui (lui) estoit.
295   'Biaus dous sire,' fait il, 'qui croire vous vorroit,
La cortoise Edea le pris en porteroit.
Si ne desdi ge pas que ses veus biaus ne soit,
Mais d'or est et d'argent et autant en feroit
Li orfevres demain, qui bien l'en paieroit.
300   Plus seroit mes amis se son cuer me donoit,
Et l'ounor de son cors et se por moi moroit
Que se .v. cens trezors d'or fin m'abandonoit.
Grant veu fist Aristés quant de bon cuer vooit
Que dedens Ephezon Phezone serviroit,
305   Ne ja por (ma) [nul] besoign(e) ne s'en departiroit
S'Alixandres li rois de ce ne l'enforchoit.

Et quant il ne savoit qu'a avenir estoit
Fors chose est a vassal qui si preus se sentoit
Car ch'avient en .i. jor qu'a .v. cens n'avenroit,
310 Et vassaus qui est preus adiés estre vorroit
Ou les proëches sont, car la set son esploit.

Col. II Et plus li seroit grief qui l'en destorneroit
D'une tele jornee ou haus pris escherroit,
Que cil qui par bel fait .ii. cités li tolroit,
315 Car au bien trespassé avenir ne porroit.
Dont plus fist Aristés quant a ce s'aloioit
Que chil qui tous les veus ensamble aüneroit.
Car (toute a) [a toute] autre honnor qu'a celle renonchoit,
Et por tant, de ma part, voel que le pris sien soit,
320 Car bien l'a deservi; et qui m'en desdiroit
A tort et a pechiet debat i meteroit.'
Alixandres en rist, si le prist par le doit.
'Antigonus,' fait il, 'mais qu'il ne vous anoit,
Nes est qui sans pechiet bien faire le saroit.'

.viii.

325 Lues qu'Antigonus eut faite la quinte vois
Alixandres lor dist par uns mos si cortois
Et si bien afaitiés, si sages et si cois,
'Seignor, se j'ai soffert, pas n'est outre mon pois,
Car g'i fai que compains, ce n'est el qu'esbanois,
330 Por ce, se sires sui, n'i doi avoir mon cois,
Ne dire a daarrains por ce se je sui rois.
Ens ou moiien estage, ne trop caus ne trop frois,
Gist seüre vertus, ce nous descrist li lois.
Et por tant orendroit mon avis en orrois.
335 Molt fu li veus Porus hautains, ce n'est nus nois:
De vaintre la bataille contre tant de Grigois
Que li dieu ont donné des armes les esplois;
Qui telle bataille vaint, il n'est mie avalois,
Ains est outremontans et sans nombre et sans pois.
340 Et de tant fu ses veus doublés et plus qu'en trois
Quant tolli le ceval au duc archadanois,
Le preu Emenidon qui est diex des tornois,
Paremens des estors, estandars des conrois.
Tant en di, et s'en lais plus a dire cent fois,
345 Por tant soit a Porus du pris fais li otrois:

Ja de la moie part ne li escondirois.'
Lors dist Emenidus, 'Boins rois macedonois,
Passés vous ent briement, autrui en est li drois.'

.ix.

Lues que li rois des Griex fu del tout acoisiés,
350 Emenidus parla, qui bien fu enseigniés,
De toutes boines teches il en estoit li chiés.
'Boins rois,' dist li vassaus, 'bien estes afaitiés
De Porus essauchier se sivis en estiés,
Et se ne di ge pas que cause n'i aiiés:
355 D'ounor est singulers et en armes triiés,
Et li plus preus de qui fusse onques aprochiés,
fo. 177r.   Gadifer esseuté por qui je sui iriés.
A celui n'en mech nul tant soit haut rouegniés,
Mais por son bien n'est pas Porus amenuisiés:
360 De vaintre la bataille es[t] fais molt adrechiés.
Ce (soroit) [seroit] trop por moi mais bi[en] i est tailliés,
Et endroit de mon fait affiert que vous taisi[é]s.
D'aquerre mon ceval ne fu preu traveilliés.
A ma sele ne sui ne gliués ne poiiés,
365 Ne je ne sui faés ne si privilegiés,
Que ne soie souvent cheüs et redrechiés.
Et se fusse aussi preus qu'orains me devisiés,
Ce fust trop li plus fors, mais de trop mesprendiés.'
Li uns l'autre bouta s'ont les vis embronchiés.
370 De s'umilité s'est cascuns esmerveilliés,
Car c'estoit li plus preus qui fust mors ne haitiés,
Et s'estoit de son pris oïr tous annuiés.
C'est li riules dont bien iestre ne puet cangiés:
Li vanteres cuide estre adiés poi essauchiés,
375 Et li preus, que plus est ses bienfais annonchiés,
Plus se crient qu'il ne soit escarnis et mokiés,
Car li biens d'autrui est si en son cuer fichiés
Qu'adiés se vuet conter avoec les mains prisiés.
'Hé,' dist Emenidus, 'ou fu teus veus puchiés
380 Que Perdicas voua? Tous (en) sui ensonniiés
De penser comment cuers par fu si esragiés
Qu'a tel veu embrachier fu mis et atachiés
Que de combatre a piet armés enmi le riés.
Gentil home estre a piet de ses armes cargiés,

385 Et villain a cheval, s'il ne le set de viés,
Est plus fors qu'a combatre a (.iiii.) [.x. huis] vierilliés.
Adiés chiet teus villains com fort qu'il soit loiiés,
Et frans homs longement ne puet estre sor piés
Por les armes qu'il porte dont li fais li est griés.

390 Dont li veus Perdicas fu plus (con) [c'ou] trecuidiés,
Car cascuns vaut a ce a quoi il est loiiés.
Quant aucuns a cheval et il est trebuchiés,
S'est il en aucun lieu et pris et detrenchiés,
As cevaus defoulés, se il n'en est aidiés.

395 Dont fu bien li siens veus doublement enforciés,
Et por tant de par moi li soit li pris bailliés.
De droit l'enportera se il n'est forjugiés.'
'Sire,' dist Filotas, 'le parler me laissiés,
A mon avis sui miex de voir dire aaisiés.

.x.

400 Quant Aimes ot parlet le parler renovele
Filotes, qui avoit la langue aspre et isnele.
Col. II 'Seignors,' dist li vassaus, 'par les diex de Tudiele,
Plus puet avoir d'ounor et de biens, sans favele,
En un tout seul penser ou quel m'amours m'apele

405 Et ou joieus jouvent ou boine amours revele,
Qu'a vaintre et reculer d'une ost la maistre eskiele.
Se bienfais n'estoit fors qu'en sang ne en cervele,
En lanches, en escus, en destriers de Chastele,
Dont n'i averoit riens dame ne damoisele.

410 Por Ydorus le di, la cortoise pucele,
Qui de fin cuer voua voiant mainte danzele
A estre son ami loyaus que torterele.
Loyautés sorvaint tout, ce droit nus ne rapiele.
Bontés et loyautés tous lius guie et caiielle:

415 Loyautés est li fus, proëche est estincele;
Loyautés est fontaine, proëce est la ruissele;
Loyautés est roïne et proëce est s'ancele.
Dame par est plus grande adiés que sa baissele.
Uns mauvés est plus preus et chinglans que harcele.

420 Proëce sans bonté ne vaut une estincele.
Nous jugons ensement que brebis qui aignele
Ce qu'on voit par dehors; mais dedans la cambriele
Du cuer est loyautés qui les biens amoncele.

Et por tant Ydorus de ce pris encapiele,
425 Qui de loyauté fu comblee que turiele.'
'Seignor,' dist Festïons, 'ciex por nïent flaiele.
Ce samble que li cuers de joie li sautele,
Mais de trop plus bel fait vous dirai la nouvele
De droit et de raison sans menchoinne isnele.'

.xi.

430 Lors que Filotas ot dite sa volenté,
Festïons, s'amoustra qui le cuer ot sené.
'Seignor,' dist li vassaus, 'j'ai molt bien escouté
Le parler de cascun, mais poi m'a savouré.
Je croi que vous aiiés Caulon entroublié.
435 Ou ert pris li haus veus que Caulus ot voué
Que de tollir son hyaume a home si ozé
Que le soudant de Baudres, ou tant a de fierté,
Et qui li diu ont si de proëche paré
Qu'au riche roi des Grius, qui tout a sormonté,
440 Ala tollir s'espee enmi son parenté?
Molt par fu li hons preus et de tres haut pensé,
Qui en plain estor a si haut veu achievé
Qu'a vassal de tel pris (a le hyaume) [le hyaume a] desclavé.
Il ne le conquist pas a la buske n'al dé
445 Mais a force de bras a desir eslevé.
Encore i a raison qui son veu a doublé,
fo. 177v. Car Caulus ne l'a pas souspris ne engané,
Ains li avoit piecha nonchiet et enformé
Que l'elme de son chief avroit outre son gré,
450 S'a son chief ne l'avoit poiiet ou engliué,
Ou il n'avoit le brach brisiet ou defroué,
Ou par force averoit le chief du bu sevré:
Et hom qui est garnis double sa poësté.
De tant mech je son veu plus en auctorité
455 Quant sor ces poins l'a si sousmis et sormonté
Que par forche li a le chief si desnué.
S'on donnoit por le pris empire ou roiauté
Si l'avroit bien Caulus de son droit conquesté.'
'Sire,' dist Licanors, 'vous avés bien parlé,

460 Mais veś moi chi tout prest de miex dire escolé.
     Ains que parte de chi en orrés mon pensé.'

.xii.

     'Seignor,' dist Licanor, 'par les diex des Chaldains,
     Bien tieng que nus de vous n'est de voir dire fains
     Selonc l'ententïon de quoi ses cuers est plains,
465 Mais encore n'est pas li voirs dis ne atains.
     Li cuers Lÿone fu de grant proëche empains
     Quant voua a jouster a .i. (de ses) [des] souverains,
     Fiex au fort roi Clarus qui d'aïr estoit plains.
     Et se fu si li tamps abregiés et restrains.
470 Qu'en cel meïsme jor n'atendi plus ne mains,
     Li jors des autres veus li sambloit trop lontains.
     Li preus vorroit adiés estre des premerains,
     Mais li couars falis trecule au daarrains.
     Por Lÿone le di qui n'iert couars ne vains,
475 Tant estoit desirans de mostrer ses caukains.
     Lues que il ot voué avoec les premerains,
     Combien que les servist li viellars hermitains
     Saveur ne li avoit ne li vins ne li pains,
     Ne sausse ne pevree ne entremés certains;
480 Mais lues qu'on ot mangiet cevaucha sor les plains
     Au tref le roi Clarus priier a jointes mains
     Jouste a son fil l'aisné, qui d'ounor estoit plains;
     Et tant fist que il l'ot, je n'en sui pas doutains.
     Se par haut veu pooit grans pris estre ratains
485 Lÿones deveroit resner avoec les sains.
     Dont le pris avera de droit, c'est li certains,
     Car d'ounor est floris et feullis comme rains.'
     'Sire,' dist Elÿos, 'molt fu li fais grevains.
     Molt bien li ot mestier li estuve et li bains.
490 D'un poi trop l'eslevés mais poi vaut li levains.
     Encore i a bien veu qui molt est plus hautains,
Col. II En verité a dire, et li plus souverains.'

.xiii.

     Quant cascuns ot son cuer mostŕe par mainte voie,
     Elÿos qui a point et bien ses mos emploie,
495 Resgarda Marciien et en riant rougoie;

Bassement li a dit et par parole coie
'Sire, dirés vous plus s'il vous plest je diroie? '
Signe li fist du chief et elle se desloie.
'Sire,' dist Elÿos en qui tous biens ondoie,
500 'Preste sui de parler si vous pri que on m'oie.
Je di que Fezonas, et bien le prouveroie,
A fait le graindre veu. S'argüee en estoie,
De bouche non d'espiel bien m'en deffenderoie.
Voirs est que tout li veu, bien les renommeroie,
505 Furent grant et peniu: blasmer ne les porroie.
S'estoie chevaliers ou demoisele soie
De tout le plus legier assés en averoie,
Nonporquant le plus grant bien entreprenderoie
A l'aiue d'Amors s'a accord le trouvoie.
510 Mais le veu Fezonas emprendre n'ozeroie,
Car contre Fortune est, se moustrer le savoie,
Contre Droit et Amors qui tout sorvaint et ploie,
Car Fortune avoec Droit Amors a li aloie.
Quant Regars s'i embat qui Plaisance i envoie,
515 Et Volentés i keurt et Desirs i envoie,
Et Cuidiers le pormaine et Souhais l'esbanoie,
Et Espoirs le repaist et Cremeurs le castoie,
Et Pensers le retient et Souvenirs desploie
Les biens qui sont en cuer qui dame sert et proie,
520 Je di endroit de moi, s'en ce point me trouvoie,
Por promesse ne veu ja ne m'en astenroie
De prendre mon ami se priie en estoie.
Et se blasme i avoit, pas ne le clameroie,
Car ce feroit Amors, ne pas ne le feroie.
525 Il n'i a riens en moi par droit que clamer doie,
Amors dedens mon cuer escondit i otroie
A son gret. Autrement, ce m'est vis, mefferoie
De dire a mon ami: Je vous aim, vostre soie,
Ne de mi refuser se de mi le faisoie.
530 L'un tieng a cruauté, de l'autre me hontoie
Quant g'i pens; mes Amors de ce fait me desloie.
Bien seroit contre Droit se de cel riule issoie,
Et se d'avoir mari aillors me porqueroie.
Dont ai ge bien prouvé s'a raison souffissoie
535 Qu'a Phezonas affiert le pris. Je li donroie,
Et par mon serement, s'a assener l'avoie.

fo. 178r.   Fortune est en Amors et Drois bien s'i aroie,

Dont ciex qui boute l'un, l'autre sake et desvoie.
Qui fait hounor as .ii. li tiers pas ne le noie.
540 Dont s'Amors est en mi et vuet qu'amie soie
Fors chose est a vouer — contre Amors voueroie,
Et encontre tous trois, s'ensi dire voloie —
Que ja n'avrai mari se d'autrui ne l'avoie.
Que d'Amors qui tout pert bien avoir le porroie
545 Se Fortune et Amors en descorde trouvoie.
Mais Fortune ne puet, mes cuers a ce s'apoie,
Fors ce que boine Amors le consent et otroie,
Et se de vrai desir mon cuer en li entoie,
Drois me seroit nuisans se desobeïssoie,
550 Si qu'a autre seignor mari requerre aloie;
Voire, et si nuement que je n'essentiroie
Mon (anui) [ami] ou autrui ou donnee m'estoie:
Fors a a contrester cuers qui Amors guerroie.'

.xiv.

Quant la bele Elÿos ot a poi de dangier
555 Dite sa volenté por Fezone essauchier,
Li rois des menestreus ne se vaut plus targier,
Ains ala sa parole en haut recommenchier,
Por l'amor Gadifer qui molt fist a prisier.
'Seignor,' dist li varlés, 'molt me doit annoiier
560 Quant de la verité vous voi si desvoiier.
La flor estes del monde et li mieudre guerrier,
Et d'armes ne savés parler nes que bregier.
S'on vous voit sor les camps ordener et rengier,
Angelot empenné samblés au desrengier,
565 Et joint esmerillon as lanches abaissier,
Ou sauvage lÿon as escus embrachier
Marcheant de prouece qu'on ne puet engignier
Por haut pris achater et ounour bargennier,
Et quanques gens cors puet et frans cuers assigier
570 En espesse mellee et en estor plenier;
Et quant vient au voir dire et au droit denonchier
Vous n'en savés parler, ains vous volés aidier
D'aucun trouble samblant d'espoir et de cuidier.
Les hiraus resamblés au bien contremoiier
575 Qui n'en sevent ouvrer, s'en veulent fabloiier.
Un poi sai parler d'armes mais l'estor n'ai pas cier,

Et vous amés l'estor, si n'en savés resnier.
Mais chiex qui vuet amer, jouster et tornoiier,
Penser, parler, ouvrer tout ce a bien mestier
580 Ciex qui des armes vuet savoir tout le mestier:
Penser et porpenser haute oevre et convoitier,
Col. II Ouvrer por ce grant fait parfaire et commenchier,
Parler por loyaument des fais d'armes jugier,
Car c'est molt gran(t)[s] pechiés de vassal forjugier,
585 Et quant vous le volés tollir a Gadifier
Et point n'estes d'accord, ains vous voi defoukier,
L'Inioranche vous fait errer et desvoiier,
Ou Cuidiers ne vous laist le voir certefiier,
Ou Plaisance vous fait vers le tort atachier,
590 Ou tout a ensciënt volés le droit niier,
Ou vous le debatés por moi contraliier.
Pensés se je di voir, si vous laissiés brisier,
En aucune maniere vous couvient amesnier,
S'en voir cognoistre n'a blasme ne reprouvier.'

.xv.

595 'Seignor,' dist li varlés, 'par les diex des Gadrois,
En voir cognoistre n'est outrages ne desrois.
Se li Baudrains osta au roi machedonois
S'espee hors des poins, et Caulus li cortois
Li ala deslachier son hyaume viënois;
600 Et li preus Floridas a force outre son pois
Le livra prisonnier au roi sans nul deffois;
Et Porus (s'avancha) [se vanta] devant les Phezonois
A vaintre la bataille encontre les Grejois,
Et qu'a Emenidon jousteroit tant de fois
605 Que il avroit Ferrant, a qui que fust anois;
Et li preus Aristés voa, ce n'est nus nois,
A sivir Phezonas et desresner ses drois;
Et Perdicas se mist entre les deus conrois
Avoec les gens pietons a guise de bourgois;
610 Et (Elyos) [Lÿones] jousta au fil Clarus l'Indois;
Et Edea a fait d'or fin arrabiois
Le paon restorer qui est biaus et norois;
Et Ydorus la bele au chef et as crins blois
A amé(r) son ami sans penser villains plois;
615 Et Phezone a eüt en mari tout son cois

De par le roi des Grius sans conseil d'autre vois;
Encontre Gadifer n'en donroie .ii. nois,
Car ce puet avenir le jor .ii. fois ou trois,
Mais ses veus est si grans que quant le contrepois
620 Ce samble visïons, fantoismes et gabois.
Dont li veus Gadifer que vous me debatois
Se preuve de li mesmes et est des autres rois,
Sans autre raison metre, ou je ne m'i cognois.'
'Non voir,' ce dist Danclins, 'mais qui se tenroit cois
625 De vos sens asserriés le pris tout a rebois.'

.xvi.

'Biau sire,' dist Danclins, 'a droit jugement faire
fo. 178v.   Ne vous doit anoiier se je di le contraire,
Voire, endroit du Baudrain—des autres me voel taire —
Sans le veu Gadifer anientir et deffaire,
630 Car parfais hardemens dedens son cuer resclaire,
Et quanques il couvient par proëche parfaire,
Mais autres le puet bien passer et contrefaire:
Por le Baudrain le di en qui tous biens s'aaire.
Car se li diex qui est de plus poissant afaire
635 Voloit de tous les preus sa proëce refaire
Et metre en un (val) [vassal] por lui a tout bien traire,
Et por faire a tous boins miroir et examplaire,
Ne porroit il de lui plus grant proëce estraire
Que de tollir s'espee a celui qui n'a paire,
640 Le rice roi des Griex qui tous les plus preus maire,
Si com fist li Baudrains au douç ris deboinaire,
Maugré tous ses amis pardevant lor viaire,
Par qui il a conquis quanques solaus esclaire.
N'i a cel qui por tant ne se lairoit detraire
645 Qui li laissast tollir le pris d'une piel vaire,
Et quant devant tel gent li ala des poins traire
S'espee, a cestui veu ne doit nus autres plaire.'
'Sire,' dist Martiiens, 'de ce ne vous siuc gaire.
A Floridas me tieng com pau qu'a mes dis paire.
650 A mon avis me samble il n'a nul examplaire.'

.xvii.

'Seignor,' dist Martiiens quant .i. poi se fu teus,
'Du voir determiner ne sui pas scïenteus,
Ne du tort soustenir ne me truis convoiteus,
Mais par mon serement mes avis en est teus
655 Que li veus Floridas est li plus precïeus,
Li plus biaus a vëoir et de cors plus cousteus.
S'a moi en eschëoit li hounors et li preus,
Autre ne coisiroie entre les plus crueus
Dont ciex qui l'achieva est preus et outre preus.
660 Encore i a raison qui le fait plus nareus:
Li Baudrains estoit durs, fiers et cevalereus,
Et de nouvele amor espris et desireus.
Si vëoit Edea as murs et as pailleus,
Et as haus fenestris des tours et des osteus
665 Qui souvent li donoit un resgart amoreus,
Et il li renvoioit le sien cuer a piteus.
Tout ce doit bien doner corage as corageus
Et vigour envoiier tous les mains vigereus,
Et de tant fu li veus li plus aventureus
670 Et fors a achiever et trop plus perilleus
Quant Amors s'en melloit qui les cuers fait jüeus
Col. II   Et qui done fierté a tous les plus piteus,
Et quant sor tous les fais par fu si euereus
Que par force sor lui fu achievés ses veus
675 De Floridas loër ne doi estre honteus,
Ne de ses grans proëces dont il fu si crueus,
Car le pris doit avoir qui qu'en soit anïeus.'
'Sire,' dist Tholomers, 'ne soiiés desdigneus.
De miex dire ne sui mie molt desireus.'

.xviii.

680 'Seignor,' dist Tholomers, 'on voit apertement
Que nus des veus n'estra fors qu'a lui seulement.
Mais a bien regarder a point et loyaument
Li restors du paon tous les autres comprent,
Et donne a tous les veus biauté et parement.
685 C'est uns drois mirëoirs qui figureement
Moustre le fait passé et done enseignement

Que cascuns des boins faice ou miex ou ensement.
Encore en ert des preus par cest remirement
Car a toute riens faut cause et commencement,
690 Et main(t)[s] grans biens avient a poi de movement.
Quant li boin le verront et penseront comment
Lor boin ancestre i ont voué si hautement
(En) [Et] l'ounor qu'on aquist en l'asouvissement,
Il enprenderont plus amaneviement
695 Un grief fais plain d'ounor, se besoins (le) [les] sousprent.
Dont s'aucuns biens avient par cest avouement
Li restors en sera cause a mon enscïent.
Dont plus fist Edea en ce restorement
Que tout, qui en vorroit faire un jugement.
700 Et s'Antigonus dist que d'or est et d'argent,
Et qu'autant en feroit li ouvriers liement
S'a son gret en avoit salaire et paiement,
Por metre le sien veu a aviutissement,
Sauve sa grace, il a erret tout plainement.
705 Uns de nos maistres dist, et raisons s'i assent,
C'on ne doit pas loër un don ne un present
Selonc ce que il vaut ou liu ou on le vent,
Mais selonc ce que ciex qui le done i entent.
Dont s'Edea voua a ce point ensement,
710 (Que) [Nous] devons susposer tres amiablement
Que ce fu por le miex et le plus hautement
Que elle pooit voër selonc son enscïent,
Et por plus essauchier la feste et le jouvent,
Et por l'Indois Porus sor tous principaument,
715 Qui estoit occoisons de cel embatement;
Dont cascuns le doit bien loër communaument.

fo. 179r.

Car ciex (qui) fait [moult] por moi qui la voie m'aprent
A aler droit chemin, se li dieus le consent,
Comment on cache hounor et comment on le prent
720 A forche de desir desmesureement,
Car teus desir[s] ne veut mesure nullement,
Tout ensi que proëche est prise en hardement,
Et vigeurs les ensiut qui de ces .ii. descent.
Mesure est en cremeur cascuns le voit et sent,
725 Et mesure i amaine .i. atievissement,
Qui fait sivir hounor voire si lentement
Qu'a paines i vient nus qui par leur lés emprent.
Car mesure et cremeurs i font empechement,

Et nus ne le(s) rataint si nel siut asprement.
730 Si qu'Edea nous moustre en ou repetement
De son trezor qui est escole a toute gent,
Et sert ou tans passé et en ou tans present,
Et au tans a venir qui les vivans atent.
Si qu'a nul autre veu li miens cuers ne s'asent.'
735 Lors dist Antigonus aprés ce parlement,
'Biau sire Tholomer, par les diex d'orïent,
Se cascuns de nous tous voloit dire ensement,
Vous averiés prouvé, mais je di autrement
Qu'au grant veu d'Aristé nus autres ne se prent.'
740 Ceste chose est certaine se li escris ne ment.

.xix.

Quant Tholomers ot dit par parole soutiue
S'entente, Antigonus dist en sa raison griue,
'Seignor, cascun[s] de vous por nient son tans aliue.
Li grans veus Aristé tous les autres desliue.
745 Se celle boine gent et latine et ebrieue
Samblerent au vouer et mouvans et hastiue,
Et au bien achiever vigereuse et melliue,
Se fu cascune pars a acomplir assiue.
Mais li veus Aristé a la chiere desriue
750 Fu teus (qu'il) [que il] n'est nus autres qui l'aconsiue,
Quant voua que feroit a Fezonas aïue;
Et dedens Epheson, si c'oiziaus pris a gliue,
Estoit jusques en fin avoec la gent caldiue;
Et si ne savoit fin prochaine ne tardiue
755 De la guerre qui fu crueuse et feleniue.
Et vassaus qui est preus vuet que tous tans porsiue
Tout ce en quoi il voit honnor plus seignoriue.
Si que selonc mes dis, com poi que on m'ensiue,
Ciex qui fait son voloir, com soit honnors peniue
760 Ne fait pas tant que ciex qui par forche l'eskiue.
Chiere qu'on fait a lui est trop plus malasiue
Col. II Qu'a celui cui on het sans merci et sans triue.
Se li autre ont voué peniue oevre et forchiue,
C'est drois lor volentés en estoit volentiue.
765 Mais ciex qui por joquier en .i. seul liu se liue
Trueve sa volenté contraire et horneskiue.

Car persone qui est a haute hounor pensiue
Et voit la gent qui est du sivir ententiue
Quant il n'i puet aler, amer li est que siue.
770   Mais ciex qui va partout aussi que gens corliue
Plus de bien i aprent et plus de gius [i] giue
Que li vassaus renclus qui n'a terme ne liue.
Or die autres aprés, ceste raisons est miue:
A mon avis n'est nus qui de ce me desliue.
775   Aristé doins le pris car l'ounors en est siue.'
Lors dist li rois des Griex que persone humle et piue,
'Biau sire Antigonus, en brief heure et tempriue
Mousterrai miex comment en qui li drois s'ariue.'

.xx.

Si tost qu'Antigonus en ot dit son samblant,
780   Alixandres parla hautement en oiant.
'Seignor,' dist li boins rois, 'poi sommes cognissant
Quant au pris assener alons tant varïant.
Cascuns le deveroit savoir faire en cluignant.
Je n'i voi si bel veu, si grant ne si poissant,
785   Que Porus i voua au gent cors avenant.
Car tout li autre veu vont simplement avant,
Mais Porus en fist deus, encore est apparant:
De vaintre la bataille a qui que fust nuisant,
Et qu'a Emenidon iroit tollir Ferrant,
790   Se li diex le gardoit en qui il sont creant
De mort et de prison et de membre perdant.
A celui qui plus fait doinst on loiier plus grant.
Dont quant bien vois le droit au vif examinant,
Le pris ne sai doner fors au miex tornoiant,
795   Et vaintre tel bataille et (estre) [estour] si p(r)esant,
Couvient cors aduré et cuer parseverant,
Et a deschevauchier Aymon le combatant,
Et faire aler a terre, toute la gent voiant,
Vigeur, forche et eür, roide lanche tenant,
800   Et vassal d'armes duit et cheval remuant.
Teus vassaus ne chiet pas a manache d'enfant,
C'est uns veus de .ii. lés renforchiés en doublant,
Dont le pris doit avoir por le mains soffissant:
Li plus des autres veus finent en commenchant,

805 Et sont soudainement acompli en passant,
Mais ciex qui vaint l'estor el non du miex faisant

fo. 179v.
Est preus au commenchier et plus preus en finant
Toute jor du matin jusqu'au soleil couchant.
Boin commench, mieudre fin et tans bien moienant

810 Doit avoir, et ce eut Porus en guerroiant,
Et s'a meschief fu pris par forche en afolant,
Nus ne l'en doit blasmer selonc mon ensciant,
Car pris fu et trouvés en hardi couvenant,
Et le boin desirier qu'il ot de remanant

815 Doit on conter por oevre au los de mon samblant.
Et s'Emenidus dist orains en argüant,
Por Porus essauchier en lui humiliant,
Qu'a avoir son ceval en lui deschevauchant
N'a proëche sor lui, ains sont fait peu coustant,

820 Ce n'est pas verités, par les dius d'Abilant;
Car je vorroie miex vouer en afrumant
A conquerre la terre et derriere et devant
D'a la fin d'orïent jusques en occidant,
Mais que cil de ma court me fissent boin garant

825 Et m'en sivissent tout de cuer en confortant,
Qu'a tollir son ceval a homme si vaillant,
Si preu et si hardi et si bien chevauchant
Qu'Emenidus d'Arcade au fier vis leonant.'
Emenidus rougi si fort en tresmuant

830 Que li sueurs del front l'en aloit degoutant.
A une part se traist honteus en sousploiant.
Quant .i. poi muset ot lors dist en sorriant,
'Biau sire, rois des Griex, passés vous en atant.
Vous le poés bien faire, par foi le vous creant

835 S'il estoit qui fesist, mais mie ne m'en vant,
Bien sariés figurer un preu en devisant.'

.xxi.

Lues que li rois des Griex la parole fina
Emenidus aprés en haut recommencha.
'Seignor,' dist li vassaus, 'ja nus ne m'aidera

840 Qu'il soit nus plus grans veus que Perdicas voua.
Autant com orendroit ne sai qu'il avenra
Que de combatre a piet ensi qu'il achieva.

Mais il vit que cascuns si haut veu embracha
Qu'a tels veus n'afferroit nus s'outrage n'i a.
845 Et por tant a Raison pas ne s'en conseilla,
Vigors et Hardemens et Cuidiers l'i loa,
Proëche et Boins Espoirs qui l'en asseüra
Par les quels il emprist et promist et paia.
Dont je di qu'en vouant molt se desmesura
850 Quant avoec les pietons a piet s'acompaigna.
Qui a piet se combat de son cors cure n'a.
Col. II Sachiés a enscïent en molt grant peril va.
Ayse va en l'estor qui a .iiii. piés va.
Il voit comment cascuns au camp se contenra
855 Et se sa gens se part avoec se partira.
S'il vaint son anemi, decachier le porra.
Et s'il vient au jouster ses cops li doublera
Li forche du ceval, si grans saus li donra,
Son elme et son escu et son cors portera,
860 Et le fais du haubert qui sor lui pesera,
Et de toutes les armes quanques il en i a.
Mais s'a piet se combat autre confort n'avra
Qu'a la forche du cors fera ce qu'il fera.
Et se sa gens s'en fuit ens ou camp demorra
865 S'il n'en s'envole en l'air, morir li convenra.
Ou il ne vaint la gent qui l'avirounera,
La prendera sa fin, la vivra, la morra.
Je ne sai que penser de quoi il s'avisa,
S'il le fist sans avis ou s'il le porpensa,
870 Mais estraigne proëce emprist et commencha.
Por tant li doins le pris car bien deservi l'a,
Et s'on le donne autrui, je di qu'on li tolra.'
'Sire,' dist Filotas, 'on s'en avisera
S'Ydorus ne le vuet, bien avoir le porra,
875 Car par voie de droit autrement n'avenra.
Et s'ensement avient oiïés qu'on en dira:
Cascuns des boins par droit nous en apelera
Trubers et ignorans et nous en mokera
S'il l'emporte sans plus, por bien faire l'esta.'

.xxii.

880 Quant Emenidus ot tant dit que ne pot mais,

Par uns mos bien assis, que de faus, que de vrais,
Filotes li cortois recommencha les plais.
'Seignor,' dist li vassaus, 'qui vorroit faire assais
Dont hounor est estraite et tous biens est estrais,
885 Reviaus, joie et jouvens, tornois, guerres et pais,
On verroit que d'Amors vienent de plains eslais.
Amors est de son droit uns principes parfais
(Que nus n'aime) [Qui nous maine] et conduist et sorporte
nos fais.
Et se semblance engenre es cuers par dous atrais;
890 Par Amors est tous maus laissiés et tous biens fais.
Et ciex qui de plus prés puet resambler les fais
C'est ciex par droit de qui plus grans biens est retrais.
Amors aime sans fin et quite tous fourfais,
Dont miex siut Ydorus ses traches et ses trais
895 Que ciex qui d'armes est et afflis et estrais
Quant voua a amer sans relenquier jamais

fo. 180r.   Betis son loyal dru qui n'est ne bruns ne bais
Mais blons, vairs et rians, avisés et soustais,
Et en toutes manieres frans et gentiex et vrais.
900 Boine Amors ne va mie es presses ne es tais,
Ne en compaignie verde ou on fait les agais
Ens ou bruit des cevaus ou sang ne es marcais,
Armés ens es estors, agregis ne irais
Por detrenchier le cuir ne l'achier ne les ais.
905 Li sustance d'Amors est amors sans relais.
Amors en est la flors, proëche li retrais,
Et li amors de dame est de merchi li rais,
Ce tient a cas samblable a droit riule portrais.
Mais se je sui jolis, chantans, nobles et gais,
910 Et des armes sivir desirans et entais,
C'est li prueve sans plus qu'Amors est a moi trais.
Mais qui done merchi sans nul penser mauvais,
Il represente Amors sans visce et sans mestrais.
Dont es armes sivir ne gist mie meffais,
915 Ains en est cascuns biaus bien parés et refais.
Mais tout adiés vaut miex li gros que li eskais.
Dont bien a Ydorus, dont des autres me tais,
Les drois riules d'Amors sivis et contrefais.
S'en avera le pris s'il ne li est fortrais.'
920 'Compains,' dist Festïons, 'tu te vis et repais
De trés grande merveille, ains tele ne fu mais,

En ses fais essauchier, mais a molt peu de frais
Te porras perchevoir qu'en ce cas ne nous plais.'

.xxiii.

Quant Filotes ot dit ce qu'il li plest a dire,
925   Festïons se drecha liement a poi d'ire.
'Seignor,' dist li vassaus, 'sans point de contredire,
Cascuns vuet ses raisons conforter et redire.
C'est drois, mais elles sont legieres a descrire,
Car nus n'avra le pris par forche n'a maistire,
930   Mais par voie de droit car li cas le desire.
Dont ne couvient il pas que Caulus s'en consire,
Car nus ne puet a droit enditer ne escrire
Que Caulus achieva qui de proëce est sire.
Dont le pris avera, nus ne m'en puet desdire,
935   Por ce se mes raisons si noblement n'atire
Que li aucun de vous, en qui sens je me mire,
Il ne doit pas son bien perdre por mon mesdire.
Et se vous li donés, qui qui le tiengne au pire,
Ja n'en dirai por lui, combien que m'en detire,
940   Nesun seul grant merchis ne que diex le vos mire,
Mais grace en ait Amors qui en son cuer espire
Col. II   Desirs de tant valoir que tel veu vuet eslire,
Que de tollir son elme au meillor de l'empire.
C'est li Baudrains qui fist nostre roi si afflire
945   Que par forche le fist dessus ses archons gire,
Et li osta (du) [des] puing[s], qui qu'en laissast le rire,
S'espee aussi briement que s'il fuissent de cire.
Et quant de si poissant fist (qu'amors) [Caulus] son martire,
Et son elme esracha on le puet bien descrire
950   Por le plus souffissant quant au cler le remire.
Nus hom ne doit le pris a tel veu escondire.'
'Sire,' dist Licanor, 'trestoute jour a tire
Ne porroit on loër car nul boin n'en empire,
Mais ne vous anuit pas se de meillor voel lire,
955   Car de toutes les choses fait le meillor eslire.'

.xxiv.

'Seignor,' dist Licanor, 'par nostre diu Marcus,
Nus biens si ne doit estre ne celés ne repus,
Ains doit cascuns boins fais estre ramenteüs.
Cascuns le fist si bien, bien m'en sui percheüs,
960   Que par mon los n'en ert ja uns seus debatus.
Cascuns por tant ç'avant doit estre retenus;
Mais a droit jugement, haïne et amor jus,
(Et jones) [Lÿones] ne doit pas estre avoec le refus,
Mais au fuer des meillors doit estre recheüs
965   Quant voua au jouster a l'ainsné fil Clarus,
Canaam, qui estoit crueus et irascus,
Fel et fiers et gaignars et a mauvais tenus.
Et quant il formenoit ses amis et ses drus
Bien deust estre par droit de Lÿone cremus.
970   Mais non fu, ains ala as tres et as palus,
(Ains) [Et] trouva un vallet enmi les pres herbus,
Vestu d'un tornequel tout semenchié(s) d'escus.
Menestreus ert au roi, teus estoit ses argus.
'Amis,' dist li varlés, 'foi que tu dois Venus,
975   Fai me .i. message au roi, bien te sera rendus.
Di li c'uns cevaliers est cha dehors venus
Qui prie a Canaam une jouste sans plus,
Et ensi l'ai voué, car teus estoit nos jus,
Ensi fu devisés des grans et des menus.
980   Et a ton repairier, quant seras revenus,
Avras le parement de quoi je sui vestus.'
Et ciex l'ala nonchier as boins et as chenus,
Tant que Lÿones fu de jouster porveüs
En achievant son veu, qui molt fu esleüs,
985   Encontre Canaam qui est grans et corsus.
Et quant Clarus estoit a tous si malostrus
fo. 180v.   De grant proëche fu Lÿones pourveüs
Quant en ses las estoit si avant embatus,
Car il i peüst estre et mors et confondus,
990   Des membres affolés et en prison tenus
Ains que de riens i fust aidiés et soucourus.
Mais li grans hardemens dont il est enbeüs
Ne li laissoit cuidier que ja i fust vencus,
Ains entendoit toudis avenir au dessus,
995   Et quant a son grant bien est a ce parvenus

Si biaus fais ne doit pas par droit estre perdus.
Dont le pris avera s'il ne li est tollus.'
'Sire,' dist Elÿos, 'foi que doi Dyanus,
Autres l'emportera se drois est sonstenus,
1000   Car il est bien seü comment ala li jus.'

.xxv.

'Seignor,' dist Elÿos, 'ce est chose seüe,
Se cascuns a s'entente par ruze soustenue
Sans resgarder comment Raisons soit percheüe,
Mais ainsi que Cuidiers vous anuie et delue,
1005   C'est tout por nient gasté et parole perdue.
Voirs est que cascuns sos essauche sa machue
Mais vous n'estes pas teus comment que je m'en jue.
Ains estes gent de bien et d'ounor parvenue,
De grant scïence plaine et partout cogneüe,
1010   Et tant seroit en vous plus grans blasmes creüe
Se gens de si grant bien se trouvoit decheüe.
Si loch qu'en la fin soit juste voie tenue
Car se vos fais nous plaist et autres vous en hue
Qui plus cler i verra ch'iert grant descogneüe.
1015   Riens ne vaut, ains en ert grans blasme retenue.
Aucune gent en vont estrivant par le rue
Que dans Porus qui a la bataille vencue
Doit bien avoir le pris, et li autres argue
Qu'estre doit Gadifer qui l'enseigne a rompue,
1020   Et celui qui au roi a s'espee tollue,
Ou le preu Floridas a la brache membrue.
Ensement a cascuns s'opinïon tenue.
Tant avons miex mestier que bien soit maintenue,
Et se faire en volés loyal et vraie issue
1025   Fezonas en sera paree et revestue,
Qui a nostre roi est de marit atendue.
Car li vertus d'Amors qui toute autre esvertue
De Fortune et de Droit, dont pas ne sui tenue,
Estoit a son avis ens ou roi contenue,
1030   Car bien moustra qu'Amors est dedens li esmue.
Fortune fait que tout autre pooir s'esnue,
Col. II   Et sa droiture moustre a gent grant et menue.
Dont eut droit Fezonas s'en son voloir se rue.

Mais quant Porus avoit au roi guerre esmue,
1035 Et ja estoit por lui d'un dart d'Amors ferue,
Molt li fu l'oevre griés et estre doit rendue,
Quant sor ce point chi vaut estre au roi si tenue
Que sans lui ne seroit ne espouse ne drue,
Si nuement que riens ne mist en retenue,
1040 Ne Porus ne autrui, molt fu sa raisons nue.
Et quant li veus fu tes qu'a ce s'est assentue,
S'elle n'en a l'ounor elle li ert tollue,
Et ert villainement fraudee et forcourue.'

.xxvi.

'Seignor,' dist li boins rois qui tant ert seignoris,
1045 'Cascuns de vous en a si bien dit son avis
Qu'a paines sai li quels en dist ne miex ne pis.
De premiers deuissons avoir auditeurs pris
Par quoi li jugemens fust au cler esclarchis.
De s'entente porter est cascuns engramis,
1050 Dont por estre en acord et oster tous estris
M'asench que nous faisons de commun .xi. escris.
En ces .xi. brievés soient li veu compris,
Cassamus fu douzimes mais ou camp fu ochis.
Elÿos les avra dedens ses poins quatis
1055 Et puis feront .i. sort et quant il ert sortis
Nous prïerons a diu qui est superlatis
Par dessus les natures, et au boin Mercuris,
Que par aus soit li sors vers le droit convertis.
Un brievet saquerai sans riulle et sans avis,
1060 Mais que de vostre assens i soie si commis,
fo. 181r. Que ciex que j'en trairai en puist porter le pris.'
Lors s'escrïerent tuit, 'Ja n'en serai desdis.'
Trestout communement sont a l'escrire assis,
Et quant furent escrit ensamble (se sont) [les ont] mis.
1065 Si les ont toueilliés que nus n'en est souspris.
La cortoise Elÿos a les brievés saisis,
Et lors fisent le sort qui molt biel fu bastis,
Cascuns sacrefia as diex de son paiis,
Et lues que cascuns ot (aouré) [ouvré] a son devis
1070 Li rois passa avant, si a un brievet pris,
Et lues que il l'a liut si en fu abaubis.

'Seignor,' ce dist li rois, 'i a nus cestui mis?
Je trueve chi dedens Cassamus du Laris.'
Cascuns s'est de ce fait vivement escondis,
1075   'Foi que je doi,' fait il, 'au diu d'Ephezonis,
Mon pere Philippon et ma mere Olimpis,
Je ne li retaurai tout ne soit il pas vis.
Miracles font por lui Mercurus et Jovis,
Mars li diex des batailles, Jupiter et Venis,
1080   Cui il servi de cuer; or li sera meris
Li services de quoi li bers les a servis.
Le pris doit bien avoir puis qu'a ce est eslis.
En son nom le doinst on a son neveu Betis,
Fiex de son frere fu, si ert oirs de son pris.
1085   Par devant son sarcu qui ert de marbre bis
Le ferai atachier et remaindre a toudis.
Bien en ert de son droit Cassamus revestis.'
'Voir,' ce dist Martïens, li sires de Persis,
1088a   'Que c'est fais outre fais d'aidier ses anemis.'
'Sire,' dient Gregois, 'vos cors soit beneïs,
1090   Car par vous est li drois aprovés et descris.
Nous i acordons bien et en fais et en dis.'

.xxvii.

Quant li rois des Grius ot la parole finee,
Elÿos se drecha qui bien fu emparlee.
'Sire,' dist la pucelle, 'a boine destinee
1095   Avés la haute hounor de ce pris assenee,
Et par l'assent des Griex de Gresce et de Chaldee.
Or couvient bien qu'on sache en quoi elle ert donee,
Et par quel joielet elle ert representee.'
'Bele,' dist li boins rois, 'bien estes assenee,
1100   Benëois soit de qui vous fustes engenree.
Sor Marciien en ert la parole jetee,
C'est bien li plus sachans qui soit en l'assamblee.'
'Sire,' dist Marcïens, 'ma scïence est secree;
Nus ne s'en apperchoit; ou l'avés vous trouvee?
Col. II 1105   Vo volenté dirés car ja n'ert recopee,
Vo parole (samble) bien [soit] ou fable ou averee.
Puis que le commandés j'en dirai ma pensee.
Espriviers est oiziaus de molt haute volee,

Mais sa conditïons n'est pas si esmeree
1110 Que por estre a tel pris mise ne comparee.
De chapiel ai veü donner mainte huee,
Car li rondeurs de quoi la cierne est confremee
Moustre perfectïon que pas n'est mesuree.
Car fin n'i doit avoir, anguelet ne entree,
1115 Nient plus que la rondeurs quant bien est compassee,
Mais la florete dont l'escliche est aournee
N'est en perfectïon mie parconsumee,
Car li biautés de flor est en brief tans passee.
Mais quant tant a souffert que elle est meüree
1120 Dont est digne d'ounor et en grange entassee.
Ensi est de proëche en quoi est ramenee,
En grant bien commenchie et miex perseveree,
Par la parfaite fin lo' on la bele entree.
Et par ceste raison est la flors reprouvee
1125 (En) [Et] l'ounor du chapiel estainte et arrieree.
Mais la couronne d'or l'a de deus poins passee
Car elle est bien taillie et autour cretelee,
Et de pierres luisans autour avirounee.
C'est signes de regner sor toute chose nee,
1130 Et que toute vertus est en li parcomblee.
Por tant affiert a pris de proëce afinee
Quant ceste proêche est de toute autre exeptee –
Nus n'en set se bien non, c'est verités prouvee –
Et li veus est si haus que nus plus haut ne bee,
1135 Loch que on doinst au pris l'aigle d'or courounee
Car ce est li oisiaus de plus haute volee,
Et regne comme rois, de ce est hiretee.
Et ceste proëche a toute autre sormontee,
Et por tant que double est et haute la vouee
1140 Ert la coroune d'or avoec l'aigle ajoustee.'
Lors respondirent Griu a molt haute alenee,
'Molt bien dist Martiiens. Ne voi qui le devee.'
Quant Elÿos l'entent tant forment li agree
Que de joie fu si garnie et assazee
1145 Que s'en lait fust baignie et de miel arousee,
Car Martiiens ot si sa parole riulee
Que tout l'ont otroiie(t) et de cuer acceptee.
Lors se leva li rois, si s'est sa gens levee,
D'ostel en ostel ont une aigle demandee.
fo. 181v.1150 A un ostel en vinrent s'en ont une trouvee,

Et li sergant le roi l'ont errant aportee.
(Et) .i. coroune d'or li ont el chief posee.
Des menestreus huchier fist li rois grant maree
Tout entour le paiis a droite avirounee.
1155   Cascuns aporte trompe ou vïelle atempree,
Nacaires et tabors de grande renomee.
Vers la feste s'en vont chantant de randounee,
L'aigle fu devant yaus qui bien fu empenee.

.xxviii.

Dedens sa feste entra li rois et si sivant
1160   A renc porestendu vont le liu comprendant,
A force et [a] viertu vont la feste fendant.
La charole s'ouvri, si les vont ataignant.
Elÿos par accort aloit par dedevant,
L'aigle en haut paraument portoit desor .i. gant.
1165   Emenidus l'aloit de molt pres costiant,
D'autre part Martiiens qu'on apele Persant,
Qui affaitiement l'aloient adestrant,
Et por li alegier le keute susportant.
Les trompes font taisir, si vont en haut cantant:
1170   'Ensi va qui Amours demaine a son commant.
Col. II   A qui que soit dolours, ensi va qui Amours,
As mauvais est langours nos biens, mais nonporquant,
Ensi va qui Amours demaine a son commant.'
En ce point qu'Elÿos aloit la pietiant
1175   Et cascuns a son chant hautement respondant,
Griu et Macedonois s'aloient merveillant
A quoi ciex fais servoit qui ert en apparant.
Et ciex qui le savoit lor aloit denonchant
Et disoit en basset et lor aloit nonchant
1180   As dames, as pucelles qui Amors vont sivant,
Et en qui Amors maint et font tout sen commant,
'Ce est li pris des veus qui tant furent parant.'
Et Elÿos l'aloit as plusors portendant
Por metre et rasachier et puis repouroffrant,
1185   Et de pluseurs autour s' aproche en dariant.
Par devant Fezonas va souvent ampassant,
Et devers Edea se traist en sousploiant,
Et puis vers Ydorus; s'en va ratraversant

Par dedevant Porus, (Ydore) [Lÿone] et Floridant,
1190   Caulus et Aristé et Gadifer l'enfant,
Perdicas, le Baudrain qui le vis ot luisant.
Tout ensement en va devant tous remoustrant,
Et que plus fort (sera) [se va] sor aus abandonnant
fo. 182r.   Plus ont les iex en bas et le vis rougiant,
1195   Car cel n'i a qui ait le cuer a ce tendant,
Ains avoit cascun[s] d'eaus cuer si humiliant
Que por nient se contoit et autrui porfaisant.
Et quant Elÿos ot tant alet ourdiant
Et l'aigle a cascun d'eaus offert en rasachant,
1200   Par dedevant Betis demora en estant.
'Sire,' dist Elÿos hautement en riant,
'Vous retenrés ce pris, voire, en representant
Vostre oncle Cassamus le hardi combatant.
Hoirs estes de son pris de (faire) [frere] descendant.
1205   A son los escheï sans visce et sans beubant,
  — De droit et de raison ce sevent li auquant —
Et par l'assent des diex qui sont li plus poissant.
Mais vous le porterés demain ou maintenant
Par devant son sarcu et maintenrés vivant
1210   Tant que l'aigle i porra estra vive en mengant.'
Tout en disent grant bien et lor fu mol[t] plaisant.
N'i ot nul envïeus ne nul cuer murmurant.
'Bele,' dist li vallés, 'bien m'i vois assentant.
Oiant tous le rechoif et par tel couvenant.
1215   Loët soient li diu qui por lui sont veillant.
Amis por ami veille, on le trueve en lisant:
Pas n'oublia les diex cha jus en conversant,
Et li diu ne l'ont pas oubliiet en morant.
C'est mauvaise bontés qui d'un seul lés respant.
1220   En la paine morut or li sont merissant.
Et benois soit nos rois que voi si souvenant
Qu'en s'occoison ne vont nul bien amenuisant,
Ains l'avoie a droit port quant il le voit waucrant
Et le bien afoibli renforche en redoublant.
1225   Por ceste hounor le di dont il ne (fu) [fust] noiant
(Sa) [Se] par sa grant bonté ne fust remise avant.'

.xxix.

Quant la bele Elÿos ot parfait son mestier
Entre les envoisiés s'est alee ataquier
Et li rois et tout cil qui vaurent festoiier.
1230 Molt bien se sot Betis de l'aigle cointoiier
A point, et gaiement porter et debrisier,
Mais la bele Edea qui ot grant desirier
De son veu porsivir sans villain reprouvier
Par deseure le dois fist .i. piler fichier,
1235 Et la fist le paon hautement atachier
Et a l'eslever fist la feste renforchier,
Col. II Tromper et orgener, taburer et buschier:
Il n'i ot jouglëor ne fesist son mestier.
Cascuns des preus sa main i mist au sushaucier.
1240 Feste i ot tres pleniere, grant deduit et plenier.
Riens n'i ot qui deüst par raison anoiier
Fors ce que on vëoit le jor amenuisier.
Molt i ot grant deduit jusques a l'anuitier,
Et la nuit toute nuit jusques a l'esclarier
1245 Que la bele Edea en qui n'ot que gagier
S'en ala en la cambre ou erent li ouvrier.
Cortoisement les fist et largement paiier,
Et li uns por yaus tous respondi sans blangier,
'Dame, nous sommes tout vostre sans racointier.
1250 A vo congiet vauriens en nos lieus repairier.'
Et elle respondi, 'Che fait a otroiier.
De ma court vous poés a tous jors mais fiier
Si qu'a Dieu sans adieu vous di sans eslongier.'

.xxx.

Lues que li solaus fu levés et apparus,
1255 Betis se descoucha cui soins estoit creüs
Du pris son oncle metre el temple de Marcus
Ou on aloit servir Dyane et Cupidus.
Ses freres Gadifers n'i mist mie refus,
Erranment sont monté sor les cevaus grenus,
1260 Et li rois estoit ja et cauchiés et vestus.
Quant vit les jouenes gens par les camps estendus
Et dessus les corssier[s] faire les saus menus.

Par .i. sergant manda qu'il fust contreatendus,
A briés mos est montés et aprés aus courus.
1265 Cascuns d'yaus qui que miex est contre lui venus.
fo. 182v. Parfont l'ont encliné, il lor rendi salus.
Et puis ont chevauciet au temple Dyanus,
Dont ont aviroré le veillart Cassamus,
Entour a la rëonde nus n'i est remasus.
1270 'Seignor,' dist li boins rois qui d'orgoel estoit nus,
'Le service des mors ou quel est lor salus
Faites faire, car chi sont de langhes li plus,
El nom del boin viellart par devant son sarcus.'
Lors furent alumet les cierges et li fus,
1275 Philosophe poëthe i ot molt revestus.
Sacrefisces i ot fait de molt grant vertus
Et de l'orison fu cascuns d'yaus secourus,
Et Cassamus en chief et li Indois Clarus,
Mais por le pris estoit Cassamus au dessus.
1280 Et a l'aigle atachié(s)[r] (cointement) [cantoient] a grant(t)[s] hus
Un ver qui portraioit: te deum laudamus,
Qui chans estoit de joie adont selon les us.
Et puis sont repairiet parmi les pres herbus
Ou chastel d'Ephezon qui n'est mie repus.
1285 Bien fu tans de disner, teus estoit lor argus.
Si dona a mangier li preus Emenidus
Gadifer et Betis et dame Phezonus
A qui ert apaisiés et de coupe absolus,
Et por yaus le donna as grans et as menus
1290 Car de tout rechevoir estoit bien porveüs.
Nus plus riches mangiers ne fu onques veüs
Car entremés i ot estraignes et testus,
Fuison de mes pleniers et tant de noviaus jus
Que ciex mangiers avoit tous autres sorvencus.
1295 Il n'est nus hom vivans qui en puist dire plus.
Aprés disner mains biaus mos eut ramenteüs
Du restor du paon qui ert si esleüs
Que de tous les boins fu en boin gré recheüs,
Car en grande biauté estoit si parcreüs
1300 Que nus d'yaus ne pooit oster ses iex en sus,
Ains disoient partout, 'Bien (le) [l'a] fait Edeüs,
Comment que li pris soit a autrui escheüs
S'a li siens veus de tant les autres forcourus
Que li siens restors est occoisons du sorplus.

1305 Par li et par son fait fu li pris ramentus
Qui tous fust amortis, anientis et fondus.
Mais par Edea fu nos rois a che meüs
Que il en fist l'accord en la chambre Venus.'

.xxxi.

Ensi bele Edea le paon restora,
1310 Sor un noble perron le mist et esleva
Col. II Ou cascuns qui (le voit) [voloit] le vit et esgarda.
Et cil qui le vëoit en son cuer le prisa.
A son quinzime jor cortoisement paia
Si que tous li barnages molt bien l'en merchia.
1315 L'endemain Alixandres ses hommes assambla,
Porus et le Baudrain et (ses hommes) [Marcïen] hucha,
(Marciien) [Betis et] Gadifer, (nul n'en i oublia) [et si lor
presenta]
S'aïde et son confort a tel effort qu'il a
Dist que s'on lor meffait que il lor aidera,
1320 Et s'il en a besoing que il les mandera.
Tout le remerchiierent du bien qu'il lor moustra,
Cascuns ala au liu que li rois li donna
Et li preus Alixandres en Babilone ala.
Las por quoi i aloit: on l'i empuisouna.
1325 Mais sachiés tout acquist a forche conquesta,
Et lues qu'il l'ot acquis tout errant le laissa.
Ce consenti li Sires qui le mont estora
Qui tous jors a esté et qui tous jors sera.
Chi finent du paon li veu qu'on i voua.
1330 Benis soit qui de cuer por celui prïera
Qui la matere emprist d'Alixandre et rima,
Et qui en la proiiere i acompaignera
Celui qui du paon les veus i ajousta,
Et especïaument celui qui i enta
1335 Le Restor du Paon que ciex entroublia
Qui tous les autres veus emprist et commencha,
Et comment Martiiens Elÿot espousa,
Et comme Emenidus sa nieche maria
Au jouene Gadifer quant a lui s'acorda.
1340 Explicit du paon, bien ait qui le lira
Et qui en tous endrois le dit en prisera.
Du bien doit on bien dire, ch'oï dire piecha.

VARIANTS

Manuscripts omitting a line are mentioned first, the abbreviation 'om.' standing for 'omit/s'. Lines transposed are noted thus: 846 W 847/846. Initials indicate words preceding or following the variant which are the same as P. Such initials are not given where the variant is another form or tense of the same word, nor usually where it begins a line or is at the rhyme. 'All' means all the manuscripts but P, and where only one or two manuscripts differ from the others their variant (or agreement with P) is placed first and the word 'Rest' used for the remainder.

Modern forms such as 'dit' for 'dist' and the dropping of a flexional s in the nominative singular of masculine nouns and its addition in the nominative plural are not usually noted. Such forms are found most often in O and Q1.

VARIANTS: PART I

Laisse I

Variants for Part I, Laisse i, continued

47	P6 m. Clarus li roys Indois.
48	P7 E. ses enfans trestous t.; N6P6Q1S1W s. e. tous.
49	P7Q1 Gadifer e. Betys.
50	P7 C. trova le r.
51	P7 om. N6P6Q1S1W e. le b. 51a N6P6P7Q1S1 A L'issie de Caldee ou vainqui les (P6 ou val que li) Caldois.
52	All: m. son harnois.
53	S1 font; Q1 f. poigneïs.
54	N6S1 Bien i; Q1 Adont f.
55	Q1 l. tint; P7 C. li cortois.
56	P7 o. buses; S1 fer n. cep, W c. n. fers; P6 o. buie ne nul f. e.
57	S1W e. a table assis au (W el) p. haut d.; N6 e. assis a table ou p. haut d.; P6P7 a p.
58	P7 P. a L'arc.
59	Q1W om. N6 A. ne f. m. rostis n. pares n. e.; S1 f. rostis ni parez li e.
60	Q1 Qui m. f., W Qui f. m.; N6 grant.
61	N6 A; P6 v. perillous e. destrois; P7 v. mervelleus e. norois; Q1 e. p. e. sourdois.
62	P7 s. destriers espaignois; S1 a. sus l. destrois n.
63	W Edeas; P7 e. si j.
64	N6 Que e. l.; Q1S1 Que le (Q1 Qu'el le) restoreroit; P6 Le paon r. P7 K'elle r. 64a P7 Le paon k'ot ochis Porrus al arc manois.
65	P7 r. dont ne fist pas esplois; Rest: r. ce ne fu pas esplois.
66	P7 cest, W cel; All: j. l'a. sans gabois.
67	N6S1 l. Maionois, P6 l. roy indois; P7 Parfait a. l. m. le rois Clarwus yndois; Q1 m. Clarvorin li Indois.

Laisse ii

68	N6 om. fais.
69	P7 om. P7 69a-k see Notes.
71	P7 Si; P6 q. avoit n.
72	P7 s. ert.
73	W om. P7 Varlet.
74	P7Q1 l. princes, contes e. d.
76	N6S1W O l. d.; P7 d. revont.
77	P7 p. l'amour de P.
78	P6 c. dist bielle E.; P7 c. a dit E.
79	P7 'P. foit, ' fait il, 'Madame, g..; N6P6Q1S1W d. il, 'Dame . . .
80	W om. N6Q1S1 Et (Q1 Car) selonc l'a.; P6 V. selonc la paine; P7 Selonc les aventures.
81	P6 Que; Q1 M'ont l. d. tant aidié q. je s. e.
82	W c. que je ainme el m. p.; N6S1 c. que j'a. ou monde p.; P7 c. au monde cui j'aim p.; Q1 c. du m.
83	N6P6S1W t. que; P7 Et t. ke i. p. est.
85	N6Q1S1W vit.
86	W e. eux levast sus, Rest: contre euz se levast sus.
87	Q1 s. puiz se rassisrent; W s'assieent. 87a P7 Sour les tapis de soie moult noblement tissus.
89	All: D'armes e. d. s. f. d'amours e. d. s. j. (P6 drus)
90	P7 Et dient, Q1 P. dient, S1 P. dirent; P6S1 nos dieus.
91	N6P7S1 Que.
92	N6S1W A. qu'il.
94	N6 mort; Q1 e. m. e. recreüs.
95	P7 W e. entre riches (W n.)
96	P7 l. armes; N6P7 s. ne d., Q1W se nes d., S1 se ne les dolons.
97	W om. P7 Aquerons; P6 k'il; N6S1 s. biaus; Q1 b. salus.

Laisse iii

98	Q1 j. aprés.

99 All: d. f. (Q1 joie) de soulas e.
100 P7 q. plus en seut f. l. fasoit, P6Q1S1 moustra.
101 P6 n. et l. g.
102 N6 Que, SI Qui; N6S1 s. cors; P7 c. si p.
103 P6 P7 Chou qu'e.; N6P6Q1S1W s. vëoit.
104 P7 Ke ains f. n. n. crëassent li diex.
105 W om. P7 Ne; N6S1 puisse; N6P6P7Q1 ens es.
106 P7 E. s'avoit e. eaus tous amour; Q1 a. ami.
107 W om. N6S1 Car; P6P7S1 e. gentieus.
108 P7 sovient; N6 v. signoris.
109 P7 q. il fu t. e. l.; S1 t. et fu l.
110 Q1W s. est, P7 s. fu; P6 q. plus ert, P7 q. fu li p.
111 N6 p. posteïs, P6 p. signourieus; P7 j. tantos ke par trestous s. d.
112 All: devant l. r.
113 P7 O. a mandet j. m. e. v.; N6 j. ne.
114 Q1W om. P6P7 C. e. Arabieus.
115 All: e. y vint d. (P7 de) f. volentiex (P7 entalentius).
116 N6 Raëmpli...garni; P7 El palais descendirent garni d. lor o.
117 P7 c. ki n'e. felenesse ne crieus.
118 P7 L. r. dochement de son cuer ki ert p.; S1W L. retint; P6 p. vrais; N6S1 u. mes.
119 P7 Car; P6 Q. sans p. ses p.; N6P6Q1S1W sambla; P7 p. estoit d. comme m.; Q1 d. com.

Laisse iv

120 Q1 E. a l.
121 P6 a recëus e. joïs; W om. 'et conjoïs'.
122 P7 Et tout en saluant les a p. le m.p.
123 W assiet; P7 s. les; N6Q1S1 s..i. riche.
125 N6 l. diex; P7 l. nostre dieu J. e. V.; P6 e. Jovis.
126 P6 d. boine aventure joie e. p.; P7Q1 h. et grant plenté d'avis (Q1 d'a.)
127 W om. P7 S. nombre e. s. m. tot a vostre d.
128 N6 Mais; P6 M. messagiers.
129 All: v. est.
130 P7 Et p. tant; N6Q1S1W r. et graces et m.
132 N6Q1S1W v. q. me f.; P7 v. me faites.
133 P7 p. de fin or.
134 W A p.; N6 piere.
135 W om. P6 V. que soient eslites si nes et si p.; P7 V. ke s. colorés, ensigniés e. p.
136 All: f. iert li paons a.
137 P7 E. si; Q1 s. mandez; P6 ca .vii. ca .ix., P7 cha .v. cha .viii., Q1 ca .vii. ca .v., N6S1W ca .i. ca .vii.
138 P6P7 Ce n'est, N6 N'est, Q1S1W N'est ce; P7Q1S1W m. cuers; N6 om. 'cors'.
140 All: Par quoi il l'e. b. et p. e. e. (P7 b. p. e. entrepris).
141 All: Mais.
142 P7 p. maistres; P6P7N6Q1W trueve on; P7 plentet d'a.
143 W om. N6P6Q1S1 E. que d.; P7 d. demoustre.
144 P7 C. k'uns m. ne voit v. b.
145 Q1 c. n'en v. pas; P7 u. autres m.
146 P7 e. auchun; Q1 p. a a. quant on a a l.; N6P6S1W a. quant o.
147 P7 S. p. ke vos ostés d. v. c. t. despis.
148 W om. N6 om. first 'ne'; N6Q1S1 n. n. outrages; P6 E. que n'i nourissiés ne orguel n. despit; P7 E. ke v. eslongiés de vos cuers tous estris.
149 N6 g. ne sera, Rest: g. n'en sera.
150 P6 c. ysi.
151 Q1 Com; P7 l'u. tout seul f. et fais e. f.
152 N6S1W D. quanquel l., P6 D. quanque l., P7 D. che k'elle; N6 om. 'pria'; P7W p. li fu f.; P6 f. l. estris.
153 P6 d. q. en furent s.; P7 q. furent s.; Q1S1W l. a s.
154 Q1 sa chambre; P7 E. sa cambre l. mande s. l. a b. saisis.

Variants for Part I, Laisse iv, continued

155 S1 d'Arrable; N6P7Q1S1W q. fust; P7 en son; P6 d'A. de trestout le p.
156 Q1 Leurs; P7 h. demandont; N6P6S1W a l'ouvrer (S1W l'o.) sont assis 156a
  P6 En moult petitet d'eure font grant marteleis.
157 P7 Dedens la f., Rest: E. e. la f.
158 N6S1 Cassien; P6 B. Marsias l. Persis; P7 B. li preus et l. g.
159 P6P7Q1S1W voit.

Laisse v

160 P7 S. ce d. Edee.
161 N6 paierés; P6 p. les drois; P7 se faveresse.
163 P7 d. vostre o. j. n. me c.
164 P7 Dame.
165 P6 p. k'avoir ne c.; P7 m. le p. k'aler ne c.; N6,S1 p. ca a.; Q1S1W c. et v.
166 P6 Mes G.
167 P6 .xx. b.; P7 e. a trait, Rest: e. traist hors.
168 P7 La les, Rest: Puis l.; N6 en v. p.
169 Q1 S. si n.; P6 p. pour t. que q. s.
171 P7 E. E. rogist e. a souris de joie.
172 P6 B. trait; All: e. loie.
173 P7 n'e. n. hons vivans; W s. enferms; P6 q. ne d.
174 N6P7Q1S1W q. set.
176 P6 e. et s.; N6 om. 'et'.
177 P6 p. p. si com; P7 e. p. p. c. espriviers s. p..
178 W a. ot.
179 P6W S'assieent; P7 S'a. au parler; Q1 q. tout m.
181 N6P6S1W p. en l'a. (P6 s'a.); P7 p. a s'a.; All: q. (S1 que) pent.
183 P6 Plus; All: d. ne; P7 M. en f. merchiés q. d. ne poroie.
184 P6P7 q. a sage; P7 d. son don m. b. l'e.; N6S1W d. tres b. 184a P7 Et li
  ovrier overent a cui mie n'anoie.

Laisse vi

186 P6W M. y p., N6 M. si p.; P7 s. painent ovrier; Q1 c. d'acomplir; P7 m. lor.
187 W om. 187-91; P7 s. et toute l. m.; N6 m. de l.
188 Q1S1 Leurs; P7S1 m. ke v. d.
189 All om.
190 P7 Et l. b. E. l. b. et l'e.
191 S1 Lors; P7 L. fasoit mies servir k'e.; N6Q1S1 n'estoit s.
192 N6S1 Aymes li dus, W Aymenidus, P6P7Q1 Emenidus; N6 ceste.
193 All om. second 'et'; P6 A. Filotias de Boudie.
194 S1 Edyos.
196 P6 l. vit a h. v. s'e.; N6S1W a plaine v. s'e.
197 P6 S. fusse orfaveresse p.; S1W f. li, P7 f. vos.
198 N6 les drois.
199 Q1 j. sanz b.; N6P7Q1S1W p. ne m'e.; P6 p. ne m'escaperiés.
201 P7 N. nos rendons prison a vous sens departie; N6P6S1W rendons; P6
  departie (om. 'et').
202 N6P6P7S1W q. v. (W nous) faites.
203 P7 n. recevés.
204 N6 Si.
205 N6S1W N'i; N6Q1S1W v. qui (W q.) nous; P7 v. nul ki nos p.; P6 n. nous p. f.
  millour a.
206 Q1 l. danzelle; P6 p., et jou l.

Laisse vii

207 N6S1 Aimes li dus, Q1W Emenidus.
210 P7 Et dames e. pucelles dont il i ot plentet; N6 l'a environ.
211 W S. ce d. l. d. v.; P6 S. ce d. l. d. bien v.; P7 S. che d. l. d. c'est fine v.; Q1 S.

dit Aimes bien v. l. v.

212	N6S1W De; P7 p. cui nos s.; P6 q. fumes; N6S1W q. si s. a.
213	P7 Avons nos achievee et a la fin menet.
214	N6 om. 'qui'.
215	P7 o. longement desiret.
216	P7 Et; P6 Et aient chou k'o.; N6W p. ou p.
217	P7 G. estommes; All: acordé.
218	All: p. de qui d. a. pité.
219	P7 Et.
220	P7 por; P6 s. c'on.
221	P7 p. ki.
223	W o. biens a a plenté, Rest: o. des biens (P7 de bois) a plenté.
224	P6 k'il die; Q1 q. li a.g.
225	N6 S'ira, P6 G'irai, P7 Jou irai; P7 por Lydone, Rest: pour m. c.
227	P7 C. c. e. autre chose v. f. par s. g.
228	Q1 G. c'est de vostre bonté; P6 c. vous v. de bonté; N6P7W d. vo bonté.
229	P7 p. tout ensi ke l'a.; N6Q1S1W s. quanqu'avés.
229a	P7 Tout nostre dieu en soient benit et aoret.

Laisse viii

230	N6S1 Aimes li dus.
231	P6 e. a l'autre b.
232	P7 b. les p. lor d. et l. u.
233	All: t. le.
234	P7 c. est venus; P6P7 p. haut.
235	W t. Se; P7 l'a trovet et l. d.
236	P7 E. li rois l'o.
237	P6 Et lors m. li dus e. c. d. s. lignage.
238	N6P7 chevauche; N6W p. prés p. plains; P6 p. bos p. plains e. p. boscages; P7 p. p. p. bos et p. rivage.
239	P7 q. e. e. grande e. l.
241	P7 d. a tenir; P6 s. cens; N6P6Q1S1W e. s. cavage.
242	Q1 om. P7 P. dedens est entrés d. un gant r. N6P6S1W gaut sauvage.
243	N6 p. prez e.; P7 p. chaut et o.
244	P7 C. nului n'en devoit ne treü ne passage, Rest: C. ou (N6S1 en) lieu ne devoit ne treü n.p.
245	All om.
246	S1 Si.
247	P7W om. Q1 Q. t. et lieu s. bien f. r.; P6S1 E. lieus.
248	Q1 v. diron d'A. et de son j. e.; P7 r. del duc. l.
249	All om.

Laisse ix

250	P7 damoisel.
251	P6 g. singuler, S1 g. reguliere.
252	All: A. avés; P6N6Q1S1W o. souvent l. r. o. (N6Q1 repete on); P7 e. le vos r.
253	W q. cuer ot; N6P6Q1S1W d. baron.
255	N6Q1S1W aquist.
256	P7 Et doi dansel.
257	P6P7 Dans Clins; P7 Tholomes.
258	Q1 Et en I. a. querre.
259	W om. Q1 Porron; N6P6P7Q1S1 a. roy C. (S1 Charuon).
260	P7 Et le preu G.
261	N6P7 C. en.
262	S1 Dauri, W Daurry; W Florida, Rest: Floridas; P7 F. par d.; P6 d. lor.
263	W D. D. lor; P7 De la cit de Defur p. f. c.
264	N6S1 Gracien; Q1 Gadifer l'i.
266	S1 Caulu, W Caulon.
267	P6 Perducas; P6P7 Lincanor, N6 L. et Canor; All: Sanson.

Variants for Part I, Laisse ix, continued

268	P7 Antiocus d. geste, S1 Ainthiconus d. G., W Antigonum d. G.; P7 d. Anticonum, P6 d. Ethyocon.
270	P7 om. 'Et'; Q1W Pyrron.
272	P6 p. moult fausse ocoison.
273	P7Q1 E. conquist.
274	All: m. a f.
275	All: o. ne l.; P6 conte.
276	P6P7Q1S1 f. Alixandre; P6P7 c. jusques en son.
278	P6Q1 c. Emenidon.
282	P7 282/281. N6 o. de l. c.; P7 o. et l'acomplission..
283	N6Q1S1W C. dame; W q. cuer ot; P7 Et comment E.
284	P6P7 Restora le paon; P7 d'or fin et s. l.
286	S1 m. des.
287	N6P6Q1S1W Les; P7 Et les h. p. ke on f. e. son nom.
288	N6 m. tençon, P7 m. canchon, Sl m. traçon.
289	P7 E. del preu.
291	W G. de la cit d'E.
292	P7 d. Lydone aussi nieche a E.
293	N6 Et; P7 Car c. l'e. ki l. v. jusk'a s.; N6 om. 'fist'; P6 ki fist ceste canchon.
293a	P7 Ot fait et estoret ensi ke les lison.
294	P7 f. d'augier ne de lanchon.
295	N6P6Q1S1W s'en f.
296	P7Q1 Ceste; P6 o. en fust, W o. fust.
297	N6 s. mention.
298	N6P6W Caton, P7 Cathon, S1 Caston.
299	All om.
300	N6P6Q1S1W a. que on (Q1 l'en) s.
301	P7 D. q. lieu, Q1 D. quelx genz.
302	S1 d. y; P7 v. de quel c.
304	All: Mais il ot b.; P6P7 e. si ot b. m.
305	P6 feroit; P7 f. departison.
306	All: s. lor (Q1 leurs).
307	All: simulation.
308	N6 f. declaration.
309	N6 e. s. non; P6P7 g. ne s. non.
310a	P7 Por che ke cascuns sache k'il fu de bon renon
b	Comment ke foliast quant il fu jouenes hon
c	Par maise compaignie ensi ke le dist on.
311	P7 Mais; Q1 C. tous ceus q. folient et p. t.; N6 q. foloient f. p. temption.
313	N6 d. si l. vrai p.; P7 s. les.
314	N6P6S1W E. ou; Q1 E. la ou a p. v.; P7 E. la u p. a visces; W d. vices.
316	All: madres; N6Q1S1W b. au r.; P7 b. et revient.
317	P6 q. fu fais s. c., P7 q. fu fais et s. c.; Q1 f. s. par c.; N6 s. et s.
318	P7 e. chi; N6P6Q1S1W l'espiration.
319	P6P7 C. apert, Q1 Et ce a.; All: a. par D.
320	P6 n. vot, S1 nombre vot, W n. volt, P7 Q. vot nombrer.
321	N6S1 E. ce, W E. se.
324	N6Q1S1W om. 324-34 P6 E. es sains Euangilles; P7 Et la sainte Ewangile.
325	P6 l. Canee, P7 la Chanaee; P6 Canoon, P7 Chanaon.
326	P6 om. 'de'.
327	P7 p. par ta c.
328	P6 d. ne s. p. incarnation; P7 d. n'en s.
329	P6 P7 vostre; P7 b. k'il o. v. faon.
330	P6 S. aussi q.; P7 q. d'un.
331	P6 m. des t. fait sa r.; P7 d. table p. sa r.
332	P6 d. vostre, P7 d. ta.
334	P6P7 om. 334a P7 Chi vorai abregier si je puis mon sermon.
335	P7 En.
336	N6P7W Sens; N6 f. que vive; P6 b. et se conversion.
337	N6Q1S1W f. mie t. l., P6 f. mie tante c., P7 f. mie t. de c.
338	Q1 Com; P7 l. porsiete faite de la male fachon. 338a P7 Et tout che se

demonstre par moult bonne raison.

340   P7 Ki fu dou noble d. qu'o. appelloit B.; Rest: F. fu d'un r. d. qu'o. apela (P6 apielloit, W a.) B.
342   P7 Il; N6S1W r. orgueilleus e. f.; P6P7 m. cruel.
343   P7 d. d'autre part Carphanun.
344   N6 P6Q1S1W C. (P6 Chil) li o., P7 Chis rois o.
345   P7 d. s. nation.
346   P6 n. vot f. mal ne o., Rest: n. daigna f. o. (P7Q1 l'o.)
347   S1 c. qui, P7Q1 c. k'il; P6 v. si petit v., P7 v. .i. jouene v.
348   N6P6S1W g. sa.
349   W Que n'i; P7 Ke on n'i fist; Sl n'i se fist; All: a. (Q1 onc) puis.
350   P7 Et par faute d. g. s'i norissent griffon.
351   N6S1 e. lupars serpent, Q1W e. liepart serpent, P7 e. l. tygre et e.
352   N6S1W f. f. destruction, P6 f. misent a destruction; P7 Et de fis e. d. filles f. divortion.
353   P7 s'e. en moult g., Rest s'e. menant g.
355   P6P7Q1 c. mescheance.
356   All om.
358   P7 g. destruction.
359   P7 a. l'enmenerent.
361   P7Q1 m. et ot d.; P6 pardon.
362   P7 D. ce k'il gaagnoit, Rest: D. quanqu'il aqueroient (P6 c.)
363   S1 l. cité de Dames; P6 D. faisoient m.; P7 Dedens D. fasoient l. habitation.
364   N6P6S1W c. qu'ensi f., P7 c. k'il fust la.
365   N6Q1S1W a. l'anete ou l'o.; P6 Gieter pour le malart ou l'o. pour h.; P7 J. a .i. marlart u aprés .i. h.
366   N6 Qui n'e.; W s. chaperon.
367   N6 368/367. N6P6P7Q1W h. et b. (P6 blasons).
368   Q1 espie; N6 hyame; P6 Et espee e. e. et helme e. e.; P7 Et espee e. espiel plates et haubregon; W Espee, espiel et elme, plates e. e.
369   P6 baniere.
370   P7 om. W om. first 'et'.
371   All: F. mis par s. f.
373   N6 P. avoir p. n. p.; All: e. ton.
374   P7 Deïssent k'il fust diex d'armes aprés J.; Q1 n. d. Marcon.
375   Q1 E. faire r. et i.
376   P7 C. il e. diex d'armes a.
377-8   All om.

Laisse x

379   P6 S. en; Q1 a celi; P7 t. ke jou.
380   P7 A. a M. l. nobile cytet; W le n. loyauté.
381   P7 Philppon par v.; N6Q1S1 Phelippe, P6 Philippe, W Phlippe.
382   P6 E. ot c. r.; All: f. en s.
383   P7 384/383. P7 A. l'avoient p. d. n. appellet.
384   N6Q1S1W a. mout ert d. j. (S1 noble, W joie) a.; P6 a. tant ert d. P7 a. petit avoit d'a.
385   W E. se.
386   N6Q1S1 p. quant; P6P7W p. si l'a a.
388   N6P6P7S1 v. v. en; Q1 J. vaurroie avoir f. s'il v. venoit en g.
389   P7 om. P6W enpesé.
390   P6 M. tost au C., Q1 Que m. au C.; P7S1W vostre.
391   N6P6S1W o. mout.
392   P7 loialtet, Q1 verité.
394   S1 e. na n'en; P7 e. ne sera desloet.
395   W b. e. e. puis l'a s.
396   W A .ii. b. l. charce; N6 b. les.
397   All: Et quant f. m.
398   P7 T. cevauchent; S1 p. c. p. b. e. p. cité, Rest: p. camps e. p. b. e. p. p.

Variants for Part I, Laisse x, continued

399   N6 as B.; P7 B. le soir a l'avespret.
400   N6 f. de; P7 Moult f. de Califre servit et honeret.
401   P7 o. lavet.
402   N6P7Q1S1W Le b. l. ont baillie (W bailli); N6P7Q1W l'ot, S1 il ont; P6 L. lettres l. d. q. ot le brief q.
403   P7 i. l'ot b. p. et tres bien aviset; Q1 l'e. leu e.; N6S1 esgardé, W esgarder. P6 avisé.
404   P7 c. mais n. l'a pas m.; P6 l'a i.
405   N6 i. pensoit; P7 t. de; Q1 f. en grigneur d.
406   P7S1W o. moult o., N6 o. ot mout, Q1 t. a; P6 d. bonté.
407   N6P6Q1S1W n'e. pas; P6 a. celle heure, P7 a cel tens; S1 d. cele.
408   W Com; P7 puis che tens; N6S1W p. ses armes; P6 Q. i. fu p. saciés par verité; Q1 Comme i. fu p. p. s. fiere aspreté.
409   N6 om. 'li'; W bien soiiés vous.
410   S1 c'e. li roys que m'a m.
411   P7Q1S1W t. ce.
412   P7 M. vos d. le roi; N6P7Q1S1W q. en s. ralé (Q1 alé).
413   N6W Que n.; P7Q1 t. mie; S1 Que je n. l. tieng p.; W a despit n'a v., P7 a desdaing ne v.
414   P7W Car; All: f. ai.
415   W Qu'est d., P6Q1 Trop e. d.; N6 b. y a r.; S1 e. g'i ay b. P6 esgardé; P7 S'est trop j. d'eage si ke j'ai aviset.
416   P7 m. sachiés en veritet.
417   P7 E. c. ont respondu, Rest: E. li mes r.; P7 furent.
418a   P6 K'otroie n'avés chou dont nous sommes pené.
419   P7 et si l'o. merchiet, Rest: si l'o. mout mercié.
420   N6 D. la; P6P7 Q. furent.
421   P7 Il montent; P7Q1 m. quant i., S1 m. des qu'i.
422   P7 Juskes a r. Phelippe.
423   All: Bien.
424   All om.
425   Q1 i. ne m. s. pas c.
426   P7 i. ont respondu; N6Q1S1 r. no t. a. g., P6 r. si a. tant tasté.
427   All om.
428   P7Q1W Car; S1 f. iert; P6 j. et n. a on conté.
429   P7 Quele ke s. por tant, Rest: Quelle q. s. p. si (Q1 ce); N6 s'en est il e., P7S1W s. t. por e.
430   P7 l'o. de grant duel a suet; N6 d'a. est.
431   P7 Tantos jure; P6 Et a juré s. d. a qui doit aourer; N6Q1S1W q. mout o. p.
432   W i. esmouvera; P7 son ost; S1 e. sa g.; P6 e. tout son p.
433   P6P7 Et; P7 n. et si en ait mal gret. 433a S1 Ne ja pour ses amis ne li est destourné.

Laisse xi

434   All: destroit.
435   All: escondit li avoit.
436   All: voloit.
437   W m. bien; P6 m. l. reconfortoit.
438   P7 M. cis c. moult petit l. v.; N6 l. sien confors, P6 l. reconforters; Q1 o. neant v.; N6P6S1 n. y v.
439   P7 A. jura A. tous les d. u il croit; N6Q1S1W ses d.; S1 om. 'il'.
440   P6P7 e. son ost.
442   P7 f. li torroit.
443   P7 E. c. tans; P6 p. e. sa, W p. a l.
444   N6 Que p. enchantent; W soudoioit, P7 sorduisoit.
445   P7 Car; S1 Que e. l. nus g.; N6Q1W n. contre l. si g.,; P6 n. hons contre l. g. n. s. donroit.
446   P6W Que.
447   N6P6S1W v. c'A. ensi; P7 A. ki si.

448   P7 p. s'en vint ki m. simples e.; S1 t. que.
449   N6Q1S1 S. dist le larron.
450   P6 v. ne c.
451   S1 Que; P7 a quel paine ke soit; P6 que il a.
452   Q1 Que vo filz A. l.
453   S1 Phellippe, W Phelippon.
454   P7 d. si ensi.
455   P7Q1 f. le paieroit.

Laisse xii

457   P6 om. 'le'.
458   W O. empris la b.; P7 e. e. si covenanchie, P6 e. e. commencie.
460   N6P7S1W e. sa.
461   P6 E. cel p. k'Alixandres o.; N6 om. 'li'.
462   N6Q1S1 Aymes li dus; Q1 il e. s. c.
463   P7 d. Baudas e. lor herbregerie; S1 d. Dames e. une praerie.
464   P7 e. menoient lor vie.
465   Q1 e. s'estoit d. l.
466   P6 e. et pointe e. e.; P7 e. noblement e.; N6S1W p. e. bien e.
468   N6P7Q1S1 Et p. l. (P7 eaus) s., W l. a s.; S1 e. s'escrie.
469   Q1 d. Aymon.
470   P7 t. et forment o.
471   N6P6W yriés.
472   Q1 au B.; P7 q. est si r.; S1 t. ert.
473   P7 i. ont respondu; S1 r. qu'il n'i yroient m.
474   P7 e. d. Surie.
475   P7 P. dieu; N6P6P7Q1S1 ce est (P7 chi a) g. couardie.
476   P7 m. donnoit d'or fin u. p.
477   P6 G'iroie; P7 Jou iroie a la nuit; Q1 encores nuit; P7 de Surie.
478   P7 Et a. e. donroie; Q1 c. a s. p.
479   P7 otroiont m. ki les s.; N6 m. qui l.
480   S1 est, Q1 soit.
481   P6 Et c. c. v. e. ou f. ou laissie; P7 Et c. sa v. e. emprise et repairie; S1 entretaillie.
482   Q1 Emenidus respont; P6 E. Emenidus respond; N6P7 vilonnie.
483   N6 Et.
484   S1 Et d. et a p. j.; N6P6 d. par (P6 al) matin.
486   P6 v. la; P7 v. provet ma gagerie; Q1 m. gaaigne.
487   P6P7 plaist; P7 om. 'et'; N6P6S1W orent; N6S1 lor m.; P7 q. il orent l. chose.
488   P7 c. s'en va.
490   N6P6S1 Erroit, P7 Aloit; N6 om. 'par' & 'lui'; Q1 l. qu'il ne s'atargoit mie.
491   N6 om. 'forment'; All: sa f.
492   N6 om. 'tost'.
494   N6P6Q1S1W Au; P6 c. et a l'oevre coitie; P7 A p. bellement contreval la cauchie.
495   N6Q1S1 C. si (N6 ensi) comme .i.; P6P7 C. ensi.
496   P6 S'avanca d. B. li leres Fols s'i fie; P7 T. il B. ne vuet k'on l'oie mie.
497   P7 f. ke il v. a l. grant manandie; Q1 manantie.
498   P7 La li f. Califfre.
499   P7 C. par c. k'il ert v.; P6 e. que f. n'ot mie, P7Q1 e. s. f. f.
500   P7Q1 L'avoit (Q1 L'ot a) u. sieue ante; P6S1W sieue, N6 seue.
501   All: c. hardie.
502   P7 m. en a. obliie; Q1S1 entroublie.
503   N6S1 Que; P7 v. del laron la m.
505   P6 a caaines d'or, Q1 a grappes d'a.; P7 a bons traus de fier e. bien atachie.
506   P6 l. l. sachie.
507   P6 e. que il point n'i detrie; P7 Et il fu entrés ens sens nulle atargerie.
508   S1 tout; P7 sa m.
510   P6 D. quoi.

511   P6 om. See 533a. P7 E. l'a viestu.
512   P7Q1 Entre s. b. le prent e.; N6Q1S1W enchargie.
513   P6W s'i. en l., N6P7S1 si vint en (P7 a) l.
514   P6 v. de.
515   P7 ara; S1 a. la.
516   P6 om. N6Q1S1W folie, P7 vantrie.
517   Q1 c. au B. le m.; S1 B. la mene; P6 518/517:
                Pour chou que on n'oïst ne crie ne huerie
                Le mena a Baudas en la cave enforchie.
518   P7 qu'o. n'i, S1 n'en i o.
519   P7 A. tot adés.
520   P7Q1 jura; P6P7 s. il.
521   P7 taura.

Laisse xiii

523   Q1 au B.; P7 e. guiee.
524   P6 u. pucielle.
525   N6P6S1W D. mais, P7 D. maus, Q1 D. mal; N6S1 esprite, P6Q1 esperit, P7 esperis, W esperites plains.
526   P6P7 q. l'ot avisee.
527   N6S1 B. v.; Q1 B. v. r. b. et bien coulouree; P6 r. et tres bien coulouree; P7 v. e. moult b. e. bien e.
528   P7 Dont f. s. v. d. desir e.
529   N6P7Q1S1 p. enversa.
530   P7 P. a p.
531   P7 d. l'avoit.
532   P6 e. apercut; Q1 e. apperçoit qu'e. est; P7 p. ke l'ot.
533   P7Q1 E. cria; P6S1 m. que m.; P7 c. trop. 533a P6 Esranment le viesti et quant il l'ot paree. Cf. I 511 which P6 om.
534   P7 jura.
536   P7 ki ert m. esploree; N6Q1S1W f. (N6 ert) esplouree; P6 que m. f. effraee.
538   P7 D. bien g. s'onour et ke bien fust sauvee.
539   P7 q. fu.
540   S1W t. c. e. si e.; P6 s. c. e. si fremee; Q1 enserree; N6 om. 'si'.
541   W om. P6 Que li leres malvais n'i trouvoit n. e.; P7 Ke n'i pooit trover l.; Q1 C'onques n'y pot trouver yssue ne e.
542   W Qu'il s.; W P6 c. ou.
543   P7 f. p. m. d. l.; All: formenee.
544   N6 f. d. l. m.; P6 demenee, P7 tormentee.
545   All om.
546   P7 Et q. v. ke e. l. n'aroit p. t.
549   P7 d. de cuer l'a r.
550   P7W Car; P6Q1 d. grande.
551   All om.
554   W om. P6 h. mes cuers espoire e. b.; P7 h. ai ma vie ordiné; Q1 c. tent e.
555   P6 c. ke chi s. ensi v.; P7 c. ke chi je s. v. 555a P7 De ce mavais larron ki chi m'a aportee.
556   Q1 q. a v. fui d.
557   P7 d'o. a l'eure ke f. n.; N6 t. com.
558   N6P7S1W V. d. cest peril, Q1 V. q. d. c. peril; P7Q1 s. tost; W çoie a.
560   P7 o. vos ai or.
561   N6S1 Prieus, W Prius, P6Q1 Peril n., P7 Por la necessitet; N6Q1S1 aprestee.
562   P7 Fait.
563   P6P7Q1 ce mot; P6 A. s. fais, P7 A. son plour.
564   P6 D. c. se hasta, W D. courrir s'enforca, N6 D. corir s'e. s'a. et sa h., P7 Adonkes s'enforcha.
565   P7Q1W .i. bocler d'achier prist (W fort); P7 ki li pent.
566   P7 Puis a traite l'e.; Q1 Et l'e. t. hors; All: et quant.
567   P7 Au laron a. droit et l. f. escriee; W a. si; Q1 li dist d.

Variants for Part I, Laisse xiii, continued

568 P7 l. d. mar l'avés destorbee.
569 P7 l. ke vos a. robee, Rest: 1. mar (N6 mal) l'a. vous (W or) e. (S1 embler).
570 W om. P6P7 Onques, S1 N'onque; N6P6Q1S1 m. n'acointastes, P7 m. n. veïstes, N6 S1 c. journee.
571 P7 Li leres l. respont ki l. c. a levee; Q1 l. teste o.
572 P6 K'ançois k'il ajournast; Q1 Gronchast qui en vausist; P7 A c. ke il anoie a moi sera p.
573 N6 s. le menroit, P7 s. l'enmenrai, W s. l'enmenra; P6 e. qui que il.
574 P7 u. lance, S1 u. hante.
575 N6S1W t. enniervee.
576 P6 Emenidus fiert s.; N6S1 E. A. la feri; Q1 E. A. y feri e. l'a si a.; P7 s. ki bien l'a a.
577 P7 En .iii. m. l'i fent toute l'a t.; W f. e. effroee.
578 P6 s. deffent bien.
579 All om.
580 N6P7Q1 sa; N6Q1S1W p. esprouvee.
581 All: B. en l. fin fu l. c. s. (P6Q1 a chou) m. (Slom. 'fu').
582 N6S1W du r. la t. ot tronçonee; Q1 l. l. si ot l. t. tronçonee.
583 All om.
584/5 N6P6Q1S1W combine: Et l. pucele fu rescousse e. remenee.
584 P7 Et l. p. f. de ses mains delivree.
585 P7 Et fu moult doucement ariere remenee.
586 N6Q1S1W om. P7 m. la dont; P6P7 emblee.
587 P7 o. entre eaus .ii. porparlee, P6 o. ançois d'iaus revelee, Rest: o. ançois deus r.
588 P6 om. P7 Et.
589-90 P6 om.
594 P7 Si en a. m'amour a.
595 W om. N6Q1S1 se; P7 e. vo; S1 l. paie.
596 P7 M. petit sui encor d.; N6S1 encor s. je p., W encor s. p., Q1 encor sui moult poi.
597 P7 om. P6 v. entencions bee.
598 P6 q. en vous; N6 o. et b.; Q1 a bonne e. belle; P7 p. se v. o. a bien estet ovree.
599 P6 b. perseveree, Rest: b. continuee.
600 P6 Emenidus respont; N6S1 r. que; P7 p. avisee.
601 P6 s. cest.

Laisse xiv

602 N6S1 Aymez li dus; All l. dame.
603 P6 c. le.
605 P7 M. a son r. la dame d.
606 P7 m. il respondu li a.
608 P6 E. a; P7 E. en Baudas m. son hostel l. n. 608a Q1 Et que ce fust secré doucement li pria.
609 Q1 Bien retint son hostel et du tout enterva; P6 r. moult b. et si bien l'encita; N6P7W l'enterva.
610 P7 d. la dame.
611 N6P7Q1S1W Et; P7 e. son hostel; P7Q1W e. puis l.; S1 e. cil li defferma.
612 P6 om. N6P7Q1S1W l. se coucha.
613 P7 o. persone nulle g.
614 P7 e. puis s.
615 P6 De sa mise que pour sa dame e.; P7 d. s'emprise. 615a Q1 Adonques au retour se mist et retourna.
616 N6Q1S1W A; P7 v. son; Q1 v. la perche.
617 P7 om. Q1 o. eslachie; P6 ala.
618 P7 Quant a l'ostel r.; P6 om. 's' en'.
619 P6Q1 m. pas; P7 m. le fait l. cela.
620 P7 om. 620-1.
621 Q1 p. l'amour; N6P6Q1S1W d. a tous jours le c.
623 P7 Ke Emes devint; P6P7 e. a c.; N6S1 l'ordena, W l'estora, Q1 l'assena.

Variants for Part I, Laisse xiv, continued

624 S1 M. p. dieu a.; P7 l. de piecha, P6 W g. pieça.
625 N6P6Q1 E. (N6 En) n. trueve o. q.; P7 E. si trovons q.; W Ne trouvons nous q.
626 P7 A. bon; N6P7 e. si.
628 P6 B. le laron; P7 e. li rois.
629 P7 Et.
630 P7 t. et illuec s'esconsa.
631 P7 Et oï k'il d.; Q1 d. Dame or.
633 P7 E. sa femme.
635 P7 P. ja; Q1 P. ja mez p. n. vivra.
636 N6 f. la ou l.; S1 f. la u on l., W f. ou l'en l.
638 Q1 Car son frere fu Charles e.
640 Q1 Q. l'oy li t. s.
641 N6 t. l'e.; P7Q1S1W t. son.
642 P7 B. salli.
643 N6S1W S. retint.
644 P6 Puis revint; P7 K. tout l.
645 P6Q1 K. se r.; P7 s'en retorne.
646 P7 om. P6 Car; N6 Encontre c. f. bien p.; Q1 f. puiz ce jour.
647 N6S1 Aymes li dus; P7 Ensement nostre sires le s. d.
648 P7 De mort; N6S1W p. l. larron, P6Q1 p. larecin.
649 N6 q. me.
650 N6S1 A. que; Q1 A. que li mons h.
651 P6P7 q. l'e.
652 W Resones, P6 Rosette, P7 La belle.
653 P6 d. chou; N6 s'entrecuida.
654 P6 l. nulement.
655 All: e. s'amie.

Laisse xv

656 N6S1 Aymes li dus.
657 P6 b. fu; P7 Por c. ke s. b. li aloit ensement.
659 P6 Et puis; P6P7 s. et l.
660 P7 c. a. laissiet son g.
661 P6 d. si s.
662 P6 m. devant.
663 P6Q1 A; N6P6Q1S1W B. s'en; N6Q1W a. qui; P6P7 courant.
664 P7 Et truevent; All: estequie.
665 P7 L. mise; Q1 s. vivant.
666 P7 Or, S1 Si; All: entrelairons du duc Aymon (P6 d'Em.)
667 P6P7 Rosette; N6 d. a g.
668 P6 e. forment va p., P7 e. se va porpensant.
669 P6 poroit; N6P7Q1S1W om. 'a'.
670 P6 om.
671 N6 Q. li s., P6W Q. li samblast.
672 P7 i. son signour a.; S1 ensaiant.
674 W Ele s'en v. a c.; P7 s'e. va a l. c. p. .i. pret d.
675 W om. S1 Dont; N6P6S1 h. et s.; P7Q1 h. l. petit et li grant.
676 P7 Q. li p.; P7 W s. l'ala e.
677 All: Fille dist; P6 talant.
678 P6 Grans; P7 a. E. d. en riant, Rest: a. et elle d. e.
679 P6 om. S1 malades; N6P7Q1 s. si.
680 Q1 l'o. s'en; P6 dolant.
681 P7 arriere e. avant.
682 N6P7 Vostre t.; P7 p. d'or fin; N6 om. 'plains'; P7 om. 'luisant'.
683 P7 c. moult; Q1 o. tout l. c. d.
684 P7 m. maintenant. 684a P7 Quant elle fu dedens d'or fin i trouva tant.
685 P7 Ne l. portassent mie; P6 l. menroient.
686 All om.

Laisse xvi

687   N6 e. li; All: biens.
688   Q1 E. e. mallars e. f. e.; P6W pietris, N6Q1S1 perdris.
690   P6 Que s.; N6P6S1 toudis; P7W tous v.
691   P6 l. malart fussent p. les faucons q.; N6 caitis, S1 castis.
692   N6Q1S1W E. s'estoit; N6P6Q1S1 q. le; P7 v. toudis.
693   N6 p. volaisent; N6P6P7Q1S1 d. les; P7 tos vis.
694   P7 E. avoit; P6 p. d. ciens et g.; N6P7 d. de.
695   N6P6S1W Que b. s. chascuns d.; P7Q1 E. b. s. (P7 s. b.) cascun d.
696   P7 E. de; W d. petis; N6S1W a. yriez, P6 a. engrans; P7 talentis.
697   P6P7 l. g. (P6 bos) tous f.
698   N6 Et c.; N6Q1 losenges; P6 l. d'estormiaus de maus vis; N6P7 d'a. et d. (P7 om.) mavis.
699   Q1 L. corps; P6 t. e. estricies et l. p.; Q1W e. et estriquies, P7 e. et eslevés.
700   P6P7 E. les; Q1 les b. aournez; N6W les b. ont ouvers, S1 l. b. ont ovriers; P7Q1S1 engiens; P7 moult s.
701   P7 Et f.; Q1 d'o. massis, N6P6S1W d'o. polis, P7 rainseles pollis.
702   P7 g. grans.
703   P7 a. de courre les chiers a.
704   S1 om. 'dains'; P6 L. s. e. l. d.; N6P7Q1S1W b. e. gris.
705   P6P7 engramis, S1 agremis.
706   P6 o. les, Rest: o. des; P6 e. les.
707   P6 m. et p. e. polis.
708   P6 om. P7 I. ert, W I. est; N6Q1S1 Et d'a. p. enfer terestre p. (N6 et p.)
709   P6 711, 712, 709, 710. W E. les; P7S1 E. la mer; P7 li iawe d. cui.
710   P7 E. si e. d.; Q1 p. dessus; S1 bris.
712   All: l. l. estoit faite; N6 du s.
713   P6 L. nues les e.; P7 Et l. m. stoiles.
714   S1 Les r. paissoient.

Laisse xvii

715   P6 C. dont s. f. fiestier; P7 f. festoiier, N6S1W f. rescrier.
716   P6 Ses cles; P7 S. c. prist a sa bourse si a. d.
717   N6 i. forgeit s'e. sache, P6 f. en s., Q1 u. huisset s'e., P7 .i. escring si en traist.
718   P6Q1 dist i.
719   P6 om. 'je'.
721   Q1 t. com c.; P6 q. terre e. c.; P7 Ke on poroit trover en t. ne en mer.
722   N6P6Q1S1W p. par; P7 E. plus v. les pieres che sachies sens gaber.
723   N6S1 q. la, Q1W q. le; P6 Q. toutes mes grans terres que j'ai a gouverner; P7 Ke t. la g. t. ke jou ai a garder.
724   P7 d. et li prist a conter; P6 devider.
725   P6P7 o. a l'o.
726   W Rosenne; P7 Q. sa fille a o.; P7S1 p. si.
728   All om.
729   N6P6P7S1W Le (W Au) bon duc qui e.; Q1 A Emon qui e. tous jours e. s. p.; P7 e. toudis, S1 e. assés.
731   P7 la clef de; P6 m. c. pour g.; Q1 m. bailliez.
732   N6 om. 'i'; P6 f. m'en irai.
733   N6P6Q1S1W n. f. pas a g.; P7 n. f. a creanter.
734   P6 p. conquester.
736   P6 m. deüssiés.
738   P6 p. grant.
739   P7 e. le plait ensi e.
740   P6 Li peres c. que le fille le d. o.; P7 C. elle quidoit b. tost le lairoit aler; Q1 C. i. cuidoit moult b. qu'el d. o.; N6S1W c. bien qu'ele le d. o.
741-7   All om. They have instead 740a-d:
740a   N6 Mais sa clef li ala mout soutiement enbler
b   Et a une pucele fist le cofre aporter
c   A Aymon a Damas et li dist sans guiler
d   C'a son ostel alast le bon duc demander.

740a P6 M. elle l.; P7Q1 M. la; P7 a. subtilement e.
740b Q1 E. par; P6P7Q1 c. porter.
740c P6 a Baudas se l.; P7 A. en; P7Q1 s. gaber.
748 S1 l. seit; All: trouver.
749 N6S1 Aymes li dus; P6P7 E. l. (P7 lors) qu'Aimes l. v. en la maison e.; Q1 E. lors.
750 P7Q1S1W P. a, N6 P. c'a, P6 P. bien en son cuer c'a; N6Q1S1W l. venist.
751 P6Q1 Si; P7 Biel l'a. r. e. moult biel; All: honorer.

Laisse xviii

752 P6 f. a; P7 l'o. ke d.
753 P7 Emenidus se se m. errant; P7 e. en sa v.
754 P7 m. ke.
755 P7 A. a n. Emon. P6 om. 'li'.
756 P7 Lors li d.; W 'Chiers sires,' ce d. ele; P6P7 m. d. v. e.
757 P6 S'amisté et cest c.; N6Q1S1W B. et c.; P7 B. cesti c.
758 N6P7Q1S1W p. et s'a; Q1 q. moult m. a.; S1 averoie; P6 Et sa grace autresi que moult m. a.
759 P6 e. s'en.
761 P7 Et; Q1 M. la pucelle dit; P6 n. le feroie, P7 nel p., W n. le p. 761a P7 Car mal gret de ma dame chertes en acquerroie.
762 P6 Dist Emenidus, 'Belle, t.; P7 B. che d. l. d. t.; S1 A. mes c. a vous s'o.
763 P7 s. en quel lieu ke je soie; P6 d. quant que j.
764 P6 A ce mot prist c. al r.; P7 Q. celle o. p. c. si se remet a voie.
764 P7 Vers s.
766 P6 Q. celle; P7 p. coi ke n.; N6P6Q1S1W noveles.
767 All om.
768 All: Et ele li c.; P6 li c. k'Eimes li dus.
769 N6Q1S1 De f.; P6 s. a. qu'i. a.; P7 s. en quel lieu ke le voie; W om. 'en'.
770 P7S1 B. ce d.; P6 Rosones, W Rosenne, P7 Rosete; Q1 p. dieu se je savoie; N6P6S1W d. de Savoie.
771 N6 c. vers; Q1 om. 'a'.
772 P7 om. P6Q1 Car; N6S1W restorer, P6 restor.

Laisse xix

773 P7 Emes a recheü n.; N6S1 Aimes li dus.
774 P6 Et; P7 Et b. l'ont regardet t.
775 W dient; P7 E. demandent ke ches p. d. son g.
776 P6Q1 volons; P7 N. en volons a c. nostre p.; P6Q1 c. droite p.
777 P7 i. a respondu.
778 P6 om. 'en'; Q1 v. y f.
779 P.7 c. les.
780 P6 Et; P7 M. de b. e. assés en s.; P6 grant.
781 P6 c. qu'il.
782 P7 Et; N6Q1S1 r. si comme a; P6 r. ensi qu'a; P7 r. par devers u.
783 P7 c. i v. pendant droit a .i.; Q1 v. atachie droit a .i.; P6 e. droit en .i.
784 All om.
785 W l'ouvrie; Q1 trouvent.
786 Q1 E. le.
787 P7 q. voient qu'i. ont gaigniet a t. f.; N6 om. 'orent'; P6Q1 g. a. f.
788 N6P6Q1S1W d. en, P7 d. vers; P6 s. mansion.
789 P6 om. N6P7Q1S1W Ne n'o.; P7 p. talent.
790 N6Q1S1W r. en; P6 Emenidus r. a D. le royon; P7 E. Emes demora tous seus a s. m.
791 P7 Ne n'i avoit o lui n. p.; P6 s. qu'il n'avoit n. p.; W om. 'ne per'. 791a P7 Ki o lui demorast en celle region. Q1 Et mena bonne vie soy tint com gentilz hom.

Laisse xx

792 P7 Ensi E. fu t. s. a Damas; N6 Aimes li dus.
793 P7 p. aprés che t.; N6 a. la.
794 S1 desmanné (?)
795 P6 P. tout son; Q1 s. contree a.; P6 a lapidaire; P7 t. lapidaires.
796 P7 S'on les aporte p.; P6 aporte p. a v. ne c. n. l.
797 All: C'on; N6 p. a c.
798 P7 A; P6 c. tans; All: li dus Aimes; P6 f. se pensa.
799 P7 Ke peu avoit deniers s. p. v.
800 P6 lapidaire vient; P7 lapidaires; All: p. li (P7 lor) moustra.
801 P7 En dementiers ke c. d. l. l'amusa; P6 c. d. la bole l. tient e. asota.
802 P7 E. a; P6 E. a C. .i. sien nies envoia; P7 l. manda.
803 Q1 t. com l.; S1 t. qui l.; N6S1 sa gent; P6 se g. rouver ala; P7 t. ke l. s. .i. mes
     i e.
804 P6Q1 om. N6S1 om. 'i'; W venus; P7 c. conjoit.
805 P6Q1 om. N6S1W l. ne v.; P7 l. dont petit s'enfrea.
806 P6 d. je Emon on en mena; P7 d. plus prison on l'e.; Q1 On prist Emenidus
     tantost et admena.
807 P6 om. N6P7Q1S1W C. et.
808 P6Q1 om. 808-10. W q. l'ensi; N6S1W le mena; P7 h. forment se mervella.
809 P7 s. tantost.
810 N6S1 om. W r. qui. 810-40 P7 see Notes.
811 N6S1 om. Q1 L. C. errant d. p. demanda. 811a Q1 Ou il les avoit prises et qui
     les li bailla; 811b Q1 Et Aymes tant ne quant onques respondu n'a.
812 Q1 l'onnour l. d. a tous jours le cela; P6 n. l'acusa.
813 P6Q1 om.
814 All: q. le; P6 f. recognut.
815 S1 C. pour; N6Q1 C. errant a prendre (Q1 p.) l. j.; P6 p. errant le commanda.
816 Q1 q. la dame voit; P6 v. que A.
817 N6P6S1W Du m. que elle (P6 qu'e. en); Q1 Du grant m.
818 W om. P6 om. 818-22.
820 S1 relevé.
823 N6Q1S1W Au Calife s. p.; P6 Droit a s. p. vint a .i. les le sacha.
824 All om. 824a Q1 Erranment S'est levee et au Califfe ala.
825 S1 om. 'cha'. P6 combines 825/6: 'Sire, 'd. l. p. 'cils h. a. t. m.
827 P6 l. c. ala.
828 P6 om. N6Q1S1W Trestot c. et (Q1 que) n'e.
829 P6 a. en m. l. si m'e.
830 P6 om.
831 Q1 A; All: l. c. h.; P6 a force me porta.
832 P6 om. 832-4; N6Q1 a. que.
833 N6Q1S1W E. com m'e. (S1 me portoit) le l. e.
834 N6Q1S1W B. le; N6 jusques au; S1 l. et a.
835 P6 Et cils m. racoust sire e. 835a Q1 Et si croy de certain que bon sang l'engenra;
     835b Q1 Pour moy se combati et le larron tua.
836 P6 om.
837 P6 Q1 om. 837-8. N6 ce ci; N6W1 a. que je v.; S1 c. ci m'avancay(?) ne vous
     n'en tiray j.
838 N6S1 d. que b.
839 P6Q1 d. par m. l. a.
840 P6 om. N6Q1S1 S. certainement; S1 a. n'en v.
841 P6 Q. ses; P7Q1 f. se (Q1 s'en) merveilla.
842 All: Fille.
843 P7 e. aime m.; Q1 qu'il vous porta; P6 f. m'a.
844 P6W om. P7 l. mes cuers mais ne hara.
845 All om.
846 W 847/846. P7 p. vos a sauver son cors abandona.
847 P7 Parmi t. m. p.; S1 Je veil qu'il ait m. terre b.; P6 m. terre b.; Q1 De t. m. g. p.
     par Dieu qui me fourma. 847a Q1 Ne m'orrez plus parler nulz ne li meffera.
848 Q1 C. Emenidon manda. 848a Q1 Voiant toute sa gent le fait li pardonna.
849 P7 om. P6 om. 849-50.

850   P7 Et d. en b. f. ke bien l. m.
851   P7 e. ordina.
852   Q1 om. P6 om. 852-4. N6S1W v. le servi et hanta, P7 v. le chieri et ama.
854   N6P7Q1S1W qu'a son enfant fait a (P7 moustra).

Laisse xxi

857   P7 M. par f. A.
859   P7 s. et.
860   N6 s. peres; P7 n'est pas r.
861   S1 e. et pris e., Q1 e. ou pris ou r.; P6P7W o. ou.
862   S1 m. et q. sont esmeuus, P7 m. et puis s'est esmeüs; N6P6Q1W q. les (N6 le) o. esmeüs.
863   P7 a. couchiés; P7S1 e. irascus.
865   W N6P6Q1S1 Contre lui vint l. C. et (Q1 a) toute sa (P6Q1 t. s.) v., but N6 om. 'lui', P6Q1S1 om. 'li'; P7 Si le conta Califfre .i. de ses privés drus.
866   Q1 f. chevauchier.
867   N6P7Q1S1W Qui s. b. s'i p. (P7 prova); P6 b. le faisoit; P7 k'il e. s. creüs, Q1 e. e. tant c.
868   P6P7 l'ensengne.
869   S1 l'i charcha; Q1 l'e. ne fu m.
870   N6Q1 h. et t. troa d'e., P6S1 h. t. i troa d'e., P7 h. et i troa d'e., W h. et esfroa d'e.
871   P6Q1 om. S1 Tant y; P7 E. t. copa d. b. d. testes e.; N6P7S1W bus.
872   W om. 872-3. P7 E. f. tant d. chevaus estraiiers et perdus; Q1S1 d. chevaus e. d. destriers crenus (Q1 cremus); N6 e. chevax; P6 cremus.
873   P7 om. P6 p. le; N6S1 d. chevax; Q1 e. mors et abatus.
874   P7 l. rois e. e. irascus.
875   N6 Et nonporquant e. (Rest: Nonporquant e. (S1 de); All: son cuer; P6 c. de tel g. iert creüs, P7 c. fu d. g. conchus, Q1 c. est d. tel guise entus; N6W d. tel g. encus (W enpus), S1 d. fol g. enceus.
876   P6 s. s. e. sus.
877   Q1 a. qu'il.
878   P6 Mes; N6S1W f. f. Aymes si qu'il, P6 f. f. Emes com s'il, P7 f. f. ensi ke il; Q1 Et Aymes a l. f. f. si com f. m.
879   P6 om. 'si'; S1 respondi q. t. se fu; P7 Puis r. aprés quant .i. pau ert; All: teüs.
880   P6 Qu'a l.; P7 d. che n. f. p. nus p.; N6 om. 'plus'.
881   P7Q1 Jusqu'atant; S1 s. s. soit m., P7 q. se s. soit u m.; P6 sera.
882   All: d. s. (P7 la) g. (P6S1 terre) maintenir.
883   N6S1 om. 'tant'; P7 l. dist il bien q.
884   S1 S'a son; P6Q1W ce, P7 cel.
885   P7 K'il f.; P7 886/885.
886   P7 Et ses conseaus ensi pooit; P6P7Q1 creüs.
887   All om.

Laisse xxii

888   Q1 om. P6 e. large. Q1 888a-m see Notes.
889   P7 Ensi p. a. l. g. d. mon o.
890   P7 t. si a; S1 a moult.
891   S1 e. en f. m.; P6 om. 'le'.
892   P6 d. grant baronnage, P7 d. rice b.
894   N6P6S1 v. en; Q1P7S1 heritage.
895   P6Q1 e. et f., P7 e. et fist.
896   P6 d. qui t., N6 d. tuitement, Q1S1W d. quittement; P7 d. bonnement s. triewage.
897   P6P7 d. l'en.
898   P6 E. aida a c. s. trés g.; P7 c. a. son trés g.
899   P7 a. destruire a grant h.

Variants for Part I, Laisse xxii, continued

900   W Que; N6S1 e. sus; P7 t. autre.
901   S1 Et l'o., Rest: Li o.; P7 q. li f. grant d.; N6 domage, S1 d'outrage.
902   P7 Par; P6 q. ordenance; P7 e. cel.
903   N6Q1S1W D'a. por, P6 D'a priier, P7 D'a. querre s. nieche; All: en A.; S1 l. sage.
904   P7 G. la belle; S1 a. fier.
905   Q1P7 f. le h. (P7 hansage); P6 s. hontaige, S1 s. hainage.
906   All om.

Laisse xxiii

907   P7 li dus Emes.
908   P6 p. les .ii. m.
909   P7 est.
911   S1 om. P7 e. d. fosses d. viniers e. d. p.
912   Q1 t. il sa niece; P6 d. vous oï avés; P7 e. penés.
913   P7 Il; P6 c. receüs et f.
914   Q1 Q. il o. bien beü e. m. a plentez.
915   P7Q1 A sa nieche c.; P6 s'est, P7 fu, Q1W est. 915a S1 repeats 915.
916   N6 A; P6 iert, P7 fu.
917   P7 d. si sommes c.
919   S1 E. pour t. n'en s.; N6W t. m'en, P6 t. me; P7 l. maltalens passés.
920   P7Q1 p. rien refuser nel d.; P6 r. cangier.
921   P6 C. vers tous li s. e. li p. alosés; P7 Entre l. plus s.
922   Q1 om. N6S1 Entres; S1 e. il.
923   N6 e. de grande, P6Q1 e. g. sa b., S1W e. grande sa b.; P7 Si est entre l. b. .i. des plus beaus clamés. 923a N6P6P7 Et entre les plus preus est li (P7 .i. des) plus alozez (P6 redoutés).
924   P7 Oncles; Q1 p. si com vous commandez; N6P6S1W c. (S1 que) vous vorrez.
925   N6 n. desvoudra, S1 n. demoura; P7 r. n'escondirai q. vos; N6Q1S1W m. conseillerez.
926   P7Q1 Nieche che d.
927   P7S1 Tantost: Q1 C. lors; P7 v. monter; P6 m. c'aprestés s.

Laisse xxiv

928   N6P6Q1S1W r. acesmee.
929   P6 Emenidus.
930-1   All om.
932   P7 E. ont tant chevauchiet e.
933   P7 K'il voient E. et la plus maistre e.; P6 c. droit l. plus maistre e.
934   P7Q1 om. S1 Qui; P6S1W que elle i f. entree.
935   P6 Q. vinrent droit a.; N6Q1S1W il (N6y) furent; P7 a. piet.
936   Q1 om. P6 om. 'dus'; P7 d. a sa nieche del mulet d.
937   P6 E. le mena, P7 Et puis si le mena.
939   All: De toutes et de tous c'e.
941   N6P6Q1S1W q. tant.
942   P6 b. E. l'orent bien saluee; P7 Y. l'aine, Q1 Y. mainsnee.
943   P7 l'enmainent en l. c.; P6 En l. c. V. l'ont conduite et menee.
944   P6 d. souvente fois paree, Q1 d. vestue et r.; P7 Et l'ont de r. d. e. viestue et paree.
945   P6 m. r. f.; Q1 r. garnie; N6P6Q1W e. assazee; P7 m. tres r. de joeaus acesmee.
946   W om. Q1 D. canque l'en pooit desirer p. p.; P7 D. trestout che ke p. d. p. p.; S1 d. de p.
947   N6Q1S1W Q. se f. soulacie; P7 Et q. f. solacie.
948   All: cortoise; S1 E. par l. m. l'a.
949   Q1 G. et B.; P7 m. l'ont honoree, Rest: m. l'ont enamee.
950   P6P7S1 L'o. en; P7 guiee.
951   P7 v. le p. de h.; P6 l. grant.
952   P7 om. P6 E. oiant; N6P6Q1S1W c. par.
953   All: Pour q. (P7 cui) c. o. f. commencie e. vouee (S1 n'ouvree?).

Laisse xxv

954	P7 Dedens; N6S1 desor, Rest: desus.
955	P6W S'assient; All: ont.
956	N6P6P7Q1W A; S1 a a Marcius.
957	All om.
958	S1 B. ce d. Marcius; Q1 desseulé, P6 esseulé, S1 assanlé, P7 acordet.
959	P6 om. 'sont'; P6P7 assené, Q1 assemblé.
960	P7 s. par v.
961	P6 Donnee v. seroit; P7 s. point d'i.; P6Q1 n. fausseté.
962	P7Q1S1 q. le c. o. s.; N6 q. lor ot s.
964	W om. 964-5. P6P7Q1 E. li; P7 s. dist, P6 s. hons dist; P7 trovet.
965	N6S1 On; S1 tous ceus; N6P6P7S1 e. q. (P6S1 qui) il a b.
966	P6 v. signes de dignité.
967	P7Q1 a moult grant f.
968	P7 p. che p. l. d. e. rechoif; P6 prenge; N6P7W a bon gré, P6Q1S1 en bon gré.
969	P6P7S1 autretant; N6P6W doins, P7Q1 v. di, S1 doing; P6 om. 'ont'; N6P7Q1W recordé, P6 regardé.
970	All: Q. tout l. a. a.
971	Q1 om. 971-1098. W Entreulz q. i. parolent; P7 Dementiers ke p.
972	All om.
973	P7 Est .i. varlés venus ki les a e.; P6 varlés q. les a ascriés.
974	P7 r. vos a mandet.
975	P7 Chil; P6 L. sont issut des cambres.
976	P7 S'enmainent; P6 Avec vont l.; N6S1W m. a; P7 o. tant a.
977-80	All om.
982	N6P6S1W om. P7 d. Bien s.
983	All om.
984	P6 m. l. saisi.
985	W om. P6 l'a. al dois; P7 a table.
986	P7 om. P6 g. honour; N6S1W deduit.
987	P6 E. o. m.; N6W li uns l'a., S1 l'un vers l'a, P6 li un a l'a.
988	W om. 988-90. P6 988-1003 see Notes. N6S1 c. us d. gas; P7 d. et g. e. d. jolis pensers.
990	N6S1 om. P7 O. mies il n. f. en t.
991	W Par devant Alexandre s.; N6S1 s. li s., W li servant, P7 li subget.
992	N6P7 portoient.
993	P7 W om. N6S1 m. orent a g.
994	N6P7S1W om.
995	N6S1 e. quant s. (S1 il) s.; P7 p. si.
997	N6P6S1W om. 997-8. P7 Et d'une chose e. d'autre.
998	P7 d. d. quoi il.
999	N6W s. et.
1000	S1 qu'i. soit; P7 Si alerent couchier et quant f. a.
1001	P7 Li bons r.
1002	N6 d. T. i ot.
1003	P7 v. a s.

Laisse xxvi

1004	P6P7 r. se.
1005	All: l. les (P6 s., P7 si) .xii. p. ens (P6 om.) ou palais entra.
1006	W om. S1 ont; P6P7 s. mais (P7 ains) n. li a. 1006a P6 Por l'amor de Porron que moult forment ama, 1006b P6 Tantos qu'il fu garis .i. varlet preuc l'ala.
1007	P6P7W Lors; P7 a. et.
1008	P6 Marcias s. c. qui grant honour porta; P7 c. ki m. f. l'ama.
1009	P7S1W Cassiel d. B., N6 Cassion d. Badres, P6 Cassiel li Baudrain.
1010	P7 A. ki; N6 A. qui g. j. en m.; W A. qui moult g.; S1 A. g. j. en demena.
1011	P6 virent.
1012	W om. P6 enclina; N6P6S1 t. et moult l. (P6 om.), P7 t. et il les.
1013	P7 E. s'en v. devers; P6 a. qui.
1014	N6P6W Dessour; P6 d. ouvré; P7 s. ke on a.

155

1016	S1 B. avec s'a.
1017	P7 t. les.
1018	P7 c. des .v.
1020	P7 M. ert poischans l. s. ki r. v. forfera; S1 q. ja; P6 r. vers v.
1021	All om.
1022	P7 v. forfait; P6 om. 'ce'.
1023	S1 s. et mon corps i v.; P7 m. s. vus v.
1025	P6 n. s'en va. 1025a P6 Tout cil i sont venu a qui on le manda.
1026	P6 om. 'et'. All: a. y a. 1026a P6 Molt i ot de barons et de cha et de la.
1027	N6P7S1W E. a sa g. G. c.; P6 Gadifer .i. serjant maintenant apiella. 1027a P6 Molt debonairement li dist et commanda.
1028	P6 Pavillons faites tendre u l. f. s. 1028a P6 Et li varlés respont volentiers le fera.

Laisse xxvii

1030	P6 p. d'e. et d'e.
1032	P6 Dames e. damoiselles; P6P7 i ot a grant f. 1032a-c P6. Parees noblement du cief dusqu'en son, De rices dras de soie et de vermel siglaton, Si ot maint mantel gris, maint hermerin pliçon.
1034	P6 t. au.
1035	P6 v. tente ne tref de si rice f.; P7 om. 'si'.
1036	W om. P7 e. d'argent l. 1036a P6 Moult fu grans li noblois qu'illuec vëoir pot on.
1037	P6 A. d. j. (om. 'Lors'); P7S1 d. A. hors.
1039	P6 q. cuer o.
1040	N6S1 ert.
1041	P6P7 (om. 'Et') M. li Persans.
1042	S1 Gardifer; P6 Perducas. 1042a P7 Et tout li .xii. per et maint autre baron.
1043	P7S1 om. P6 Et Aristés li preus od lui E.; 1043a P6 Tholomers et dans Clins od iaus Antigonon.
1044	P7 om. 1044-5. P6W Dauris; P6 F. Lincanor et F.
1046	P7 Dont; P6 p. li boins rois; N6P7S1W arestison.
1048	P6 r. lor a d. O. r. cest.
1049	P6 Phezon, W Fezone; All: l. clere f. 1049a S1 Qui tant a de biauté qu'espriseroit nus hon.
1050	P6P7 V. l'a.; P7 l'a. par amours p. le me dist o.
1051	P7 E. par; N6S1 l. empristes; P6 W l. empresistes; S1 l. male a.
1052	P6 As, P7 Des; N6 f. a m.
1053	W om. All: Dont; S1 D. je fui m.; P7 D. nos f. bien pres de g. d.
1054	N6P7S1 Moult, W Lors.
1055	W om. P6 D'une g. piece a.
1056	W E. puis prist a p.; P6 q. il ot pensé s.; N6 v. a p.
1057	N6W d. il sire (N6 r.); N6P6W a grant; P7 a moult rice don.
1058	P7 M. de.
1059	W om. N6P6P7S1 j'aie; N6P6 a. b. e. h.; P7 b. ne t..
1060	P6P7 ore (P7 ja) n'a. quisençon.
1061	P6 Car j. ne di ains riens nulle se p. b. n.; P7 j. aie dit chose ki s.
1062	W om. 1062-5. N6 s'a b.; S1 vostre; P6 Et par le foi que doi a mon d. M. 1062a-b P6 Que se j'estoie a quieus de tous les preus del mon, Sor tous hommes vivans et t. l. p. d. m.
1063	P7 om.
1064	P7 om. 'je'.
1065	All om.

Laisse xxviii

1067	N6S1W convoitans.
1068	P7 h. et d'e. b. v.; N6S1 s. biens (S1 b.) veillans.
1070	N6P6P7S1 t. que.
1071	P7 Et.

Variants for Part I, Laisse xxviii, continued

1072   P7 jou estoie tes c.
1073   P6 Je; S1 a. les jors; P7 a. ke passast li a.
1074   W Qu'en sa vie ne t.; N6 Que onques n'e. eüst l.; S1 Qu'o. en euust l.; P7 C'ains
       en toute sa vie en tenist r. P; P6 Tant que mius en seroit tous mes apartenans.
1075   P6 P. mon chef; N6W j. ne; P7 p. mentans.
1076   P7S1 F. ke s.
1077   N6S1 P. dist li roys; P6 P. de haut pris ore s. r.; W P. je vous prie que s. r.
1078   S1 c. d'un; N6S1 c'onques f.; P6 p. preu q. a. fu en n. t.; P7 ki onkes f. vivans.
1079   P7 om. P6 e. fors e. h. seurs et entreprendans; N6S1 p. combatans e.; N6S1W e.
       auques (S1 avec) enprendans.
1080   W om.
1081   P6 a fait p. v.; P7 a par; P6P7 l'en (P6 l.) mercians.
1082   P6 f. moult c. e. entendans.
1083   P7 W om. 1083-5. P6 Biaus c. o. e. sorcius que o. f. r.
1084   P6 regardure l. iex vers et rians.
1085   P6 b. avoit vermelle; S1 v. le.
1086   P6 d. basset t.
1087   P6 D. vous plaisirs biaus sire et v. c.; P7 f. et tous les v. c.
1088   P7 p. p. .i. a.
1089   P6 Q. mari n'averoie; W s. n'estiés li g.; Rest: s. ne l'e. g. (P7 creans).
1090   N6P6 P. mes diex, S1 P. m. dieu, P7 P. ma foi; N6P6S1 m. ces, P7 m. les
       contrewans. W combines 1090-1: P. mes diex d. l. r. ja n'i s. p.
1091   P6 c. aviés d. n'en s.
1092   P6 om. 'en'.
1093   P7 Dont; P6 L. e.
1094   N6S1 T. le, W T. la.
1095   All om.
1096   P6 I. Menour; W M. li; P7 I. M. li d. dont la terre estoit g. 1096a-k P6 see Notes.
1097   P6 W om. N6S1 d'Illande; N6P7S1 q. moult e. (S1 e. m.); N6 om. 'bien'.
1098   All om.

Laisse xxix

1099   Q1 resumes. 1099a-b P6 Et le Baudrain de Baudres et la bele Edeas, Betis et
       Ydorus u il n'ot vilain cas. Cf. 1101, 1104 which P6 om.
1100   S1 D'A. d'Alir; P7 d'A. l. rois machidonas.
1101   P6 om. 1101-1106. P7 B. et.
1102   Q1 om. N6S1 Norvede, W Norvege, P7 Morenge l. grant t. les donna haut et
       bas; W t. li; N6S1W donna.
1103   P7 B. de che; N6Q1S1W e. ce.
1104   N6P7Q1S1W A; N6P7Q1S1W cas.
1105   W l. l. li; P7 l. l. les d. sens debas.
1106   W om. N6P7Q1 biaus dons; N6Q1 f. onques j. l.; P7 f. il onkes l., S1 f. onques
       eschas.
1107   P6 Apiele M.
1108   P6 E. resai; P7 E. k'il tenoit p. l. dras.
1110   N6S1 preigniés, Q1W prenés.
1111   W om. P6P7Q1 vos; P7 m. avoir repas.
1112   Q1 d. pieça q.
1113   W om. 1113-4. P7 Elle v. a jettet .i. ieu p. plain d. l.; P6 r. iex vairs clers tels que
       mas; N6S1 u. gius si (N6 p.) p., Q1 .i. gieu p. plain.
1114   P6 om. 1114a P6 Vous convient par force estre nel tenés pas a gas.

Laisse xxx

1115   P7 Marcias.
1116   All: Mout vous; P6 v. ricement m.; P7 v. hautement c. m'e. v. m.
1117   P7Q1 E. e. moult.
1118   P7 d. moult haut linage; N6 l. et l.; W n'ot.

1119   P6 b. avec; N6P6Q1S1W l. (N6 le) preus c. (P6 Q1 nommer).
1120   W om. 1120-1. P7 p. preus; S1 q. vous.
1121   P7 o. moult b. e. e. presenter; Q1 o. eslire et sanz faillir compter; P6 p. et e. e. nombrer.
1122   P6 M. ne le veul refuser; P7 sauve v.
1123   P6 om. W r. o lui vous vueil donner; P7 l'os bien affermer. The following passage is found partially in all but P, W:
1123a   N6 Dont li marchiés se puet aques bien acorder.
      b   'Sire,' dist Martien, 'ne le voel refuser.'
      c   (Chose ke vos veulliés dire ne commander.') P7 only
      d   'Ne je.' dist Elyos, 'puis qu'il le veult greer.'
      e   'Par ma foy.' dist li rois, 'si deves conquester.
      f   Qu'a ma volenté faire et du tout accorder Q1 only
      g   Avez plus gaaignié que ne poez penser Q1 only
      h   Car je le vous cuit bien et richement solder Q1 only
      a. S1 s. prent.   b. P7 M. je n. v.; S1 l. quier.   d. S1 Elyas; P7 p. ke.   e. S1 P. f. ce d. l. r. ci; P7 f. fait l. r. che fait a merchier; Q1 s. poez bien jurer. P6 has only 1123c-d.
1124   S1 Frisse e. t. Hillande; W H. sans riens ent d.; P6 v. veul quite clamer.
1126   P6 assener.
1127   N6P6Q1S1 Avecques l., W Avoec l.; P7 A une des p. belles; P6 q. soit de cha la mer.
1128   P7 Niece le d. Emon, Rest: L. n. Emenidon (Q1 W Emenidus); N6S1W douter.
1129   N6S1 A. v. li donne, P7 avoec l. v. donrai; P6 s. nului apieler.
1130   S1 Gabois; N6P6P7S1 e. Escoce.
1131   P6 Lindoine, P7 Lydone, Rest: Lidoine; P6 p. cest.
1132   S1 d. son; Q1 e. les freres g.; P7 e. de lui afermer; N6 p. acorder; P6S1W p. afremer.
1133   Q1 om. S1 vostre; P7 Q. le sien pere o.; All: G. al (N6S1 a) jouster.
1134   N6P6Q1S1W fort.
1135   P7 t. devoie, Rest: t. soloie.
1136   W om. 1136-7. N6 C'ert; N6P6S1 Pieres (P6 Porrus) d. M. q. f. gentis e. b.; P7 Pieron d. M. dont il me doit peser; Q1 Pirron d. M. q. t. fist a. loër.
1137   P7 om. S1 o. devant G. sans per.
1138   Q1 m. s. p. pardonner; N6P6S1W p. quiter.
1139   P7 Par; P6 v. v. v. la moie q.; N6W m. pooir.
1140   S1 r. les m.; P6 espouser.
1141   All om. 1141a P7 Aprés ches mariages commence a fiestier.
1142   S1 om. 1142-3 here but has written them in at the foot of the same page, f. 156v., after l. 1170. P7 Par dedens les grans t. prendent a c.
1143   W om. 1143-4. P7 L. bons; P6 A. fait; Q1 honnorer, P7 agreer.
1144   N6 C. oians, P7Q1S1 C. devant; P7 t. hautement; P7 Q1 chanter; P6 Signour baron font il commençons le festier.

Laisse xxxi

1146   P7Q1 P. a; S1 P. Betis et Y.
1147   Q1 Au; S1 B. Elyas M. Ydorus.
1148   S1 E. aprés G. et le sage Elyas; N6P6 le sage Lindonus (P6 Lindeus), P7Q1W la belle (W serour) Lydonus.
1149   Q1W om. P6P7 n. Emenidon; N6S1 a. duc A. 1149a S1 De noz .v. mariés dont grans biens est venus. Cf. 1159.
1150   S1 om. W t. furent mises; N6P6Q1W et q. p. (P6 tans) f. v.; P7 c. q. li tans f. v.
1151   All: r. ala; S1 l. li autre s'irent j.; N6Q1 e. touz, P6W e. tout; W s'assient. 1151a P6 Porrus porta coronne cel jour et Phezonus.
1152   All om.
1153   Q1W om. 1153-4. N6P6P7S1 Quant bien f.
1155   P7 S. d. l. bons r.
1156   P7 f. soit durans .xv. j. voire p.
1157   P7 J'en; N6P7S1W .xi.; P7 s. bien sui entendus.

1158   All: les .v.; P6 m. cois; P7Q1 Esleüs.
1159   N6Q1S1W D. nos, P6 A nos, P7 A vous; N6 mariees; P7Q1S1 venus.
1160   N6Q1S1W Ara chascune (Q1W chascuns) .i. j.; P7 j. et en nom de Martus; Q1 j. en; P6 n. de d.; N6 om. 'diu'.
1161   P6 Car; P7 E. en; N6 c. erés; S1 c. qui les a p.; P7 i. a tous p.
1162   Q1 om. S1 Les; P6 De tous .v. r. et t. lor; S1W r. et t. l.; P7 r. a t. lor; N6 revenoir et t. l. a. deus.
1163   P6 E. les a. .v. j. ai je bien e.; N6S1W les .vi.
1164   P7 P. vos, P6 A vous; N6P6Q1S1W mariees; P7 m. je n'en devise plus; S1 m. or; P6 n. me tenroit n.; N6 om. 'ne'.
1165   Q1 tenrons; P6 p. de g. e. de; P7S1 p. a g. e. a (S1 as).
1166   P6P7 om. 1166-7. N6Q1W teüs, S1 teuus/tenus?
1167   N6S1 A. les; N6 j. me a.
1168   Q1W om. N6S1 verrons p. .v. j. et (N6 om.) lor feste et lor; P6 venrons p. .xv. j. lor solas et lor; P7 Et verons ces .v. j. lor f. et lor. 1168a-b P6 Or veul je departir, je m'en sui assentus, A cascun le sien jour, detrier ne veul plus.
1169   P7 om. P6 Les .v. premiers ferai, ja n'i ara refus.
1170   P6 L. s. je d.; N6 E. les s. d. je; S1 s. d. j. P. S1 inserts 1142-3 here.
1171   N6 E. les, W E. la; P6 Le s. a., P7 Le s. avera.
1172   P6 Et Betis l. w. l. n. Ydorus; P7 Y. ait l'uitime; W la w. la; S1 le .x. B.
1173   S1 Elyon; W E. la.
1174   N6 Lydone l., P6 Lindoine l., Q1W Lydoine l. (W la), P7 Si ara l., S1 Li doint je l.; N6P7Q1S1W li m.
1175   W La; P7 t. Lydone; P6 Li t. avra et l. B. corsus; S1 Le Baudrain a. li t. au s.; Q1 Avera le t. l.
1176   P6 F. le .xiiie. Ede le sorplus.
1177   S1 W j. d. k., P7Q1 j. e. k.
1178   S1 S. ce d.
1179   S1 Li; P6 Li r. n. a tous mis en plus grant fieste jus; P7S1 m. festoiiés et repus.
1180   S1 om. N6 Q. si e., P6P7Q1W Q. s'il; P7 e. donnet de m. .xiiii. u plus; Q1 e. doublé n. m. d.

Laisse xxxii

1181   W M. o. dedens les t.; P7 Dedens les t. ot g.
1182   Q1 M. a b. A., P7 Et m. f. d'A.; N6P6S1W M. f. b. d'A; N6S1W rescriee, P7Q1 recreee.
1183   N6Q1S1W .v. j. p.; P6P7 j. pleniers; S1 c. est f.; P7 joiie e. festiee.
1185   P7 Bien.
1186   P7 Et q. v. au quinseme d'E.; S1 qu'Edeas l'assenie.
1187   S1 A. desus aimmont n. e. j. sa pensee; N6P7Q1 esgardee. P6 gardee.
1188   Q1 om. 1188-90. P7 l. estoit e.; S1 talentee.
1189   All: c. quant l'iaue fu cornee (P6 tornee).
1190   All om.
1191   P6 saisist.
1192   W om. N6Q1S1 Qui; P7 Ki f. m. l. aisie; P6 m. l. est s.; Q1 f. richement; S1 l. et s. e. festee.
1193   W Et.
1194   Q1 Aloit de t. e. t.; N6S1 a. a moult g.; W a. la gent a moult priee.
1196   P6 Dehait que i. d. s. q. forment m'a.; P7 M. a. a c. d. car a moi bien a.; Q1 s. forment m'a.
1197   P6S1 q. plus l.; N6P7Q1W q. plus fu l. gent e.
1198   Q1 En; S1 c. a orfevrers et g.; Q1 o. s'est; P7 e. Edea t.
1199   Q1 om. P7 damoiseaus; S1 d. d. e. m.; P7 e. amee.
1200   P7 t. paree
1201   Q1 D. r. Alexandre s'estoit h.; P7 r. de Gresce est moult h. S1 c'est.
1202   P6 m. Gregois, Yndois e. g. C.
1203   P7Q1 p. il n'a; P6 n'est p.
1204   P7 Par l. h. p. ke por li f. m.; P6 p. qu'est en s. n. m.
1205   N6Q1S1W Q. l. restoreroie; P7 r. or.
1206   P6 Vees e.; All: restor; P6Q1 d'o. tres esmeree.

Laisse xxxiii

1207 N6S1W E. l. noble; P6S1 om. 'et'; N6S1 l. vaillans.
1208 P6S1 Vees chi; P6 r. gaie; P7 enjoissans.
1209 P6 d. estre d'o. de femes d'e.; S1 e. e. d'omne.
1210 All: Car; P6 om. 'i'.
1211 N6 1212/1211. P6 Memoriaus a. o.; P7Q1 a. obliiés, N6S1 a. oublieus; P6 rices; N6 r. a m.
1213 W Or; N6S1W se; P6P7 s. s. el, S1 s. s. aus; S1 luisans.
1215 All: e. e. cuer; P7 k'est en a. m.; N6P6Q1S1W a. est.
1216 W om. P6 om. 'bien'; N6 p. au perron, P6 p. el p., S1 p. aus p.
1217 Q1 Car cilz ci represente l.; P6 Cels p. s. l. grans cops poissans; P7Q1S1 l. mors e.
1218 P7 Ch'est li v. a. p. e. a b.; S1 a. biens.
1219 P7 Ne n.; P6 om. 'fu'.
1220 P6 S'il; N6P6Q1S1W n'avoit amé (W a.); P7 n'estoit amés; N6 o. o il, Rest: o. il.
1221 Q1 l'espoir; P7 e. eü en; P6S1W d'amer.
1222 P7 Premiers i s. en; S1 P. li.
1223 W riche; N6Q1S1W l. poi c.
1224 N6P6Q1S1W e. armes.
1225 S1 Apré sist l. s. q. les g. f. p.
1226 Q1S1W vertus; P7 e. amours.
1227 N6 om. P6 le cuer; P6 W amour; P6 b. taians/caians?
1228 P7 m. e. bien seans; S1 q. est m.
1229 N6 l. gens, Rest: l. cuers (S1 om. 'les'); W se n., N6P6S1 ce n., Q1 et n.
1230 P6 om. 'd'amant'.
1231 P7 om. Q1 Simple s. vanterie; S1 s. beuberie; N6P6W e. simples, Q1S1 e. courtois.
1232 P6 L. p. e. i est a. sivans; P7 Le quarte est l'e. ki auques est samblans; S1 La quarte est emaude et est preus ensuivans; Q1 l. quarte; N6 om. 'la'.
1233 P7 a. k'envoisiés s. amans e. j.; P6 s. d'envoisure j.; S1 s. enoisiés.
1234 P7 Et l. quinte p; All: est l'e.
1235 P7 e. amours c.; Rest: e. t. (P6 tous) s. contenans.
1236 P6 Et p. esluminer l. c. de ce gardans; P7 K'il puist e.
1237 N6S1W s. achoison du bien d. ignorans; P6Q1 d. ignorans; P7 de bien as ignorans.
1238 S1 A. si est ceste encostes; P6 l. jagousse, W l. jaconce; P7 l. escuse c'est p. as escusans; Q1 e. c'est la; N6Q1S1W p. esconsans; P6 p. est estonçans.
1239 All: s. secrés; W e. bien c.
1240 S1 om. 'Se'; P6 o. ni; S1 o. e. entreprenans; P7 W om. 'et'.
1241 S1 e. agonse.
1242 P6 s. s. descombre d'enerbure, Rest: s. s. destourne d' enherbure (P7Q1 d'enherber).
1243 P6 s. paisiules e.
1244 N6P6P7Q1W s. et t. g.; S1 s. en amour asés biens est partans; P7 nuisans.
1245 All om.

Laisse xxxiv

1246 P7 om. Q1 E. l'envoisie la f.; S1 E. l'envoie la f.; N6W om. 'et'.
1247 P7 e. de; P6 om. 'le'.
1248 S1 Si n'i; P7 Car il n'a r.
1249 P6 Qu'il n'i ait bien mestier a g. s.; P7 Ke n'a grande m.
1250 W om. N6 E. a. ne, S1 E. a. est; P7 o. li b.; S1 o. mes b.; P6 om. 'boins'.
1251 N6P7W p. dehors; S1 p. samblant noble est la remembrance; P6 d. belle s.; P7 paranche.
1252 P7 b. e. d. grande s.; Rest: b. e. p. d. g.
1253 N6P6Q1S1W Et cis p. (P6 paons) n.; P7 C. p. nos senefie e. d. demonstranche; P6Q1 souvenance, N6W a. d'omme soveneanche, S1 a. d'omne senefiance.
1254 N6Q1S1W Car; P6 Q. il; S1 q. est en armes; N6P6P7Q1W e. armes.
1255 S1 E. gracieux d. d.; P7 despitance.
1256 S1 recreance.

1257   S1 Queue et c. e. c. t. sans desplasance; P6 k. col; P7 c. e. c. tient en droit par u.; N6P6P7Q1W usance.

1258   S1 E. est; Q1 g. apparance.

1259   P6S1 om. 'et'; P7 c. et t. est; N6 t. c. en; P6 t. cest r.

1260   Q1 d. venir; P7 t. par.

1261   S1 j. et desevir.

1262   P6 E. del p., P7 E. de p.

1263   All om.

1264   P6 d. v. par sanlance, S1 d. v. sans faillance; N6Q1W e. se lance, P7 e. il lance.

1265   N6P7S1W Mostre; All: a forme eage (P6 pooir) et poissance (P7 'eage' obliterated).

1266   P6 a. son sestance.

1267   N6 Dedens; W D'a. l'un; N6Q1S1 e. en tres h. h.; P7 D'a. soi sorlever et avoir honorance.

1268   P6 E. les; S1 t. sus.

1269   P6 c. par; P6P7Q1S1 mesceance.

1270   P6 monstrent, Rest: moustre; S1 e. lieu.

1271   N6 A. aist, S1 A. est; P6 s. kaïr, P7 sens defaillir, N6S1W sens (S1 cens) de cuellir.

1272   N6P6Q1W L. faoncel, P7 L. paoncheaus; P6 c. cognissance.

1273   S1 Que n.; P6 e. gie h.; S1 j. hons (?)

1274   All: representance.

1275   N6P6Q1S1 Senefie; P7 Monstre; P7 b. si en f.

1276   P7 cui l. m. desavance.

1277   P7Q1 parseveranche.

1278   S1 om. P6 Convient .i., N6P7Q1W Conchoivent .i. (Q1 il); P7 q. les; P7Q1 beance.

1279   N6Q1S1W Des (W D.) tres b.; P7 b. costumance.

1280   N6P7Q1S1W p. ce point c.; P7 om. 'tout'; S1 tous li boins refourmance; N6P7Q1W restorance, P6 rescriance.

1281   P6 om. 'Et'; P7 l'alieue autant d'i. p. sa d. o.

1282   W Senefient; P6P7S1 p. quoi.

1283   S1 d. cuer f. s. nule d.

1284   P6P7 c. qu'il; Q1W de p., S1 de plume, P6 d. plume; P7 e. legiers de plume, N6 e. legiere de p.; S1 om. 'legiere'.

1285   P7 om. S1 debrise.

1286   N6Q1W moustrent, P7 N. demonstre merchi; P6 de savorance.

1287   P6 Elle d., P7 Et l.; Q1S1 e. retrait; S1 p. d'avisance, Rest: p. d. nuisance.

1288   N6 C. que il; P6 C. que il a, P7 Et c. k'il a; P6 om. 'luisans'.

1289   P6 E. que n., N6P7Q1W E. qui n.; P7 moustre, Rest: moustrent. P7 dechevance.

1290   P6 C'a. ne doit m. avoir sans d.; N6P7Q1S1W Qu'a. a a m.; S1 la lueil p.

1291   P6 amensisance, S1 aveuliance.

1292   P7Q1S1W l. biens, N6P6 les biens; Q1 e. ist; N6P6Q1S1W v. passe l., P7 v. par droite m.; Q1 mescheance. 1292a P7 Met el cuer amoureus une bonne esperance.

1293   P7 Quant; P6S1 o. en e., P7 W o. y e.; P7 e. de n. acointance.

Laisse xxxv

1294   S1 Sire d. Elyas des l. e. des marcis; P7 d. quens e. d. marchis.

1296   N6Q1S1W achoison; S1 de f. li; N6 f. le; P7 f. as; P6 om. 'les'.

1298   S1 E. ce ce e.; P7 E. si e. li v. a p.; P6 s. c'est; S1 gentis.

1299   P7 E. a v.; S1 E. au; N6P6 l'amor, P7 q. amour; Q1 apris.

1300   P6 Et autre r.; Q1 a drois est q.; W q. les; S1 Et une a. r. y a ce m'est avis.

1301   S1 Et l. p. si est v. l. queue polis; P6 p. de sa k. et n.; P7 e. cointes e. j.; N6P6Q1W polis.

1302   S1 E. c'e.

1303   Q1 om. P6 d. proieres, Rest: d. proesce.

1304   S1 A; P7 o. l'afection.

1305   P6 om. See 1315a. S1 Et p. l. queue f.; P7 f. de che sui je t. f.

Variants for Part I, Laisse xxxv, continued

1306	P6Q1S1W d'un (P6 d'une) ouvrage, N6P7 del ovrage; P7 e. tout p., N6 e. li p., S1 e. premerains b.
1307	P6 E. plus.
1308	P7 E. tant, N6 om. 'tout'; P7 l. ne r.; P6 E. si est e. b. l. nicement.
1309	P7 c. en l.; N6W f. en; P7Q1 f. est haus et a.; S1 Et l. c. est l. f. en h. et a.; P6 c. et l. f. en faut et a.
1310	P6 e. de t. et de fors poingneis; P7 e. de t. de guerres et d'estris; S1 Et ainsi e. de joustes de t. de p.
1311	S1 Et c. p. armes p. suour e.; P6P7 commence. 1311a P7 Soient tout demenés et a darains finis.
1312	P7 t. ces mestiers; All: f. oublis.
1313	P6 j. l. e. h. e. p.; Q1S1 honour.
1314	S1 om.
1315	N6Q1S1W cremeurs, P6 cremir; P6 dur. 1315a P6 Par le keue est la fin mes cuers en est tous fis. Cf. 1305 om. in P6.
1317	All: giex.
1319	All: gagiés; S1 gagiés a a. m.
1320	Q1 Petit mal; N6P6Q1W m. qui puet e.; N6Q1 grant bien; P7 P. amans ki puet en grant bien estre mis; S1 Mays que petit peuust e. e. bien c.
1321	P6 p. s'est; P6Q1 e. la roe, P7 e. sa roee.
1322-23	All om.
1324	P7Q1 Lors; S1 Quant i.; N6Q1W p. en e.; P6 p. s'est t.; S1 p. si e. e. a.; P7 p. est il t. amatis.
1325	S1 Ainsi f. l. paons; W e. as a.
1326	P7 e. par.
1327	P6S1W h. puet, P7Q1 h. puist; S1 amas et conjoÿs, Rest: a. n. conjoïs.
1328	All om.
1329	All: r. a s.; P6P7 p. et c.; N6P6Q1S1W i. fu.
1330	P6 E. des; P7 s. cors; S1 e. parés.
1331	P7 n'e. pas; P6 des biens r.; S1 d. biens.
1332	N6Q1S1W apertient; P7Q1S1W telle: P6 Qu'i. a. d. telle d. estre o.
1333	P7 d. sour; N6S1 esbahis.
1334	P6P7 e. grant, Rest: de grant; P6P7Q1 aquellis.
1335	P6 om. 'Et'; P7 v. en che cas ke si fait valent pis, Rest: v. q. si fait en armes valent pis.
1336	S1 l. en; P6 l. ses cuers est raëmplis.
1337	P7 portrais; W l. p. por tant s.
1338	N6P6P7 Des a. e. des; Q1 p. e. doit c., Rest: p. doit e. c. (S1 conjoiés).
1339	P7 Car i chis r. e., Rest: Cis ci (Q1 Cesti) q. r. e.
1340	S1 joustis.
1341	All om.
1342	P6 Q. devant h. f. t. et d. P. o.; N6 om. 'fu'; P7 d. Porron.
1343	S1 l. mes; P7 s. petit; P6P7 om. 'i'; P6 escris/estris? , S1 destris.
1344	Q1 Que; S1 Qui a.; P7 Ke d'offrir tout premiers d. e. e.
1346	P7 e. B. l.; P6 gentis.
1347	P6P7Q1 marié, S1 mariés; P7S1 m. a m.
1348	S1 A. et; P6 A. ore lor a s. meris.
1349	P7 om. 1349-50. N6S1 e. le d. e. a tous (N6 om) deservis; Q1 l. resserst sanz estre desservis.
1350	N6 c. que D.; P6 l. adés a servis.
1351	P7 Ke; P6 Que cascun a il f.; N6S1W qu'i. ont.
1352	N6 om. 'aprés'; P7 o. l. conte et l. m.; S1 a. marris.
1353	P6 o. le; P7 o. voés l. v. h. e. a.
1354	S1 q. nous a t. c.; P7 aquis.
1355	P6P7Q1 A che (P6 cest) mot s'e. (P7 e.)
1357	P6 conjoïs. 1357a S1 Si ca l'en devons rendre et graces et mercis.

Laisse xxxvi

1358	P6 f. nobles; S1 f. bele.

1359   N6P7Q1W o. o. tout; S1 Q. orent tout s.; P6 Q. ont assés mengiet le n.; N6 l. na;
P7 s. et tans fu de laissier; S1 f. oster.

1360   S1 t. font oster.

1361   All om.

1362   P6 A. m. a.; P7 A. laver se vont l. b. sus drechier; Q1 arrengier.

1363   P7 om. All: l. p. vindrent a.

1365   P7 d. et: All: la f.

1367   Q1 Eslut donc p.; P7 a. si.

1368   P7 estoiier, S1 adrecier.

1369   S1 a ces; W E. assés; P7 c. departir sens noisier.

1370   P7 qu'e. voloit; Q1 qu'il ne voloit.

1371   P7 g. a manestres et les vot essauchier; P6 m. baindrer; Q1 f. n'a.

1372   Q1 E. que o. n'e. a. p. f.; P7 n'entendist p. fors a p.; N6P6 n'e. fors c'au; S1W n'e.
fors au.

1373   P6P7Q1 V. en; N6 V. .i. tresor; P7 c. ne puissent corochier; N6 parçonnier, S1
clarchonnier.

1374   All: e. que t.; P6 t. en.

1375   Q1 Lors c. cascun, Rest: D. commanda cascun.

1376   P6 o. ont; P7 o. o. tromper juer e.

1377   P7 Les; N6Q1S1 orgues; N6P6Q1S1 e. busquier; P7 t. flautier; W combines
1377-78: Orgues harpes citoles b. e. p.

1378   Q1 om. P7 om. 1378-79. P6 b. e. kontoiier.

1380   N6Q1S1 efforciement; P7 e. et canter e. t.

1381-86   P7Q1 om. 1382-86 N6S1W om.

1383   P6 Ensanle s'a. trestous sans d.

1384   P6 p. se peuist.

1386   P6 l. a s.

1387   P6 om. 1387-9. S1 o. ost; N6 f. qui f.; S1 f. point de; P7 f. ke tens fu de l. Cf.
P7 I 1359.

1388   N6W Desour.

1389   P7 E. puis a.; Q1 e. ala; S1 p. jus.

1390   P7 b. salirent por eaus plus avanchier.

1392   P7 om.

1393   P7 Porron.

1394   S1 a. mariees; N6P7Q1S1W m. estoient.

1395   P7 Et en t.; S1 En.

1396   P7 om.

1397   P7 En.

1398   P7 E. en; P6P7 e. li; S1 r. estoient t. a. p.

1399   Q1 o. grant; P6 m. i fist.

1400   S1 offroy.

1401   P6 c. que t.; S1 c. qui t.; P7 qu'i. conquist.

1402   S1 d'Arcage; P7 d'A. a l.; N6 l. abrisier.

1403   P6 de. .M. mars; P7 de .ii. C. mars.

1404   P6 s. branc forbi d'a.

1405   S1 P. Caulu; P6 a. a A.; P6S1 aracier, P7 enrachier.

1406   P7 om. S1 U m. d. la g.

1407   P7 Et de son pesant d'o.

1408   N6P7Q1S1W om. P6 f. or qu'on p.

1410   N6P7Q1S1W om. P6 t. est grans.

1411   P7 De .ii. C. mars d'argent l.

1413   All om.

1414   N6P6Q1W S'offri, S1 L'offrison; P6 son c. d. rice paille cier; P7 Le c. d. soie d.
s. confanelier.

1415   P7 En; P6 O. restor l'e; P7 detrenchier.

1416   N6P7Q1S1W om. P6 f. en.

1417   All: A quoi l.; N6 s. devot saluer.

1418   P6 om. 'i'; P7 o. un; N6P6Q1S1W legier.

1419   All om. P6 has 1424 here.

1420   N6P6P7S1W Ens; P6Q1 esracier, P7 enrachier.

1421   All: Cassiel.

Variants for Part I, Laisse xxxvi, continued

1422	P6 destrier, P7 chevalier.
1423	P7 Qu'i. ot fait de fin or et poindre e. e.
1424	All. om.
1425	P7Q1 c. ke F.; N6P7 faviier, Q1S1 fabloier.
1427	P7 Ke; P6 n. vauroit; P7 v. eslongier.
1428	P7S1 J. 'a tant; N6 c'a C.; W qu'a C. p. apaisier; P6 c'a Porus poroit pacefier; P7 C. le poroit apasier; Q1 apaier.
1429	Q1 om. P7 S'A. li rois, W S'A. se s.; N6P7S1W l'en (N6 le) venoit chacier (P7 sachier).
1430	N6P7Q1S1W om. P6 s. doit a lui souploiier.
1431	P6 Perducas; N6 d'o. fin a.
1432	All om. but see 1435 P6.
1433	N6P7Q1S1W om. P6 s'o. taint (caint?) .i. b.
1434	P6 P. c. qu'il v. chiaus de piet a a.; S1 om. 'a'.
1435	N6P7Q1S1W om. P6 om. 'fu'. P6 1432 follows 1435.
1436	P7 Et B. offri .i.; N6P6Q1S1W B. (N6 Bris) o. autel q. valoit m. d.
1437	P7 c. k'a P.; P6 Perducas.
1438	P6 r. au; Q1S1 p. en; P7 p. a loi de; P7 soldoiier, P6 boucier, Rest: bouvier.
1439	N6 om. 'lanche'.
1440	P6P7Q1 aquitier.
1441	P7 K'en; S1 Charus; P7 atargier.
1442	P7 P. jouster a s. f. l'a. sens desfiier; P6 assaiier, Q1 tournoiier.
1443	All om.
1444	P7 E. F. aussi offri .i. p.; N6S1 o. si comme .i. p.; W a. com p.
1445	All om.
1446	S1 B. offri.
1449	All om.
1450	N6P7Q1S1W om. P6 1451/1450: Que jamais ne voloit a homme nocoiier, Ne c'a nul mariage ne voloit repairier.
1451	N6Q1S1W Que jamais n. v. a homme m; P7 K'a nul h. v. n. v. nochoiier.
1452	Q1 Se li roys A. n'e.; P6P7 l. rois; P7 nel voloit otroiier; W a alalyer.
1453	P7 om. N6 decriier, S1 destrier.
1454	N6 .II. amans; P7 k'e. avoit f. forgier; Q1 f. appareillier; P6 atirier.
1455	P7 c. qu'a; Q1 volt jurer.
1456	P7Q1S1 Que; Q1 a. Betis d. c. e.
1457	N6P7Q1S1W om.
1458	P7 j. sens plus de prolongier; P6 om. 'je'; S1 eslongier.
1459	P6 om. All: largement; P7 targier, Rest: dangier.
1460	P7 Meismes A. n. se vot relaissier; P6 m. n'en s'en vot.
1461	All but P7 om. 1461-2. P7 Ains i offri a. p. s'o. e.
1462	P7 De p.
1463	P6 A. i o.; P7 .I. saffir moult tres rice et moult fist a prisier.
1464	P7 Il ne le d. pas, Rest: Qu'il ne le (P6 om.) d. pas; P7 p. plain d'or.
1465	N6S1 o. m. bel; Q1 m. m. bel d. e. l.; P7 m. d. e. maint l.
1466	P7 l. l. le beaus d.; N6Q1S1W desploiier.
1467	N6Q1S1W om. 1467-8. P7 D. a m. q. present.
1468	P7 f. enlargir; P6 e. et b. et t.
1469	P6P7Q1S1W v. aver; P6 laissent; All: mengier.
1470	S1 Au; P7 As ores (?) e. a v.; N6P6Q1S1W v. car p. l. fol cuidier.
1471	P7 om. 1471-1484. All: Aiment miex lor a. a. l. (N6P6Q1 le) r.
1472	All: la grace. 1473-84 N6Q1S1W om.
1475	P6 om.
1476	P6 q. n'a que gaigier.
1477	P6 ala e. l. c. o. erent l. ouvrir. P6 om. 1478-80.
1481	P6 C. lor.
1483	P6 acointier. 1483a-d P6 A vo congiet vouriens en nous liu repairier. Et elle respondi Bien fait a otriier De ma court vous pöés des ore mais fiier. Si c'a diu sans adiu di sans eslongier.
1484	P6 om.

VARIANTS: PART II

Note Ya = N1N6OQS1U   Yb = N5S5S6S7

Laisse i

1   O le I e. t. ses.
2   P7 en r. par; S5S6S7 r. o g.; OQ r. et en; Q1 e. et par d.; P6S1 r. et.
3   O rendus.
4   Ya 5/4 P7 P. l'onor; S7 l. biens, N5 les biens; N2 om. 'qui estoit'; P7 venue en. N2Q1Yb v. de; O p. son o.
5   Yb faire d., Q1 faites d., P7 fisent en; P7Q1S7 offrandes; S6 o. le; OQS1 o. au d., U o. et d.
6   P7 Semblantes, N1 Sambletes; Ya l. diex; N5S5S6U repentation, N1N2N6OQS1 repectacion, Q1S7 repetition, P7 presentation.
7   N2Q1 om. U P. afermer e. eulz; N5S7 P. euls en affirmer l.; P7 P. eaus a rafermer en m.; P6 renfermer.
8   P6Q1 q. cuer o. d. Yb combines 8/9: Alixandre apela E. p. s. n.
9   N2P7Q1Ya E. belement; P7 b. a bas ton.
10 N1 Marci, Q Marssi; P7 l. preu; P6Q1 Antigonon, Rest: Anthiocon.
11 N1 Fesonus(?) L., S1 Phezom et L.; P6 Lincanor, P7 F. T. Lincanor; N6 Clichon Q1S5S7 W Clicon. 11a Q1 Filotas et le duc c'on dit Emenidon.
12 O om. P6P7Q1 E. de.; P7 q. a.; Q par, S1 partie; N1N2YaYb p. en; U l'avocion; P7 a l'envoison; N6QS1 l'acoison.
13 Ya D'une p. l. a trait (Q a traist); N2 p. se; P7 t. et l. d. son sermon. N2Q1YaYb t. et l. d. abandon.
14 N1N6QS1U A. or oes, O A. escoutez; P7 mon sermon.
15 OYb. om. N1U a eu t., N6QS1 a en t.; Q p. sa r.; P7 t. por voir le vos dison.
16 P6Q1Ya om. 'et'; N2P6 l. moiene; N5S5S6 m. c'est l. f. et (S6 om.) l. c.; P6P7S7 f. et l.
17 P7 Quant; OQ D. la c.; S6 D. une c.; N2 La c'est b. emprise; Q1 c. bien emprise; WYa c. prise; P6P7Yb emprise; S6S7 om. 'en bien'; Ya om. 'quant'; N2 q. a. b. moielon.
18 N2 Et si desierre bien qu'ait b. c.
19 O Homme q.; P6 a. vraie, P7 a. bonne.
20 Yb om. P6P7 d. aquerre ou (P7 par) c.
21 N1N2P7QQ1S1S6U Proece h.; N5OS5 Proece h. s.; OQ s. et renom.
22 S6Ya om. P6 p. s. ire; P7 s. noise e. s. tenchon; Q1 façon, N5 foison, N2S5 fricon, S7 s. fra . . .?
23 P6 a se mission.
25 N1N2OP6QS1S6S7 biaux; N6Q1W b. fait.; N6P6 f. je croi n. v. n. h.; N5S5 n'avint ce c.; N2Q1S7W v. ce; O v. onques h.; P7 v. nus vivans h.; U croit; N2 hons.
26 P6 C'on f., N5SQ1S5 Comme o. f., S1 Q'om *per*vist(?); S7 por o.; N5 l'o. et; Q1S5Ya l'o. Ph. (Q1 Fezonie).
27 N6P7 P. (P7 Por) hardement v., OQ P. hardement nous, Rest: P. hardement voé; Ya firent ice s. (S1 c'est) o.; S5S6 b. ce.
28 Yb om. P6 Et.; P6P7Q1W achievé, N2 achevez, Ya achevee; N2P6Q1Ya par n. e. par t. (S1 tenconcon); P7 a. tot por voir le dist on.
29 O om. W Huchon, Yb Huchier; Q H. en ot c.; P6 c. les, S5S7 c. ces, N6QS1U c. de; S1 m. a n.; U m. le n.

Variants for Part II, Laisse i, continued

30 N2N5S6S7Ya Si; N5 diron c., S5S6 dirons c.; O Si dy je et d. c. son intention;
    P7 S'e. dira cascuns d'eaus de bonne e.; S1 d. que c. die s'e.; Q1 si en dirons
    c. selon s'e.
31 P6 asserions, N1N6Q asenione, O asonime(?); N2N6QS1S7 similation.
32 N2 per; N5 e. par description, S7 e. d. escription, O e. discreetion; P6 s. sans
    simulation.
33 P6 S'asseons, N5U S'avrons, N2W as P, Rest: Si avrons; U l. tiers de p. d.; P7 d.
    nostre entention; P6 om. 'no'.
34 U l'atour; P6 loiers, O loer.
35 S1 Da g., OQ La glose; P7 .ii. pars; P6P7 c. dist.
36 P7 37/36. P7W E. pris; Ya preu; N2N5P7WYa heneur; U h. Miex; P7 m. asseir,
    OQ m. en a.
37 P7 Ch'est li profis a preu; N2P6Q1Yb au petit; N1N6P6P7QS1U l'o. a. h.
38 S6 om. Q1 Car; N1 E. ce.; P7 p. p. a bons; S1 a. bien, Yb au bien, Q1 es b.
39 Yb om. 39-42. Q1 Et l. g. es h.; P7 p. a honour et vie et n.; N2N6P6 p. as h.;
    Q h. peisture; O h. pecune n.
40 Ya Grant homme (O om.) s. h.; P6 honnors; U confection.
41 Ya v. pas il l.; N1OQ om. 'et'; W mor; N6Q1W conte on, P7 l. tient on.
42 P7 om. 'Et'; Ya honore; UW e. empris d'a.; N1N6S1 e. empre d'a.; OQ e. em
    preu d'a. (O en a.); U d'a. et adonc; N2Ya tenroit; P7 d'a ensi le nos vent on.
43 S6 om. 43-5. S7 h. h. s'amie; N5 'sa vie' crossed through and 'honnour'
    written above. N1 haute; S5S7 porçon; P7 A .i. h. h. d'armes en s. d. p.
44 P7 Car; N2YaYb e. son; P6 sourplanter; P7 veroit, N2YaYb n'avroit; U la b.;
    S1 om. 'sa'.
45 P6P7 E. s., Rest: Ne s.; Ya amener; Yb amourir ne por quant: P7 e. p. che;
    N2P7YaYb l. doit. 45a Q1 Sceürement celui qui en est la parçon.
46 N2OS1U S. com; U n. procon; P6 reprovoison; P7 donner s. c'o. n'en ait b.
47 N2P6WYa ces mos, P7Q1 ce m.; N5S5 A ce c.; S6 ces gens c.; S7 A ceus a c.;
    P7 m. a mander a f. a u. g.
48 U Lyoine a queroller; P6 karaloler, P7 a chls=chevaliers or charolers?; Q1 d. la.
    48a P7 Ke tot facent grant joie entour et environ.
49 P7 M. par o.
50 N2 L. y peust; P6 puist; N2U o. veoir; P6P7 m. noise e.; N2N5Q1S5Ya ton.
51 W. om 51-4. O om. 'Et'; P6P7 m. noble.
52 P7 De g. et d'a.; S1 De la gent amoureuse; U g. ris a.; N1N6OQ g. a.; P6 om.
    'i'.
53 S6 de B.
54 P6 Et P. et Y., N2 Fezonne Y.; Q1 Y. et le vassal Beton; O e. messire E.; N1 d.
    Armenidon.

Laisse ii

55 O Quant a; P6 fu f.
56 U Et d. m.; N5S5 m. du leu, S6S7 m. du veu; N1 print, U pris; N5S5S6 le roy;
    P7 r. grant, N2 r. sa.
57 N1OQ est.
58 O Le; Q1Ya r. par s. g. courtoisie; P7Yb r. a (N5 et) noble (N5S5S6 sa grant,
    S7 belle) compaingnie.
59 P7Ya Assis; S6 A. deleis; YaYb l. sus.
60 P7 c. e. envoisie.
61 U om. Q1 Marcien d'a. p.; S1 p. eu Marcien, N1N6OQ p. en mercie; N2N5P7W
    Marcien, S6 Marcoen.
62 N2QUYb s. a. sus; S7 les jons; N1 q. verdure.
63 S5U Et l. r.; N5S7 regarde.
64 Yb om. 64-5. P7 S. ce d. l. r., W d. il a eulz; Ya r. qui a fort (U fet) c., N2 r. qui
    a force partie.
65 N2Ya om. Q1 66/65; P7Q1W d. vous; P7 signorie.
66 S5 Que s., S6 Tout s.; Yb l'aucion (S6 l'accion); O q. vous; S1U a. ouye.
67 P6 Il, N2YaYb C'on; S1 li d. a., U d. bien a., N6 d. a. amer; N1OQ om. 'faire';
    N2Q1YaYb com l.; S6 r. Emenie, S7 r. Termenie, O d'Armenie, Q1 d'Aumarie.

68   P7 om. Yb V. n'i; N2U V. n'i alez; N1N6OQ om. 'i', Ya q. .iii.; N1OQ om. 'vail'; N2 voil, P6 vaue, S1 veil, N6 voi.

69   N1N5S7 tous; Q1S6 a. a; N2YaYb u. route; P7 Serés v. t. les moi amant et druerie.

70   O e. affin d.; S5S7 q. en; O vostre.

71   Ya Face c. honour.

72   Yb a. a. jeu; N1N5N6OS1U a l'o.; N2 e. l'eure; U que est.

73   N2 c. sa pensee en d.; P7 c. sa volentet en die; Ya c. s'e. ait (N1 est) mise; S6S7 s'e. en die.

74   P6 esgarda se; Ya s. d. (Ü d. a) par druerie.

75   N2N5Ya L. premiere; N6S1 p. voee, N1 p. voir; All: de; N1S1 de no, N2P6 de nos; S6 L. premiere nous vous donnons d. v. o.; S7 L. premiere vous donnons si est drois c'on l'o.

76   O S. ce d.

77   U Ses; P6 om. 'Mais'; N2S6 s. soit vo p.; O v. grace; P7 p. ensi n'ira il m.

78   OP6U Marié.

79   W om. N5S5S7 Moy (S7 Mes) s. ai m., S6 J'ai s. a m., Ya Seigneur ay et m.; P7 Et a noble seigneur q.; N2 m. que m. S1 m. qu'a m.

80   S6W om. Ya Mesire vous serés t. q. seray, N2 Mesire et vous soiez t. com s., N5 Mes sires et vous t.; S5 Mes sire est vous t. com vous s. ou v.; S7 Mes sire serés vous t. com s.; P7 M. est vos homs t. ke sera.

81   S7 Mes; P6 plaist; N1 p. aus d.; N6U a no; P7 q. tant s.; N1N6QS1U s. si.

82   N1 om. Q1WYaYb t. dessus; Ya l. soye si atardie, P7 l. por nient m'e.; P6 m'eshardie.

83   O om. N5S1 est; P7 o. toudis a; Yb a. a l.; Q l. parie, S1 l. saisie.

84   Yb v. se m.; N1QU l'otrie, O l'otroie.

85   S1 i. n'a m.; P7Q1YaYb qu'o. le c.; O om. both 'il'.

86   N2 Proumetre; N1 m. cors et cuers et terres h.; OU terres et h., N2N5N6Q S1S5S6 terres h., P6 terre h.

87   OS5S6S7 M. regarda, N5 M. la regarde, N1 Mar les garda; N1N6P6QS1U pot; N2S5S6W p. lessier n'en (N2 ne) r., O p. mieulx qui n'en r.; N1N5N6P7QQ1 m. (N1 rimer) n'en r.

88   O om. 88-93. Q Sa main tenant s., P7 S'a maintenant s. v. et s.; S7 m. mist d. s. v.; N2N5S5S7Ya v. s'a sa c.; Q1 c. a e.; S6S7 enfronchie.

89   YaYb L'un a l'a. c. (Ya rignoient); N2 Slun a l'a.; P7 om. 'et'; N1 om. 'en'; S6S7 et a se croy; P6 pincie, P7 s. a le fie; YaYb pitie.

90   P7 Ke; N1 C. ci; P6 s. tresbien; N1 Mahonnie.

91   Ya E. entour lui a. sa; Yb E. encor a. si; N2YaYb s. mesnie; P6 engensie, P7 aguisie, Ya agaitie.

92   P6 t. icelle g.; S1Yb est; N2YaYb arengie; P7 Ke la g. ki l. e. en est esmervellie.

93   U Et; P7 Et e. dient grant b. et en tout b. p.

94   Q1Yb B. ce d. l. r.; N2P6P7 Ya l. bons r.; O m'atente; P7U marie.

95   Yb Nostre; N6QS1UYb e. sus, N1O om. 'sor'; P7 s. le h.; S1 si grant b. rengie; N1 legie, P6 forgie.

96   P7 Je n. v. ose p.; N5S6S7 Q. n. v. ose p.; Ya Plus pres n. v. et (S1 est, N6U v. os dire) que (U et q.) je ne (N6 ne me, S1 vous) m.; P7W p. presser, N2Yb p. prier; S7 desdie.

97   Ya Marsille (U Marseilhe, N1 Marceille); N2YaYb l'o. et; O s'il l'a d., U et a la destruirie.

98   S6 om. N2 chascuns; N5S5S7 n'i a c. nel guerpie, N2 n'a c. qui nel guerpie; N6QS1U t. il n'est que (QS1 qui) les (Q cel, S1 le) desdie, O n'y est qui tel desdie, N1 t. il veult que il desdie; P6 c. nel contredie; P7 E. a c. l'offri mais il l'ont resoignie.

99   P7 om. 99-100. N2 f. pourporte, Ya f. portee, P6 f. pour offier; Q1S1U peublie, N1 peuplee, N6 peuploiie, OQ peu plorie, Yb oïe.

100 N1OQ Se; Ya escondit, N2 escondire; S6S7U et de p.

101 S7 l. crestiens; P6P7 f. en la fin b. (P6 laissie); N2Q1YaYb c. lessie (O laissee).

102 S6 om. P6 p. euandement e. e. carcie, P7 p. amendement esmeute e. cargie; Q1S7 e. e. enchargie; O om. 'et'.

103 Q S. se; P6P7 S. d. l. bons r.; O A vous c. d. l. r. seigneur e.; Yb r. avon nous

avouie; P6P7Q1Ya envoïe.

104   S6S7 C. se p., S1 C. vous y savés p.; N1N6OQU om. 'le'; O p. vous s., P6P7 p. en s.; Yb s. q. m. y s. m. (N5S6 si) d.; Ya et q. (N6 om.) plus s. se (N1 si) d.; P7 s. n'est nus ki m'en desdie.

105   O Des; S1 c. a l.; P6 batelerie, Yb bataillerie, P7 cevalerie.

106   S1 om. N5W Les; Ya Les j. chevaliers; P7 e. norie.

107   P6P7 Q. j'ai (P7 je ai) en ma main ma boine h. (P7 ma. g. hace) e,; Q1Ya Q. je tieng en (N1QU a) mon p. (N1 a main sur) une lance (OQ blanche) fourbie; N2Yb Q. je tieng (N2 tient) en mes mains (N2N5 poins) une (S5 ma) g. lance (N2 ante) antie.

108   N2P6P7Q1YaYb Mon (N6 Moult) h. e. mon d. (S6 dors, Q1 h. endossé) e. ma t. v. (P6 voiie, N6S1 vestie, OQ deslie, U destie, N1 cestie, N5Q1 enpoignie, P7 ma coife lachie). 108a P6 Et j'ai en mon cief mon elme qui brunie.

109   P7 om. W 109/110, Rest: 110/109. Q1 E. je sui as plains c., Ya E. je sui (U E. le suivi) as (S1 a ces, N6 a) c., N2P6Yb E. je sui s.; OYb c. en b. r.

110   P6 enfoukiés, S1 esfourchiés, N2Yb enforciés, P7 haubregiés; P6 d. d'Arabie.

111   P6S5 om. W as P. Rest: Et (P7 Se) je sui b. r. u je fais l'e. (P7S1 f. e.)

112   N2YaYb Cil (N2 C., N1 Ci) q. (N1 qu'il) en (N5S5 s'en, S6S7 se, N2 ce) vont e.; N1N2N5N6OQS1 v. cele partie, S5S6S7 et n'ont (S6 vont) telle partie; P6 v. cele estormie, P7 v. celle envaie, W v. cele a.; U entour a batailhe rengie; Q1 c.e. d'une et d'autre partie.

113   P6 om. Ya Bien (U Si) doit (OQU doi) s.; N2P7Q1YaYb c. j'ai (N6 ja) ma l. e. (OQS1 versie, N1 bersie, N6U brisie); W a enpoingnie.

114   O om. U c. le recoit, P7 c. j'ai rechu, W as P, Rest: c. je recoif; P6 c. je l'en r., P7Q1 c. je l. renvire (Q1 renvoie); N5S5 r. et com bel l. r., N2N6S6S7U r. com bel je le r., N1Q r. com bel r., S1 r. com bel cop je r.

115   P7 om. P6Q1 C. ma g. s. p., W as P, Rest: C. ma g. depart; S5 et c.; W c. il, Rest: c. je; N2P6Q1Yb le r., OQ1. dalie, S1 l. deslie.

116   N2Ya Q. je q. ay ma t., P6Q1Yb Q. (Yb Et) je q. ma t. ai (P6 a), P7 Et comment ma t. ai; Q1Ya en mon h. embuschie, N2P6P7Yb en mon h. embronchie.

117   OYb om. P7 Et ke j'ai mon c.; N2P6Q1Ya q. ai; Q1 p. de ire.

118   O D. mes, W as P, Rest: D. mon; N2N5P6S6Ya p. (P6 piet) esgarder, S5S7 p. a garder; N2P6 n. m'ensoignie, YaYb n. me soingnie, Q1 n. messonnie, P7 n. m'estudie.

119   N1 b. qu'elle v., OQ b. que; P6 q. les; S6S7 q. l'envoit; N2N5P6Q1S5S6 v. qui p., S1 v. et p., P7 v. et ki p. nel oblie; N1N6OQU om. 'que'; U p. je n. l'e.

120   O E. pourtant; S7 p. ce vous ai je l.

121   P6 l. maistre, S7 j. pourserie.

122   N1OQ q. giue chiez, S1 q. giue les chiés; N6 q. giue ciez li p.; U q. giue sus li de p. l.; N1 d. le v.; O larie.

123   Ya e. pas; P7 p. n'i estudie.

Laisse iii

124   N1 om. 'Filippon.

125   Q1W om. Ya om. 'rices'; U de Gresce; S1 G. y est q.; N1O G. que; P7 L. bons. r. Alixandres ki nuli n. d.

126   N1N6OQS1 om. W r. de; P7 m. tous.

127   P7 Soi l., P6 Ses levés; OQ e. e. et p.; P7Q1W capitre, N2P6 as P, Rest: capite.

128   O a. avoir; P6 a. la f.; N2Q1 a. a. pale f.; S6 f. plane, Ya f. plate; S6 e. afficte, N1 e. flice, OQ e. flite, S1 e. pliche.

129   W om. P7 Belle b. e. c. ki p.; P6 c. que p.; N6OQS1 c. e. si n'e., U c. e. n'e. pas p., N1 c. ci n'e. pas p.; N5S5 p. n'avoit.

130   P7Q1 Ya Un; N2 Ya e. l'autre faisoit l'e., S5 e. li autre l'e.; P6 om. 'et'.

131   Q1W om. Ya E. c. viex (N6 bien) b. (U bectus) ou contrais ou abisse, N5S5S6S7 Come n. ou b. comme contrait (S7 traitre ou) herite (N5 habite); S5 b. comme contrais herite; N2 b. et contrais i abite; P6 om. 'com'.

132   WYb om. Ya L. uns tient a couars (N1 cornars) et (N1OQU om.) les autres (Q ends at 'autres', N6 a. avise, O a. il despite, S1 a. pour bisse, U a. bien assise, N1 a.

bien . . . se; P7 c. c. et ribaus et herite.

133   Q1 om. N6QS1S5S6S7W E. com, P7 Ausi com; P6 p. mius plaire encite.
134   Ya s'a que; S1 c. le enhite, N1N6OQ c. l'enhite, N2 l'i enhite, U l'en habite, Yb
       li enditte, P7 c. s'i delitte.
135   N1N2N6QS1 d. uns vallés, O d. ung varllet, N5 le varlet, S5Q1 l. vallet; N6 t. le,
       N2 om. 'les'; P7 Freres dist il au roi p. t. l. sains d'E.
136   N2 om. P6P7Q1 ai dedens m. c. e.; O om. 'bien'; N6 escrites, S6 eslite.
137   N2N6OQS1U jouste; N2P6 t. de; O q. l'on.
138   N2Q1W Ai veu, P6 A un d., Yb Ai oï d., Ya Li (U Les) uns d., P7 Bien voroi d.;
       N5P7Q1S5 om. 'le'; O p. aucune; P7 enlite.
139   S1 om. N2P6P7Q1 Ya guerre mortel (P6 mortele, N2N6 as P); W d. grace; P7
       est de; N1U Yb q. (N1U om.) en champ est c.; OQ m. host en champ c., N6 m.
       e. e. camp desconfite; N2 e. e. champ c.
140   Q1 om. O l. mendre; N5 est aquise; N1 om. 'est'; U et afflite, S6 aduite.
141   O om. 141-2. S7 p. erreur d.
142   Q Pris e.; N1 Pas n'i v.; S1 P. v. d'onneur p.; Ya elle (U elle est) desconfite; P7
       b. enlite, S7 b. escripte.
143   S1 E entre l. b. p. doit elle estre dite; N2 l. biens, W l. uns; S6 b. parans; P6 l.
       plus poissans u s. e. bien dite; N6 p. par droit doit estre dite, N1OQ p. doit
       estre dite, U p. devroit bien estre dite.
144   N1 p. de; Ya p. (U p. qui) est ainsi mais dite (S1 adite), P7 p. la u li biens habite;
       P6Q1 c. al (Q1 a) mal, N2W c. est.
145   Ya Le pris soit; N1 a nostre; Q1 g. je n'y r.; U g. je n'e. quier estre habitre;
       N1P6S6 n'e. quier; N6OQS1 n'e. querre par (S1 om.); W n'e. quic; S7 g. je n'en
       veul nuls a.; N2N6OP6QQ1S1S5S6W arbitre; P7 g. se j'ai chose mal ditte.

Laisse iv

146   Yb Sire; P7 S. dist dont l.; N1N6OP6Q om. 'ce'; W r. de; O r. trestouz or
       escouter; N1N6QS1U c'e. (N6 chet) moult c.
147   O om. 'Que'; N5S5 guerres m., N2N6S5 as P, Rest: guerre mortel; P7 m. n'oi
       ains pris d.; O m. je v. pou p. d.; N1N6QS1S5U p. de p.
148   N1 d. de c., N6OQS1 U d. ses, W c. jeus, P6 d. cel pris; Yb d. a autre ses (S7 yces)
       f. a (N5S7 om.) c.; U f. autre; O f. aux; P6S1 autre, N1 autri.
149   All om.
150   Q1 Ya F. a. par revel f. leur (N1 le) veu donner; Yb Fines a. regnans f. leur v. v.;
       N2 r. leur fist l.
151   N2YaYb om. 151-2. Q1W valoir, P6 valeur, P7 valour.
152   P6 il plot; P6P7Q1 a diu; P6 j. pot.
153   U Nul; N5S5 la moienne, S7 la monnoie, S6 d. en monie; N2YaYb f. (O om.)
       en,; P7 f. a j. tourner.
154   O l. p. vueil.
155   OS5 Je, S6S7 Jel; Q1 q. fu; P7 e. hardis e. b.
156   O b. sens f. assis; S5S6 f. atrait, S1 f. effrais; OU il l'osa.
157   All om.
158   Q t. cels.
159   All om.
161   P6 om. Ya Au p. p. (N1N6Q preu); N1OQ1 d. ses (N1 ces) gens; W l. p.
       agarder; N2YaYb p. le pris agarder (S1 esgarder), Q1 p. son pris amonter, P7 p.
       petis eskiewer.
162   S6S7 M. cil, S5 M. cilz; P6 M. i abati bien e. s. c.
163   S1 om. 'Et'; S7 l'ala il decoper; O j. gecter.
164   All: Tel chose n. f. o. (P7 ains, N2 anc) faite d. (Q1 d'un) b.
165   Ya Et, N5Q1S6 Qui; O peut; N6P6OQS6S7U un o.
166   N2Q1 Ya Yb Et; P6 Yb e. (P6 ne) les gens; P7Q1 e. (P7 ne) l. g. decoper; N1
       desrancher.
167   Yb v. ferir, N2U v. fouir; P7 f. ne; P6 trestourner.
168   N1N2N5N6QS1S5S6U r. me v., O r. je me v.; Ya recorder.
169   S6 om. Ne; S5 j. je n'e., S7 n'e. m'en; P7 j. ne m'en tairai, N1 n'an i tarai;
       S5S6S7 istrai, O isray, N2 istera; S6 s. j. ne vous oy; P7 s. ne voi; P6 j'en ot,

N1N2N5N6QQ1S1S5U j. n'os; O m. compter.

170 N6 om. 'merchis'; N1S1Q d. Orton; O d. Coiton (?) je s.; S6 je y s. a a., P7 jou
i s. amender.

171 P7 Non por tant; Ya n. v. (N1 v. je) mie b.

172 N1N6OQU n. puet; S5Ya h. de.

173 U s. bien fet; P6P7Q1 n'e. nus si biaus (Q1 preu) qu'on (P7 ke); N5 qu'o. n'i;
N2 ne ruist, OP7S7 n. treuve; P7S7U om. 'bien'.

174 N5OQ1S6S7 v. du, P7S5 v. au; P6P7 f. mies, Q1 f. moult; P6Q1U relever, Rest:
reveler.

175 P6 n. n. pot; P6P7S5S6U p. haut; N1OQ loër.

176 N5 d. aiment; O d. veult t. vostre; P7 d. si voloient n. r. tant amer; S6S7 n. loy
a.; N1 n. r. amer, Q1 n. r. honnorer, N5 n. r. et monter; P6 Car l. d. qui font
sour tous le r. a.

177 Q1 Qu'il l'o.; N1OP6Q il ont; N1 s. d'aire, Q s. d'are; Yb s. et d. t.; P6U om.
'air'; O s. tant de t.; P7 s. de t. e. d. la m.; Q1 d'a. et d. t.

178 P6P7 haute vertu; P6 l. v. bien p., P7 l. v. coroner.

179 P7 Et c'on s.; S7 en l. en.

180 O om. N1N6QS1 b. et b., U b. moult b., Yb b. en b., P6 b. a a b.

181 N5 Par son veu par r. t.; Q1W r. puis, O r. par, U r. de; P6 r. puet tenir s. v. a. s.;
P7 s. voi; S6S7 t. et s.; N6 t. et a singler.

182 N6OQS1U e. l. veu; P7 l. v. s. lever, P6 li vorent amonter, Q1 l. vaurrent
eslever, Rest: l. v. eslever.

183 P6 E. encontre p., P7 Encontre l. p.; N2 Ya Yb c. l. voloir; W les, Rest: le;
N1P7S5 firent, S7 vi, Rest: fist; N1P7S5 om. 'tant'; N2N6OP7QQ1S1 avaler, Yb
devaler, P6 eslever, N1U avancier.

184 N1 om. N5S5 Que ou m., Q1 Qu'el m., Ya Ou m.; P6 l. vient, Yb l. vi; N2O
l'espee.

185 O n. cuide, P7 n. croi; Ya q. mes (O mais) h.; P6P7S7 h. osast p. (P6 si) h.
penser (S7 voler); O h. plus peüst; N1N2N5N6OQS1S5S6W p. h. oser, Q1 p. h.
penser, U p. h. monter.

186 U Si; S7 alast; N1N6OQS1 desroër, U derreer, Yb effroër, P7 decoper.

187 P7Q1 a ki l.

188 O Car l'e., P7 Car l. standars; S6 s. ou t., P7 s. veoir, N6 s. n. taire, S1 s. n.
braire, O s. n. tuer; S7 t. n. lancier.

189 S1 om. 'Ne'; S7 W s. ami, P7S1S6 s. anemi.

190 U om. 190-1; Yb S. tous; P6 c. voloient; Q1 c. s'en vont fuiant q.; P7Q1S5W l.
doivent garder (W t.), N5S6S7 l. v. amer, P6 l. devroient t.

191 Ya l'e. et cheïr et.

192 Ya n. y; P6 amer, Q1 tenser, Rest: garder.

193 P7 Ya om. P6 c. a g.; N2 g. de.

194 S6S7 P. deffense; P7 P. faute d. bon c. v.; S1 vorrions, Yb c. volentiers.

195 O om. Q Se n.; S7 Se nous avons b.; N1QS1 r. donnier, N6 r. bonnier, U r. bon
niert; P7 om. 'rois'; Q1 Yb bon cuer; P6P7Q1 d'u. preudome esgarder; N2 Ya
Yb h. h. encontrer.

196 N1N6OQS1 d'envaïe; P7 c. de lui; S5 Ya c. p. (S1 om.) li.

197 P6 E. t., OQ De t., U E. d. telz; Yb E. pour ce f. l. v. (S5 veulz, N5 l. v. f.)

198 Ya S. il, N5S6S7 S. ce; N2 n. fu; N6 QU q. sus; P6 q. tous n. d. guier.

199 O e. voulisse; P7 v. encor p., Yb amener.

200 Ya d. le veu v.; N5S5S6W l. n'en; S6 v. si; S6S7 h. pas; S5 amener, N2N5P7Q1
S6S7 WYa raconter.

201 S6S7 Devant o. (S7 l'o.), O P. s'omme, N1 P. s'om ni ere (?); Yb doit on s.

202 P7 Par; Q1 d. amonter; P6 e. reporter, P7 e. reparer, N2S5S6S7 e. renforcier,
N5 e. reconforter, Ya e. enformer.

203 N2Yb M. pour tant, Ya Et pour tant; N5Q1 n'en; P6 n. f. mie; O p. les faiz,
N1Yb p. le fet; N6OQU f. mielx a; YaYb priser.

204 All om.

205 W De; P6 l. coze, P7 l. chose; Q1 c. en c.; Yb c. reprenre; P6 e. avieler, N2 e.
avueuler, Ya Yb aviller.

206 S1 t. le; N6P7Q t. a B.; U B. vuelhe p.; N5 B. le p. miex a.

207 N1N5N6QU E. dit; N5 q. par; O de bon; S1 d. s'en d.; OP6 d. le d.; S5S6S7 d.
sur tous l'e. doit p.; N6QU d. sus t.

209   P6 vo parole; N1 p. p. en b.; OYb b. a paine (S7 b. apanre) apeler (O parller).
210   S1 Et q. l.; Ya fu preux p. itel (OS1 tel) f.; P6 p. itel (om. 'fait'); All: outrer.
211   W as P, Rest: D. f. c. souffisans (P7 plus poissans) q. l'ala e.
212   N6 E. a v.; P6P7 v. le; N1 om. 'le fist': P7 r. li ala presenter.
213   N5 Pour, P6 A, U Et; P6P7 g. d'un.
214   U q. ci volst; Yb s'i vi.

Laisse v

215   N6 Pliçon; N1OQ om. 'je'.
216   U Q. ce.
217   P6 Toute c. du diu q. p. est p.; P7 Yb q. sont plus, Q1 q. moult s.
218   P6P7 om. Ya E. li e.; S6 l'e. par a.; N2N5Q1S6S7 WYa d'acort; O om. 'a'.
219   P7 i. por; P6 i. p. lui; O i. pas m.; Yb e. greignur p.
220   N5S7 Com; N6QUW s'espee.
221   P7 r. et s'enclina; O e. son.
222   U om. Yb s. (S6 s. et) dous amis.
223   O m. louez; P7 m. loés i t.
224   N1N2S5U q. iere, N5N6QQ1S1 q. g'iere; N5 entrepris.
225   S5 M. biau sire dous amis (cf. 222); N6 n'il ai de r. m.; O d. r. je n'ai m., Rest: d. r. n'i ai m.
226   OQ1 om. N2 U d. du; S1 d'u. renteour; S6 v. je y a.; N2 i avrai je p.; Ya po amis.
227   OYb om. N2P6 Atant, Q1 Or tent, P7 Or vieng; N6QS1 t. avons, N1U t. a. vos; N2N6P7QS1 propos; P6 p. veul estre r.; UW p. ou j. s.; Q1 p. au quel s.
228   S7 Si l. veus f. ytieus; N6QS1UW fust; N2S6 t. com p.; Q1 Ya t. com en (S1 j'en) p. (OQ parlast) d.; P7 t. que jou chi v. d.
229   S5S6 veu d. F. furent p.; O F. si fut p.; N5S7 f. le p.; P7 f. de t. p. floris; N6U fust t.
230   S7 Q. o v.; N6QS1U v. se, N1 v. ce; W l. livrai; P6 v. iel uic a e. e. p.
231   S5S6S7 p. q. preus; P6 q. fu p. c. s. e. b.
232   Q Soit; U Si d. p. desus l.; Yb p. desus l.; P6 om. 'lui'.
233   O Et; N2N6QS5S6S7 t. com; N2P7Q1Ya a (OQ en) q. i. est; Yb p. doit on estre c.; P6W i. sont.
234   O D. n'estoit F.; P6S6U F. pas le pris e.; O l. preus, N1 l. pres, S1 l. pies, Rest: l. pris.
235   O donne que que s.; N1N6QS1U de quoy q.; N5S5 de qui s.; P6Q1 de qui qu'il s.; P7 de cui soie; N2Ya s. les (N2U le) dis (N6 dist), Q1S6 s. desdis, N5S5S7 s. escondis.
236   All om.
237   S1 M. ycil, U M. se il; P6 i. n'euist; P7 l'e. mie; Ya ne sot (O scet) pas; Q1 M. pas ne li donnasse s.; U p. que; N2P6 fu; N6 bis.
238   N5 Mes; N1 o. mes p.; P7 p. fiers v., N6 p. haus voes; P7 f. fais ne b.; N2P6Q1 YaYb e. cuer b.
239   O Et; O q. estoit, Q1 q. fu, S1 q. est.
240   P7 E. voa qu'il seroit p., U Que d. loier iert qu'il p.; N1N6OQS1 d. loer qui ert (S1 est, O estoit, N1 om.); O a grant.
241   Q1 Se a m., Rest: S'a m.; Q1 t. contre; P7 e. ses anemis.
242   S1 q. se, O q. si; P7 c. pensa.
243   P6 d. mais, N5S6S7 d. mauvaise, Q1S5Ya d. male (N1N6O mal); P7 d. male oevre; N2 N. plains d. mauveise i. m.; S5 p. mes amour; P6 p. ne d'avoir s.; S6 om. 'si'.
244   N1 Et a p.; P7 p. puet; N1N6QS1 h. nus, O h. cil, N2UYb h. nul; N6 que li; Ya l. fet l.; Yb l. feist (N5 fest) p.
245   S7 D'aidier; P7 ses a., Rest: son anemi; S1U morte, N1N2W as P, Rest: mortel; N1 forcis, U forreis.
246   N2P6P7Q1WYb Est, Ya Et; Q f. d. fait; S6 fait par dessus fait; N2OU h. contre h.
247   OP7 om. P6 Que c. q. j. au vin e. t. p. q. hardis; N2 q. gaaigne e.; Ya j. aus (N1 au) des e. (QS1 et); Q1 j. trop p. est q.
248   O om. 248-50. Q1 Qui ce, N1 Q. il, U Q. se, Rest: Q. ce; U d. aus ribaus,

P6P7QQ1 d. a r.; N2U r. qui; N6QS1U sus l.
249   Q1 Car; N2Q1W s. puis j. (N2 gaaigne) a l.; Ya s. plunge (N1U pluge) a; P6 q. i
e.; N1N2N6QU regramis.
250   N6QU qu'a fin; N2Q1 s'en t., U le t.; P7 t. mal ballis.
251   O E. dit.
252   O a. Charnus, Q a. chascuns; S6 C. dont il e., S7 C. qui de li e.; U d. ce que iert;
P7 q. il iert.
253   S6 om. P6P7 s. partis.
254   U om. 'Le', P6 Les; Yb L. pris doit (S6 doit bien) a.; Ya g. don a. elite (O om.,
N6 elide) a m.; P7 d. eslire apres a m.
255   S7 om. P7 t. le huee de c. v. et l. p.; N5N6QS1S5S6 d. ses v. (S6 nons); P6 le hue.
256   S7 Floridas le doit bien avoir ce m'est avis; N2Ya q. d'amours e. (N1 en) f.; N5
q. est d'o. f.; P7 ki tant est signoris.
257   O om. N1 om. 'le'; P7 m. emploiier.
258   Q1 om. 258-60. W t. qui estoit, P6 T. moult i.e., P7 T. vos e., N2YaYb T. si e.;
O e. se a.
259   U q. j'en iere p.
260   P7 hastans; S7 si m'en t.
261   OP7 P. ma foi, Q1 P. mes dieus; N1OQS1 r. si; All: affiert.
262   N5 om. N2O Respons n., U Respousez vous; N2 n. a .i. po; Q1 p. mes tres
loyaulz amis; N2P7YaYb p. si ert (O sera); Ya f. vos.
263   P7 Et; N5 S. vous; S6 h. louier; N2 Ya v. que (O qui); P6 v. n'en soiés a.
264   All om.
265   OQ1 om. Yb n. p. (S7 suis) p. ensens, N2 n. suis p. aus s., U n. suis p. a seulz, N1
n. p. p. mes s., P7 p. p. a ceaus; P6P7W estre, Rest: geter; P7 atentis.
266   Q1 om. S7 Vostre s. l. c. et moy s.; N2N5P6P7S5S6WYa c. et v. l.; N2 escris.
267   N6OP7Q S. vos; P7 u. petit r.; W afrescis, S6 regehis, S7 resjoïs.
268   Yb Et T. (S7 Tholome) a.; N2N6QQ1S1UW averoit; P7 c. del estre.
269   N5 v. par; P7 flatis.
270   S7 donnoient; P7Q1 f. de; N1 viz.
271   P6 lues, Rest: lors, N2N6OQS1W qu'o. b.; Q1 qu'il ont b.; N1 c'orent en ha b.,
S6 l. quant o. b., U l. tout maintenant a p. a r.; N1N6OQQ1S1W b. a l. p., P6P7
b. le p. o. (P6 a); N2 ont a p., N5S5S6 ont leur p., S7 b. leur p. ont r.
272   S6 Et T. d'E.
273   P7 Non por tant, O Neantmoins; Q1 d. respondre; P6Q1 ne fu m.; N5S5 n'e. pas,
S6S7 n'e. point; Ya n'e. pas apprentis; N2P7WYb esbahis. 273a P7 Ains
rainoit com vassaus sages et bien apris.
274   All om.

Laisse vi

275   P7 d. li vassaus; P6 reprendre.
276   N2 seroie; Ya s. apenser, S6 s. enseignier.
277   Q1 Car c'est; O l. p. saige; W qu'ens e. m.; N2P6Q1Yb qu'el (N5 qu'au) m.
saroie p., P7 Ya q. je saroie p.
278   N1 n. v. je p.; N1N6QS1U t. ces; P6 t. les biens d.; P7S7 entendre.
279   P6 m. aucuns, O m. i aucun, P7 m. sovent, N5S6 s'aucun, Q1 se aucun;
N5OP7S1S5S6U pour a.
280   All: Sont: O S. partout e.; P7 u. pas en .i. autre s.; Ya p. et d'autre p. s.; N5
point et en a. s.; N2W a. (W autres) pas; P6S5S6S7 e. a. point s. m.
281   P6 n. n. pot, N6 n. n. set, O nous n. p., U nul lie p.; P6Q1W le sens tout s.; Yb
sens ne (S5 om.) s.; P7S1 p. savoir tous les (P7 tot le) sens n. c.; N2QU
contendre, N6O entendre, W aprendre; N1 p. savoir les tous savoir n. c.
282   U Nonporquant; Q1 E. p. ce; N6OP6P7QS1U sauf t. d., S5S6S7 sur t. d.; OQU
n. volt; N2 c. allors n. v., P7 c. a lor dis v. t., P6 d. a autre n. v.; Q1S7 el v.
entendre.
283   P6Ya D. povre; U rendre.
284   N5S5 D. a E.; S5 om. 'le pris'; P7 d. d. i puis a.; Ya d. d. l. puis; N5OQS1
entendre, N6U contendre, N2 aprendre.
285   N1L. resors.

286   U Com; Ya e. sus (N1N6 s.) son pooir (N1 poier); P7 sor le p. seans comme c.; Q1 p. cueillant comme c.; N2N6OQS1UW c. com. c. Yb p. lorians com (S6S7 que la) c.

287   O les bons, N2 l. bons, S5 le bon; W q. ore; P7 s. s. devenu c.

288   U v. il; N2 om. 'venront'.

289   S1 Que; P6 l'o. fait p. le c. esprendre; Yb l'o. par oïr dire entendre; P7 poet on trop mies raprendre; Ya p. p. a (U au) c. reprendre; Q1 esprendre.

290   N5S5 Que qu' aucuns v. (S5 voirroit); S6S7 Que quanque uns verroit pour o.; OQS1 voiroit.

291   P7 P. tant; S6 om. 'ce de'; Q1 s. bon fait, N2 Ya Yb ce b.; N2 l'en v. b.; P7 li v. le l., N5S5 l'en v. le l., Ya l'en (S1 U le) veult (S1 v.) le l. n.

292   N2 N. de biauté d'autrui ne m. p. sourprendre; P7 W N. bontés; P7 d'a. rien; U b. d'autrui n.; Q1 Ya n. me; P7 soprendre, S1 souprendre, W as P, Rest: sorprendre.

Laisse vii

293   N5S5S7 om. 'tout'; N1P7S5 UW c. qui, N5O c. qu'il l., S7 c. que il l.

294   P7 estoit, Rest: seoit.

295   P7 om. 'il'.

296   N2 Ya Yb E. assez (O om.) emporteroit.

297   N2 Se, N6OP7QS1UW Ce; P7S7 d. je mie, P6 desdie pas; O om. 'ge'; Yb q. son v.; Ya q. cilz (U cist, N1 ce) vers (N1 ver) bel n. s.

298   N2 Ya Yb M. d'or (S6 de or, S1 om.) et d'argent est (S6 om.) et a.; Q1 est esmeré et a.; P7 d'a. et autre tel f.

299   S6S7 L. offrende; Q1 b. les p., N1N5S5 b. le p., P6 om. 'bien'.

300   P6P7W P. feroit; P6 a. qui s. c. m. donroit; OQ c. m'en d.

301   Ya om. 'se'; S1 U moi y m.

302   Ya Et s. (N1 ce, S1 si) vostre (N1 notre, S1 un) tresor (OQ t.); Yb Et (N5 Q.) de .v.; P7 c. restors; P6 t. de fin or me donnoit.

303   P7 Dont fist plus A. ki d.; S7 G. rien f.; S6 om. 'veu'; S5 v. dist; S1 c. veoit, N1 c. reçoit.

304   OQ Q. de dedens Phezon.

305   All: p. nul besoing; P7 b. il ne s'e. partiroit.

306   OQ om. S'; Q1 S'A. ses sires; N1N6QS1U n. l'efforçoit, OS6 n. le forçoit; P7 S'A meismes a forche nel ostoit.

307   S6 il le; P6 s. que a a., N1N5P7Q1S6S7 s. que avenir, S5 U s. qu'avenir li (U om.) e.

308   O Forte; N2S5 e. au, Q1 e. en; O v. que; N6Q1 s. preu, P7 s. pres, S1S5S6U si fort; N6 s'en s., N5S5S6S7 se tenoit, P7 s'en prendoit.

309   In P7 309 follows 315. N2 Que c'a., Yb C. ce a., P7 Et s'a.; Ya Ce avient a (OS1 en, N1 om.); S1 j. que en .v. n'avroit, N5 j. que en .vi. n'a., S6 j. qui en cent n'a., S5S7 j. qu'en .vi. c. n'a., N1P6 as P, Rest: j. qu'en .y. c. n'a.

310   P7 Car; Ya q. preus est a.

311   P7 La l.; P6 U ses p. s. c. l. sont si e.; Ya sont que (U qu'il); N2 set ses e., W s. con e.

312   P7 p. l'en s., S5S6S7 p. en s.; Q1 l. feroit mal, P6 l. s. griés; N6OQS5U q. li, N1Q1 q. le; P7 departiroit, U destour.

313   P7 om. P6 D'u. haute, Yb D'u. seule; P6Q1 o. grans p., N1 o. le haust p.; N2N6OQS1S5U j. un h. p., S6S7 j. un h. pas; OQS1 encharroit; N5 repeats 302 here.

314   S6 om. N6OQS1U Et, S7 Car; N5 p. bel bet, P7 p. beaus fais; N2 par .ii. bel fais c. l. t., Ya fait .ii. ités l. t.

315   P7 C. a b.; Yb aus biens trepassés; OQ avenir, Rest: revenir; S1 ni p.

316   Yb om. 316-8. N6P7W D. fist p.; P6 A. si com il me sambloit; N6P7 A. qui; Q1 ce se looit.

317   N1N6OQS1 om. 'Que chil'; N2W Q. touz (W tout) q. t.; U Q. t. l. v. e. a ce s'il avenroit; S1 e. chascun li avenroit; N6OQ avenroit, P6 acompliroit, P7 prenderoit.

318   P6P7Q1W C. a toute a.; N2 Ya Que (N2 Qu'a) trestoute (O toute) autre h. que

(N2 qu'a, O a) c. r; P6 autre amor; P7 autre chose; Q1 qu'a celui.
319   P7 E. par che; U E. de ma part je v. q. l. p. siens en s.; O m. p. le pris v. q. s. s.;
P6P7Q1W p. siens.
320   U om. P6 Et b.; P6 q. me d.
321   N1N6 et p., S6 p. le d. y metroit; N1 d. il m.
322   S1 A. n'en r.; OP7 en r. (O om.) et l. p.
323   P7 A. dist i. m. ke n.
324   S6S7 Neis; O est s. p. qui f. l. s.; P6 p. assés mius dire s.; N2 l. porroit.

Laisse viii

325   W Oues qu'A., Q1 Sors que A., P7S6 Lors (S6 Puis) quant A., S7 Ains que A.,
N2 Puis qu'A., Rest: Puis que A.; N2P6W ot f., Rest: ot fet; S1U q. fois.
326   P7 A. les; P6 p. vrais, W as P, Rest: p. biaus; P6Q1 m. mult, P7S6S7 m. et;
OS5 om. 'mos'.
327   All om.
328   P7 S. je ai s.; S1 S. si ay s.; N2P6P7Q1 s. n'est pas o. (P7 contre) m. p., Ya s.
n'est ce pas a redois, Yb s. (S6 s. je) ne fis (N5 fist, S7 sui) pas (N5 a, S7 pas a)
outrois.
329   Q1 Je ne sui q. c., Rest: C. (U C. se) je (WYb ne) sui q. (N2 com, P7 vos, Ya om.)
c.; W et ce n'e. qu'e., S1 ce n'e. qu'e., N1OQ n'e. a (N1 pas) el qu'e.; P6P7Q1 n'e.
fors. (P7 c'uns) e. (P6 qu'e.); Yb el (S7 om.) que e.
330   O om. 'doi'; S1 d. je a. c.; U a. a c., N1N6OQ om. 'mon'.
331   P7 N. de d. a darains p. c. ke j., W a darrains, N2P6Q1YaYb au derrain (P6
darrains, S7 deerain, Q1 daarain).
332   S6 om. O En mon m., N2 E. un m., P6P7W as P, Rest: En son m. (N5S7 mendre);
All: estat; W n. tres c. n. tres f,; U t. haut n.
333   P6 G. deseure virtus, N2Yb G. (Yb Ci a) s. verité, Ya G. fine (N6 faire) verités;
S5 v. ne trop chaus ne trop frois; P7 n. despont.
334   P7Q1 orrois, S6 orrés, S7 diroi, U diroit, Rest: dirois.
335   O om. 'fu'; Ya v. por eus (N1 proeuz, U P.) et grant a (U et a) la fois; P7 h. a
tous endrois; P6 v. hautains Porrus ce; N2 n'e. mi n., Q1 n'e. pas n., N5S5 n'e.
nul vois, S7 n'e. une gabois, S6 n'est...?
336   N2 c. gent des G., S6 c. les gens g., P7 c. tous les G., P6S7 encontre les G., W as
P, Rest: c. gens de G.
337   P7 om. 337-8. Q1 Qui.
338   N6 Q. de t., N1 Que t. b. vint; N6OS1 b. vient; P6 Que telle b. vaincre ce n'e.
m. avielois.
339   Ya est (O estre) o. (S1 contremontains, O montains) s. (U s. nesun)
contredois; N2P6Q1WYb o. preus s. n.
340   Yb d. ce; S5 f. ce, P7 f. li, S6S7 om. 'ses'; O s. deuz; P6P7 d. en p. de t., N1 d.
p. que .iii., S7 p. que t.
341   P7 t. son; P6P7W arcadiois, Q1 acardiois, N5S5S6 d'Arcadonnois, S7 de
Cardonnois, N1 au Cardonnois, N2N6U acardonnois, OQS1 ahardonois.
342   P7 om. N6OQS1 q. (S1 que) en d.; S6 e. duc; P6 d. de t.; S1 cortois.
343   N2YaYb om. P6 Par armes d. e. e. de c.; P7 d. tornois.
344   O et sans; N2P6WYa lai (U les); N5S5Ya p. dire a ceste f.; Q1 d. plus en l. a d.
.iii. c. f.
345   N1 t. c'est; P7 Porron de p.; P6 P. fais du p. l.; N5 d. dit fet; N1N2N6OQS5S6U
p. (N1 pres) fet.
346   P7 Ja par; O n. l'en e.; N1S6 escondirés, P7 estorderois.
347   P7 E. beaus r., S1S6 E. au roy., S7 E. vous avrés.
348   N1N2N6OQS1 Passe (N1 Passer, S1 P.) v. iert (O est N2 e.), S6 Passon nous en;
P7 ent a mains a.; N2 b. autrement iert l. d., P6 b. a a. est l. d., Yb b. car (S6
ja, S7 om.) autrement l'orrois (S6 l'orrés); S1U a. en iert l. d.

Laisse ix

349   P6 Lues q., Rest: Lors q. (S6S7 om.); N6 r. de G., U r. de Gresce, S6 l. bon

roy d. G.; P7 f. a tant aquités; P6U apaisiés, W acoisis.

350 P6 Emes li duc p.; P7 araisnés.
351 All om.
352 P6 e. ensengniés.
353 P7Q1 Porron; Ya D. paiens e. se (U de) sire e. e.; N2 se sires en; P6 se creus e. e.; Yb se soustenu estiés (S6 fussiés).
354 P6S5 E. si, N2 E. ce; U n. dit; Q1S7 d. g. mie, N5 om. 'pas'; P6 q. vous bien dit n'a.
355 P7 D'armes e. s. en amours adrechiés; P6 a. cler et liés; N5S5 a. criez.
356 N6 om. 'Et'; S6 om. 'li'; P6P7 q. je f. o. (P7 onke); N1U feusse o. (U onc); N5S5 o. mes; N2YaYb acointiés.
357 P6 Perducas e.; W G. en exceté p. q. j. fui; N5P6P7Q1 Ya e. de q. (OQ que).
358 S6 om. 358-394. P6 A ce veu n'a nul; N6OQU n'e. est. S1 c. ne est n., N1 c. n'et n.; O n. haubert r.
359 N2YaYb p. ce; S7 b. est, U b. n'es; Ya p. por eus (N1 riens) a.; N5S5 om. 'pas'.
360 W v. tel; N2N5P7S5S7W b. est; Q1 Ya b. s'est il m. a. (Q1 traveilliez); P6S7 f. bien; P7 f. plus ke prisiés.-
361 Q1 om. P7 Et; All: seroit; S1 om. 'por'; All: bien; S7 i ert.
362 Q1 E. tant que de; U d. mot; N2 f. affier; P7S7 f. est drois; All: taisiés.
363 N1 De querre; P6W f. pas, N5S5 f. peu, Q1 f. trop, P7 c. fu moult peu t.
364 O s. n. fu; N1 n. liés n. glués; N2 g. n. tailliez, N5N6OQS1S5S7U g. n. liés.
365 S7 N. ne s. si f.; Ya j. n'i (N6 om) s. plaiés (S1 plates) n. n'i sui empiriés; N5P6 om. 'si'.
366 N1 Q. je n. s. s. chut e.; N2 s. s. et c. et dreciez; Q1 trebuchiez.
367 P6 Se je f. si p. qu'o. m. jugiés; P7 E. s'estoie a. p. comme vos d.; N2N6OS1 f. ainsi; Q1 p. que ore d., N5S5 p. comme o. disiez, O p. come vous dissiez, S7 p. corageus m. teissis; N1N6QS1 deissiez, U disiez.
368 O fut; P7S5 f. tot, N1 om. 'trop', Rest: f. tous; W p. preus; N2W mais de t., P7 mais d...t(?), Rest om. 'de'.
369 Ya l'a. si ont l. v. tous e.; Q1 b. s'orent v.; P7 b. sor l.
370 N1 D. son u.; P7 Des grans humilités est c.; OP7S5S7 merveilliés.
371 N2N5S7 Ya Que; O ce soit; P7 plus ki adont f. h.; P6 plus fors; N2P6 fu; Q1 f. dessous les chiez.
372 N5S5 E. si e., S7 E. estoit; Ya p. ore, N5S5S7 p. oiant; P7 p. a oïr a.; U enviez, N5 esmaiez, S7 ariviés(?).
373 O om. 373-8. P6W r. du bon, P7 r. des bons, Rest: r. du b.
374 S1 L. vantres, N1 Ribautere, U L. venierres; P7 estre a. estre.
375 N1N6QS5S7U p. qui p., P7Q1 p. com p.; N1N6QU e. sans; S1 s. fais, N5P6 s. biens, S5 s. biens si, S7 s. biens est, N1N6QU s. biens fes; N2N5P7S5S7 avanciez, N1 anoncier.
376 P7 P. doute qu'il; N1N2 c. qui; N5 qu'il n'estoit; Q1 e. ou m., N2N5P6P7QS1 S5S7 e. ne m.; N1 om. 'et mokiés'.
377 N5S5S7 Que; P7 l. boins; S7 est dedens s. c.; N5P7S5 est en s. c. si (S5 om.) f.
378 P7 Ya Adés; Q1 v. prisier; N2 l. bien p.; N1N6QU l. (Q le) miex p., W l. mesprisiés.
379 N5OP7S5S7 Et; P7 f. chis, N5 f. ces; S7 o. fustes vous p.; U plungiez.
380 Q1S7W om. 'en'; S5 enseigniez, S7 essoingniés, N5P6 esmaiez; N1Q. per dit as bonna t. e. s. e.
381 N2 p. conme c.; N1N2QUW enragiés, N5S5S7 s. osés.
382 S7 Car; P7 cel v.; N2S5 Ya v. commencier, N5S7 v. commencie; S1 m. ni, P7 m. ne; U atachier, O arachier.
383 P6 Comme d.; N1N6QS1U Qui; P7S7 e. les biés, N5S5 e. les viés, N2N6P6Q1 e. les r., O en mille irez.
384 N5S5 Gentis hons, Q1 Vaillant h., N1 h. entre; P6 coragiés, Ya liés.
385 P6Q1 vilains; N1N2 c. cil; Q c. si n.; N5S5S7 c. et (S7 om.) cil estoit devisiés; N6O s. dez viez.
386 N1S1S7 Et; P6 Ya f. que; N5S7 a .xviii., S5 a .xiiii., P7 a .x. ours, Q1 a .x. cerfs, Rest: a .x. huis; N5S5S7 milliers, P7 desliiés, N2P6W verilliés, N1 barilliés, N6Q1S1U bresilliés, OQ bersilliez.
387 O om. N1 Aidiés; N2N6QS1U A. siet, N1N5S5 A. si est, S7 A. est; P7 c. tost v., Q1 c. uns v.; P7 v. ja si f. n'iert l.; U c. fox qui est l.; S1 f. quel s.; S7

chargiés, N2N5N6QS1S5U liés.
388 N5S5S7 h. ne puet estre longue (S7 longement) sus ses p.
389 All om.
390 Q1 391/390. S1 li veut S7 li vies; P7 f. moult; N5S5W c'outrecuidiés, Rest: outrecuidiés.
391 Ya om. 391-5. N5S5S7 c. voult; All: tailliés.
392 Q1 om. 392-5. P7 Q. a. d'un c. a tere e. t; N5S5S7 a c. ist et.
393 P7 Il est des anemis errant p. e. loiiés, N5S5S7 Et i. est lors p. (S7 pres) des anemis e. trebuchiés; N2P6W i. des anemis lues (N2 lors, P6 liiés) p. e. d.
394 P6 Ou ceval afoulés; N2N5P7S7 A c. (P7 cheval); N2P6S7W il n'i e., P7 il n'est bien a., N5S5 il n'est a.
395 S6 Quar bien f. l.; N2P6WYb v. doublés et e. (W renforciés).
396 N5 d. ma part, N2 d. part m.
397 Ya om. P7 Par; P7 n'e. mal jugiés.
398 UW om. N6 F. or le p. l., N1OQ F. or me lessiez (O laisse) p.; S1 F. or p. m. l.
399 U om. 399-879 (twelve laisses). N1N6OQ s. viez, S1 s. bien; N2P6P7YaYb d. parler a. (P6P7 avisiés).

Laisse x

400 N5S5 Q. Emenidus o., S6 Q. li dus o., Ya Q. Philocas parla.
401 Ya la l. si i., N2Yb la (N5 om.) l. tres i.; P7 a. langhe fresce et novelle.
402 N2 Trudelle, P6 Tutielle, S6S7 Rudelle.
403 Ya P. peus savoir de bien sans (N6 om.) ni (N1 vi, S1 vis) une f.; P6 a. d'amor; P7Q1S5S7 a. de bien (S5 b.) et d'ounor s; P6S6W d. bien.
404 S6 om. P6 Ens; P7 D'un tres doue s.; Ya p. ains que la mort m'a.; N5 o. quil; N2N5P7Q1S5S7W q. amours, P6 q. d'amor.
405 OP7S6 om. P6 Ya E. en jone revel (P6 jouvent, S1 penser) o. b. (N1 revel en bon); N2 ou j. revel ou quel a.; W E. .v. j. jouvens et b.; Yb E. amoureus revel ou on a mort revelle.
406 O om. 406-7. P6S6 Que, N1 as P, Rest: Qu'en; P7QQ1S1S5W r. d'un; N1 r. dont ot la metre esselle.
407 P6N6QW S. biens fais, P7 S. buffois; N1N6QS1 n'e. fais, N5S5 n'e. fet, S6S7 om. 'fors'; N2P6P7Q1W f. en; All: s. et.
408 P7 om. S6S7 de charriere.
409 S6 Donques n'i aroit r., N5P7S5 aroient, N1 avanroit, O avront; S7 aroit r. nee d. n. d.
410 P6 c. damoiselle, Rest: c. danselle.
411 N5 Que; Q1 de bon; All: oiant (P7 v.) m. pucele. 411a=419 Ya Un mauvés si est preux et cingle la praele.
412 OS7 e. son, Rest: e. a son; P6 l. comme, N2S6S7 l. et, Rest: l. com.
413 Ya L. seurtient et le d. nous apele; P7 L. si vaut moult chou chi n. n. r.; S6S7 tous; P6 t. cest, S5 t. se; N5S5 d. ne nous r.
414 P7Q1WYaYb om. N2P6 t. biens.
415 P7WYaYb om. Q1 416/415. P6Q1 l'estincelle.
416 WYaYb om. P6 proaice l.
417 YaYb om. P6 et p. s'a.; P7 est li a.
418 P7 D. si; Ya D. est mies (O mie) vaillant toujour q.; P6P7Q1S5S6S7 g. assés; P7 Yb q. la; N2 s. baiesse, S5 Ya s. dansele.
419 S6Ya om. Sec 411a. Q1 om. 419-20. N2P7S5S7W est bien; N2 et ploians com osere; N5S5 p. janglant com ostelle, S7 p. genglant come costelle; P7W c. com h.
420 All: u. cenele.
421 OS6 om. N2 N. joignons, N6Q1 N. sommes; N5S5S7 Nus gageour e.; S1 Mais ainsi e.; N1Q om. 'jugons'; N2P7Q1S5S7 e. com.
422 S6 om. N2Q1Ya Qu'on connoist p.; S7 Cognoist on p. d., N5S5 Congnoist S5...gnoist) p. de d.
423 P7 De c.; W D'onnour est; N5S5Ya c. ist, Q1 c. gist; P6 anoncielle.
424 Yb om. N6 om. 'tant'; Ya c. pas; N2Q1Ya en apele.
425 P7 om. S5S6 Que; W c. q. tourtereule, N2Q1YaYb; comble com tourterelle.
426 N2P6Q1YaYb om. 426-9. W F. cis ci p.; P7 F. cest dit tieng a favelle. 426a P7

Tel mot li valent peu a prover sa querelle.
427   P7 om. 427-9.
428   W dirai ja.
429   All om.

Laisse xi

430   P6 Lues, S7 Quis, P7 W as P, Rest: Puis.
431   P6P7 F. si (P7 se) monstra, W Et F. s'amoustre, N2YaYb F. sermonna.
432   O j'ai bien m. e.
434   Q1 Ya avés; All: Caulus.
435   Q Or; N5S5 est, O estoit; N6 om. 'pris'; All: plus h. v. (N1 om.); OP6 ot v., Rest:
       a v.
436   S7W Com; P6 t. le h. al h.
437   O Comme, S1 as P, Rest: Com; S1 l. doudant; N1 Vaudres; O t. ert, N1N2QQ1
       t. ot.
438   N5 om. P6 Que l. grant d., P7 Cui l. d., W as P, Rest: E. que l. d. o. si (O om.).
439   N6P7 Qu'a; N1 roi de; S5S7 q. (S5 ou) tant a de fierté, Q1Ya q. tant a poesté
       (N1 a de posté).
440   Ya a tolu; O l'espee; N5 s'e. en milieu s. barné, P7 s'e. tout e. s. barné.
441   P6 h. haus et t.; S5S6S7 t. grant p., Ya d. grant poesté, Q1 d. riche p.
442   P7 Ki a en p. e. si; P6 plaine; N1 assené.
443   N1N2N5 Que v., P6 Qu'a homme; P7 a l'eaume jus rué.
444   Yb Et; S5 c. mie; W a l'esbuque; P6P7Q1 la (P7 om.) boule (Q1 bille, P7
       billes) ne au; S1 b. ni al; N1N5N6OQS5 b. valdé, S6 a b. de valdé, S7 a b. n'a
       truel.
445   OQ a la f. des (Q de son) b.; P6 f. des; S1 a desir d. b. a force e.
446   Ya E. la r.; N1N6Yb r. que.
447   N1N6OP6P7S1 Que; N1N2Q1S7 sourpris; O n. enginé, N1 n. anginnié, P7 n.
       encanté, N5 n'e.
448   P7 A. n'en a. moult bien n.; W A. l'avoit.
450   W om. N2 l'a. poisie et englumé, P6 l'a. u poé et glué, Yb l'a. cloé et (S6 ne) e.,
       P7Ya p. et (O ne) e. (P7 aglué).
451   S6 om. P6S7 Ou s'il, P7 Et s'il, S5W Se il; N2 il avroit, Q1 n'eüst, N5N6S5S7
       n'a. les bras brisiez; Ya b. et desloé (S1 dessolé); N2Q1Yb ou desnoué (S7
       desnoués).
452   S5 om. 452-6. S1 Et; N5S7 aroit, P6 l'avroit; P7 c. de; S6 d. corps; S1 d. bus
       osté.
453   S6 om. W om. 453-6. S7Ya A; N5 E. a h.
454   Q1 Et t.; P7 Et d. t. met son; S6 t..je met; Ya j. ce (S1 se) v. si (S1 ci, N1OQ om.)
455   P6P7 Q. en ce point, N2Q1YaYb Q. a ses p. (Ya piés); N1P6Yb si seurmis, Q1
       si surpris.
456   Ya Et; N5 a si l. c.; P6 om. 'si'; S7 c. tout desmué; O defraié, P7 desiewé, S1
       dessevré.
457   P7 Ke s'o.; N6S7 S'o. devoit; P7 om. 'le'; N1OQS1 por ce; N1 e. en.
458   N6 S. airoit; S5 b. Porrus.
459   N2 om. 459-61.
460   P7 M. je sui chi tous pres assés m. e., YaYb M. veez m. t. p. d. m. (S7 moy) d.
       apresté.
461   All om.

Laisse xii

462   N2 Sire d. L. p. le dieu; P6 de C.
463   N1N6QS1 tient, N2 B. say, P7Q1 B. croi; N6 n. de nos; S6 v. ne de v.; N2 d.
       voer mi f.
465   W om. P7 465/464. Q1 M. encor n'e. par vous l.; O encores; Yb encor n'e. p.
       dit le voir n. a. (S6 v. bien plus certains, S7 v. veant ains); P7 v. dires a.
466   N6S6S7 c. de L. (S6 l'onme, S7 Loinne); N5S5 p. pains, S1 p. estains, N1N6P6

S6S7 p. (N1 presse) plains.
467 N1 Q. donna; P6S7 j. a l'un; All: des s.
468 Ya F. ier (S1 est, O estoit) au r.; P7 F. ainnet a C.; S6S7 Le (S7 Des) fils au r.; N2N5S5 om. 'fort'; OQ1 que (Q1 q.) de ire e., P6W q. d'irour e. P7 ki d'estours e., S6 q. estoit d'ire, Rest: q. d'ire e.
469 N6OP7QS1Yb E. si; N5 si le jour; N1 t. abrigier e. destains, P7Yb estrains.
470 N2P7 Que c. (N2 cest), P6 as P, S7 Que en (om. 'ce), Rest: Qu'en ce; S7 meismes l'eure.
471 P7 Car l. j. d'aucuns v.; N1 jour, N2S7 om. 'veus'; N1 samblent, P6P7 sanla; S1 s. plus, N6 om. 'trop';
472 P7 L. preu vuelent a.; N1 om. 'preus'; O v. tousjours; W e. li; S7 Tousjours v. l. preus e.
473 N1N5N6OQS5S6 le couart failli; P6 trescule a, O se reculle des, S7 recules au, N1P7 reculent au (P7 a), Rest: recule aus (Q om. N6S1 de, S6 au); S1 serrains, QS7W as P, Rest: darrains.
474 OP6P7Yb n'est.
475 P7 m. se cointains; N2Q1YaYb lorains.
476 N5 Et lors qu'il, Q Lors qu'il, P6 as P, Rest: Lors que il; S5 il l'ot, Q1W om. 'ot'; O l. Phezonnois, P7 as P, Rest: l. (P6 le) Phezonnains.
477 P7 q. le; N1N5OS5 le viellart h. (O hermitoys), S6 l. vaillans h.
478 P7 S. n. l. faisoit.
479 All om.
480 P6 M. l. qu'il, Rest: M. (Q1Ya Et) lors qu'on (P7Q1S5 qu'il); S6S7 ot congié; W c. par, Yb c. jus l. (S5 aus, S6 es); N1N2N6QS1 c. sus l. (N2 le).
481 P6 C. parlier.
482 N5S5 La j. a s. f. l'a. (N5 a Canaus); S6S7 A jouster a s. f. q.; N1 l'a. que; N2N5S5S6W d'o. iert atains, N1OQ d'o. en (N1 est) hateins, N6Q1S1 d'o. est (Q1 ert) hautains.
483 N6 om. P6 f. qu'il ot; N1O il ot; N1N5OP7Q om. 'je'; S1 l'o. de ce ne sui d.; N5P7 s. mie.
484 O Et; P6 par voer p.; N2P7Q1WYaYb par grant; N1OQS1 v. veoit, N6 v. vooit, N2 v. voloit, N5S5S6 v. vouer, S7 v. vooir; N2P6P7WYa haus p. (O om.); Yb grant p. estoit (S7 e.); P6S6 atains.
485 N1N6OS1 Liaine; P7 L. en devroit, S7 L. si devroit, N1N2N5OP6QS5 devroit r.; Q1 L. regneroit toudis a.; O r. avecques.
486 S6 Donques l.; S7 D. li pires avra; Q1 Le pris emportera d. d.; P7 Si en ara l. p. par droit; N1P6 p. avra par (N1 de); N2S5S6S7 d. droit ci (N2 si) ert de (N2S5 l.); O d. d. est l.; P6P7 droit j'en sui c.
487 O est sailliz e. flory je le tiens; Q et failliz c. riens; Yb et florist, N1W et foillus.
488 All but W om. 488-91. W m. est.
491 W q. est m.
492 All om.

Laisse xiii

493 Ya Chascun si o. m. son c. p.; P6 c. en s.c. monstra m. v.; P7Q1W o. m. (P7 monstrer) son c. p.
494 Ya a bien et (S1 et a) bel; S5 p. et bel; N2 b. les.
495 P6 om. 'et'.
496 W Sagement.
497 N1 dites; O d. v. s'il v. p. que j.; Yb p. en qui tous biens (S6 qui tout bien) ondoie; N1N2 p. si v.
498 P7 S. f. de son c.; O f. ou, S7 f. el.
499 P6P7Q1W Signeur; N5S5S6 tout bien.
500 P6 P. me le p.; O Prest; N1 sui du; OP6 p. je v. p. q. o. (O l'o.); P7 si prie q.
502 N5S6S7 greigneur; P6 l. plus grant v.; N2 l. grande; O l. grant v. si creüe e. e.; N1S1 S'argue; Yb Se (S5 S'en) sonniee en e.
503 S6 W om. P7 d'espee; N2N5N6OQS1 b. me d.
504 P7 v. ke bien r.; N2Q b. le; S6 ramentevroie.
505 P7 e. plenier; N1N2O n. le; All: saroie.

506   Ya Corageux c.; N2 c. com; P6 quoie.
507   S6S7 a. vous (S7 je) e.; Yb diroie, OQ avroie.
508   O Ne pour tant; P6 les p. grans b. les e.; Ya p. preu moult b. e.; S6S7 b. en e.
509   S6 om. N5 A li aide, Rest: A l'aide; N2YaYb s'a la (O om.) court; Q l. trovroie, P7 l'en avoie.
510   O om. 510-19; N1Q li v., S1 les v; N1 e. ne saroie.
511   P6 C. F. e. mult grant se; Q1 C. c. Raison; S1 moustre; Yb combines 511, 513: C. c. F. e. droit (N5 om.) amours a li aloie.
512   Yb om. 512-3. P7Q1 t. sormonte; N1 ploient.
513   P7 om. S1 F. a. lui A. a. l. s'aloie.
514   P7Q1YaYb e. que; Q P. li voie, Yb P. renvoie, N6 P. je voie.
515   N1 D. le convoite, Rest: D. le convoie.
516   S6 om. 516-9. N5S5S7 s'esbanoie.
517   N2Q1YaYb r. et Amours.
518   N6Q et fol venir d.
519   N2YaYb om.
520   P6P7 s'e. tel, N2 s'e. cest; Yb m. tenoie.
521   Yb P. proesce; P6Yb v. je n. m'e. (Yb m'i) a. (Yb attendroie); N2 atenroie; Ya combine 521-2; Pour prendre mon neveu (S1 nonage) ja ne m'en atendroie.
522   Ya om. Q1 s. requise; N2 p. n'en e.
523   P7 a. ja; N6 p. nel c.
524   S1 A. car, P7 W as P, Rest: A. et.
525   P6P7 Car (P7 Ne) je n'ai r., N2 Ne i a r., Q1 N'il n'y a r., YaYb Ne n'i a r.
526   W escondis; N1S5W i o., Rest: et o.
527   W g. ce m'e. v. autrement m.; P7 forferoie.
528   N6QS1 a nostre a., N1N2 a vostre a., P6 a lui amis; N1N6O v. ai.
529   P6 N. lui va refusers, Rest: N. d. lui r.; S6 om. 'se'; P6 s. d. li; N6 l. savoie.
530   N2N6OQS1S5 tient; OS1 c. et; O l'a. le.
531   NaYaYb Car; N6 g'i prens. S1 g'i pers, Yb g'i tien, P6P7 je i p.; Yb dessoie; P7 p. A. d. cel f.; Yb dessoie.
532   S5 om. 'se'; P6 om. 'de'; Q cel r., Rest: tel r. (O nulle); Ya estoie, N2 usoie.
533   Q1 pourchaçoie, N2YaYb requeroie.
534   N1N6Q Tout, S1 Tant i ai; Ya ge trouvé (N1 droissie); N2 p. la r.; S5S6S7 soufferoie; P7 p. r. ki souffir doie.
535   S7 Dont; Ya l. p. si (N6 se); P6 donnoie.
536   S6 om. N5Q1S5S7 s. se a.; Ya s'asener (O s'a seur) la pooie.
537   N2N5S5S7Ya F. et (N1 om.) A., Q1 F. avec A., S6 Quar F. et A.; Yb otroie, P7 aloie, N2 avroie.
538   Yb om. 538-53. N2Ya D. cuit (N6 cuic, O cuide) q. (N1N6O que) b. (N1N6 bonte); O l'un sache l'autre d.; P6 om. 'et'; P7 et loie; N2Q1WYa desroie.
539   P7 om. N2 f. amours; N1 h. au; P6Ya .ii. l'autre p.; N1N6OQ n. l. voie; P6 n. devoie, N2 p. n'en avoie.
540   N2P7Q1 Ya Yb om. W D. A.
541   P6 Forte; Ya est amours (S1 d'amours); O roeroie.
542   Q1 e. ces t.
543   P6Ya n'avra, P7 n'aroi.
544   N1W t. part, P6 t. paist, P7Q1 t. puet, Rest: pt=pert or part (?)
545   O Et; P7 A. a, N6OQS1 A. et; OQ trouveroie.
546   Ya M. F. et Amour mon cuer a c. s'a.; P6 s'otroie.
547   S1 Force qui b.; N1P6 le, Rest: li.
548   O om. Q1 om. 'se'; Q s. devra; N1 E. ce donray d., P6 om. 'de'; N1Q encoie.
550   N6OQS1 Ce, P7 Se a a.; O que a.; P6 autre mari signor querre i a.; N2Ya querre.
551   Q1 om. 551-2. For 550a-e see notes. P6 s. meïment, Ya s. me vient q.; W q. l'en esseuteroie; N2Ya je en sentiroie; P6P7 j. (P6 jel) n. (P6 nel) sentiroie.
552   P6S1W M. ami ou, P7 M. ami a, Rest: M. ami ne; P6 autrui a; P7 d. seroie.
553   N2P7 F. est; P6P7W a a conquester; N2Q1 mestroie; Ya F. encontre son cuer sont qui (N6 que) A. mestroie.

Laisse xiv

554 ⸱ P6 o. sans point de.
555 P7 avanchier, N1N6Q essaier.
556 O s. peut; P7 v. attargier.
557 Yb ala la.
558 S6 om. N2Q1 Ya Yb q. tant; N1P7S5S7 fet; S1 a loer.
559 P7 l. hyraus; N1P6 om. 'me'.
560 N5S5 Q. a; S6 Q. l. v. pure v. v.; OQ om. 'de'; O l. v. si v. v.; N1 v. ci d.; Q1
      eslongier.
561 S6 om. 561-83. O l. mieux.
562 W om. 562-75. P6 Ne; N5S5 s. plus n'essigier, S7 s. riens du monde jugier; Q1
      p. ne; N2Ya p. (O parolles) ne esligier.
563 S1 Que v., Rest: Qui v.; O om. 'voit', Q1S1 voy; P6P7 v. as (P7 a) plains c.;
      N1N2N6QS1Yb v. sus.
564 N2 Aignelot, P6 Angeles, P7 Angle tot; N5N6S1 despennés, S7 espennés, N1N2
      OQS5 despanés; N1 au destarner, OQ au destraver, N6S1 au destraiier, P7 a
      desrainier.
565 P7 j. esmervellon a l.; N2 e. en, N1 e. au.
566 N5 om. O om. 566-9. P6P7 Et; P6S7 a. lances e. (S7 abaissier); S5 a. chevaus
      desrengier.
567 P6 M. esprové qu'o.; P7 d. provenche; P6P7Q1 puist, QS1 puis, N1 puit gynier.
568 P7 a. par grans cos b.; P6 o. a b.
569 N5S5 om. 'cors'; S7 q. getter p., P6 q. grans c.; P7 gent en armes poroient
      esligier; N2P6Q1 Ya Yb franc cuer (N2P6Q f. c.) esligier.
570 N2Q1 E. espee m. (N2 melle).
571 N2 om. 'vient'; N1OS1 v. a v. (O vray); P7 vint a v. d. et a d., N2YaYb et au
      (N1OQS1 a) voir; P7 pronunchier, N1 desnier, P6 as P, Rest: desrenier.
572 N2P6YaYb V. ne s.; P6 a. v. veul, N2 a. v. vus.
573 O om. P7 D'a tourblet; N2P6 Yb d'e. ou.
574 P7S1 r. a b.; P7 contraliier; O combines 574/5:L. h. qui ne scevent fors que
      flavoler.
575 O om. N2P6Q1YaYb Q. ne s.; P7 o. et v., N2Q1YaYb o. ains v.; N1N2QYb
      flavoier, N6 faubloier.
576 O s. parolles, S7 s. plus; N5 p. dames; Ya d'a. et; N2 l'e. ne p.; N1 d'a. et de
      tournes p. c.
577 P7 l'e. et, W l'e. se; YaYb si ne s.
579 N2YaYb o. et (N2Yb om.) haute oevre (N2 o. et) conter (N5S7 commencier,
      N2S5 convoitier); P7 ce i a m., Q1 ce a bon m.; 579a Q1Ya Parler pour (N1
      puet) loialment jugier (Q1 les) fais d'armes (O d'autruy, Q d'autres) jugier. See 583.
580 P6 om. 580-1. N1N6QS1 Que q., Q1 Car q., O Et que d., Yb Qui d. a. (N5
      d'armes); P7 Dont chis ki d'armes v. s. le droit m.
581 Q1YaYb om. 581-2. N2W P. pour p.; P7 Doit penser porpenser h. o. sans
      tenchier; N2 om. second 'et'.
582 N2 om. P7 por cel; P6 por .i. g. f. p. u c.
583 Q1 Ya om. See 579a. P6P7 l. les; P6 f. d'amor.
584 Ya Ce est (N1 C'est); P7 g. mesfais; 584a Q1 Et de tolir honnour car elle couste
      chier.
585 Ya q. le (OQ les) volés or (O om.) t. (N1 taillier).
586 W om. Ya Ne pas (O om. N2 p.); P7 desvoiier, N2YaYb forvoier.
587 All: Ignorance; Ya f. (S1 voy) durement d. (O forvaier); P7 f. vers le tort
      atachier; S5 forvoier.
588 P7 om. 588-9. P6 Vous; S1 O C.; W laist, P6OQ1 laisse, Rest: lait; S7 lait vers l.
      v.; P6 le droit.
589 P6 Vous, O en; P6 vers tort, N2N6W v. la cort, N1OQ v. le cuer, S1 v. le hurt,
      N5S5 v. les tors, S6S7 v. les corps.
590 P7 Et; P7 l. voir n.
591 W om.
592 N2 om. 'je'; W v. se; S5 lessier.
593 All om.
594 P6 W En; P7 En v. a reconnoistre; N2Q1Yb En c. le (Q1 om.); S1 En c. le bien
      sans mauvés r.; N1N6OQ En c. le voir (O vray) de (N1 du) r.; N2P7 n'a point
      de r.; S6 n'a mal ne r.; N5 reprochier.

Laisse xv

595	Q1 om. 595-1043, laisses xv-xxv. P7 l. hyraus; P6S1 diex de; N1 Galdois.
596	S5 n'e. blasme, N1 n'e. avantage n.; P6 n'a o. n. destrois.
597	O B. osa.
598	P6Ya L'espee; S6 Son e.; N1N5S6 om. 'hors'; P7 fors d., N5 de ses p.; N1 p. mes; OQ et conquis l. conrois.
599	O Si; N5 a. desclaver, P7 a. enrachier; N5OQ le h.; N1 viannoies,
601	N5 a. bon r. des Greiois, P6 r. macidonois; S1 a. mal; N1N2 n. desrois (N2 desroy), S6 n. desfoirs.
602	N1N6QS1 s'en vanta, O as P, Rest: se vanta; P6 v. voiant l.
603	P7S6Ya De v. (S1 vaintr'a, N1 v. en) l.; P6 b. a e., Q b. contre, N5 b. au bon e. l. G.
604	P6 j. sans defois.
605	S1 Q'il a., P6 Et qu'il a.; OQ om. 'Ferrant'; P6S1 a. qu'il.
606	S6 om. 606-7, N5S5 A. veue c. n'e. nul vois; N2Ya c. n'e. pas (N2 mi) n. (OQ rois, S1 bois, N6 drois), S7 yce est drois, P7 ce est li voirs.
607	P6W A servir, P7 A aidier P. a sortenir s.; N2YaYb A vengier P. a d. s (O se d.
608	P7 om. O m. contre; P6 les .ii. rois.
609	N5OP7S1S5S6W Aveques; P6 A. le pieton avec les b.; All om. 'gens'; S1 p. aguisiés d. b.; N5 p. entre les .ii. conrois; N2OYb p. en.
610	N1OQS1 A; All; Lyones; S1 f. Charle; Q ly Indois.
611	S5 a f. au filz Claruus l'Yndois; N1 arabias.
612	P7S7 courtois, N1 noirois; S1 b. air (?) drois.
613	P6 b. as vairs iex as c., P7 b. ki porte les c., Ya b. qui avoit les c.
614	P6 om. See 621a. S6S7 De amer (S7 s'amer), N2W Ya A amé; P7 om. 'penser'; N1 p. bisel; N2 plaiz, OQ v. plains.
615	N2P7S5Ya om. 'Et'; N2P7YaYb Fesonas; S7 om. 'a'; All om. 'en'; P7 e. le m. a son c., N2P6WYa eu m. t. a son c., Yb eu ami (S6 ami tout) a s. c.
616	N2 D. part; Yb r. de Gresce; Ya s. parler autre fois, N2Yb s. penser (N2 penser a) autre v.
617	W n'e. douteroie, O n'e. donne, N1 n'e. diroie.
618	P6 ce pooit.
619	N1N6Yb M. ce (N6 se, N1 ces); O ses deux sont si.
620	O Ce me s.; N1N6S1 vision; P7Yb vision et (S7 ou, N5S5S6 om.) fantosme ou (P7 el) vision; N1P6 f. ou; O babois.
621	N5S5S6 combatois; 621a P6 A amer son ami sans penser vilains pois.
622	Ya p. bien de li mes est aux (N1 a, N6S1 d.) a. r.; S6S7 et des a. est (S7 om.) r.; P7 m. si ke me samble voirs.
623	O om. Ya a. raençon m. o. je me c.; P7 r. dire; Yb o. noiant m'i.
624	S6 om. 624-5. S1 C'est; Yb N. vous; P7 dans Clins, N1O Dandin; P6 q. s'en; P7 s. tairoit, S1 s. troit; OQ q. s'en teroit c. (O roys).
625	N1 Ge; N6 D. nos; OQS1 Se vous s. (O seul); W v. s. sens lesseriés et feriés a; P6 assenés, O asevrés, N6 asenrienz, N2QS1 asevriez, Yb asseneriez la (S7 bien la) court a; N1 p. tost; N1S7 rebois, Rest: redois.

Laisse xvi

626	P7 dans Clins, O Dandin.
627	OQ Que; W om. 'doit'; S1 d. au nier; S1 contraille.
628	N2YaYb Veil dire du; P6 e. le.
629	OQ l. bien; Ya G. ne mantir (S1 matir?) ne, N2N5 G. mantir e. (N5 ne), S5 G. a. ne, S7 G. noiantir ne, S6 G. desmentir ne, P6P7 G. amenrir ne.
630	W om. 630-1. N6 Car par sez h.; OQ h. de tout s.; All: repaire.
631	P6 E. quanqu'il i c., P7 E. tot che ke c., O E. quancuns c.; All: c. a; P6 p. faire.
632	N2P7Ya b. penser, S7 b. peser; W b. p. par.
633	Ya d. a; N1 Yb q. tout bien; P7 Yb repaire.
634	S7 q. sont; S6S7 om. 'de'; S6 p. p. a ce fere.
635	N1 t. ces; N1N2P7Yb p. la, P6W p. leur; All: retraire.
636	P6 un vaissel, Rest: un vassal; S7Ya a tous bien t., P7S6 a bien (S6 biens)

atraire.
637 N5 om. 'Et'; P7 om. 'por'; Ya om. 'boins'; N2Yb f. aus bons (S7 autres) m.
(N5S5 mireour, S6S7 mirouer) et (S5 om.) e.; P7 t. les b. Ya mirouer (S1
mireoir) d'examplaire.
638 P7 p. de nullui p.; N2P6 traire, N1N6OQYb atraire.
639 Q Et; N1QW s'espee, Rest: l'e.; P7 q. tout maire.
640 W om. OQ G. que; P7 G. a cui nus ne s'apaire; S6 q. de t. preus est m.
641 OQ Si se, P7 Si ke; P6 B. a d. vis, P7 B. a gent cors d.; S7 a. regart d.,
N5S5S6 a. bon roy, OQ a. deus r., S1W d. roy
642 P6 M. de s.; N6OQYb p. son.
643 W om. 643-5.
644 P7 a nul; P6P7 n. se (P6 om.) laisast; N1 traire.
645 OP6P7S1 Que; N2 Qu'il li; N6 lairoit; P7 le poil; P6 d'u. penne, N6 d'un p.; S7
nere.
646 Ya Quant d. tele g.; P6 d. del.
647 P7 L'e.; N6 S'e. d'autrui v.; N1OQS1 a autrui ber (N1 per, S1 n'est); P6P7 v.
nus a. ne doit p. (P7 ne s'apaire); N5S5S6Ya d. nul autre p., S7 d. a autres p.
647a P6P7 Dont il ara le pris s'on ne lui veut fortraire (P7 sortraire).
648 P6 n. soin ge g., S1 n. sui je g. S7 n. v. sai g.
649 P6 t. comment que m. d. plaire, Yb t. plus que a tez (S5 tel, S6S7 om.) .X. p.
S6 .x. autre p.), N2 Ya t. bien plus qu'a (N2 que a) .X. (S1 .IX.) p.; P7 p. ke m.
650 All om.

Laisse xvii

651 P7 Sire d. M. ki .i.; P6 M. .i. p. me sui trop t.; N2 p. sui t.; P7YaYb om. 'se'.
652 P6 D'onnour d.; P7 De v.; S1 v. desermouner; N2YaYb p. deceus.
653 P7 N. de tot sortenir; N6 du voir; N2P7WYaYb ne sui pas (O point) c.
654 P6 a. i est.
655 N2 l. bel F.; S5 F. fu.
656 S6 om. P7 Et p. b. a voer e. a c. p. c.; N1 Le cors p.; S7 et li p. precious; O p.
corsus.
657 P7Yb Se a (N5 S'a) m. e. estoient l. h. (P7 profis); O en estoit; N1S1 li
honores li p.
658 P7 A. je ne saroie; S5 l. creu c.; O creneus.
659 Yb D. cuit (S7 De ce) qu'il a.; Ya D. cuit (S1 tuit, O soit) que li chevaus
est (S1 et) p.; P6 q. la cieu; P7 p. deseure p.; OW et contre.
660 S1S6S7 E. (S7 Encor) la r.; OQ En apraia r. que; P7 noreus, N1 vareus, Yb
varieus.
661 N5 Ya e. fors (O fort) d. et; N2 d. fors; S6 d. et fort c.; S5S7 d. et fors e.
chevelus.
663 N2Yb om. P7 S. le v. amours encoste les p.; WYa combine 663/664 thus: W S.
v. E. a. tours as fenestreus, N1 A la voir au fenestres d. t. et d. sotiers,
N6OQS1Si avoit as (OQ a) fenestres (O senestres) d. t. et d. o.
664 WYa om. P7 E. a; P7Yb hautes fenestres; P6 f. de t.; P7 del hosteus.
665 S1 s. le, S7 s. si; W l. jetoit; P6 d. vrais regars.
666 Ya l. remenoit (N6 menoit); N2 r. .i. sien; S1 c. si, P7 c. tres, Yb c. en.
667 W om. Yb Dont (S7 om.) c. (S6 om.) devoit b.; S1 T. iche d.; P7 ce puet; N6
ce donner doit; Ya om. 'bien'; N1P7Q c. a c., O c. et c.
668 S6 W om. P7 v. en voer, Yb v. as honneurs, N2Ya v. et honour; N5 l. plus; Ya
l. miex euereux.
669 N5 d. tout; N1OQ f. (Q fust) il (OQ om.) moult plus; P6 f. ses; N2N6P6P7S1
WYb v. moult p.; Q aventurer.
670 P7 om.
671 S6 om. 671-2. Ya Mes; S1 s'amour; P6P7 q. fait les c. joieus; N1N6QS1 q. le
cuer; Yb f. uiseus; N1 f. miex, OQ f. muer.
672 Ya q. (N6 om.) a donné force; N2 Yb d. force; Yb p. pereceus.
673 N2P7 q. par, Ya Yb q. sus; N1N6P6P7QW t. (P6 om.) ces, Rest: t. ses; N2 f. fu
si tres e.; N5S5 om. 'par'; S6S7 f. il fu s. (S6 bien) e.; P7 f. refu s.; O fu li; S1
envieux.

674   S6S7 s. l'un; N2 fust; P6P7 f. acomplis, O f. asené; N1 f. a ces fes v.
675   P6 l. n'i d.
676   All om.
677   N2 Et, S1 Qui, N1N5N6OQS5S7 Que; O a. que; P7S1W envieus, N2 Yb airex, N1N6OQ eureuz.
678   P6P7 n'en s.; P7 envieus.
679   P6 s. trop diseteus; S6 mie trop; N5S5S7 om. 'molt'; W m. tous diseteus; N1 m. m. desirier; P7 Car d. m. d. orains ne s. pas diseteus.

Laisse xviii

680   Yb T. or voi.
681   N1 nus de, Q n. tez; N2 v. n'afiert; P6P7 Ya v. ne sert f. a l., Yb v. ne fet f. que (S5 om.) lui (S5 le sien).
682   P6 a droit r. et bien e.; N5S5 b. esgarder; P7 r. a droit.
683   N1 Le recort.
684   N6 t. ces viex viaire et; N1OQ l. viex, S1 l. siens.
685   O m. que; P6 q. donne ensegnement; S7 q. les autres comprent.
686   P6 Moustrant l. f. p. si figureement; P7 l. tens.
687   Ya om. 'Que', N5S5S7 Car; N2 d. homs f. ensi m. e.; Ya b. i f.; W om. 'faice'; Yb f. aussi (S6 si) o. m. e.
688   Yb om. 688-9. O en y a; W ert de; P6 preus en ce; Ya par ce.
689   N6OQS1 toutes r. (O choses), P6 t. veus; N6 contenement.
690   P7 Yb E. moult g. (S7 de) bien a.; N2P6W mains; Ya m. bien (N6 om.) si a.; N1S5S6S7 p. d'esmouvement; S1 d. monnestiant.
691   Q l. bons; O les verront; P6 v. si.
692   Yb Li; Ya L. tres (N1S1 tous) b. ancesor c'ont v. (N6 om. c', N1 ancesour couronné) noblement; N2 Yb ancientour (N2S6 ancesor) qui (S6S7 om.) o. v.; N2S6S7 s. noblement; P7 L. a. voerent s. tres hautainement.
693   OQ A, Rest: Et; Yb l'o. a (S6 ont) conquis a (S6 si a) la fenissement; P7 l'o. qu'il aquisent a l'acomplissement; S1 qu'o. aquiert, N1N6Q qu'o. a quise; Ya a l'a; N2 a. a l'achevissement, P6 a. a le sovenissement.
694   OQ om. P7 Il entreprenderont p. amoreusement; N2 Il emprendroient p. a mon avisement; S7 enprendront bien p.; N1N6S1 amenuisement, Yb anciennement.
695   Yb om. N6OQS1 U. griex, P6P7 U. grant, N1 U. grain; N1N2 f. plus; N6 f. d'o. p.; N2P7W b. les, P6 b. lor; Ya consent. 695a Yb Un de nos mestres dist et raison si assent. See 705.
696   Ya p. grant; P7 p. cesti voement; S6W c. avoiement.
697   O om. 697-8. Ya r. e. vouant (N1 recors estrovant) sera commencement; Yb s. creü m.; N2P6 om. 'a'.
698   P7 D. fist p. E. en son r.; S6 Donques; Yb om. 'plus'; N2WYb e. cest r. (S6S7 recouvrement).
699   S6 Q. ceuls; N5S5S7Ya tous; N5 om. 'qui'; N5OP6S5S6 voudront, P7 vaura; P7S7 f. droit, S1 f. maint, N1 f. autre, Rest: f. vrai.
700   P6 om. 'Et'; S6 E. se A.; P6 A. li d.; P7 E. s'aucuns d. ensi k'il est d'o. et; S1 d. qui est d'o. et; S6 om. 'est'.
701   Ya E. qu'atant. N2N5S6S7 E. (N2S6S7 om.) qu'autretant; P7 E. un autre en; S6 f. l'orimiers, S7 f. l. ormiers, O les o., N1 f. .i. o.; P7 bonnement.
702   N6P6W a. solaire, P7 a. loiier; N6 pairement.
703   P6P7 P. cesti v. mener; P6 om. 'a'; P6WYb anientissement, N2P7 amenrissement, N1N6 amatissement, OQ amarissement, S1 amassissement.
704   N2P7YaYb e. trop; N5P7 malement.
705   N6 U. dez m.; Q vos.
706   Ya don ou.
707   OQ om. Yb il v. (N5S6S7 a voué) et je m'assent; P6 ou li ou o. l. prent; P7 au l. u vent; N1N6 on l'atent; S1 tent.
708   O om. N6 om. 'que'; Ya cis en donne et a.; P7 l. donner e.; Yb d. l'entent.
709   P7 Et; O se E.; P7 a tout che e., Yb a ce mien enscient; P6W c. dont, N2 c. dons, Ya v. ases (N1 a ces, QS1 a ses) dons (N1N6 dous, O doux) e.
710   All: Nous; OQ d. composer; P6P7 s. tout.

712   S6 Que on p., S7 Q. ne p., Rest: Qu'ele p. (P6 pot); Yb s. mon (S5 mien).
713   P7 Ni p. p. esjoir; W om. 'por'; N2P7WYaYb couvent.
714   Ya om. P6 p. Porus l'I.; P7 Porron trestout p.; Yb l'I. proisier; S6 om. 'sor'; N2Yb t. (S6 tout) especialment.
715   N5P7 d. cest, N1OQS1S6S7 d. tel; All: esbatement.
716   O om. 716-34. N2N5P6W c. l'en; S6S7 c. si (S6 om.) l'en d. l., Ya c. l'en devroit l.; N5S5 b. prisier; P7 d. faire bien covegnaulement.
717   S7 om. 'Car'; W c. fait p., S7 c. fet assés p., Rest: c. fet moult p.; Q moi que; N6Q l. moie, N2 l. voe; P6 v. mi a.
718   All om.
719   Yb C. ou ce se mort; N2 o. c. amours, Ya o. haste amour e., P6 o. acate h.; N6 et c. elle p.; P6 vent.
721   Q om. P6P7 C. desiriers n.
722   P6 T. e. est, N2N5N6S5S6 T. e. com; S1 p. emprise, N1N2N6P6P7Q p. esprise.
723   N2 A vigreus; N1 e. car, S1 e. que; N5S6S7 q. des .ii. d. (S6 se d.); S5 om. 'ces'.
724   P6 Vigeurs; Ya est entre amour; N5 om. 'en'; P6 v. souvent.
725   S7 om. N1 m. amoine, P7 m. si maine; Yb y a meismes .i. aatissement; P6 m. en cremeur c'est acevissement; N6 a. lui asoufissement; N1QS1 assouvissement, N2 atainisement, P7W achievissement.
726   Q om. 726-7. P6 f. sour, P7 f. servir; N2YaYb s. (Yb seur) amour; S5 Ya v. se (N1 ce) il l'entent (N1 antant, S1 le tent).
727   P7 vint; N1 p. les las, N6 p. loi le, P7 por l. los, Rest: p. l. los; P7 l'aprent, N5S5S6W l'emprent, Rest: le prent.
728   P7 om. 728-9. P6 c. li; N2YaYb appensement.
729   N2P6YaYb ne le (N2Yb la) r. (Yb retrait); N2P6WYaYb s'il (N1P6 si) n. (N1P6Yb ne, N6 ne le) s. (Yb fuit).
730   P6 qu'E. voa autre presentement; Ya m. entre presseement, N5S5 m. en (S5 a tous) presentement, S7 m. appartement, N2P7S5W m. en (W ou, P7 a) representement.
731   N1N6Q s. (Q sont) rector, S6 s. retor, Rest: s. restor; P7 est estoile.
732   W om. 732-3. Ya E. s'iert (N1 si iert), Yb E. (S6 om.) si (S7 om.) est, P6 E. fu; N2P6Ya et ens, S6S7 et est, N5S5 om. 'en'; P7 E. ert en t. p. et che t. p.
733   P7 E. en, N2P6Yb E. ou; P6 v. que; P7 l. venans, S6 1. amans.
734   N2YaYb v. nul (Q om.) autre ne, P7 v. nus autres n.; P7S5 se prent.
735   P7 Dont; P7W a. cest.
737   P6 om. 'de'; N1N6OQS7 de vous; N1N6O om. 'tous'; S1 S. vous voliés tuit dire vostre enscient.
739   N1N6OP7 Qu'a; P6 v. Aristes N1 v. benaiste, Rest: v. Aristé.; N6 om. 'se'.
740   All om.

Laisse xix

742   P7YaYb d. en (P7S6 par, S7 sa) parole g. (P7 brieue); N2 s. langue g.
743   Ya v. tout son t. i a.
744   OQ Les; N2 v. d'A.; N5 om. 'tous'; Ya A. trestouz l. a. siue; P6P7W desiue, S5 destiue, S6S7 aliue, N2 deseure.
745   Yb De; Ya g. latinier e. e. (O brieue); P7 S. ceste b. g...(?) iewe.
746   N6 S. a; P6W au moivoir, P7 v. esmovant e., N1 v. armorant e., OP6 e. joians e., Q e. joranz e., N2N6S1Yb e. morans e.; Ya estiue.
747   P7 E. a b.; Yb E. qu'a b.; Ya E. as (N1 au) biens (S1 veus) a. est (S1 et) dit (S1 dist a) moult reveliue; N2 v. e. mellice; S7 om. 'et'.
748   OQ om. P6P7 Si; N1N6S1 Ce (N1 Se) f. pas contre pas a a. (N1 acorder plir) l'asiue (N1 le siue); N2Yb Ce f. cas comme pert (S6 il pert) a a. asiuue (N2 assiure); P7 a achiever.
749   N2 d'Aristé; N1 la riche; P6 la tiere dessiue; S7 desiue; P7 A. del quel on or estrieue.
750   N2YaYb Tiex fu; P7S5S6S7W que il; Ya que nus n'estra (N1 n'est) certes (N1 certains) qui (N6 que, O qu'il) l'a. (S1 le consiuue); P7 nus ki de rien le consiue.
751   N2 om. 'voua'; N2N5P6P7S5S6 qu'il f.

752   S6 Par; OQ d. E. (O Phezon) o oisel, N1N6S1 d. E. com oisel, N5P6P7W d. E. com o.; N1 grue.

753   All: Seroit; P6S5 jusqu'en la (P6 om.) f., N1S6S7 jusque la (N1 a) f., N6P7 j. a f., N5OQS1 jusqu'a la (OQ om.) f.; N1N6QS1S6S7 a. (N1 aveque) sa; O f. a sent c.

754   P7 si n'en.

755   P6P7 q. iert; N1N6QS1 cruel, OP7 cruelle; O feliue, N6 fenieue, S1 felentiue, P7 malasieue.

756   W om. 756-7. Ya p. qui velt (N6 vec) son temps p.; P7 p. est drois ke il p.

757   Yb om. Ya T. convient a h. porter et signorie (S1 seignoriue); P6 om. 'plus'.

758   P7 q. se vos m. dist; P6 p. c'on me porsiue; N1N6 o. me siue, S7 o. n'ensiuue, P7 o. l'ensieue.

759   P6 f. tout son; Yb om. 'son'; P6W v. tout s. ce oevre p., P7 v. tant s. chose p., Rest v. tout s. oevre perriue (Yb pareniue, N2 penible).

760   P6 f. par; N2N6OP7Yb t. com; P7 qui a f. l'achieue.

761   S1 Oeuvre, P7 L'oevre, Rest: Guerre; N5 que on; P7 f. envis, Yb f. en lieu; P6 om. 'plus'; S5S6 Ya male asiuure, N2 malensiuure.

762   P6P7 Que c. (P7 celle) que o. h. (P7 fait); YaYb Car c.; W c. con o., N2 Yb c. que o., O c. que l'o., N1 c. qui en est s.

763   P6 v. p. o. e. fortiue, P7 v. pesant o. e. penieue, S6 v. sans merci et sans triue, Rest: v. estrange o. e. fortiue (N6 O forteuue).

764   Ya om. P6P7 en est (P7 ert) entalentiue, S6 en e. ententiue.

765   O om. 'qui'; N2YaYb p. couchier (OQS1 conchier); P7 q. le porquirt en; S7 s. bien; S5S6S7 s'acliue, N5 s'encliue.

766   Yb Trouvasse v.; P7 Et t. son voloir comment ke il li grieue; P6 v. et contraille h.; W om. 'et'; N5S5 honnestiue.

768   N6 Avoit l.; N2 e. de luy suivre; P6P7 d. (P7 de) servir, N6OQYb d. (Yb de) fuir (S5S7 suir); P7 talentieue.

769   N1N2N6OQS5S6S7 a. amours, S1 a. a mort; N2N6 l. en; P7W e. c'on s.; Yb e. qui s., N2 Ya e. cassiue.

770   All: p. si que (P7 p. comme) la gent; N2 curiue, Yb turbiue, P7 coriele.

771   Ya d. gier i (N1S1 om.) a. (N1 l'a.) e. de p. d. (O om.) gent g.; P6 d. biens i a. e. p. d. jus i jiue; N2W e. de p. des gius (W de gieu) jue, N5S5S7 e. (S5 om.) de p. gius on miue; S6 a. n'est nuls qui m'en desdiue; P7 e. p. d. gent i grieue.

772   Ya Yb om. P6 Et; N2 Qui n'i a sans revel r. q.; P7 v. renchus, W v. reclus; P6 n'a bonne, W n'a terre; P7 triewe.

773   Yb om. P6 Ore di; N1 aprés car c. r. en m.; P6 siue.

774   All om.

775   P7S5S6S7 p. et, N1N6OQ p. que; N5P6 om. 'en'.

776   W L. a dit Alixandres com p.; P6 G. com; N2 Yb G. qui p. h. prise (S7 et prise); N1N6OQ G. qui (N1 que) moult si (O om.) s'umelie (O se humilie); P7 G. parole noble et p.

777   WYaYb en (N1O om.) b. (O om. N6Q bries) oevre et (S6S7 est) t. (S1 emprise).

778   N1N6OQ Moustera; N2 M. bien, N5 M. ore miex a qui; P6P7 M. m. assés a q. (P7 coi); W Moustrai m. et c.; N1N2N6OQS5 c. a q.; P6 s'en riue, N1N6OQ s'aïue; S6S7 Menesteraus (S6 Menesterel) scet miex c. (S6 om.) a qui le d. s'acliue. 778a P7 Car j'en sui enformés s'en dirai sens estrieue.

Laisse xx

779   P6P7 qu'A. ot tout d. (P6 d. tot) s.

780   O en voiant.

781   N1N6OQ S. ce d. l. r.; OQ r. personnes c. (O nuissant); P6 entendant.

782   N5P7S5S7 Q. a p.; N1OQ p. donner; S7 a. valen t. (va l'entant?); P7 alons si.

783   N1N5N6OQS5 Que (N5 Et, S5 Quar) c. l. (N1 ne, Q li, O om.) devroit (O d.) S6S7 C. si (S7 om.) l. devroit; P6 d. assener en; N5S1S5 e. clinant, S7 e. chantant.

784   N1 J. n'an; P6P7S5 veu si fort.

785   N2N5N6S6S7W Com, N1OQ Comme P. v.; P6P7 P. a voé au (P7 a); N6 om. 'i'.

786   OQ om. 'li'; N6 om. 'veu'; S6 veu sont simple voirement, S7 voeu tot s.; P6 vont folement a., N1 vont si s. a.

185

787   OQ om. 'deus'; O encores; S6S7 avenant; N1 M. qui droit li fist ancor e. a.
788   P6 A v., Q Del v.; N1 Dont vaindre a la; P6S1W qui qu'il, N2 qui qui.
789   N1OQ E. que E.
790   OP6P7S7W l. dieu le gardoient; N2S1W en quoy estoit (N2S1 i. s.); N1N5N6OQS7 i. est, P6 i. ert.
791   OQ persant.
792   N2OP7WYb f. doit o., S1 f. dont ont; N1N6QYb o. l'onnor.
793   S6 om. N1N6OQ Et q. le d. au (N1 en) bien e.; Yb Doit qu'au bien l'en (S7 l'en y) voit au bien e.; P7 q. je; N2 b. voit l. d. a bien e.
794   N5S6S7 scet; N6P6P7 f. a m., N2S1Yb f. qu'au m.; P6 combatant.
795   N2P6P7WYa A; O v. telle, N1S6 v. la; N1N6Q et (N1 a, N6 en) un estour pesant, Rest: et (P6 en) estour s. (O om.) pesant.
796   OP7Yb om. N1N6P6Q c. adurer e. ozer (N6 ovrer, Q orer, P6 c.) seurement (P6 p.).
797   Yb om. N2WYa E. adés chevauchier avec (N2W au non, S1 A.) l. c.; P6 om. 'a'.
798   All om.
799   N1N6Q f. d'eür, P6 f. et irour et r.; O f. la l.; W l. et t.; S6S7 l. et (S6 om.) devant; N1N5N6OQ puingnant.
800   Yb duit fort.
801   Q Cel, N1 Se; N5S5 c. mie; N2P7 pas par, N1N6OQYb pas pour; N5 menaces.
802   W om. 802-4. N2 YaYb C'est (N2N6OQS5 Ce est) u. v. des .ii. (S1 .ii. les) r. (N5S5 enforciez, N2 renformez) e. (N2 et); P6 r. et; P7 Ch'est u. renforchiés veus de .ii. los e. d.
803   N6OQ om. 'avoir'; N6 om. 'por'; P6 p. l. plus, N1N5N6OP7QS5 p. l. miex; P7 combatant.
804   N6 om. 'autres'; P7 v. furent.
805   W Li autre veu sont tuit a.; N1 s. aidement a. e. pansant.
806   N1N6OQ q. maint estour ont (N1 ont eu) du; P7 l'e. en n. de.
807   S1 Et; S7 E. plus p. c.; N6P7 p. a, N5S5S6 p. en; S1W suivant, N5S5S7 faisant.
808   W Tous jourz d. main; N1 T. joie; S6 j. au; P6 jusques s., Rest: jusqu'a s.
809   O om. P6P7 B. commencement bonne f.; S6S7 B. conmant bonne (S6 bon de) f. e. bon moiennement; N1N5N6QS5 c. bon de f., N2 c. bonne f.; P6 e. mius en m., P7 e. tres b. m., N2QS1 e. tant b. m., N1N6S5 e. bien m., N5 e. bon m.
810   W et souvent, S1 et convent.
811   Yb om. N1N6OQ E. qu'a m. f. par f. e. combatant (N1 ot batant); N2 en combatant.
812   N1N2N6OP6Q ne le d.; P7 Yb b. par le mien e., N5 b. par m. e.
813   O p. et trouvez fut en h. c.
814   N1N6OQ om. P7 d. ot il del; S1 ot du; P6 d. raviant, Yb ot derrainement.
815   S1 om. 815-6. P6 c. al; N6 au lez; P7 Dont le doit o. c. a los.
816   N2 om. P7 Yb E. se (S5S6 si, S7 om.) E.; O E. si Emedus si d. en a.; P6 E. s'Eimes li dus d.; N1N6Q d. adés.
817   Yb e. et l.
818   Yb Car vëoir s.; P7 Que il rot s.; N5 c. et.
819   N6 Ne p.; P7 W p. son lieu, Rest: p. sans (P6S1 sen, O en) l. (N6 om.); P6 l. sont fait ains p.; N2 a. son; S6 sont li f. c.; P7 f. si pesant, S7 f. en c., N5S5 om. 'peu'; N6 courant, OQ cointant, N1 cemant.
820   O n'e. point; Yb p. cités; N1N2N6OQP7Yb d'oriant.
821   All: C. (P6 Que) j'ameroie; P6 m. a voer, P7 m. jurer, Yb m. vëoir; N1N6OQ aprenant.
822   N1N2N6OQYb Et; N1N6OQ et arriere e. avant.
823   P7S1W De la, Q Del f., N1N2N5N6S7 Des la; P7 f. d'occident j. e. oriant.
824   N2 q. cis; N1 ma c. feüssent b. g., Rest: ma c. en (N5S5 m'en, P6P7S1W me) fussent b. (P7W bien) g. (P6 aidant).
825   N1N5N6OP6P7Q E. (P7 E. si) me fuissent t.; Yb m'en (N5 me) fuissent d. c. (N5 f. d'acort) trestout (N5S5 tout) reconfortant (N5S5S7 e. c.); P7 c. bien confortant.
826   N2P7 Que t., N1N6OQ Et t.; P6 t. le.
827   OP7 om. P6 combatant.
828   N2 Yb Comme li dus d'A.; P6P7 K'Eime le duc d'A. au (P7 a) f. contenement (P7 v. l.); O Au bon duc d'Arcage a. f. v. et puissant; N1N6Q Si com li dus d'Arcage.

829   O om. 828-30. N1 Armenidus r., S1 Aimes li dus r., W Lymenidus r., P6P7 Dont
r. li dus Eimes (P7 li bons dus) s.; N2N6P6P7Yb tressuant.

830   N6 om. 'li'; P6P7S7 f. li ala (S7 a.).

831   P7 p. s'encline; N1 t. hons tex; N2P7S1WYb simploiant; O Emenidus s. t. a part
honteusement.

832   P6S5S7 Q. un p. ot m. (P6 pensé), Rest: Q. ot un p. m. (O pancé); S1W lors,
Rest: si; S1 en sourissant, O en se riant.

833   OQ Et, N1N6 E; P6 om. 'sire' and 'vous'.

834   All om.

835   OS1 om. N1 Cil; S5 e. que tel fusse m.; N6 q. de ïst; N1N2N6 ne me, S7 ne s'en.

836   OP7S1 savés; N1N2N6OP7QYb s. deviser u. p. e. figurant.

Laisse xxi

837   N1 Hores l., O Alor l., Q Lores l., N6 Lors l., N5P6 as P, Rest: Lors q. l.; N1 r.
de; All: G. sa.

838   S1 Aimes li dus a., N2 E. a pris e. h.; Yb E. en h. aprés r.

839   P7 S. ce dist l. dus; P6S1 ne m'adira, W ne ma, Rest: ne me (N2 m'en) dira.

840   OP7 Qui s.; P6P7 p. biaus.

841   P7 Et tant ke, Rest: En tant c.; N1 n. se; N6 qu'il l'avera.

842   N1N6OQ Et; P7S1W qu'il l'a.; N2N5P6S5S7 e. com a. (P6 l'a.); N1N6OQS6 e.
com a cheval.

843   P6 M. quant; O il dit; S7 vit si grant veu que chascun embronca; N2N5P6P7S5S6
Ya si grant v. (P7S5 fais); P7 encarga.

844   P7 k'a tel veu, S1W as P, Rest: Que tel veu; P6 n'afiroit; P7 n'afroit n. se
autre jeu n'i a; N1N2N6OQ n'a. se (N1 s'a) o.; N5S5S6 v. ne feroit se o.
(S5 outrages), S7 v. ne voua se outrages.

845   N2 om. 'a'; OP6P7Q ne se c.; N6 om. 's' en'; N2 conseillera.

847   N1 Et P. e.; S6S7 E. si; N5S5 om. 'qui'; P7 E. del tout l'a; S1 E. qu'il l'en.

848   N2 Parlers que il l'e.; P7 il l'e.; P6 il promist e. emprist; S6 il voua, S7 il
l'eu; N5 O poia.

849   S1 d. que v., W d. en; N2S7 qu'e. voiant; P6 m. de joie sura.

850   S6S7 Qu'avec l. p. (S7 compaignons); N5S5 Qu'avecques l.; N1N6OQ l. p. avec
(O o eulx) s'a.

851   N1OQ Que; N2 combatent.

852   All om.

853   Yb Assez (N5 Asse); O A. vait; P6 en stour; N2S6S7 qu'a .iiii. p. y va; Q .iiii.
preuz v.; S7 repeats 845 here.

854   P7 854-8 thus: 856, 854, 857-8, 855. P7 Et; Yb v. c. (S6S7 comme) c. en c.
(S7 c. aus champs); S1 c. u c., N2 c. el c., N6 c. es c.; OQ c. c. eschapper s. c.;
P7 c. c. a eaus se maintenra; P6 combatra.

855   P7 g. s'enfuit a. eaus en ira, S1W as P, Rest: g. s'en p. a. s'en p.

856   O om. 856-61. N1N2 Si v. (N1 voit), P6P7 S'il voit, N6Q S'il vient; P7 a.
encauchier.

857   N2P7 E. si (P7 se) v.; P6W v. a j. s. c. y d.; Yb j. corps a corps d.

858   Yb c. qui s. g. s. saudra, N2WYa c. qui grant (Q g.) saut (N1N6Q s.) l. saura;
P7 c. la force l. d.; P6 li saura. N6 repeats 855.

859   N6Q om. first 'et'; N1 om. both 'et'.

860   Ya Yb q. sus; N1S1 pensera.

861   All om.

862   N1N6OQ c. nul c. (O reconfort) n'a. (N6 n'avera, N1 il n'ara).

863   S6S7 Que l.; P7 f. de; N1N2N6P7QYb c. faire; P7 ce qu'i. pora, S1 as P,
Rest: quanqu'il f.

864   P7 sa gent s'en fuient; N2 g. se f.; O f. seul, N1 f. e on c.; S1 om. 'ou'.

865   N1N2N6OQYb S'il (N6 Yb Se il, N1 Si) ne vole, P6 Se i. ne veut. P7W S'il ne
s'e.; OQ l'a. monter le; N2N5P6P7S5S7 m. le, N1m. les.

866   O om. 866-7. N1N6Q n. (N6 n'i) vient; N5 om. 'la gent'; P7 q. entour li sera.

867   S6S7 Yleuc (S7 Ja ne) prendra; S5 L. prendra il s.; N1N6Q Et la (N1 La il)
perdra (N6 p.); P7 p. son lieu l. morra et vivra; N1N2N6QYb la (N1Q que, N6
qui) mort le (N1 les) marira (N1 maira, Q marrira).

Variants for Part II, Laisse xxi, continued

868 N1 om.
869 W om. N1 Si l.; O S'il f.; N6OP6 ou il l., N1 ou si l.
870 N1OWYb om. N2 om. 'proëce'; N6Q p. en fist e. porposa (Q pourpensa); N2 pourparla.
871 Q li doint; N6 t. le d. p.; N1N6QS1 p. que, P6 p. moult; O Ainssi le pris lui donne c. d. il a.
872 N5S6S7 d. a autre; P7 j. croi; S7 di com.
873 N6 d. Phezonnas; O F. l'on.
874 O om. P7 Se Y. nel v.; P6 S'en estiés creüs b.; S7 b. s'en avisera.
875 N6O Et, N1 Que; P7 C. de; Yb a. ne l'avra, P7 a. n'en ira; W d. d. autres ne l'avera.
876 OS5 om. N5P7S6S7W E. s'autrement; N6Q E. sa sement y vient, N1 E. ce ce ment vuet; S7 om. 'oiiés'; P6 o. qu'en d., N6 o. que on d., Q o. qu'on avendra, N1 o. quant on d.
877 N1N6 C. de vous p.; N5S5 C. bon p. d. l'en a. (N5 apera); S7 C. veu par d. et l'en a.; P7 Plusour cascun de nous par d. a.; P6 des voirs jugans n.; S6 om. 'des'; OQS6 d. vous en.
878 P6 T. i.; N1N6 i. si; S6 et vous en; OQ i. nous.
879 N1N6OQ Si (N6 S'il) le porte; N2P6S5S6S7 S'il e.; S7 sen p.; P6 om. 'sans plus'; N6 por faire l'estra, P7 por bienfait l'avera; P6, e. grans mercetes sera; Yb f. les a.

Laisse xxii

880 U resumes. S1Q Aimes li dus. o.; Yb o. dit t. qu'il n.; P6 d. qu'il n., OQ d. qui n.; N1 om. 'tant'; P7 n. vuet; O p. plus.
881 W om. P6 P. vrais, S1 as P, Rest: P. biax; P6 a. tant d. f. com.
882 N2N6P6P7UYb recommence; P6 ses p., S1 les fais.
883 N1 l. courtois; Yb f. drois, N1N6OQU f. ancois.
884 S6 Donc; S1 D. touz biens est e. e. t. b. e. e.; N1N6OP6P7QU h. e. venue; S7 et honnour est, N2 et dont bien est.
885 O om. N1 Biaus joune jouvant, P7 R. et j. e. jeus, N5N6QU R. j. (Q joies) jouvent, S1 as P, Rest: R. joie j.; N5S5S7 tournoi; N1N5N6QS5 guerre, S7 et gerre.
886 N2OQUYb Trouveroit q., N6 Convenroit q., N1 Stonveroit q.; N1N5OQS5S7U plain; S1 Ou d'amours qui verroit v. d.; P7 d'amour est venue a eslais.
887 S7 A. et; P6 de ses drois vrais p.; S1 u. princes si p.; N1QU u. principel; N6 O d. du principel.
888 All: Qui nous (Yb vous) maine; P7S1 soupporte, P6W as P, Rest: susmaine; Yb vos (S7 ses) f. (S6S7 drois).
889 Yb E. soulace et e. es c. p. d. estrois; N1N2N6OQU E. s'enlace (U se lance) et e. (N1 en guerre) escuier (N2 e. c.) dous (N6 touz, N2 par d.) estrais; P7 E. samblance engenree en cuer; N5S1 e. en cuer; P6 engenre pardon es cuers arais; W estrais.
890 Yb om. N1 P. A. et.
891 N2 A; P7 U om. 'de'; N1N2N6OQUYb p. p. vuet; P6 puet porsuir ses trais, P7 puet ensiewre ses bons f.; N2WYaYb r. ses (N1 ces).
892 Yb om. 'de'; S6 p. dont g. b. e. atrais; S7 b. est et trais, N5S5 b. est cartrais; P7 Ch'e. gieus p. quoi de droit p. de bien e. estrais; N1N6OQU p. quoy de (N1 et d.) q. p. grant bien e. (N1N6 en) estrais; P6 droit je quic de p. g. b. estrais.
893 N2 om. 'fin'; P6 t. biens fais, S7 t. ses fais.
894 All: D. moult; P7 siet Y.; N1N6P7 e. s. fais. 849a N5 Bonne amour ne la pas espressé ne essais, cf. 900.
895 S1W om. N1OQ om. 895-9. P7 Quant. N6 U Et; P7 Yb q. d'amours; N6 ki est d'a. est; Yb et (N5S5 om.) emplis et atrais; N6U et esliz et.
896 N6U om. 896-9. P6 a anter, N2 Yb a amours; All: s. relenquir; N2 je mais. 896a N6 C'est cil par coi de qui plus grant biens en estrez, cf. 892.
897 N5S5S6 dru ne l'a pas essaiés (N5S5 espressé ne essais), S7 dru qu'elle n'a pas essais; P7 lais.
898 P7 Ains est blans v. r.; N2 b. vrais, S5 b. bers; P6P7Yb a. en ses

trais (P6P7S6 fais); S1W soutais.

899 All om.
900 W om. 900-4. Yb n. l'a pas espressé, P7 n. vaut m. en; N1N6OQU A. si n'est m.; P6 A. empressés n. entais; N2 m. as; N6OYb ne essais, N1QU ne es ais.

901 All om.
902 O om. 902-4. Q Ne li b.; N1N6 Ne u b. de, U Ne de b. de; P6 E. o. sanc d. c. en boe n'en m., P7 E. en b. de c. ne en son de marteaus; N2 b. de; N1 c. un s. n. ou harnas, Yb c. y ert L'autre harnais (N5S5 harnois); N6QU n. u m. 902a-b U Car bonne Amour si fet fere moult trés grant fais, Et gens deschevauchier ce sachiés a .i. fais.

903 Yb om. 903-4. P7 Armee en ces e. agregie; N2 A. en es estriers; N1N6QU ens en l'estour a. (N1 agregir, Q et gregis); P6 A. en l'estour a. et i. U repeats 903.
904 P6 P. trencier l. c. et le fer et l. a.; S1 detrenchiers l'escuier n. la char n.; N1 n. lassier, N2 n. lancier.

905 P6P7S1W est (P7 n'e.) amer (S1 amers) s. (P7 ne) r. Rest: c'est a. s. r. (U delais).
906 S1W Amers; S7 est l'amour; P6P7 p. est l. r. (P7 relais).
907 N2P7Yb a. des dames; N1N6OQU a. des (O de) fames.
908 N1N6P7QU om. O om. 908-11. W C. tiengne, N2 C. tieng, S1 C. tien ge a, P6 Je tieg, Yb Si tieng a (N5S5 je a); N5S5 droite.
909 Yb om. P7 j. tous tans n.
910 P6 E. as a. sui; P7 a. porsiere volentis et; S5S7 d. est entrais; N5 e. entrais, S6 e. estrais, N2 e. enrais, N1S1 e. entairs.
911 Yb Car la p.; P7 p. por voir qu'A.; N2P7 p. en; Yb qu'A. a a m. t. (S7 tret); N1 e. a. centaris, N6QU a ce t.

912 S7 p. ne m.
913 S1W Je, P7 Cis; U s. viuté; N1N6OQU om. 'et'; P7 retrais.
914 O om. 914-16. Yb D. aus, P7 D. en; N6QU a. servir, N1 a. fuir; P6 m. li fais, Yb mestrais.
915 Yb Ains (S6 Aincois) est; N1N6QU est chascun bien (U b. c.) parés e. bien r. (N6 faiz); N2P6P7S1W c. bons; N5S5 c. bons et b. pes e. r., S6 c. bons b. preus e. bien r., S7 c. bons et pensis e. r.
916 P7...(?) mies l. grains ke l. esclais; S6 estrais, N1N5S5S7 estrois, U eschas.
917 S7 Doings b. a.; S6 A Y. le doins dont; P7 D. a bien Y. mais; P6 b. Y. et des a. mestrais.; N1N6OQU Y. que, N2S1WYb Y. car.
918 S1 Et les r., S5 Le droit riulle; Yb d'A. su ïr, N2 d'A. suis je et, N1N6P6Q d'A. suis.
919 S6 Si en avra; O Si avra l. p. se n.; N1P6 p. si n.; S7 fourfais, N6OQU pourtrais.
920 Q Et c.; S7 tu ta vis, W t. le jus, N5N6OQS5 t. te jus, U t. te joue, S6 t. te tais; P7W et refais, N6 e. te tais.

921 All om.
922 N1N6QUYb E. tes; O m. pas ne nous plaist; P7 a petit d. fais; N1 om. 'a'; N1N2N6QUYb d. fais.
923 O om. Yb Tu; P6 p. que c. qu'as ne; P7 k'en tes dis ne me p.; N1N2N6U cas n'a nul (N6 nus) p. (N1 fais), Yb cas n'as (S6S7 n'i a) mais; W n. m'i p.

Laisse xxiii

924 OU Philote, N1 Philotain; N6P6P7 c. que l., N5S5UW c. qui l.; All: plot (S1 plost).
925 N1 A F.; N6 F. s'adreca; P6 l. sans plus dire.
926 Yb v. a poy d.; O om. 'de'.
927 U C. veu s'est reson conforte; N1 C. bels ces r. set c. e. dire; P7 C. v. confermer sa raison et r.; N5 sa raison; S7 r. reconter.
928 N1N6OP7QUWYb desdire.
929 Yb om. N1N6 Canaus a., OQ Lairaus a., U Caciaus a.; P6 pris a f.; S1W f. ne, N1N6OP7U f. de; P6 mestrire, N1N2N6OQ mestrise. P7 ends here.
930 N6U om. 930-2, N1OQ om. 930-3. Yb d. d. que; P6 l. tans l., S5 le cuer l.
931 Yb D. n. (S6S7 om.) c. que C. nus (N5S5 om.) ne m'en puet nulz (N5S6S7 om.) desdire.

932   Yb om. 932-4. N2P6W p. plus bel veu (P6 ne) diter (N2 dire) n. e.; S1 p. plus bel n'enditer ni e.

933   N2 Q. C. a cheval; N6U Qu'Erculuz (U C'Herculus) a. par force et par bien dire.

934   O a. vous n. m'en peuz d., P6 ne le p.; N2S1W p. adire.

935   Yb P. conserver (S7 confremer) r., N1N6OQU P. consuivre r.; P6 n. atire, N5S5 n. m'atire, N1Q n. nature, N2 n. adire.

936   Yb Qu'il a a.; U d. nous; N2 a. des veus; P6 om. 'je'; N6 m. jure, U m. vire.

937   O d. point; Yb s. droit; S6 p. par m.; S7 por moy, OP6Q por m'en; P6 descrire, O desdire.

938   O om. 'se'; S5 v. le; S1 d. q. qu'il, N2S6 d. que que, N1N5N6S5S7 q. que; N2 l'en t.; N5S5 t. empire, S1 t. aus p., N1N2N6QS6S7U t. a p.

939   S5 Je; P6 J. ne d.; N6 dira, O dire; N2 l. car bien qui m'e.; N1 c. qui, P6 c. com, N6OQUYb c. qu'il; N1 dedire, O destrire, Q descire.

940   S7 Ne .i., O Mes ung, U Nesune; N1N6OQU om. 'seul'; N5 g. mes que; N2P6S5 S6 m. nes, N1N6OQU m. mais; N1Q q. de l. (N1 les).

941   N1 om. N5S5S7 graces.

942   All: Desir, Yb de tel; S7 voloir, S6 valour; S1W v. en t.; N1N2N6UYb v. qui t.; S7 om. 'veu'; P6W v. vaut, S1 veul vault.

943   N2 De t. s. e. aus meillours; O om. 'de'; N6 e. a m.

944   N5S1S5S7 affire, N1N6OQ afflixe.

945   U f. li; N5 f. sus, P6 f. desous; N2 d. son cheval, N1N6OP6QUYb d. son arcon.

946   S7 o. l'espee, Rest: o. des poins; S7 qu'en deüst r.; N2 l. a r.

947   S7 om. N2P6 L'espee; S6 Aussi legierement; OW b. com s'ele (O celle) fust, N1N2N6P6QUYb b. com s'il f.

948   All: f. Caulus; P6S1UW s. (U sa) maistire, N5N6QS5S6 sa mestrie, N1N2OS7 sa (N2 la) mestrise.

949   U Que; Q s. royaume enracha en l.; O e. aracha l'on l.; U e. enracha; P6 pot.

951   N6O N. (O Nul) homme; S1 h. le; S6 h. si ne devroit; Yb om. 'le pris'; N5OS5 a cel.

952   P6 trestout le j.

953   N2P6S1W Le, N6 Nul, OQU Nel; N6 om. 'on'; S7 l. que; P6S1S5 W nus boins; S1 b. ne e., P6 b. ne l'e., U b. ne posdire, N1N2N6OQYb b. ne despire.

954   N6 om. 'vous'; O v. ennuye; U p. de se m.; P6 om. 'se'; O s. des meillours; N1N2N6OQUYb dire.

955   All om.

Laisse xxiv

957   N2WYa b. estre (N6 i e.) ne d. ne c.; N5P6 om. 'si'.

958   N1N6OQU om. Yb d. estre chascun bien f. (N5 fet) r.; P6 c. biens estre.

959   P6 f. moult; N1N6OP6QU b. je m'e. s. p. (N1 O aperceus, P6 pourveüs), N5S5 b. que (S5 qu'il) voult estre retenus, S6 b. n'en doit estre repus, S7 b. que il n'i a refus.

960   N1N6OQU om. 960-1. Yb om. 960-4. P6 ert uns tous s.

961   P6 om. N2S1W t. qu'il vaut; W receüs.

962   N2 a. gius.

963   N2P6WYa Lyones ne (N6 net); P6 d. mi; OP6 a. les. 963a S5 Pour Lyoine le di qui d'onnour n'estoit nus.

964   O M. avec les m.; P6 a. fait d.; O recus.

965   N1N6U om. 965-7, OQ om. 965-8. S7 Liones qui jousta a; N2N5P6S5S6W v. a j.; S1 jouste.

966   N2P6S1WYb e. en (P6S6 de) tous biens (P6 tout bien) parcreüs (S7 revestus). 966a N2P6S1WYb Mais li peres estoit crueus et irascus.

967   W om. Yb g. et pour; P6 grignars.

968   N1N6U om. 'quant'; N1N2UYb il surmenoit; N6 il menoit seur s.

969   N2 B. d. par d. estre de; N6OP6Q doit; S7 om. 'par droit'; N5 p. d. des hommes c.; P6 de li leone c.; S6 Par droit devoit bien estre des estrangez c.

970   O Car il ala a. tours et a. p.; N1 ala as estours e. a. plains; N2N6QUYb ala as tours; N2 paulus.

971   All: Et; O v. parmy.

972 W om. 972-3. N1N6OQU V. fu d'u. tunicle qui est (U ert) a or batus; N2 d'une
tunicle, S6 d'u torniquet; P6S1Yb t. (S7 tous) semencié.
973 N1N6OP6S5U Menestrel e. (O estoit, S5 fu); P6 e. le r. et s'e.; N1OQ r. des e.
974 W d. il a lui, Rest: d. l. vassaus, S6S7 d. Marcus.
975 N1N5N6S5U F. (N1 F foy) mon m.; OS7 om. 'me'; N2 om. '.i.'
976 S1 De; N2 c'u. messagers; U e. s'a d., N2P6 e. de ca (P6 la) hors, S1W e. c.
defors, O e. par decza v.
977 O Que; S5S6S7 om. 'a'; N1N2N6OQUYb C. d'une; P6 Et p. une j. a C. s. p.
978 N1 Car; N2N6P6QS1UWYb qu'ensi l'ai (P6 Yb l'a); P6 v. et tel e. lor j.; S1 c.
temps; N1QU e. vos j.; Yb e. ses j. (N5S7 ws); O E. tel l'ay ainsi voué telz e. ses
argus.
979 All om.
980 N1N6OQS5U q. tu s. venus.
981 P6 Tu a. l. p. d. qui.
982 N2P6S1W as (S1 a) blons, Rest: as (N1 au) blans; S1 et a c., N1 et au c.
983 N6 om. 'fu'; All: d. jouste.
984 W om. S7 om. 'son veu'; N1U V. que; S1 q. tant est e.; Yb esseüs.
985 N1N6OQS5U Encontra; P6 q. ert, N1OQU q. fu; N6 q. grans fu et.
986 O t. ses maleureux.
987 O p. estoit; S1W fourmeüs, Yb sousmeüs, N1N2N6Q surmeüs, O esmeüz.
988 S6 l. s'e.
989 P6 Que; S1 C. li p.; U il li; N1N2W om. 'i'; N1 estre mors.
990 S7 om. S1S5 De; N2 a. ou.
991 N1 r. il; N2 fu; U f. a joie s., O f. s., Rest: f. a. ne s.
992 U om. 992-4. N6 g. harmenenz, Yb g. biens; N1N2S1S6W d. i. ert; P6 d.
estoit raviestus; O eslëus, S1 esmeuus, Q esbeüs.
993 O om. 993-4. P6 q. il f. ja v.; N1 j. il f.
994 N1N2N6Q A. atendoit; P6 A. entendi ades devenir; S7 t. au venir.
995 N2S1W q. par s. (N2 ce), S5 q. de ce, P6 as P. Rest: q. a ce; N1N6OQU b. vous
estes p., S6 b. fu ainssi p.; N2 avenus, S7 pormeüs.
996 S6 e. teüs, P6 e. repus, W perdue.
997 N2 D. li preus; N1N6S5 a. si ne, P6 a. se ne.
998 O S. ce d.
999 U A. le portera cist d.
1000 All om.

Laisse xxv

1001 OS1 Sire; N5 E. c'est bien c. s.; N1 E. c'est c.
1002 S1W c. s'e. a p.; O c. aparence s'e. s.; N2 a par ruile sa raison s.; N1N6QUYb a
par ruse s'e. s. (Yb maintenue); P6 p. visce.
1003 O r. vertus c. R. s. porsue; U c. amours s. perseüe; N1N5N6QS5S7 porsiue,
P6S6 porveüe.
1004 N1N2N6QUYb a. com; U v. anuise, Rest: v. amuse; Yb dessue, N2 deslie.
1005 S6 Ce est t., N1 Cet t., U S temps, N6 C'e. tant, N1N2OP6Q C'e. tans, S1C'e.
seus, W C'e. chans; N5S5 p. n. (N5 ni est) gaster; S6 om. 'gasté'; S7 g. c'est.
1006 N5S6S7 c. scet essauchier, W c. sols e., S1 s. essante, O c. soit ensauce, N1N6QS5
U sot ensance (S5 e., N1 ensauce, U essaute?)
1007 O n'e. point; S7 p. telle; N2 t. conme; N5 q. me jue; N1N2N6OP6QS5U j. me
jue.
1008 N1N6OQU estes de ligniage et; N2 g. d. lui; All: pourveüe
1009 N1 Et d.; Ya plain, W plains.
1010 P6 om. 'tant'.
1011 N5S5 Se a g., S7 S'a g., P6 De g.; N5 s. g. pris; W b. s'en, S1 b. o t.; S6
confondue.
1012 P6 Je loc, S1 Se lo; N6 Si qu'a la; N1 l. que en.
1013 N6OQU Que; S7 C. si; N1 Si que nos f.; N5N6UW nos; P6 v. plais n.; N2YaYb
f. vous p.; N1 om. 'et'; W a. nous; N1 v. annuie, P6 v. eskiue.
1014 W Que; N6 p. i v. cler; Yb c. les remire (S7 mire); N5 om. 'ch'; N2 v. si ert,
N1N6QU v. ce ert. S1S7 v. c'est, O v. si ait; P6 c'ert plus g.; N1N6OQU om.

'grant'; N1OQUWYb desconvenue.

1015 S1 R. n'i v. a. i ert; O v. mes aincois une g. b. eüe; N1N6QU ert une g. b. eüe; N2P6S1WYb receüe.

1016 N1N6OQU escriant, Yb eschignant.

1017 S6 De; O om. 'dans'; Yb P. de qui est l. parole (S5S6 l. parole est); N1N2N6OQU l. parole; S6 meüe, U entendue. Q repeats the line: Q. dant P. q. a l. parole v.

1018 S1 Doint; O e. l'autre si a.; N5 e. .i. autre l'a.; N1N6P6QS5U l. a. l'a.

1019 N2 Que ce d.; N5S6S7 Qu'il d. (S6 doint) a; S5 Qui dit de G., N1N6OQU Qu'est dit de G.

1020 N6 Qui, U Por, Rest: Ou; N1OQ om. 'qui'; O om. 'a'; N6 a l'enseigne rompue; N2OP6 l'e. t.

1021-4 N1N6OQU om.

1022 P6 a a; S1W ferue, P6 freue.

1023 Yb a. bien; S1 a. m. mesfies; P6S5 q. soit b.

1024 P6 volons; Yb l. ne.

1025 S1 s. polye.

1026 S7 om. 1026-41. U Q. au, N5S5S6 Q. en; O om. 'roi'; N1OQU c'est, Rest: s'est.

1027 O C. les; N5S5S6 C. la verse; P6 tot l'a.; N1N6OQU t. (U toutes) riens argue.

1028 N1N6OQU om. N2N5S6 om. 'et'; N5S5W teüe, S6 remue.

1029 S1S5S6 E. en; W repeats 'a son'; N6 a. a .i. r. c., O a. au vroy (?) c.; U e. au r.; N5S6 maintenue, P6 deceüe.

1030 N1N6OQU om. 1030-2. N2S1W moustre; P6 qu'A. estoit en l.; N2N5S5 l. (N5S5 om.) meüe, S6 l. sceüe.

1031 S6 om. S1 f. qui; P6 a. point; N2N5P6S1S5W desnue.

1032 P6 E. se fortune m.; S1 a grant gent.

1033 N5S5S6 F. se s., P6 F. s'a s.; N5S5 v. s'arue, S6 v. ne mue, P6 v. s'amue; N1N6OQU Et Phezonnas si ert (O estoit) de voloir (N1 valoir) esmeüe.

1034 S6 a. la bataille vaincue; P6 tenue, Rest: esmeüe. 1034a N1N2N5N6OQS5S6U Et ses peres Clarus (N1 Traian) a la teste chanue.

1035 N1N6OQU om. 1035-43. S1 E. la; S1W l. du; N2N5S5S6 E. (S6 Qui) pour Porus estoit (S6 s'estoit) du d.; S6 repeats 1035 and 1036.

1036 S6 f. l'eure; S5 g. estre li d.; P6 M. fu li outrages g. e. doit estre r.

1037 P6 om. N2N5S5S6 Q. a (N2 en) c. p. vaut e. ainsi a r. (N2 au r. ainsi) t. (N5 tenu).

1038 P6 s. espouse, N2 s. n'espousee, N5S5S6 s. espousee.

1039 P6 S. vivement q. de r. n'i m. r.; N5S5S6 S. menuement q. r. n'i (S6 ne).

1040 N2N5S5S6 f. a raison mue (N2 n., S6 meue).

1041 P6 q. ses v.; N5S5 ce c'est.

1042 N2 Sella, S1 Yb li est.

1043 WYb om. S1 E. est; P6 fortornue.

Laisse xxvi

1044 Q1 resumes. Yb t. est; N1QU q. si e., O q. estoit s.; Q1 t. fu. 1044a Q1 De vos diz escouter sui forment esmahis.

1045 N2 d. nous; S7 a dit s. b. s.; P6 om. 'si'.

1046 N1N6OQU A; P6 q. a dit mius u p.; Q1 en a dit m. n.; N1N6OQUYb d. ou m. ou.

1047 N2S1Yb D. (N5S5 Du) premier, N1OQQ1U Au (Q A) premier, N6 Premier; OQ a. tenu (Q tenuz) le p.; N1 a. inditeur du p.; N2N6UYb a. auditour.

1048 Q1 om. 1048-9, N1N6OQ om. 1048-58, U om. 1048-60. N2S1WYb P. qui; P6 f. al mius e., S1 f. tantost e.

1049 N2S7 D. sentence; N5 esgarnis, S6S7 desgarnis.

1050 N2P6S1WYb estre d'acort; Q1 Et pour nous accorder et; W et d'o.

1051 P6 Je m'a. q. f.; S6 Couvient q.; Q1S1WYb facons, N2 faissons; S6S7 c. .xii.

1052 P6S7 Ens (P6 Et) en c. .xi. bries.

1053 N2 fust; P6 f. li .xiie.; S6S7 d. ens; N5S5 m. en; S1W fenis.

1054 Q1 1053,1056, 1058, 1054. S1 d. s. puis, N5P6S6S7 d. son poing, Q1 d. les p.

1055 Q1 om. N2P6S1WYb ferons; N5S5 il est, P6 q. sera.

1056 Q1 Puiz p. aus dieus q. sont s.

1057 Q1 om. N2 Et; S1 P. desur; P6 n. au b. roi M.

1058 S7 sors envers li c.; N5 v. li d.; Q1 li drois approuvez et descrips.

1059   P6 Les s. s.; N6 Ou briement secherai; Yb b. chaceray, N1 b. sachera; N1N6OQ sans livre et (O ne); N2 om. 'et'; N1N6OQQ1S7 s. escris.

1060   N1N6OQ om. Yb d. nostre a. (S7 absens); N2Yb i (S7 et) soiés; Q1 soie ainsi.

1061   P6 Et; O Qui cy, U Q. cist, N2 Q. ce; S7 q. je t. p. p.; P6 q. j'enterai; O en peut.

1062   P6 om. N1N6OQ om. 'tuit'; N1N6QQ1U J. (U Je) n'i sera, N5OS7 J. n'e. serés, N2S1W n'e. (N2 ne) sera, S5 n'e. soit contredis.

1063   N2N5S5 communaument; N6 c. se s. a terre a., N1OQU a la terre a.; P6 mis.

1064-65 All om.

1066   N6 E. si a l. briez s.

1067   N5P6S5S7 f. leur sors, S1 f. lors s., Rest: f. leur s.; N2U s. que; N5Q1 m. fu b. b. (Q1 sortis), P6 m. fu bien b., S5 q. biau furent b., S6S7 q. furent bel (S7 tel) b.

1068   N1N6OQQ1UYb om. 1068-9. N2 C. certifia; S1 s. a d.

1069   N2S1W E. lors q. c. ot ouvré.

1070   OQ r. si passe, P6 om. 'rois'; N5S5 passe; N1N6QU a le (Q li) b. luis, O a les brevetz luis.

1071   N1N2S1UW E. lors; N6OQ1 E. lors qu'il; Yb E. quant il ot (S6S7 l'ot) l.; N2N6QQ1S1U l'ot l. (S1 U om.), N1P6 il ot l., O y ot l.; All: s. (N1 om.) fu (O om.) tous esbahis (P6S1 a.)

1072   Yb S. d. l. bons r.; P6 om. 'ce'; S7 r. qui y a c., OQ ja (Q i a) nulz cecy; U om. 'nus'; S1 n. de nous m.

1073   Q1 Yb J'ai trouvé.

1074   N5S1S5U C. c'est, P6O C. est; N2 de cest; N1 om. 'fait'; S1 f. vistement encondis; W s'e. vivement de c. f. e.; O esbahiz; U repeats 1074.

1075   Q1 doi dit; N5S5 doi as diex des Fezonnis, S6S7 doi aus diex qui sont d'E.; N2N6OP6QQ1U il aux diex; P6Q1W des Phezonis.

1076   O om. 'et'; N1 Olimpe.

1077   N1N2N6OQQQ1S1W Ja; P6 Ja voir n. tolre com ne; Yb l. toudrai mie (S6S7 pas) t. (S6S7 cor); N1N6OQU r. (U tolre) dont; N6 om. 'il'.

1078   S7 M. fist; N1N6OQ M. pour l. (N6 om.) f.; Q1S1 l. Jupiter; Q1 et Venis.

1079   W om. Q1 om. 1079-81. S1 Marc; P6 Marcus diex, S7 Mes le duc, N1N6QU M. l. dus; S6S7 de bataille, N1 de b.

1080   P6 C. a s., U Que j'ai s., Rest: Que il s. (S7 sera, O servis); P6 c. ore; Q s. me m.; S1 mercis.

1081   N1N6OQU om. Yb b. sera s.

1082   N6 om. 'bien'; N1N6OQQ1U a. quant a (N6 li) ce e. e. (N1 essis); N5S7 p. que c'est (S7 c. e.) essis; S5 p. que il e., S6 p. qu'il y e.

1083   N1N6OQU om. Yb n. li doins o. (S5S7 ou); S1 l. doit.

1084   O si estoit o.; P6 si est; Yb e. (N5S5 est) hons d.; N1 e. iert.

1085   N1N6OQQQ1U om. 1085-7, N2 Et; Yb d. le; N2N5P6S5S6 q. est.

1086   N2N5P6S5S7 fera; Yb a. si (N5 si y) remaindra t., N2 e. remaindra t., P6 a. a remainbre a t.

1087   N2P6Yb en est.

1088   N2P6Q1Yb Voire d. (N2S5 c. d.), N6 V. de c. d.; N5 M. le signeur; N2OP6QQ1 S1UYb s. des.

1088a   P om. Yb f. contre f.; N1N6OQU c'e. (U cens) faus contre faus entre s., P6 son a.

1089   O S. ce d.

1090   O om. 'Car'; N6OQU d. et prouvez et, N1 d. esprouvés; P6 d. provés e. esclaris.

1091   All om.

Laisse xxvii

1092   P6 om. 'des Grius'; N2P6Q1 Ya Yb ot sa; N2 fine. 1092a All: Et au pris acorder sa gent toute acordee. S6 p. assener, P6Q1W p. acorder, Rest: p. esgarder; Yb toute s. g. mandee; N1QU g. acoardee, O g. couardee, N6 g. a commandee, P6 ordenee.

1093   N1 d. que; N2 q. fu b.; O q. moult; S7 emparles.

1094   U p. par; N5S5S7 p. qui fu sage et senee, S6 p. qui fu bien assenee.

1095   N1N6OQU om. 1095-6. P6 d. cest; Q1 A. si com moy semble ceste chose ordenee.

1096   Q1 om. N2P6 p. les sens (P6 sains) de (N2 d.) diu (N2 diex), S1 p. la sens d. G.; Yb p. les diex de Grece qui sont (N5S5 om. 'qui sont', S6 G. et de ceulz) et (S6 om.) d. C.

1097   P6 Ore; O om. 'bien'; N1N6OQU s. a qui e. est; N5S5 elle est.

1098   N1N6OQS6U om. P6 p. confait joiel, S7 p. quelle jouelle; N5S5 elle est.

1099   Q1 B. ce d. l. r.; U r. or; All: avisee.

1100   N1N6OQQ1U om. In P6 1100 follows 1103. P6S1 Benois; S1 s. ciex d.

1101   N6QS7U Sus; N1N5O en est; N5 esgardee, S5S7 garee, S6 posee.

1102   N1N6OQU om. S6 Ce est l., Q1 Car c'e. l.

1103   N1 secrete, Q secretee, O sechee.

1104   N1N6OQQ1U om.

1105   N1N6QS5U Vostre v. dites, N5OQ1S7 V. v. dites, N2 Vous v. en dites; P6 d. n'en ert j. r., N2 Yb d. ja n'en ert (S5 soit) r., N1N6OQQ1U d. ja ni (Q ne, OQ1U n'en) iert (O sera) refusee.

1106   N1N6OQQ1U om. Yb V. (S6S7 Vos) paroles bien soit; P6 V. volenté en b. soit f.; N2S1W p. bien soit; N2 Yb o. f. (S7 soit f.) o. (N2S7 om.) navaree; S1 aversee.

1107   S6 Quant vous l.; N1 Puis li; QU q. li; N1N6OQQ1U c. je d.

1108   N5S6S7 El premier (N5 premiers) e. Cassamus d.; O l'oisel; All: m. grant renommee.

1109   N2 Ma; N1N6OQU sa conscience; N5S5S7 n'iert; N1 espuree, Q1 ordenee.

1110   N6QU Com, O Comme.

1111   N1N6OP6QU Le; Yb c. donner a. v. m.; N6 c. a v.; P6 d. a m., O d. et m.; N1 hue.

1112   N1N6OQU om. 1112-22. Q1 om. 1112-15. P6 Mais l. r. d. q. sa c. e. parfondee; Yb l. lierne; N2 la la sierne; N2S1Yb e. (S1 et) fourmee; W mesuree.

1113   Yb om. S1W p. qui p.

1114   P6 Yb f. ne d.; N2 anglet; N5S5S6 a. a (S6 ne) guerre, S7 a. agueire (?); N5S5 ni e.

1115   Yb om. 1115-23. N2P6S1W p. qu'en; S1W l. rouseur; P6 q. est b.

1116   N2P6 l. flourceste; N2 l'esclipse, S1 l'aclisse; Q1 Mais l'esclicete dont le cerne est aournee, 1116a Q1 Va. debrisant au vent s'est en brief tans passee.

1117   Q1 om. 1117-25.

1119   N2 e. iert.

1120   P6 et. grande e., N2 en grace entesee.

1122   P6 g. bointé commence.

1123   N1N6OQU A; N2 loe on, O f. la on, U loons, P6 f. puis c'on a boine e.

1124   N1N6OQU revelee.

1125   N1N6OQU om. S7 d. chapelet; Yb c. et (N5S5 om.) tainte e. arree (N5S7 airee).

1126   Q1 outree.

1127   N1N6OQU om. 1127-8. N2P6Q1S1W est bretesquie e. entour (S1W a.) c. (P6 crenelee); Yb est a breteiches e. entour c. (S7 cercelee).

1128   Q1 om. N5S7 E. des; N2P6WYb l. entour.

1129   N2N6QUYb r. sus, N1 r. cest; S5S7 cree.

1130   N1 om. 'Et'; N1N6OQ en (N1 om.) par (O om.) l. comblee; U v. si soit par l. comblee, W parcomplee. 1130a Q1 Et pour ce que le pris est de tel destinee.

1131   Q1 om. 1131-3. N1N6OQU om. 1131-4. Yb P. (S6S7 Par) tout; N2S7 a. apres d., P6 a. au p., S6 a. asprece et p.; P6 finee.

1132   S5 Car; P6 esentee.

1133   All om.

1134   N2P6Q1S1WYb v. si (S7 plus) hautains q.; P6 p. biaus n'i b.; S5S7 vee.

1135   N1N2N5 Los, S6S7 Lors; P6 L. c'on; OU q. l'on; N1O doit; Yb d. apres l'a.

1136   N1N6OQQ1U om. 1136-41. P6S5S7 C. c'est.

1137   S7 d. ceste.

1138   N2 En teste p.

1139   S6 p. ce; P6 doublee est se aünee; S6S7 est ert (S7 soit) h. l. lancee, N5S5 est h. lancee.

1140   P6 posee.

1141   P6 r. tout; W m. haut, N2P6S7 m. (P6 om.) grant.

1142   Yb M. dit b.; P6 n'i v.; N2 v. que; S5S6S7 q. l'en, P6 q. li.
1143   N1N6OQQ1U om. 1143-8. S7 Q. l'entent E.
1144   P6 f. moult.
1145   N5 om. N2P6S1 fu; P6 e. en vin; S5S6S7 Qu'il sambloit qu'elle f. b. et a.
1146   N2Yb Quant; P6 Que M. a si la p.; N2 o. dist; N5 acceptee, S6 contee, S7 finee.
1147   N5 om. P6 otriie, N2 outroie, Rest: otroie; N2 d. touz acetee; S7 e. tuit l'ont a.
1148   N2P6 Yb si est.
1149   P6 e. o. vont u. a. ont d.; N1N6OQQ1U L'aigle d'or a li roys tantost (Q1 roys en l'eure) dont (OQ1 om.) demandee.
1150   All om.
1151   S6S7 s. du, N2N5P6S1S5W s. au; N1N6OQQ1U s. li ont ilec dont (Q1 o. prestement) a.; P6 r. li o. tost; N2S1S6W r. li o. lors, N5S5S7 r. lors li o. a.
1152   P6 Coronne d'o. fin, S1 Une c. d'o., O Et couronne d'o., Rest: E. couronnete d'or.; O ont au; N1 pesee.
1153   S1 De; N5S5S7 om. 'huchier'; S6 m. y fist l. r. moult g. m; N1N6OQU Li menestrel (Q menesterel, O m.) i ont mout grant feste aree (O aidee); Q1 Li m. y ont mainte note sonnee.
1154-55   All om.
1156   N1N6OQQ1U om. 1156-7. N5 Nacaire; N2P6S1WYb t. mainte trompe doree (N5 sonnee).
1157   S7 A, N5S5S6 Hors; P6 v. courrant.
1158   All: L'a. par; N5S7 q. fu b., N1N6OQU q. (N1Q que) b. est (N1 ert); P6 emplumee.

Laisse xxviii

1159   N1N6OQU Devant, Q1 Enz en; P6Q1 la presse N2WYaYb la f.; N6 f. esta; N1N6QU s. (N1 ces) sergant; N5S5 sivans.
1160   N2 Au; N1N6OQQ1U Tout arengie (U arengiee, Q1 arrengiement, O arrengiez) v. (O vous) l. l. (N1 les luy, O la place, U l. l. si) porprenant; N2Yb porprenant.
1161   N1N6OQQ1U om. P6 Par; All: et a v.; S7 v. le lieu porprenant; N2N5P6S5S6 rompant.
1162   S7 om. N5 L. feste; S5S6 Et l. feste s'o.; N1N6OQU c. (O trompete) sonner s. (N1 ci, O se) v. esbaudissant (N1 en baudissant); Q1 s'o. qui l. va; Q1W achaignant.
1163   N2P6 p. a. si (P6 en) a. par devant.
1164   N1N6OQ L'a. portoit sur un gant (N1 grant, O hault) hautement (O ornement), U L'a. portoit hautement sus .i. g.; P6 Et l'a. coronné portois; Yb en (S7 om.) h. par amont p. desus (N5S5 sus); N2Q1 h. parement; N2P6S1W p. desus.
1165   S1 Aimes li dus; OQ E. l'avoit; N2 cointoiant, S6 convoitant, S7 conduisant.
1166   Q1 M. d'a. p.; N1N6OQU Marsillon (O M.) qu'o. apeloit. 1166a N1N6OQQ1U Li jugleur y vont de leur mestier fesant (O sonnant, Q1 joant).
1167   N1N6OQQ1U om. 1167-9. N2 Q. afestiement, S1 Q. efforcieement; Yb l'aloit adestriant.
1168   P6 les keutes soustenant, S1Yb la queue s. (S5 seurportant).
1169   N2I-bS1WYb f. t. (S6 bondir) et en (P6 om.) h. vont c.
1170   N1N6OQ v. que; N1N6OQS6S7U A. maine; Q1 d. en; N2S1 talent, OQ amant.
1171   Yb om. N1N6OQQ1U om. 1171-82. S1 Et qui sont si sougis et font tuit si commant.
1172   N5S5 om. 1172-3. N2 l. mes/mus (?); P6 A nous est grant doucours solais et fieste grant. S1 En joie sont tout jours baut lie et joiant.
1173   S1 om. S6S7 v. qu'A. (S6 qui A.) maine.
1174   S1 Et ainsi qu'E., S7 Ensement qu'E.; P6 p. E.; N2 a. le; S1Yb a. le pavement (N5S5 paiement).
1175   N5S5 E. a c.; S1 Yb c. en son; N5S5S7 om. 'chant'; S6 c. moult h. chantant.
1176   S5 M. a.
1177   S6 De q. cela s. q. ert si a.; N5 q. ce afferoit q. est a.; S5S7 q. cils (S7 cis) s. (S7

seroit) q. e. a.; S1 De la feste qu'il ooient et qu'est senefiant.

1178	N5S6S7 q. les; S5 le servoit; P6S1 savoient l. aloient d. (S1 noncant); Yb s. les a.
1179-81	All om.
1182	P6 C'est les p. de v.; S1 Yb q. f. si pesant; P6 vaillant.
1183	N1N2N6OQQ1U om. 'Et'; N1OP6Q E. aloit a (N1 au); N2N5S5S7 l'a. a; N6Q1 U E. si l'a. (N6 a.); P6 denoncant. 1183a N1N6OQQ1U Et devant (O d'avant) toz (O om.) aloit li aigle d'or mostrant O demoustrant).
1184	N1N6OQQ1U om. 1184-8. N2N5S6W Proumettre; P6 e. pour sacier, N2 e. rasaucier, S1S7 e. ressaucier.
1185	S7 om. P6 De parole a tour sa proaice ataignant; N2 p. auctours sa proesce entariant; N5S1S5S6 p. acors aloit (N5S5 om., S1 moult souvent) enchariant.
1186	Yb Et d.; S1 Et p. d. Fezone aussi en trespassant; W apassant.
1187	P6 e. pouroffrant.
1188	N2P6S1Yb v. Y. (N5 Elyos) reva reconversant (N2P6 r., S5 en conversant).
1189	N2N5P6S6S7 Et (S7 om.) p. devant (N2 om.); N2P6S1WYb Porus Lyoine; N1N6OQQ1U P. devant Ydorus et Porus ensement.
1190	Yb om. O om. second 'et'.
1191	N1N6OQU P. et (O l.) B. (N1 Baudrier) q. ot l. v.; P6 l. cuer o.
1192	N1N6OQQ1U om. 1192-7. P6S7 e. s'en; S1 Yb remontant, N2P6 demonstrant.
1193	S1W E. com; P6S1S7W f. s'en va s. (S1S7 sus), N2N5S5S6 f. se va sus (S6 vers).
1194	S1Yb P. ot; N2 om. 'ont'; P6 et les; W rougissant.
1195	S6 C. il; P6 q. a l.; N5S1S6S7 ait a ce le (S7 a celle) cuer t.; P6 atendant, S5 baiant.
1196	P6 Tant; W chascuns cuer; P6S7 d'e. le c. si (P6 om.) h.
1197	S7 om. S1 om. 'Que'; S6 e. autre; N2N5P6S1S5S6W bienfesant.
1198	S7 om. 'Et'; O ot tout; S1S5S6 o. alé t.; S1 Yb tournoiant, N1N6OQU ordenant.
1199	S7 om. N2 offerte; P6 o. et; Q1 retraiant.
1200	O om. P6S6S7 P. devant, N1N6QU Et p. devant.
1201	P6Q1S1Yb en oiant.
1202	P6Q1S1Yb V. recevrés, N2 V. detendrois.
1203	S6 Cassamus du Larris l.; P6 l. vrai.
1204	N1N6OQU Or; S1 d. son frere, N1 as P, Rest: d. frere.
1205	P6W A, Rest: Et; N5S1S5S7 l. enchaï.
1206	All om.
1207	S1 p. les douz diex, Yb p. les diex, P6 p. les sens d. d.; O E. plaissent es diex; S6 s. de tous l. p. p.
1208	S7 om. 'Mais'; O Que; S1S6 M. vois li p.; P6 v. l'emporterés, N2S7 v. li p.; O d. au.
1209	S1 s. serquite, S6S7 s. sarqueute e. le tenrés v.; N6Q s. sarlieu; O s. aultier tant que serés v.; P6 m. itant.
1210	P6 om. 'Tant'; N2S1 Yb T. com; S6 om. 'i'; N1N6OQU T. com (O come) l'a. p.; S1S5S7 e. vif; P6 e. et v. et m.
1211	N1N6QS1UYb dient; P6 et si l. f. p.; O l. en f. pesant, Yb l. sont moult (S5 bien); N1N6QQ1S1UW f. (S1 est) moult; N1 QU pesant, N6 pensant. 1211a N1N6OQU Et sont (N6 en sont) tuit d'un acort et en vont mout joiant (Q1 joant).
1212	N1 n. enuileur, N6Q n. enulex; N1N6OQU ne n. murmurement; Q1 Nulz n'en fu envers eulz courcié ne m.
1213	All: li vassaus; U b. me v.; N1 m'i vas consentant, O m'i voy ensement.
1214	O om. P6 Voiant tout; N2P6YaYb r. par itel.
1215	O soit les dieux; S1S5S6S7 p. moi; P6 lui voient visant; S1 s. vueillant.
1216	N6OQU Amie, N1 Ame; N5S5 p. amis; P6 p. amit belle; N1N6OQU om. 'veille'; S7 v. ce t. on; U ou le; All om. 'en'.
1217	Q1 N'o. pas; P6 n'oubliiés, O n'oubliray; S1 d. sa j.; N1N6OQU d. Caulus en.
1218	N5S5 l'o. mie.
1219	Q1S7 om. P6 m. volenté q. d'u. seu lieu descent; N1N5O b. que; N6 q. bien; N6S1 s. le; N5 replant, S5S6 resplent, Ya reprant.
1220	O Et; S1 Yb m. si; P6 m. ore l. est; N1N6OQU li soit.
1221	S7 om. 1221-6. W beneois, S5S6 beneoit; W r. cui, P6S5 r. qui; Q1S1S5S6 si

v. s.; N5 om. 'si'; N1N6OQU que (N6 q. je) vois (O voiez, U veons) si (O cy) souvant.

1222   N2 Par; Ya Yb Que s'o. (S1 Yb s'oroison); P6 ne veut, S6 ne va; N1OQS5U nul bon; N6 om. 'nul bien'; S1 b. en murissant; N1N6 amerissant, N2OP6QS6W amenrissant, U amendrissant, N5 aennutrissant (?).

1223   Q1 om. N1N2 l'anvoie; O d. por ce q., Q d. pore, U d. pour; P6 i. vont variant; N1N6OQU i. va (Q vi) octroiant (N1 controiant) N5S1S5 v. vaquant; S6 Aincois l'a. a d. por tant qu'il v. vaquant.

1224   N5 om. N1N6OQU b. afaiblir enforce (O a force) entredoublant; S5 a. enforcier, S6 a. forcie, Q1 a. enforce; P6 r. il e. doublant. 1224a S1 Pour iceste raison je le di en oiant.

1225   N1N6OQU Proece h.; N5S5S6 c. reson; N2 di dun; P6 om. 'ne'; N1N2OU fu, Rest: fust; S1 Que de iceste chose il n. fust or n.

1226   N1N6OQ De, Rest: Se; N2 n. fu; N5S6 n. refust mis (S6 nus) a.; N1 f. demis, U f. tenus; N6OQS1S5W remis.

Laisse xxix

1228   OQ Et e.; N5S6S7 renvoisiés; P6 e. est a., N5S6S7 e. est (N5 s'e.) alés, N1OQS1 e. c'est a. (S1 alé); Q achacier, U fichier.

1229   S1 touz ceulz qu'il; P6 q. se v., O q. vouloient.

1230   N1N6OQU se set, N2 se sest, P6 se seut; P6 manoiier, N1N6OQU chastier.

1231   W om. Q .i. point; P6 et gaitement, N1N6OQ et coiement, U et acoiement.

1233   S1Yb v. acomplir, O v. pour a suivre, N1 v. poursuivre, Q1 v. parfurnir; OP6Q reprocier, S6 desirier.

1234   N1N6OQU om. N2S1Yb p. drecier. 1234a-k Ya Yb see Notes.

1235   S7 om. N6 f. hautement le p. a.; P6 p. bellement.

1236   S1 E. ariere refist, Yb E. au lever f. (S5 refist, S6 a fait, S7 f. on); U f. a la f.; P6Q1S1 commencier.

1237   P6S1Yb T. et tabourer o. e. b. (P6 noisier); N2 o. tabeur; N1N6OQU o. et apres vieler.

1238   All om.

1239   O om. N1 C. de; Q1S1Yb p. i mist la (Q1S5S7 sa) main; N1N6OQU p. si (N1 ce) mist s. main a atirer; P6 om. 'i'; N2W mist a; P6 m. a sourhaucier, S1 pour renvoisier.

1240   S7 om. 1240-42. N2S1Yb o. (N2 o. si) tres grant biau; N1N6OQU o. moult g. bel d.; P6 i avoit moult grande et d. moult p.; Q1 La f. y fu moult g. et le d. p.

1241   O om. 1241-3. P6Q o. que; W o. par raison q. d. a.; N2Q1YaYb p. droiture.

1242   W om. 'ce'; P6 c. c'on.

1243   P6 d. desci a, N2 d. jusque a, Q d. jusqu'a.

1244   S1 E. toute n. aussi j., O E. toute l. n. j.; S7 om. second 'nuit'; P6 n. desci a; N2N5S1S5 l'ajournier.

1245   N6S1WYb Et; S5 E. qui il n'o.; N1 e. quoy n'o. q. songer; S1 Yb qu'esgaier, N2N6OQQ1U qu'enseignier (U om. 'qu'). 1245a P6 Pour le restor si fist moult loer et prisier.

1246   P6 om. 1246-53. N5 en sa; N2 o. oeuvrent, O o. se tenoit l'ouvrier; S6 e. l. ormier.

1247   N1N6OQU C. le.

1248   N2Q1YaYb E. l'un p. y. trestous; O respont s. racointier; S1 s. targier, S6S7 s. dangier.

1249   N6W tout, Rest: tous, S7 D. tous s. v. de bon cuer et entier; S1 s. acointier, O s. chalangier, S6 s. recouvrier, 1249a-c N1N6QU, 1249c O; Et sanz nul boisement (N1 voisement) ne sanz nul destorbier, Vostre sommes en fin et par grant desirier Feron vo volenté sanz nul (O om., U point) contrelaiier (N1 contralier, O contre aller, U contrarier).

1250   N1 Ainz c., N6 Au c., Q Auc c., O Avoir c.; N2P6Q1 Ya Yb voulons; Q1S6 v. arriere r., S7 no tere, N5S5 n. pais, N1N6OQU v. a vos (N6 no, U nos) dieux; S1 retourner.

1252   S1 Yb c. a tous j. vous p. m. f.

1253   S7 om. S1 adieu sanz ma court e.; O esloingnier, S6 recouvrier.

Laisse xxx

1254 N2Q1YaYb Puis; O parus.
1255 P6 d. a qui son e. c., S1 d. qui sains e. et drus., S7 d. qui s. e. et crus; N1N6OQ
d. que.
1256 P6 om. 'de'.
1257 U O ou en a., P6 U il a., N1 Cil an a.; S1S6S7 Capidus.
1258 N2 n'i fist, O n'i mis.
1259 OP6W sor, Rest: sus, P6S1S7W crenus, U charnus, N1 querrus, N6Q quernus,
O quarus, N2N5Q1S5S6 cremus.
1260 N6 r. se leva s'est cachiez e. v.; P6 ja c.; Q et chaciez.
1261 P6 Q. ces j.; N2S1 espandus.
1262 S7 om. N2E. desur; Q le c., P6 ces coursiers, Rest: l. coursiers.
1263 N1 P. les; O fut.
1264 P6 Errannment est, O A bref mot; U om. 'aus'.
1265 Q Chascun dieu; S6 om. 'd' yaus'; All: qui miex (U om.) miex (P6 puet) est c.
l. (P6 c. l. e.)v.
1266 O Davant lui encline; P6 et si; N2Q1 Ya Yb e. et i. l. (O et lui en) rent s.
1268 P6 Puis, O La, Q1 Tout, W Et; O o. environner.
1269 All om.
1270 Q r. que; N5 d'o. est.
1271 O om. N2YaYb Ou; N1 s. de m., S1S6S7 s. d'amours; N6 o. qu'il.
1272 N2 F. i f.; W f. c. cis, P6 f. torsis de lor longeur et p.; N5S1S6S7 chi de leur gent
est (N5 a) l. p.; N1N2N6QQ1S5UW s. (S5 est) d. lor gent (Q1 leurs gens) l. p.;
O Fairent ung service de ses parens estoient le p.
1273 Q n. de.
1274 N1N2N6OQQ1U L. firent alumer; W a. li cierge, P6 a. li encens, O l. torches,
N2S1S5S6S7 l. cires.
1275 N6 om. N2Q1WYb Philosophes poetes, P6S1 Philosophes posteis (P6 et
prestres), N1OQU Pholote (U Philote) li poestez (O poete, N1 prestres);
N2N5OP6QQ1S5S7UW ot maint.
1276 N1OP6QS6U Sacrefice; N6P6S1U i (P6S1 om.) ont f. (P6 faite, N6 om.), N2S7
i o. fais; N1OQQ1 om. 'fait'; N1P6 m. grande, N1OQQ1U m. grandes, N2S1S6
m. tres g. (N2 grans) v.
1277 O om. N1N6QU d. lor raisons (QU raison); Q1 d. leur o. f. li vieux s.; P6 l'o.
d'iaus fu c. s.
1278 P6 om. 'Et'; N2 C. ou; P6 et l'Indois.
1279 N6 C. a d.
1280 N1 E. l'a.; N6Q l'a. achacier chantement, Q1 l'a. encharnier chantoient,
N1N2OP6S1UWYb atachier chantoient (OP6 canterent) Q1S1S5W granz.
1281 N1N6OQU Uns (O ung) vers que (N1U qui) porte avoit (U q. avoit non);
P6 .i. viers, N2 .i. vert; N5S5 v. qu'il porterent; S6S7 q. se disoit.
1282 W Q. estoit c. d.; O Chanté e.; All: s. leur (O leurs);
1283 P6 s. reparus.
1284 O n'estoit m., N5Q1 as P, Rest: n'iert m. (S1 pas); Yb rompus, S1 de refus.
1285 P6 Tans estoit d.; N6Q fust; N6 om. 'de'; O estoient, S1 iert; OQ1 leurs a.
1286 U donne; N5OS5 m. le preu.
1287 P6 B. o d., S1 B. la belle Ephesonnus.
1288 OS5 om. N1N6QU Et, P6 om. 'A'; N5 est; N6 apelez et, S6 rapesiez et; N1Q om.
'et'; N2Q1YaYb d. bouche a. S1Yb absus).
1289 N2 U y. li; N1 au g. e. au m.; S7 om. 'grans'; N5 e. a m.
1290 N1Q1S1W touz.
1291 N1N6OQQ1U Un.
1292 Q1 crestus, N2P6 Ya Yb menus.
1293 OS7 om. P6 Et veist on des m.; N2W Foisons d.; N1 m. plusiers i ot et; N6 p. i
ot et; U e. avec t.; N1N6QU om. 'noviaus'.
1294 N1 Car cil, O Cellui m., U Q. cist; P6 t. les a. vaincus.
1295 All om.
1296 All: A. mengier (W d.) y ot (N1Q om. 'y ot') maint (N2 m., O om.) biau mot
(N1N2N5Q1W b. m.) ramentus (O retenus, P6 r.).
1297 N2 D. estour, S1S7Q retor, N1 recort; S1 p. dont parlé est desus, Yb q. si est
ramentus, N2QQ1U q. si ert e., O q. estoit eslus; N1N6 om. 'si'.
1298 O om. 1298-9. P6 Et d., S1S7 Qui d., N6QQ1U Et (U Et en) t., N1 Antre l.; Q1

b. diz furent; U l. grans poins f. il bien r.; N1N2N6P6QQ1S1Yb en (N1 pour) grant g. (N1N6Q om.); N6 repeats 'en grant';

1299 S1 En moult g., S6 En tres g., N5S5S7 En g.; N1N6Q estoient; S1 Yb e. cil.
1300 U Q. uns; P6 p. ses i. porter e.; Q1 p. avoir; S1 Yb s. (S1 ces) i. desus (N5 d'en sus); O A le regarder avoient les i. e. s.
1301 O Et si d.; P6 d. entreus, Q1 d. trestuit; N5 b. a f., Rest: b. l'a f.
1302 N6 receüs.
1303 N5S5 Si a l., N1N6OQ Se a l., S1 Si a bien l.; Yb v. autant; P6 v. sour tous l. a. sourcreus, S1 v. li autre aconsus; N1 om. 'de tant'; OQ1UYb secourus, N1N6Q souscourus.
1304 N5Qui, N1N6OP6QQ1U Et; S7 s. retors, N1 s. recors, S6 s. veus si e.
1305 S6S7 p. ses dis, N5S5 p. ses fu, S1 p. ces fais f. ce p.; Q1 s. f. est; N2 fu cis; O om. 'fu'; N5P6S5 ramenteus, N1N6OQU remanus.
1306 N1N6OQQ1S7U om. S5 Que t. f. anientis a.; P6 f. anientis et mortis.
1307 N6 om. Q1 Car; O f. nostre.
1308 N1N6OQQ1U om. P6 Qu'il f. faire la court e.; N2 il il e. fu l'a. en la cort e. l. c. V.

Laisse xxxi

1309 S1Yb E. la b.
1310 N6OP6QS1UYb Sus; Q1S5 n. pilier; O e. le leva; N1N6QU aleva, N2 restora.
1311 All: q. vouloit, P6 om. 'le vit'; N1N6OQQ1U regarda.
1312 All om.
1313 N2N5P6S5WYa Et (OQ Ou) son (N1 le, N6 a, U au, OQ om.); N2Q1WYaYb passa (N6 parla, N1 parsa, Q pasa).
1314 P6 Et q. l.; S6S7 b. forment l'e.; N5P6S5 om. 'bien'; S1 m. si; N1N2N6OQQ1UW m. (O si) l'en (N2 le) remercia (U remenia).
1315 S1 A. ces.
1316 N5 et...(?) et.; All: et Marcien h.
1317 All: Gadifer et Betis et si leur presenta.
1318 N1N6OQU Et sa gent (O ses gens) avec li a (O o, N1 et) t. pooir qu'il a; Q1 Li et toute sa gent a le pooir qu'il a; N2 son atour et t.; P6S1 Yb c. et.
1319 W om. Q1 D. se on; N1 q. ce on, O q. si on; N1 m. q. on, O m. qu'il, S5 m. que lor.
1320 All but P6 om. P6 E. si lea b. qu'il l. m.
1321 Q1S6 Trestouz, N5S5 Et tous; P6Q1S1 Yb l'en (Q1S1S5S6 le) mercierent; N1N6QU le mercient; P6Q1 b. que fait lor a, N5 b. qui l., N6 b. que l.
1322 N2P6W a. el, N6OQS7U a. ou; N1N6OQU liu ou; N2N6QQ1S1UYb r. leur d., N1 r. l'ordena, O r. ordonna.
1323 OQS7 l. roys; W A. vers.
1324 N6 i ala; O o. le e.
1325 All: Par force tout le mont acquist (OYb conquist, P6 prist, N1N6QQ1U vainqui) et c.
1326 N2Q1WYaYb E. lors; N1N5OP6 qu'il ot, U qu'il or; P6W o. conquis la mors le desevra (W l'en desnua), N2Q1YaYb o. conquis erranment le (N6 se) l. 1326a W En brief tans le conquist et briement le laissa.
1327-28 All om.
1329 N2S1Yb C. fine, O C. furent; N5O le veu; S1 v. com il v., S6S7 v. que il v., U v. que i v., O v. c'on li v.
1330 Yb Beneoit; N2 s. il d. dieu qui de cuer p.; S7 s. de dieu qui p. li p.; S1S6 p. li si (S6 en) p.
1331 N2 m. fist, Q1 Ya Yb m. prist.
1332 O en en p. l'a., Q en p. l'a., P6 e. sa p. l'a.; S1S6 p. si a., N1N5S5U p. il a., N6 p. il l'a.
1333 S1 v. si; Q1 p. Le Restor y enta. 1333a Q1 Que cilz qui fist les Veus a mettre y oublia.
1334 Q1 om. 1334-6. P6 om. 'celui'; N1 c. que je i antai (?); S7 om. 'i'; O entra.
1335 O Retour, S7 Retor; S6 c. y ajousta.
1336 N1 Au, N6OQ A, U Et; N2YaYb compassa.

Variants for Part II, Laisse xxxi, continued

1337 S1Yb c. Elyos Marcien e. 1337a N2WYaYb Comment (N1OQU Comme, N6 (Com) li roys le prist (W pris) assist et acorda.

1338 P6 E. comment, Q1 Comment E., S6 E. a E.; N5S1S5S7 om. 'comme'; S1 espousa.

1339 N1N6Q A j. 1339a-b Q1 Et de l'estrif des veux qu'il y acompaigna, S'en dites tous et toutes .i. Ave Maria.

1340 Q1S1UWYb om. 1340-42. N6Q q. les.

1341 N1N2N6OQ om. 1341-2.

1342 P6 Et d. b.

NOTES ON THE TEXT: PART I

Laisse i

2   *aporte* P stands alone but 'acorde' and 'aferme' may be *lectiones faciliores*. Accepting the meaning 'alleges' for 'aporte' the reading in P makes sense.

3-5   The introduction of a literary work by a proverb is recorded by E. Faral in *Les arts poétiques du XIIe et du XIIIe siècle* (Paris, 1924), pp. 55-59. Brisebare has three and these do not convey a general truth relating to the work but rather serve to sanction it.

6-8   A similar apology occurs in *RAlix* Br. IV, 1610, 'Cui Dieus done le sens il nel doit celer mie'.

9-11   The poet proposes to insert an episode omitted in the Alexander cycle, namely the carrying out of Edea's vow made in *Voeux* 4076-80 to restore the peacock in gold (see *Restor* I 63-67 and 280-94).

12-46   A summary of Alexander's exploits described in the *Roman d'Alixandre*.

14-15   *seignouris, vois* Feudal technicalities expressing the lord's position and rights over his vassals, while *serviches, hommages, fois* describe the duties of a vassal to his lord. P alone has *autres* in line 15. It avoids the jingle 'hommes', 'hommages' of the other manuscripts but the author may have intended 'hommes' to contrast with 'terre et air et mer' in line 14 so P could be wrong. 'Autres' was possibly copied in error from line 17.

16-19   Reference to Alexander's submarine descent. The glass vessel and the battles of the fishes from which Alexander learned lessons of military strategy are described in *RAlix* Br. III, 364-595 and particularly in 422-64.

18   *alois* Gf. gives *'alliage'* and T-L. *'Mischung', 'Legierung'*. Possibly Brisebare intended the meaning 'alloy', a mixture of metals, for glass is also a mixture made by the fusion of sand, potash, etc. In that case the reading 'c'est' for 'ces' in N6 Q1S1W may be right. Or 'alois' may be a noun, unrecorded, derived from *aloiier* and meaning 'bonds'. The vessel is described as being bound with bands of iron in the L version (*M.F.R.A.* III):

> 488   Tant soltiument l'ot fait de fer loier entor
>   Qu'il n'atouche au vaissel de pres de demi dor;
>   De deus bendes le çaint, de plain doi le gregnor.

In *RAlix* Br. III the vessel is sealed with lead, and iron bands are not mentioned: 435 'Et fu de toute pars a plonc bien seëlés.' It is also possible that 'alois' is a misreading of 'a itel loi' from this description of the vessel in Br. III:

> 408   Molt bons ouvriers de voirre avoit aveques soi
>   Qui savoient ouvrer le voirre *a itel loi*
>   Que il ne pooit fendre ains le metent en ploi

20-22   Refers to Alexander's flight in a car drawn by griffins, *RAlix* Br. III, 4914-5098. *un cuir de biois* 'Biois' may be a rhyme variant for *biais*. The skin would be used on the cross so that it could be stretched over a frame-work of timber. In *RAlix* Br. III Alexander gives orders for the car to be made, 'De cuirs envelopee, novel soient et cru/ A las les m'atachiés et englüés a glu' (4998-99). Later, when the workmen have finished, the author comments, 'Cil ont si charpenté et le cuir estendu' (5009).

21   In Br. III, 5032 the number is seven or eight, 'Ne sai ou set ou uit en i a acouplés', but Brisebare may have taken four from 5063 which states, 'A quatre des oisiaus a les liens trenchiés'. In Br. I also four are mentioned, 'Quant

la chaiere d'or en fu lassus portee/ Par les quatre grifons a qui fu acouplee' (74-75). In the L version (409) they are two.

The birds are described as 'li oisel fameilleus' in Br. III, 5039.

22-23   P and S1 differ from the rest in reading 'par' for 'por' in 22 and 'tous' for 'prist' in 23. In the PS1 reading Alexander had himself borne aloft over the whole world in order to see Nicolas and the other persons and places listed. In the other manuscripts Alexander ascends in order to see the whole world. Then, reading 'prist', a new sentence begins listing Alexander's conquests. As Nicolas dies in Br. I he could not have been seen during the flight which is described in Br. III, so PS1 are probably wrong here.

22   *ce n'est nus nois* This phrase, found also in II 335 and 606, is not in the dictionaries. Only N6P6 (S1 partially) here and P6W in the other two instances, support the reading. As 'nois' is masculine, could it perhaps be a post-verbal noun on *nier* and the meaning 'there is no denying it'?

23   *Nicolas de Nicole* King of Caesarea *RAlix*, Br. I 776-7 and 1400. The war against Nicolas in *RAlix* Br. I 583-1656. Nicolas was killed by Alexander in single combat. The city of Nicole is not mentioned elsewhere.

24   *Surie RAlix* Br. I 2660-2676 Alexander takes Syria without fighting and gives it to Antiocus who builds Antioch.

Alemaigne RAlix Br. I 165 Olimpias brought the land to Philip on their marriage.

Persans The defeat of Darius, King of Persia, is described in *RAlix* Br. II 2965-3074, his death in Br. III 265-312.

Aufricois Alexander's desire to conquer Africa is mentioned in *RAlix* Br. I 2719-20, and Alexander himself refers to his conquest in Br. III 385 and Br. IV 550.

25   *Gresse RAlix* Br. I 146,205,243. Part of Philip's domain.

Inde Major The defeats of Porus, King of India, are described in *RAlix* Br. III, 596-877 and 1678-2148.

Babilonois Alexander's desire to conquer Babylon is mentioned in *RAlix* Br. I 134 and the battles of Babylon are described in Br. III 5149-7218.

26   *la tour de Babel RAlix* Br III 6237-9. Alexander threatens to take the tower in the battle of Babylon. He enters it as conqueror in Br. III 7217.

27   *Amazone* A bloodless conquest described in *RAlix* Branch III 7219-7707.

Rommains RAlix Br. III 383. Alexander mentions his conquest of the Romans.

Franchois RAlix Br. II 1243. Not a conquest but used to describe a brave fighter.

28   *Femenie.*The land of the Amazons, so called in the Arsenal Version laisse 390, line 5422.

29   *Tir.* The siege of Tyre is described in *RAlix* Br. I. 2678-3284 and the taking of city in Br. II 1875-2015.

30-46   A summary of the *Fuerre de Gadres* which relates the foraging expedition led by Emenidus into the valley of Josaphas to obtain food for Alexander's armies besieging Tyre. cf. *RAlix* II 1-1874. The foraging of Gadres is the subject of *M.F.R.A.* IV. For the history of Br. II and correction of *M.F.R.A.* IV see D.J.A. Ross, 'A new manuscript of the Latin *Fuerre de Gadres'*, (note 2 p. 24).

31   *.vii. cens rengiés et trois* The variant reading 'estrois' may be right as the number of foragers and that of their attackers are 700 and 30,000 in *RAlix* Br. II, 499, 'Car ne sont que set cens et cil trente mil erent', cf. *Restor* I 34.

32   *bissal* 'troop of hinds'. In *RAlix* Br. II, 29, the animals are 'bestes' and in 45 guarded by 'vachiers'. In the Latin *Fuerre* they are 'boues et oues et animalia multa' guarded by 'pastores' (Ross, loc. cit. pp. 238-39). The variant 'bestail' may be the better reading. 'Bistal' in P7 seems to be a conflation of the two words.

33   *Emenidus* The chief of Alexander's twelve peers. The name probably derives from Eumenes of Cardia, Alexander the Great's secretary. In the *Restor* his early exploits are described (I 250-896).

34   *li dus Betis* The leader of the men of Gadres in *RAlix* Br. II is not the same person as Betis of Epheson, son of Gadifer du Laris a hero of the *Voeux* and its sequels.

35   *Gadifers* Gadifer du Laris, father of Gadifer, Betis and Phezonas of Epheson and

202

brother of Cassamus.
In *RAlix* Br. II he is a prince of Egypt:

> 1189 Gadiffer de Larris ou croissent li paumier
> Qui la terre d'entour a toute a justicier
> El roiaume d'Egypte n'ot mellor chevalier.

He was a powerful enemy of Alexander's and was slain by Emenidus at the foraging of Gadres. cf. *Restor* I 46 and 900-1.

39 *Par faute de message* When the foragers were hard-pressed by the overwhelming numbers of the enemy Emenidus wished to send to Alexander for help. Each knight in turn refused to undertake this mission deeming that it would be a dishonour to leave the field of battle. Finally Aristé, sorely wounded, agreed to go.

44 *as tors ne as berfrois* Alexander was building assault towers in order to take Tyre. *RAlix* Branch II 1-12 and 1910-17. The reading in P is right here. The reading *en* for *as* in the other mss. is an alteration of a scribe who missed the allusion and took it simply as the general term for 'in safety'.

47-64 An account of the *Veus du Paon*. During a truce in the battle of Epheson knights and ladies of the opposing sides make ceremonial vows over the body of a peacock killed by Porus (cf. *Restor* I 58). In this poem the performing of all the vows except Edea's is described.

47 *Clarus* Brother of Porus, King of India, and father of young Porus who killed the peacock. He was killed by Cassamus during the siege of Epheson.

48 *Epheson* Fortress and court of Gadifer du Laris and scene of the action in the *Voeux*. The name is perhaps a deformation of Ephesus in Ionia.

50 *Cassamus* Brother of Gadifer du Laris and a suitor of Edea's in the *Voeux*. He met Alexander after the capture of Defur and persuaded him to come to the aid of Epheson.

52 *Chaldois* The other mss have 'son harnois'. The people of Epheson are called 'gent de Chaldee' I 1202 and 'la gent caldiue' in II 753. In the *Voeux* they are 'Caldain', W 606, 'Caldés', W 1331, 'Caldiien', W 3762. As Alexander commands the men of Epheson as well as his own this may have led Brisebare to think that he brought them with him.

53 *Barbarois* Probably Berbers fighting with Clarus's army. The form 'Barbarin' occurs in the *Voeux* 3825. They could possibly be barbarians, i.e. the enemy from the point of view of the Greeks.

54 *Porus* Son of Clarus (I 259), nephew of Porus of India (I 258).
li Baudrois is Cassiel, sultan of Baudres (I 107). Both were taken prisoner at the first battle of Epheson and were received in the city with great courtesy.

59 *hastiers, espois* As they both mean 'roasting spit' perhaps 'No roasting spit was ever better supplied', (sc. with a bird to roast on it).

61 *narois* This is not in Gf. or T-L. It may be connected with the German *närrisch*, 'foolish', 'extravagant', cf. II 660 'nareus', also at the rhyme, which likewise describes a vow.

63 *Edea* A lady of Epheson. In the *Voeux* she is the sister of Ydorus (W 396) 'Edee et Ydorus filles Antigonier'. She is also related to Phesonas, 'Fezonie la bele et sa niece Edeüs' (*Voeux* W 531).

65 *lui cortement es plois* The reading in P may be corrupt but the versions in the other mss seem to be emendations. Gf. glosses *cortement* as *'promptement'* and T-L. gives *'kurz'* temporally and spatially. In I 9 Brisebare claims that there is lacking in the Alexander story '.i. molt biaus plois' which may mean an episode or incident. Gf. is not very helpful under the head *ploit, ploi* giving meanings such as *'tour'*, *'situation'*, *'ordre'*, *'lien'*, etc. Perhaps the word conveys the idea of the twists and turns of the action and so in the plural could mean the story itself. I can only suggest, 'I read briefly (or quickly) in the story', (i.e. in the *Voeux*). The other mss except P7 have 'ce ne fu pas es plois' which seems to be a revision of the version in P. P7 has 'dont ne fist pas esplois', 'he did not make a success of it'?

67 *Clarus le Mazonois* Clarus was an Indian (see I 47) and Mazonois may describe the inhabitants of some Indian territory. In the *Voeux* Mazonie is considered

an oriental country, perhaps the same as Amazonie, and in W 443 'li roys de Mazonie' is Alexander. In W 2109 the spy who betrays an ambush proposed by Porus justifies his action by claiming to have been born in Mazonie, so presumably this was not Indian territory. The Mazonois are the people of that country, e.g. *Voeux* W 3384. In the *Venjance Alixandre* Mazone is a variant of Valgarni or Valgrene, the land of Alior and Candace, i.e. a country of India, and this may be what Brisebare had in mind. In his edition of *Venjance* E. B. Ham used M as the base manuscript and Valgrene occurs in 505. The variant of this in QS is Mazone and in P Mazoine.

Laisse ii

Brisebare returns to the *Voeux*. Lines 69-97 correspond closely to *Voeux* W 8256-77. Line 68 serves to link this passage with Brisebare's introductory laisse.

69   P7 omits this line and copies eleven lines beginning, 'Et quant on ot Porron a la terre mis jus', a version of Ritchie's laisse 7a (see pp. 35-36 and 38 note 1).

79   None of the manuscripts corresponds exactly with *Voeux* (W 8266) which reads, 'Madame, il m'est molt bien, loés en soit Marcus! '

84   *Marciiens* A Persian ally of Clarus of India. He is 'le seigneur de Persie' II 61, cousin of the younger Porus, I 1008 and nephew of Clarus, II 239.

88   Following this line in the *Voeux* W alone has a passage, probably interpolated, where Alexander bids Emenidus send for his niece Lydoine. He calls Gadifer to make peace with Emenidus. He will arrange marriages between Porus and Phesonas, the Baudrain and Edea, and Betis and Ydorus, after which they will go to Babylon. Emenidus sends two knights for Lydoine and she sets off on her journey (W 8278-8360). The next laisse in *Voeux* includes a short passage where Porus is informed that Alexander has released his prisoners and they have become his liege men (W 8361-66). This information is given in *Restor* I 90-97. See also laisses I .xxv.-.xxviii. note.

89   The reading of the other manuscripts seems more appropriate here. In P 'amors' and 'armes' were perhaps transposed through scribal confusion.

90   *Marcus* Perhaps Mars the Roman god of war, although here he is a god of the Indians and Persians, and elsewhere of Epheson I 160, II 1256, and of the Greeks I 777 (Marcon at the rhyme), 1062, 1160, II 956. Alexander refers to 'Mars li diex des batailles' II 1079 which may be the same god.

Laisse iii

98   *joiouse sor tous dius* 'Merrier than all the gods'(?). The form *dius* for *dieux* occurs also in I 104.

114   *Kenelius* 'Canaanites'. This seems to be an old altered derivative of *Canaanitos*. The form *Canelius* is found in *Roland* 3238,3269, but disappeared in the later Middle Ages, which may account for the variant 'Arabieus' of P6P7. Cf. 'Chananee', 'Chananon' I 325.

Laisse iv

135   *oelletés et signés* Edea wants the peacock to be decorated with 'eyes' and marked, perhaps with lines scored to indicate feathers.

136   *jolis* Nominative, agreeing with *li paons* understood? The other mss seem to show revision.

138-41 P differs from the rest in the placing of 'Mais por' which is logically expected after 'N' esse mie'. Edea is explaining to the goldsmiths the reasons why she has sent for so many of them. She says, 'It is not as though I were not confident that each one is well-skilled, but in order that all of you ('on' I 140) may undertake it and finish it well and in order that the work may be of the highest worth''. All the other mss. place 'Mais' at the beginning of I 141 and have what

I believe to be a revision of I 140. Edea's argument in this version is less persuasive and appears to be divisive rather than conciliatory. There is no suggestion of the goldsmiths working together as in P and one can imagine each one going off convinced that he could have done the job on his own and resenting the presence of the others.

It is true that P may represent the revision. The scribe could have picked up 'Mais por ce que' from I 141 and written it by mistake in I 140. If so he discovered his mistake in time to substitute 'on' for 'il' in I 140 and 'Et' for 'Mais' in I 141 to make sense and to omit 'et' before 'parfait' for the sake of the meter.

I think it more likely that the redactor of the archetype of the other mss revised the passage. He may have objected to 'por ce que' on two consecutive lines and substituted 'Par quoi il' for 'Mais por ce qu'on'. This makes sense but is less subtle than P's version. It also left the line hypometric. This fault was then remedied. presumably in later copies, in two different ways: P7 has *'entrepris'* for *'empris'* and the rest have added *'et'* before *'parfait'*.

142 *entre pluseurs sages truev'on pluseurs avis* The nearest equivalent I have found is *Autant de têtes autant d'avis* Le Roux de Lincy Vol. I p. 185. This proverb and others like it seem to counsel against large numbers because of the confusion resulting from different opinions. But Edea's argument is that somewhere among the crowd there may be someone, perhaps, even an apprentice, (I 144) who knows intuitively how best to do the work.

143 *diex moustre a l'un ce qu'autres n'a apris* cf. *Ce que l'ung ne scet l'autre scet* Morawski, *Prov.* 328. Edea underlines the idea that someone may know by instinct what others have not learnt with years of experience. By suggesting that such inspiration is God-given she is tactfully making it easy for the master-goldsmiths to accept that they can still learn from others.

144 Edea is not suggesting that apprentices in general see more than their masters. What she does, I think, is to take it for granted the master knows more than the apprentice, nevertheless, one of the apprentices there may well see something that a master may miss. She continues (I 145-46), 'And for this reason a wise master is not diminished in worth if he takes from others what has been taken from him', in other words the wise man is not too proud to learn from those he has taught.

Laisse v

162-63 'Or you would remain (*se tenir*) prisoners of the masters of our work if I had authority in the matter (or 'from them', *en*). Never would I hold back from it (*se cesser de*).'

172-73 'There is no one so morose who if he saw how she holds the Baudrain and bends him (to her will?) would not be joyful.'
ploie All the other mss have 'loie', 'binds', which seems less good as the Baudrain is constantly escaping from Edea's grasp and then allowing himself to be caught (I 176-77). The same word occurs in II 512 where the subject is 'Amors qui tout sorvaint et ploie'.

175 *dangier et broie* C.S. Lewis has dealt fully with the semantic development of *dangier* in *The Allegory of Love* (Oxford, 1936), pp. 364-65. He traces a two-fold development from the primary sense of lordship, dominion, power through the lord's power to act, therefore to hurt, and through his power to give and, by inference, to withhold. W.R.J. Barron on 'Lufdaungere' in *Medieval Miscellany presented to Eugene Vinaver* (Manchester, 1965), pp.1-18, notes the idea of withholding, refusal and resistance first in twelfth-century texts. To this was added a feeling of uncertainty and suspense and the further ideas of fickleness, of being over-nice and uncompliant. In the *Roman de la Rose* Dangier represents the Lady's resistance to love expressed by the rebuff, which may of course be counterfeit. In the *Wife of Bath's Tale* c. 1388, the word seems to have, rather, the meaning of uncompliant. The ugly, old woman says to her young husband who is reluctant to consummate their marriage, 'Is this the lawe of King Artures hous? / Is every knyght of his so dangerous? ' (1089-90). Perhaps the

meaning we are looking for is best exemplified in the *Wife of Bath's Prologue* where the Wife describes her fifth husband whom she loved best because he 'was of his love daungerous to me' (514), for, she says, women desire what is forbidden and crave what they may not lightly have (515-19).

In the *Restor* there is nothing serious about *dangier*. The Baudrain is merely being playful as is made clear in I 176-77.

broie Literally a kneading trough, it has acquired the figurative meanings of *'épreuve', 'délai'* (Gf.), also *'Zögerung', Säumnis'* (T-L.). In this context the meaning is similar to that of *dangier*.

181 *tint a* Preterite 3 of *tenir a*, 'be attached to'. The other manuscripts have altered this to the more common *pent*. The preterite of *pendre* having two syllables, the change to the present tense was necessary.

Laisse vi

189 This line must have been omitted in the archetype of all the other manuscripts which may have been due to the corruption of a difficult line. The line in P could be by a redactor but no evidence suggests that it is not Brisebare's and I have let it stand.

191 *Li dus Aimes* This is probably the correct reading here as it is reinforced by 'li dus' I 200. P has the forms Emenidus,-don; Emes,-mon; Aimes,-mon; Aymes,-mon; Ayme. The name was originally Emenidus and seems to have developed to Emelidus > Eme li dus > Emes li dus. The spelling Aymes li dus may have resulted from the influence of the common O.F. name Aymes.

193 *Caulus, Aristés* Two of Alexander's twelve peers in the *Roman d'Alixandre*, (see I 266, note). Caulus may owe his name to Calas, a Macedonian satrap, but there is no historical counterpart to Aristés.

The line is hypermetric as Marciien has three syllables in P so I bracket the second 'et' which is omitted in all other mss.

P6 supplies a different name for Marciien as he is already present in that version (see I 158, variants).

194 *Elïos, Ydorie* Ladies at the court of Epheson. *Ydorie* is a rhyme-form for Ydorus who in the *Voeux* was sister to Edea and cousin of Fesonas (see I 63, note).

197 *le plus* Perhaps 'in the majority'. S1W have the nominative *li plus* which may be correct, but P is supported by N6Q1.

199 *n'en* 'from it' is better than *ne m'*, 'from me' of the other mss.

201-03 The future *rendrons* seems better here with the subjunctive after *mais que* than the present tense of the other mss. 'We shall give ourselves up without fighting provided that you act in such a way through your courtesy that you release us on parole (*nous recreés*) and on interrupted imprisonment (*sor prison brisie*). i.e. a suspended sentence.

faire partie 'joust in a troop against another troop' (Gf.)

Laisse vii

212 *Que* of P is better than *De* of N6S1W.

217 [*acordé*] I adopt this reading from the other mss. It may be the *lectio facilior* but I can find no satisfactory gloss for 'achievé ' in this context. It may have been copied in error from I 215.

Emenidus is referring to the death of Gadifer du Laris whom he killed in the foray of Gadres (*RAlix* Br. II laisses lix - lxii). As Gadifer du Laris had already killed Pirus de Monflor, Emenidus's nephew, (*RAlix* Br. II laisses liii - liv) young Gadifer and Emenidus had an account to settle. They are reconciled by Alexander and Emenidus promises his niece Lydone to young Gadifer to confirm this (see I 901-05 and also I 1131-39 where Lydone agrees to the marriage).

218 *que* This form of the indirect object pronoun is unusual but I leave it as it occurs again in II 337. The variant 'de qui' arose perhaps because the absolute construction was becoming obsolete in the fourteenth century.

223   *Betanie* Promised by Emenidus to Gadifer this is some vague Asian land, perhaps owing its name to Bethany in Judaea or to Bithynia.

228   *de volonté* 'Of your good will'(?) The variant 'de vo bonté' may be a *lectio facilior.*

Laisse viii

234   *el plus maistre estage* The main floor, the Hall or main room of a great house being often on the first floor above an undercroft used for storage.

239   *Archade* Although Emenidus is historically Eumenes of Cardia the form Arcade or Arcage was presumably in Eustache's *Fuerre de Gadres* as the form Archadia occurs in the Vatican ms. of the Latin translation of this poem (Ed. Ross, p. 238).

241   *quitement, sans rente et sans treüage* i.e. paying no rent or tribute, only service.

242-49   Transitional lines linking the interpolated *Enfances Emenidus* to the *Restor* proper.

244   *travers, paiage* Toll for crossing and for entering (lit. setting foot in) a place. The other mss have substituted 'treü', 'tribute', for the more technical 'travers' and P7 has 'passage' for 'paiage'. They may have altered the first hemistich to avoid the hiatus in 'ne i' which was not normally permissible.

245   The line is hypometric but as it occurs only in P the added word [son] is purely conjectural.

Laisse ix

252   *repeton* Pres. Indic. 3 or 4? N6Q1 with 'repete on' indicate clearly that these scribes have read the third person singular. P6S1W with 'souvent le repeton' are ambiguous but the idea of 'souvent' with which they replace 'nous le' hardly applies to the author of the *Restor* who has only once summarized the exploits of Alexander, in the first laisse of the present work. It seems therefore that in these mss also the reading is 'repet'on.'

In ms. P other first conjugation verbs appear without a final e in the third person singular present indicative: *'truev'on'* I 142, *'cont'on'* II 41; on the other hand *'entrelaisson'* I 666 is more likely to be the third person plural. In addition, if *'nous'* is to be read as an indirect object pronoun then the pronouns are in the wrong order according to normal O. F. practice (Foulet § 203). P7 has the pronouns in the correct order but has 'vos' for 'nous'. 'Nous' would therefore seem to be the nominative case and the subject of 'repeton' in ms. P.

256-72   The list of peers differs slightly from the list chosen by Aristotle in the *Roman*, namely Tholomer, Cliçon, Licanor, Filote, dant Emenidon, Perdicas, Lyoine, Antigonon, Aridés, Aristés, Caulon, Antiocus (Br. I 688-692). Of these Aridés (historically Arrhidaius, Alexander's half-brother) does not appear in the *Restor* but other characters are introduced from the *Voeux* and the *Prise de Defur* who did not exist when Br. I was written.

257   *Danclins et Tholomers* Two of Alexander's peers; in *RAlix* Br. I 996-998 they are described thus:

> Cil dui ne furent onques en leur vie sevré
> Assez d'un aage erent et pres d'un parenté,
> D'un samblant, d'une guise et d'une volonté.

Danclins is really Clitus and appears in this text as Clitons (nom.) II 170,208,215; as Cliton (obl.) II 11; and as Danclins here and in II 626. He appears as Clis, Clinz, Cliçon and Dans Clins in Br. I. It seems that a nominative Cliz was nasalized to Clins and preceded by the title *dans*. The original appears then to have been forgotten as he is latinized as Danclinus in the Latin *Fuerre de Gadres* (ed. Ross, p. 251, section 154). The variant Dans Clins of P6P7, in the *Restor* shows an earlier form.

The historical Clitus (Kleitos) and Tholomer (Ptolomy) were both friends and generals of Alexander the Great.

258   *Poron* King of India and uncle of Porus son of Clarus.

262   *Dauris et [Floridas]* Brothers who became Alexander's liege men after the siege of Defur in the Duke Melcis interpolation. P is wrong here with Philotas who was one of the original twelve peers and is mentioned in line I 269.

264   *Graciiens* Driven from Chaldaea by Duke Melcis, Graciiens took Alexander across a secret ford to the city of Defur which was being defended by Melcis and Dauris and Floridas. Graciiens killed Melcis and Alexander left Dauris in charge of the city, taking Floridas with him into his service.

266-69   *Caulus, Arristé, Perdicas, Lyone, Licanor, Antigonus, Anthiocon, Filotas* Eight of the twelve peers in the *Roman d'Alixandre*. *Festion* was not listed among the twelve peers in Br. I but was one of the twelve in the *RAlix Amalgam* (See *M.F.R. A.* IV, p. 23, note 9). *Aridés* who appears in Br. I is omitted in the *Restor* and presumably Festion takes his place. Although not listed as a peer in the *RAlix* Alexander calls him 'un sien dru Festion' (Br. I 418) and in Br. IV 1371-75 Festion laments Alexander's death more than all the other peers for:

> 1372   Cil fu plus ses privés ainsi com nos cuidons
> C'onques n'avoit esté Tholomés ne Cliçons
> Por qant si n'iert il mie des douze compaignons
> Mais en enfance avoit esté ses norreçons.

He thus corresponds in part to the historical Hephaestion who was Alexander the Great's closest friend, but Alexander outlived Hephaestion by a few months.

Perdicas had an historical counterpart in Perdiccas who was appointed regent of the empire on Alexander's death. He was murdered while attacking Egypt.

Lyone may represent Leonnatus a Macedonian general who received Hellespontine Phrygia after Alexander's death.

Licanor may be based on one of the several personnages connected with Alexander the Great who were called Nicanor.

Antigonus took over the rule of Great Phrygia on the death of Alexander, but there seems to have been no historical Antiochus contemporary with Alexander. There were however three of that name in the Seleucid dynasty founded by Seleucus I who became Governor of Babylonia on the death of Alexander. The names Antigonus and Antiochus were frequently confused in the Alexander cycle as the variants show. The historical Philotas was the son of Parmenio, a Macedonian general. Both father and son were executed for alleged involvement in a conspiracy against Alexander.

I have replaced Cliton with Sanson in I 267 although Sanson does not, strictly speaking, belong in a list of peers. Cliton was a peer but he already appears in I 257 as Danclins. Sanson has the support of the other mss. He became Alexander's liege man in return for Alexander's help in regaining Tyre from his uncle Darius (*RAlix* Br. I 696-743). He was killed by Betis of Gadres in the *Fuerre (RAlix* Br. II laisses .xxiv. and .xxv.).

270-71   *Divinus Pater, dant Antipater* Liege men of Alexander who plotted against the latter's life (*RAlix* Br. III laisses .ccxli. to .ccxlv. and laisses .ccccli. to ccccclvii.) They finally poisoned him (Br. IV laisses .iv. to .xi.).

The historical Antipater was a Macedonian general and was appointed regent of Macedonia during the eastern campaigns. He was confirmed as ruler of Macedon after Alexander's death and was one of the few of Alexander's associates to die a natural death in old age.

There appears to have been no historical counterpart to Divinus Pater.

270   *de Monflor Pieron* Pirus de Monflor was Emenidus's nephew and Lidone's brother. He was killed by Gadifer at the foraging of Gadres. (See I 217 note).

274   *mauvais* probably means cowards here in opposition to *les boins* 'the brave' in the previous line.

sans raënchon In the *Roman* Alexander is described as ruthless in his treatment of prisoners when his anger was roused, as for example when his men seized him and try to prevent him from releasing Bucifal (Br. I 447-49);

Il en jura son chief et met sa main en son
Que, se nus le tient més, ja n'avra guerison
Du poing ou du pié perdre sanz nule raënçon.

Again, in Br. I, laisse .lxvii. Alexander sends a messenger to Nicolas to say (1477)
Ne prendroit de la teste nesune raënçon.
Nor does he show mercy to the Duke of the Rock who offered him his sword. He
hanged him and slew all his men (Br. I laisses .cv. to .cxiv.).

280   *Veus du Paon* Poem by Jacques de Longuyon. It is clear that Brisebare regards
his own work as a supplement to the *Voeux*.

288   *cruchon* Gf. gives *cresson, croisson, cruchon,* s.f. meaning *'croissance'*,
'augmentation', etc. which makes sense in this context, although the variants
suggest that the scribes had some difficulty with the word.

294   *engien de camion 'épingle de très petite dimension'* (Gf. Supplement). The
line may be an example of litotes, 'which were not composed with the skill of a
pin', i.e. with no little skill.

298   *Caton* The collection of moral sayings wrongly attributed to Cato the Elder, the
Disticha Catonis, composed probably in the second century A.D., was a much
used school text in the Middle Ages. Several French versions were made,.
beginning with that of Everard le Moine in the first half of the twelfth century.

299   *les .vii. sages* Perhaps a reference to the *Roman des sept sages* in which the
seven sages by their skill in story-telling defend a young prince against a false
accusation by a jealous step-mother. (Edited by G. Paris, S.A.T.F., (Paris,
1876)).

303-04   Proverbs usually take the opposite view e.g. 'De mauvaise vie mauvaise fin',
Morawski *Prov.* 521. With this in mind Brisebare may have used 'se' (I 304) in
an adversative sense, i.e. 'The duke had a poor beginning and yet (in spite of
this) he had a good end'.

307   *simulation* I have adopted this form as it is well-supported and occurs again in
II 31.

311-38   This section contains three examples to excuse Emenidus's life as a robber.
First the broken mazer which is more valuable after it has been repaired. It is not
clear in what way it is worth more, but it may mean that a flaw which was
formerly hidden has now been discovered and put right. (I 316-18). Second,
David who repented after a life of sin (I 319-23). Third, the woman of Canaan
who although belonging to an outcast nation was saved by her faith (I 324-34).
The examples are introduced by a statement of the poet's theme, that God
pardons sinners by His grace (I 311-15) and rounded off by an extension of
this theme, namely that it is not the sin that matters so much as persistence
in sin (I 337-38). cf. *Vulgate* Ezech, Cap XVIII, vv 26-28.

314   [*ou*] This has the support of N6P6S1W in line 314 and completes the idea
of 'la' in 315. 'leur' may be the transcription of a corrupt copy which was
revised by P7 and Q1 to 'la ou'.

316-17   [*madres*] Although 'li maisons' is a possible feminine form in this text 'il fu
sains' in the next line suggests that P is mistaken here. The other manuscripts
have madres which is masculine and makes better sense and I have therefore
substituted it.

The sentence has a proverbial ring but I have not found it elsewhere.

Mazers, bowls of maple wood or a mineral, sometimes with a silver rim and
foot, were so valuable that Richard de Swinfield, Bishop of Hereford 1289-90,
had his repaired at a cost of 10d (Camden Society Old Series, Vols. LIX and
LXII, 1854 and 1855, ed. John Webb).

319-23   A reference to David's arrogance in counting his people (*Vulgate* Lib. Sec.
Regum, Cap. XXIV, vv 1-10) and to David's lust for Bath-sheba and the murder
of Uriah (Ibid. Cap. XI, vv 2-17). Brisebare was well-versed in the Scriptures
and these references to David and in I 325-334 to the woman of Canaan may be
considered as support for his authorship of the Emenidus episode. He also
refers to David's sins and repentance in the *Tresor Nostre Dame* (B.N. ms. fr.
576, folio 115):

> David lues qu'il devint pechieres
> Fu et ses peules vergondés
> Or a muees ses manieres
> Dame en vous si qu'en nos prieres
> Est 'agnus dei' appellés.

322 *mainte lechon* In the New Testament Jesus is frequently called 'Son of David', chiefly by the poor and those who have been cured by His healing powers, e.g. Mat. XII, v 23, also ibid. IX v 27, XV v 22, XXI vv 9 and 15. When the Pharisees call Him son of David His answer only confounds them: Mat. XXII vv 41-45.

323 *par figaration* Gf. gives for *figuracion 'figure particuliere', 'action di figurer'*, and T-L gives *'Vergleich', 'Bild'*. This is possibly a reference to the descent of Jesus from David as shown in the Jesse–tree windows, or perhaps here it means 'through supposition'. There seems to be no doubt that Joseph was descended from David but Brisebare probably means that as Joseph was only the foster-father of Jesus the descent of Joseph from David does not make the latter literally the father or ancestor of God. To anyone believing in the virgin birth, as did Brisebare, only the descent of Mary from David could establish the latter as *'Peres de Dieu'*. Modern scholars have tried to do this, but it seems that there is insufficient evidence and the point may never be proved. It is clear from his other works that Brisebare considered Joseph to be the foster-father. For example in the *Tresor Nostre Dame* he explains that Joseph marries Mary at God's command:

> Pour vous servir sans deshonnour
> Et pour vostre fruit excuser
> (fol. 115vo. Col II, 33-34.)

Again, in the *Escolle de Foy* Brisebare explains that Jesus was born of woman without the intervention of any man, for, as the sun passes through glass without breaking it so surely can God who is omnipotent pass through a virgin (B.N. ms. fr. 576, fol. 102r Col. II).

The spelling *figaration* is peculiar to ms. P and I have not found it elsewhere.

324-34 The story of the Canaanite woman occurs only in P P6 P7 but in view of Brisebare's propensity for Biblical references and sermons it is probably genuine. In Matt. XV vv. 22-28 Jesus at first refuses to help the woman whose daughter is possessed of a devil for 'Non est bonum sumere panem filiorum et mittere canibus'. The woman replies, 'Etiam Domine: nam et catelli edunt de micis, quae cadunt de mensa dominorum suorum'.

P6 P7 have *ne* for *je* in I 328 which at first seems the more attractive reading: 'If I am not worthy in my unworthiness to have the holy bread which your children have...' But this opening leads one to expect that having acknowledged her unworthiness she will ask for something other than the 'holy bread'; on the contrary, she goes on to say that even the crumbs fallen from the table will suffice. Perhaps P then is after all more logical: 'If I am worthy in my very unworthiness...' She acknowledges her unworthiness but still has her faith which assures her that the smallest crumb of His blessing will be enough for her. The alteration may have been made in P6P7 because the complement preceding the verb normally causes inversion. Other examples of this construction are found in P, e.g. in I 414,560,902, II 351.

329 [*vostre*] This is better than 'nostre' as it was to the children of Israel that Jesus felt he had been sent, 'Non sum missus nisi ad oves, quae perierunt domus Israel'.

334 P6P7 omit this line but P7 has 334a which is clearly an addition. The plural 'des diex' may refer to the fact that the Canaanites were polytheists and Brisebare may have known this. The change from 'et de no' to 'de nostre' is conjectural but seems to be necessary.

None of the lines I 332-34 has a parallel in the *Vulgate*.

340 *Blaton* I have not found the name elsewhere. In *RAlix* Br. IV. 722, Emenidus is called 'li fieus l'amiraut de Tudele', but this person is not named.
apele A past tense seems preferable but as the present has the support of W I have retained it.

343   *Capharnaon* This may owe its name to the town on the north-east shores of
Galilee. It is mentioned in *RAlix* Br. III, 4883, when Alexander says he has the
lordship of all the land from India to Cafarnaon except Babylon.

348-52   The description of the land laid waste recalls a passage in *RAlix* Br. III,
369-77 describing a desert traversed by Alexander and his army after the death
of Darius.

354   'He never heeded hedge nor thicket there'.

356-57   These lines must have been omitted in the archetype of the other mss but could
be genuine. The passage makes a little scene of Aymes's meeting with the robbers
which is typical of Brisebare's style.

363   *Damas* Damascus? See note on Baudas, I 390.

364-78   Although he lived the life of a robber Emenidus's noble nature shines through.
The whole passage presents Emenidus as the natural gentleman and knight. The
idea of nature surpassing nurture is also expressed in *RAlix* Br. IV, 1661-62,
'Nature et norreture demaient grant tençon/ Mais au loing vaint nature ce dist
en la leçon'.

364-67   'But although he was there he would rather have thrown a falcon after a lark or
his goshawk after a heron than that he should have to take from a single monk
his cloak.'

365   *l'aloe* 'The lark' has become 'l'anete', diminutive of 'l'ane' 'the duck' in N6Q1S1
W. This in turn has become 'malart' in P6P7.

370   *Pumier, fraisne, sapin* All well-known lance materials.

373   [*ton*] P makes little sense with 'non' as the things in question have already been
named.

Laisse x

381   [*Philippe*] The line is hypermetric with P's 'Philippon'. However the form
adopted does not occur elsewhere in P where the nominative is Phelippes I 437,
453 and the oblique Phelippon I 422 and passim.

384   *et s'iert* P's reading has no support but in view of the diversity of the variants
I retain it. The form *iert* 3rd sing. imperfect indicative occurs also in I 869, II
474, and *si* is abbreviated similarly in 's'iert' II 264 where *iert* is the future tense.

386   *com* This and the variant 'quant' of N6Q1S1 are strange, conveying the idea that
after he (Alexander) had spoken he said ... Perhaps the meaning is rather, 'When
he had addressed him (i.e. after the preliminaries demanded by courtesy)
Alexander said ...'
      It seems that 'quant' represents a revision of *com* meaning 'when' and that
'si l'a' of P6P7W is a *lectio facilior.*

390   *nostre* This and the variant 'vostre' of P7S1W imply a feudal dependence of the
caliphate on Macedon. *Baudas* and *Damas* in I 363, presumably Baghdad and
Damascus, were to Brisebare, one imagines, simply famous Saracen towns of
whose actual geographical location he had no knowledge. For the purposes of
his story they are within walking distance of each other.

402   This line is hypometric but is difficult to adjust. The other mss. have avoided
the problem in different ways, but 'ont bailli' of N6P7S1W involves a change
of tense as well as a change of vocabulary. P6 has 'lettres' for 'brief' but
supports 'donnerent.' However this entails the problem of the agreement of
'quassé' and P6 has solved this by introducing 'le brief' into the second half of
the line. In the circumstances it seems best to leave P uncorrected.
      l'ont This form, probably due to an unnecessary titulus, I have corrected to
l'ot.

424, 427   These lines, omitted in the other mss., seem to be genuine and necessary.

429   An obscure line and the variants give no help. Perhaps: 'However it may be, by
this circumstance/ruse(?), he considers himself excused.'

Laisse xi

434, 435   P begins with the wrong rhyme and I have altered this following the other manuscripts.

448   *souples* If 'qui' refers to the robber, perhaps 'suppliant', if to Philip, then down-cast'.

Laisse xii

495   *uns clos leus* Presumably a lame wolf would be even more stealthy than an unmaimed one as his lameness would hinder his escape if surprised.

503   *le tour de sa maistrie* Gf. gives *'trait d'adresse', 'ruse'*, etc. for *tour*. Perhaps 'the tricks of his art'. It seems that Emenidus, recognizing the man for what he was followed him either through curiosity to see what he would do, or perhaps in order to see if he could learn something from his methods. In either case his interest in the man was enough to make him forget his wager.

507   *despechie*<**dispeciata*, 'broken open' (the house), or 'extricated' (the ladder)? T-L gives *'losmachen', 'freimachen'* and the gloss *'extricare: despeschier'*. This seems to be the better reading as the thief would obviously think first of unhooking the ladder, a valuable tool of his trade.

508   *la dame* The aunt who acted as guardian to Rosenés. See I 500.

Laisse xiii

524   *une cisterne* Great underground cisterns for water supply, characteristic of Byzantine civilization, are to be found for instance in Istamboul. The use of this word gives an air of authenticity to the story.

525   *malvais espris* Perhaps jinn, if this is a genuine Arabian tale.

527   The description of Rosenés may be compared with that in *RAlix* Br. IV 70-73:

> Cors de si bele dame ne sera jamais nes.
> Qui veïst son viaire, com il iert colorés!
> De blanc et de vermeil estoit entremellés
> Et li cors avenans et li cuers esmerés.

536   *espantee* 'frightened'. The Francien form *espoantee* has too many syllables and the variants seem to be revisions, either to avoid a word which was obsolescent or to avoid a dialectal form.

540-42   Eastern women who wore closed trousers would presumably be able to defend themselves more easily against sexual assault than Europeans who wore only a smock and petticoats. This, together with the *cisterne* in I 524 and the *malvais espris* in I 525, suggests that Brisebare was drawing on an oriental source for his tale.

549   *Venus* Brisebare may have introduced Venus into an oriental tale to be in keeping with the flavour of Antiquity in the Peacock cycle.

551   Omitted in all the other mss and not essential to the sense it may be an addition. Or the other mss may have dropped it to avoid a repetition of 'reclamee' in I 549.

556-57   'Lady, as surely as I am entrusted to your care through the gift of my weight in gold at the time of my birth ... ' This seems to be a reference to the ancient practice of offering the weight of a person in precious metal or goods as a gift or as purchase money. Gf. describes the custom under *contrepeser* (Vol. II, p. 277).

567   *deffiee* It appears that even a robber must not be attacked without this vital formality.

581   The line is hypermetric in P and the other mss may be correct. Simply to drop 'a' before 'fin' would leave the weak article 'la' at the caesura. By moving 'fu' to this position the difficulty is overcome.

584-85   All the other mss have traces of these lines although they are combined into one except in P7. P clearly has the right reading. The omission of 'vi' is probably due to a scribe.

Laisse xiv

625-46 Brisebare introduces another story to justify Emenidus's life of crime. This tells how Charlemagne went out to steal at God's command and so discovered a plot against his life. The only other surviving account of this story in French is a summary in *Renaud de Montauban*, see p. 60 note 2, in which Charlemagne tells the tale as part of his life story. Full versions of the story exist in Middle Dutch, Middle German and Old Icelandic, see *Karel ende Elegast*, edited by R. Roemans and H. van Asche (Amsterdam, 1959), *Der Mitteldeutsche Karl und Elegast*, edited by Josef Quint (Bonn, 1927) and *Karlamagnus Saga ok Kappa hans*, edited by C.R. Unger (Christiania, 1859).

It is certain that a *chanson de geste* on this subject not only existed but was well-known to a medieval audience, otherwise much that is unexplained in these brief summaries would have been incomprehensible.

652 *Rosenés* The historical Roxana was the daughter of Oxyartes, a Sogdian nobleman. In the *Roman* she is the daughter of Darius.

655 *sa vie* Perhaps a scribal error for *s'amie* with three instead of four minims, but the initial v of 'vie' is perfectly clear in P and as the *lectio difficilior* it may be right. The archetype of the other mss must have read 's' amie'.

Laisse xv

669 *(a)* P6 also has 'a Emon' but as the line is hypermetric and makes sense without *a* I omit it.

670-71 *nul joiiel ... samblaissent* Probably this is to be taken as a collective noun followed by a plural verb.

Laisse xvi

695 *pertrisier* Not found in the dictionaries but Gf. has *pietriseur*. In view of the syntactical construction a noun, e.g. 'partridge hunter' seems preferable to a verb e.g. 'to hunt partridges'.

696 *aherdre* Either 'to size' from **adhaerĕre* for *adhaerēre*, or 'to excite', 'to start' from *aderigere > *adergere* (Pope § 293). In this context the § partridges are depicted entering the nets or snares, ('rois I 693), so there would be no need for the dogs to take them. Or perhaps two different methods of hunting are being described.

699-701 'With their necks stretched out and their breasts puffed up (*estierkis* literally 'made taut') and their beaks opened through such subtle mechanisms(?) that they made the golden leaves on the branches tremble.'

700 *aouviers* In view of the past participles in absolute construction in I 699 P has a better reading than N6S1W which have 'ont ouvers'.
engien[s] The plural seems necessary because of *soutis* at the rhyme, and probably refers to the machinery which set the birds in motion rather than to the ingenuity which created them.

Laisse xvii

717 *forgier* 'a box'. Gf. quotes *forcerium:forgier/ scrinia: forgier* (Gloss.Lille.22b). In the *Restor* the Caliph's jewel casket (.i. cofre biel et cler) was locked up in the forgier which was presumably a large chest. The treasure-house is depicted in a miniature in P. (169 r Col. II) and all the treasure is contained in such chests. In another miniature (169v. Col II) Rosenés's maid is shown bringing the jewels to Emenidus in a small iron-bound casket.

722 *par* The replacement of *et* by *par* seems essential and has the support of all the other mss. but P7 which has rewritten the line.

725 *elles* i.e. the *pierres* of I 720. The line refers to the occult powers they are supposed to possess.

740 *deust* This may be monosyllabic in P, cf. II 969, and perhaps 'qu'elle' should

read *que le*. An alternative is to suppress 'qu'elle', introduce *le* and read 'deüst'.

741-47   P again differs from the rest. In P the action is followed clearly step by step: Rosenés stole the keys, entered the treasure-house, confided in her waiting-maid, took away the casket and sent it by the girl to Emenidus at Damas. The repetition of the formula 'qui tant/molt fist a loër' in I 741 and 743 may be due to scribal carelessness, but as the other version in I 740a-d is clearly inferior I prefer to retain the text of P with its defects.

748   [*trouver*] This reading of the other mss makes better sense than P's 'mander'.

751   [*ounerer*] The word 'ormerer' appears to be a meaningless scribal error so I supply *ounerer* following the other mss.

Laisse xviii

767   Although no more than two formulae strung together this line does serve to bring the girl into view before she relates her news to Rosenés. In the other mss, which omit the line, no sooner has the girl set out on her journey than she is telling her news.

Laisse xix

784   Only in P. Like I 767 it describes a stage in the action which can be omitted but whose omission results in an abrupt transition from one stage to the next. Such lines must have been of great use to a performer anxious to make all the action clear to his audience and Brisebare would have been fully aware of this. I think they are genuine.

Laisse xx

798   I have not altered P although the variant 'li dus Aimes' for 'Emenidus' would avoid the hypermetric line.

810   The passage 810-40 in P7 differs so much from P that I print it here instead of in the textual variants:

P7   Quant li Califfres l'ot ki noient ne l'ama,
        De ses pieres tantost durement l'aparla.
        Mais Emes de sa dame si bien l'onour garda,
        Et tant covertement la chose devisa,
        Et por che ke le fait ne cognut ne nia

815   Li Califfres Emon a pendre commanda.
        Et quant Rosete vit ke Emon ensi va,

816a   Ke por l'amor de li morir le convenra,
        Tele angoisse rechut ke toute tressua
        Par le tres grant dolour ke a son cuer en a.
        .iiii. fois est pamee, a peu ne devia.

819a   A cascun ki le voit moult forment en pesa,

819b   Nus ne sot a penser ke ce fu ne k'elle a.

820   Et quant fu revenue molt de fois souspira
        Et dist, 'Lasse chaitive, chis homs por moi morra.

821a   Et si est sens se coulpe ne deservi ne l'a'.
        Mais elle est avisee et dist ke elle ira
        A son pere tout droit et le fait contera

823a   Tout ensi com il est, ne ja ne mentira.

825   A lui vint et dist, 'Sire, a moi entendés cha.
        Je sui toute chertaine ke chis homs culpe n'a.

826a   A che dont la metés et dont parlet chi a.
        S'il vos plaist je dirai comment la cose va'.

827a   'Oïl,' dist li Califres, 'et on l'entendera.'

'Et je vous dirai voir ne n'en mentirai ja.
.i. lerres devant hier en mon lit si m'embla,
830   Et par son grant malisce en la mason entra.
En la cave hideuse moult parfont me mena.
831a   Mon cors vot vergonder et moult i travella.
De nului n'oi aiie fors de chel home la
832a   Ki me vint au secours et si m'en delivra.
   b   A lui se combati et tant la cose ala
   c   Ke le laron ochist et la teste en copa.
   d   Por mon cors a garder le sien aventura.
835   Del laron me rescoust et si me ramena
835a   A l'ostel droitement dont ichis me jeta.
Et por la cortoisie ke chis hons me fist a
Je m'avisai de che ke je vos dirai ja
D'un bel don a donner, car bien deservi l'a.
Les pieres vos emblai et de moi il les a.
840   Or sachiés vraiement ke la chose ensi va.'

824   Another line, only in P, helpful in describing a stage in the action (cf. I 767 and 784), and serving to bring Rosenés before her father to speak to him. Q1 and P7 have equivalent variants.

842   [*Fille*] 'Sire' in P is a scribal error which I correct following the sense and the other mss.

843   *fait Hounor* is usually feminine in this text but to read *faite* would affect the metre and other instances of non-agreement occur e.g. I 849 and I 987 (at the rhyme).

Laisse xxi

875-78   *enquenus* is written clearly thus in P but may be for *enqueuus* through palaeographic u/n confusion, cf. *tenus* I 879. Gf. gives *encheu de, enqueus de (son apel)* meaning '*renvoyé de*'. Perhaps, 'Not for this was he (Emenidus) dismissed from favour in his (Alexander's) heart, for through great love he followed him up and down and kept on begging him to become his true friend, and from time to time he too (Emenidus) looked as if he were affected with emotion ...'

879   *tenus* From *se tenir* 'to abstain' (from replying)? Or for *teuus (se taire* to keep silent')? All other mss have 'teüs'. Cf. 'enquenus' I 875.

887   Omitted in all other mss, with its change of tense it seems to be a personal opinion expressed by the author or by the performer.

Laisse xxii

888   Identical with I 230 and on the same rhyme. The Emenidus episode ends at I 895 and I 896, which repeats the content of I 240-41 links it to the main story.
Q1 omits I 888 and has the following thirteen lines instead:

887a   De ceste grant bataille qui fu sur .i. rivage
Vous en voeil je la fin abregier sanz outrage.
Tant i feri Aymon au tres hardi courage
Que le jour acourci et s'en vint a ombrage.
Li Califfes manda sanz faire autre attendage
Sa fille Rosenés qui molt fu preus et sage.
Lors dist: 'Belle pour vous est venu ce dommage
Et ma terre exillie et par terre et par nage.
Gardez que vous vaurrez ou guerre ou mariage.'
'Sire,' dist la pucelle, 'je respons sanz folage,
Parlez ent a Aymon ou tant a vasselage.

> Et ce qu'il en fera je tieng a seignourage.'
> 'Par dieu,' dit li Califfes, 'ci a coint respondage.'

896   *sans servage* Emenidus held Archade as a free fief for which he owed only military service and no servile tenure of sergeanty. See I 241, note.

901   See I 217, note.

Laisse xxiii

The sending for Lydoine to marry Gadifer is described in the *Voeux* in W only (8278-8360), but P2 ends with 8278-8309. In W Emenidus sends two barons to fetch his niece whereas in the *Restor* he goes himself.

923a   This line in N6P6P7 is probably an addition as there are already three supérlatives describing Gadifer.

Laisse xxiv

930-31   A description and comment by author or performer, only in P. It adds a picturesque touch.

952-53   P, 'They told her of the well-considered vow ('la parole') by means of which this work was brought about'. The rest, 'They told in well-considered words ('par parole') why this work was begun and vowed'.

Laisses xxv to xxviii

This section is part of the *Voeux* remodelled to permit the insertion of the *Restor* material. Cf. *Voeux* 8361-8411 and 8470-8537. In the *Voeux* the first line reads, 'En la chambre Venus desus .i. drap ouvré. In the *Restor* Brisebare has changed the setting to the 'orfaverie' to introduce the peacock. The *Voeux* continues with a passage telling how the knights inform Porus that Alexander has freed them all and made them his liege men, Brisebare omits this here but its content appears earlier in I 90-95. The *Restor* continues (I 955-72) with an invention of Brisebare's, Marcien's proposal of marriage to Eliot. Lines I 973-1003 follow the *Voeux* closely.

954   *desous* P may be wrong. The word is *desus* in *Voeux* 8361 as in the other mss of the *Restor*.

956   This line is awkward in P and one is tempted to alter *Et* to *A* as in the other mss. except S1. However, as S1 supports *Et* and in P Elyos is nominative and Marcien oblique it seems preferable to leave the line as it is. S1 has the preposition *a* as well as the auxiliary *a* and an abbreviated form of Marcien which may be dissyllabic to rectify the metre. Elsewhere in P Marciien is always trisyllabic and always has a final s in the nominative. Elïos, Elÿos are nominative and Elïot, Elÿot oblique. The only deviations are Elias I 1110 and Eleüs I 1147 both being oblique and both at the rhyme. It seems likely therefore that the line in P is Brisebare's with the archaic use of the oblique case without preposition: *Elÿos a parlé Marciien* 'Eliot spoke to Marcien'. This has been modernized in S1 by inserting the preposition *a* before Marc*ius* (?), and in the other mss. by putting the preposition at the beginning of the line instead of *Et* thus altering the sense.

957   Only in P, it adds a little vivacity to the action and may well be genuine.

969   *doins(t)* The first person singular present indicative seems necessary here. The form *doins* is found in P, e.g. I 1124, 1129, 1170.

972   Only in P. This line and the preceding one form the transition from Brisebare's interpolated passage between Marcien and Eliot back to the *Voeux*. I 972 is ambiguous and not essential but it may be genuine.

975   *issent de la chambre* Brisebare has slipped up here. He had set the scene in the 'orfaverie' (I 954) but this part of the laisse is simply a copy of the *Voeux* in which the scene is in the Chamber of Venus, (see above, note on

	laisses .xxv. to .xxviii.). I 975 corresponds exactly with 8369 of *Voeux* in W.
977-80	These lines, only in P, do not appear in the *Voeux*. If the workshop, as seems likely, was situated outside the main tower, Brisebare may have added these lines to suggest the longer distance they would have to cover to reach the dining hall. In the *Voeux* they were in the Chamber of Venus which was in the same building as the great hall, *Restor* I 76, and again in I 234 where the Chamber of Venus is said to be 'ens el plus maistre estage'. It may be that the archetype of the other mss was copying a manuscript of the *Voeux* not realizing that Brisebare had made further insertions.
978	*acolé* One would expect agreement with 'cascuns' but the form is guaranteed by the rhyme. It must then be nominative plural associated with 'sont' in the previous line. Perhaps 'cascuns a sa cascune' may be taken to be an adverbial phrase of manner like 'molt estroit', both modifying 'sont ... acolé.
982-83	These lines are a continuation of the insertions begun in I 977 (see above). They are only in P, except that P7 has I 982. Of the passage I 977-83 only I 981 appears in the *Voeux*.
984	*a pris* The variant 'saisi' in P6 is in *Voeux* W 8372.
986	*[de]duit* The line in P is hypometric and *deduit* has the support of N6S1W. *deduit* is also in *Voeux* in PP4Q1 but W omits the line.
988-1003	The P6 version of these lines given below is closer to the *Voeux* than P, cf. *Voeux* W 8375-82. It is even closer to the *Voeux* in P3P4.

988	Des cortois dis des gars sans nul vilain pensé
	Furent si bien servi comme a lor volenté.
	El dois devant le roi ont par humilité
	Maint jouencel servant trés ricement parés,
	Qui les servent de mes c'on lor a presenté:
	Grues, gantes, marlars orent a grant plenté,
	D'iawe douce [et] salee poisson fresc et salé
	S'eurent maint autre mes que n'ai pas devisé
	Et boin vin a fuison boin greastre et claré
	Vin de Cypre, vin grec, grenate et ysopé.
995	Quant il orent mengié, s'ont l'iawe demandé.
	Cil menestrel lor ont harpé et viellé:
	Assés ont par laiens assés ris et gabé.
	Et quant ce vint au soir que tout orent soupé
1000	Cascuns ala coucier tant qu'il fu ajorné
	Quant li rois se leva et son riche barné.
	Que vous diroie je? Tant on[t] la sejorné
	Que Porus fu garis et venus en santé.

990	and 997-98, found only in P and P7, have no equivalent in the *Voeux*.
999-1003	These lines agree almost word for word with *Voeux* W 8384-88.

Laisse xxvi

Cf. *Voeux* W 8389-8411.

1018	.v. *Voeux* W 8403 reads '.iii.' Brisebare has altered the number to include the two marriages he has added.
1021	This line develops the idea contained in 1020 but is omitted in the other mss and in the *Voeux*.
1026a	1027, 1028. These lines in P6 are from the *Voeux* (W 8409-11) and 1027a corresponds to *Voeux* W 8429.
1028	In the *Voeux* W alone has an extra laisse following this line beginning 'Moult fu liés Alixandres quant il ot et entent', which describes the arrival of Lydoine, after which Alexander calls Gadifer and they all go to the palace.

Laisse xxvii

Cf. *Voeux* W 8470-8509.

1032a-c   These lines in P6 correspond to *Voeux* W 8474-76. As Q1 omits them in its version of the *Voeux* Brisebare may have followed a similar manuscript rather than one like W.

1038   *les .v. pucelles* In the *Voeux* there are of course only three, even in W, which suggests that when the two extra marriages were added the necessary alterations were not made to the original text. Cf. *Voeux* W 8483, 'Les .iii. dames le vont tenant par le geron'.

1044   *le preu Festion* One would expect the nominative case after *fu* (I 1039). The confusion may have arisen by the substitution of *et* for *o* in I 1043. The corresponding passage in the *Voeux,* (W 8488-90), reads:

> Et Aristés li preus o lui Emenidon
> Caulus et Floridas, Lycanor, Festion
> Et Gracien de Tyr qui fu cousin Sanson.

1053   Omitted by W here and in *Voeux*. Present in *Voeux* in other mss, e.g. Q1 agrees with P but with 'Dont' for 'Puis'.

1059   Omitted by W in *Restor* but present in that manuscript in *Voeux* 8503 with 'N'i oi' for 'Dont aie'.

1060   *souspechon* Found in *Voeux* in Q1. The variant 'quisençon' is in *Voeux* W 8504.

1062-65   omitted in W perhaps because of its difficulty. *Voeux* W 8506-10 reads:

> Ne par la foi que doi a nostre Dieu Marcon,
> Se je estoie a chois de tous les preus du mont
> Pour mon cors a garder, porter mon confanon
> N'i esliroie je personne se vous non.

In P6 1062 and 1062a clearly derive from this tradition as they correspond to W 8506-07 (above). For these two lines *Voeux* Q1 has 'Car se au besoing voloie par nostre dieu Marcon', which is of course the same as I 1062 of *Restor,* a further indication that Brisebare was using a version of the *Voeux* similar to Q1.

     The difficulty in I 1062 is that 'voloie' has no object. It may be that the formula 'par nostre dieu Marcon' has replaced words such as *eslire un compaignon.*

Laisse xxviii

Cf. *Voeux* W 8510-37.

1096a-k   This passage in P6 is also in *Voeux* P1P4, and the first line only is in *Voeux* Q1. See variants to *Voeux* W 8537 (Ritchie, vol. IV, p. 437).

1097-98   Only N6P7S1 besides P have 1097 and all omit 1098. The lines are not in *Voeux* W, nor is Ireland given to Porus in that version; but it is in some versions of the *Voeux,* that is in the manuscripts with Ritchie's laisse 7b (see pp. 36-37) which relates the marriages of Porus, Betis and the Baudrain who receive Ireland, England and Norway respectively. It is clear therefore that the gift of Ireland in I 1097 and of England and Norway in I 1102 and 1105 are not inventions of Brisebare's but were in some versions of the *Voeux,* though not in W.

     Alexander refers to his conquest of Ireland in *RAlix* Br. IV, 555.

Laisses xxviii a and b. P6 inserts two laisses from *Voeux* P1P3P4P6QQ1S5S6W (W 8538-77) so that P6 has these laisses twice. As their content, the marriages of the Baudrain and of Betis, is also in *Restor* laisse xxix P6 has this material three times.

Laisse xxix

1102   *sans nul gas* 'without any jesting about it'(?)

1104 *n'ot villain[s] gas* 'there was no tendency to coarse jesting'(?) P alone has this reading, the variant 'cas' for 'gas' was perhaps intended to avoid a repetition of 'gas' within two lines.

1105 Alexander refers to his conquest of England in *RAlix* Br. IV, 554.

Laisse xxx

The two marriages described in this laisse are not in the *Voeux* except in W 8578-8612 which seems to be a later addition by the author.

1122-24 This exchange between Alexander and Marcien is rather abrupt in P and W from which some equivalent to 1123a-e may have dropped out. In 1122 Marcien seems embarrassed at Alexander's praise but before he can utter a deprecating speech Alexander breaks in with 1123 'By my faith, I dare swear it is true!', then offers them Friesland and Holland before Eliot and Marcien have given their consent. In *Voeux* W Marcien receives not Friesland and Holland but Surie from Alexander and Pyncernie from Porus (W 8604 and 8609).

1130 *La terre des Galois, Escoche* Alexander refers to his conquest of these lands in *RAlix* Br. IV, 554-55. In *Voeux* W Gadifer receives Otrente from Alexander and Thebanie from Emenidus (W 8580-82).

1131 *Lydone* The name of the sister of Pirus de Monflor is always wrong in P. Ydoire or Ydorus is of course the lady of Epheson who marries Betis. In I 1148 Ydorus appears instead of Lydonus at the rhyme, and in I 1174 there is 'Je done' for 'Lydone'.

1132 *vostre oncle* is Emenidus and 'son pere' is Gadifer's father, Gadifer du Larris.

1134-35 See I 217, note.

1143 *rescrïer* may be related to *rescriement* glossed in Gf. as *'régénération', délassement'*, i.e. 'recreation', and perhaps 'entertain' is the meaning here.

Laisse xxxi

The feast is described in *Voeux* W 8613-51 but in the *Restor* it is so thoroughly recast and Brisebare has added so much original material relating to the golden peacock that his account shows little resemblance to that in the *Voeux*.

1148 [*belle Lydonus*] The form 'Lydonus' has the support of P7Q1W and the epithet is from P7Q1. There has clearly been some doubt about this hemistich as the number of variants shows.

1149 *viel* A curious epithet for a man in the prime of his fighting life, although he was of course old compared with young Gadifer. The word occurs only in P and it may be that one of the variants is better.

1149a in S1. Cf. P I 1159.

1151a in P6. This line recalls *Voeux* W 8615-16.

1156-76 The complicated allotment of the fifteen days has confused the redactors. Alexander clearly wants the first five days for himself (I 1169) and therefore .vi. in I 1158 is wrong. This is confirmed in I 1169 and also in I 1182-83. I have therefore altered the number to .v. From I 1163-65 we learn that of the remaining ten days five will go to the bridegrooms to hold full court, and from I 1166-8 that five will go to the brides for feasting and entertainment. Lines I 1170-76 indicate which person will be responsible for each of the last ten days. It is not clear from I 1175-6 how the Baudrain and Edea will distribute the fourteenth and fifteenth days but it is made clear in I 1186 that Edea has the fifteenth.

  Returning to lines I 1159-62 we learn how Alexander will use the first five days. He will appoint for each of the bridegrooms a day in turn, and in the name of the bridegroom of the day he, Alexander, will receive the other four.

  The programme of festivities appears then to be:

1-5 Alexander's responsibility. He receives the five couples in the name

	of a different bridegroom each day
6	Porus to hold full court
7	Phesonas for feasting and entertaining
8	Ydorus for feasting and entertaining
9	Betis to hold full court
10	Elyot – feasting
11	Marcien – full court
12	Lydone – feasting
13	Gadifer – full court
14	The Baudrain – full court
15	Edea – feasting

1159   One is tempted to alter *De* to *A* as in P6P7 although *De* may be syntactically possible: 'I shall allot to each of your five bridegrooms, whose great worth is well known, a day in the name of our god Marcus; and in the name of that bridegroom *(celui)* I shall be ready *(porveüs de)* forthwith to receive the other four.'

1160   *Ara chascuns* of Q1W and *Ara chascune* of N6S1 seem less good readings as Alexander was not giving them these first five days; they were his own days and he was merely assigning one of their names to each day.

Laisse xxxii

1182   [*d*] *'Alixandre(s)* This seems preferable and has the support of all other mss save Q1.

1189   *avisee* Applied to Edea, 'with great forethought'(?)

1190   Only in P, this may be a performer's line added to give a realistic detail but could also be an integral part of the original text.

1197   *plus* P seems meaningless with 'vint' I therefore introduce 'plus' from the other manuscripts which gives an acceptable reading: 'between two courses when the folk were most talkative'.

1206   *restor* This is preferable to 'trezor' because of 'en' and it has the support of all the mss.

Laisse xxxiii

1211   oubli[*é*]*s* 'Oublis' in PP6W makes little sense and 'oubliés' of P7Q1 is grammatically acceptable and metrically preferable.

1217   *les quis* 'Quis' may be connected with *quiter*, perhaps 'the departed', but I have found no support for this gloss. The word seems to mean 'the dead' as opposed to 'les vivans' as in a similar line where Edea again refers to the peacock, 'Ciex chi qui represente et les mors et les vis' (I 1339). In I 1217 the variant 'mors' for 'quis' in P7Q1S1 suggests that the two words were synonymous.

1220   *n'avoit* This correction is necessary here, has the support of all but P7 and balances 'n'avoit' in I 1221.

1222-45   Medieval interest in precious stones is evident from the number of lapidaries that have survived. They usually consider the twelve precious stones as representing the twelve tribes of Israel as they were placed on Aaron's pectoral (Exodus XXVIII 17-20 and XXXIX, 10-13), the twelve months, the signs of the zodiac or the twelve apostles. Brisebare deals with only seven stones and for him they represent the seven virtues a lover should have. These are not the theological or the cardinal virtues but rather seven rules of courtly love.

1222-24   *li dyamans* Marbod *Pat. Lat.* vol. CLXXI, col. 1739, *de Adamante* describes powers of the diamond, but not those of I 1223. Two added lines in an Anglo-Norman verse adaptation of the *First French Version of Marbod* (P. Studer and J. Evans, *Anglo-Norman Lapidaries*, (Paris, 1924) p. 74) may be what Brisebare had in mind: 'Ke ki tele doné serra/ Ja poverté ne lui sivra'.

The other lapidaries add nothing to Marbod.

1225-27   *li saphirs* Marbod (loc. cit. col. 1743 *de Sapphiro*) calls the sapphire 'gemma gemmarum'. It has many powers of which perhaps the closest to Brisebare's 'fait les gens plaisans' is 'Invidiam superat' (1.13) and 'Fertur et ad pacem bonus esse reconciliandam'. The *Lapidaire de Modène* (before C.14) quoted by L. Pannier in *Les Lapidaires français du Moyen-Age* (Paris, 1882), p. 84, adds: 'Saphirs est buens por faire amis/ Por metre pais entre anemis'.

1227   *bien ceans* Perhaps = *bien cheans* (from *cheoir*), literally 'falling well' hence 'lucky'.

1228-31   *li rubins* In the lapidaries the ruby and the carbuncle are generally treated as the same stone, e.g. the *Lapidaire en Vers*, Pannier op. cit. p. 241:

> Premierement i fu assis
> Li rubys qui toutes par conte
> Les pierres de biauté surmonte:
> Escharboucles eut non sans doute.

Marbod does not discuss the ruby at all.

The *Lapidaire en Vers* deals with 'La Nature dou rubys' Pannier op. cit. p. 246 and 'La Senefiance dou rubys' ibid. p. 264. This lapidary praises the great beauty of the ruby and lists its curative powers and continues:

> Li oeil qui verai ruby voient
> Se pensent et au cuer envoient
> Confort dont li hom lies devient.

It is described also as a light sent from God to lighten our darkness but this is closer to Brisebare's *escarboucle* than to the ruby.

1229   *cors* The variant *cuers* may be right here. In the extract from the *Lapidaire en Vers* quoted above it will be noted that the ruby offers its *confort au cuer*.

1231   *de fais sans beubans* 'of deeds without pride' i.e. active (cf. 'deedy') without bragging about it (?). P is alone in this reading but the variants sound like revisions.

1232-33   *esmeraude* According to the lapidaries it had many powers but none suggests any connection with gaiety. cf. Marbod loc. cit. col. 1744 *De Smaragdo*.

1234-37   *escarboucle* cf. Marbod ibid. col. 1754 *De Carbunculo* The glowing light of the carbuncle described by Marbod corresponds to Brisebare's description e.g. *Ardentes gemmas superat carbunculus omnes*. The A.N. verse adaptation (in Studer & Evans op. cit. p. 89) has:

> Rubi escharbuncle done amur de seignurage
> Et maintient home en grant vasselage
> E done amur de Deu e de gent,
> D'ami et d'amie ensement.

1235-37   These lines are difficult and it is tempting to accept 'k'il puist' (P7 1236) for 'Que por'. However P7 is not a reliable text and a possible interpretation of the passage is: 'This (stone) teaches that a lover must in everything be all-conquering so as to enlighten the onlookers in such a way that he is the occasion of advantages to the fearful'. See I 1319-20 and I 1334-36.

The variant 'contenans' for 'conquerans' may be right here – 'the lover must comport himself in such a way' – although 'conquerans' seems more appropriate to the ardent brilliance of the carbuncle. It may be also that 'conquerans' conveys the idea of 'amur de seignurage' in the Anglo-Norman verse adaptation quoted above.

1238-40   *li esconse* Gf. gives only 'dark lantern' which cannot be right here, nor can the variant of P6W as 'jagones' is the seventh stone. P7 with 'escuse' may have a variant spelling of *esconse*. There is no stone in any of the lapidaries with a name remotely resembling *esconse*.

I believe that the only precious stone that can be said to grow (P 'est croissans'), is the pearl which grows in an oyster-shell (*concha*). Could this account for *esconse* < *ex concha*? Cf. Marbod, loc. cit., col. 1766 *De Margaritis:*

> Tollitur a conchis species memoranda marinis
> Unio dictus ab hoc quod ab una tollitur unus . . .
>
> At juvenes conchae dant baccas candidiores
> Ultra semi nucem sed crescere nulla putatur.

The Cambridge Version (Studer and Evans, op. cit., pp. 193-94), describes the 'Margarita' thus:

> 1185 Chascune conche par raison
> Ne doit avoir se un non.
> Unes a conches en la mer
> Qu'eschafotes* solons clamer.   * pearl oyster

In the *First Prose Lapidary* (Studer and Evans op. cit. p. xxxviii) under the head *Margarita* is the following: 'si receivent la rusee del ciel et de ceo creissent les perles'.

It is possible that Brisebare was thinking of the pearl with his 'esconse' but I have not found the word used with this meaning elsewhere and my attempt to equate it with the pearl may be far from the mark. P's reading of I 1238 is certainly the *lectio difficilior* but it may conceal the original version whereas the other readings seem to be revisions which make nonsense of the text.

1241-45 *jagonse* Of the jacinth Marbod says (op. cit. col. 1748, *De Hyacintho*):

> Confortativae cuncti virtutis habentur
> Triastiamque fugant et vanas suspiciones . . .
>
> Sed quodcunque genus collo suspendere possis
> Vel digito portes, terras securus adibis
> Nec tibi pestiferae regionis causa nocebit.

The *Alphabetical Lapidary* (Studer and Evans op. cit. p. 273, *Hyacinthus*), says:

> E Aristotle dit pur veir
> Que ses peres poent valeir
> Pur destruire ire et felun
> E pur estancher sancfusion.

The *Apocalyptic Lapidary* ibid. p. 273 under *Hyacinthus* says:

> Ja enpoysonez ne serat
> Ne ja trahison ne ferrat.

All these seem to give support both to 'murmure', P I 1242 and to 'enherbure', the variant of the other mss. However, several other stones, for example the emerald, were alleged to afford protection against poisoning; and as the 'vanas suspiciones' of Marbod and 'ne ja trahison ne ferrat' of the *Apocalyptic Lapidary* support P I see no reason to alter the reading of that manuscript.

Laisse xxxiv

1253 *souvenance* seems preferable to 'soustenance' and is well-supported.
1254 It may be that one or other 'amors' should read 'armes' as in the other mss but I keep P's reading as Edea's recommendations must apply to all lovers and not simply to those who have taken up arms.
1263 This line, only in P, may be an ironical comment on the idea of courtly love expressed in the preceding lines. Another performer's line which may or may

not be Brisebare's.

1270   *mostr[e]* The present tense seems preferable here, cf. I 1265. It is well-supported.

1274   [*representance*] in all the other mss gives a meaningful reading. In P 'parseverance' may have been copied in error from I 1271.

1278   [*Conchoivent*] I have supplied this word which occurs in N6P7Q1W although it may be a *lectio facilior* replacing the authentic version. P makes no sense although it has some support from P6.

1280   P is difficult here. Perhaps, 'And through this hope (i.e. that valiant men have of resembling the brave dead) all the brave have remembrance (i.e. are remembered). For *racordance* Gf. gives *'mémoire', 'souvenir', 'réconciliation'*. The variants seem less good.

1288-91 'The fact that there are so many eyes there (in the peacock's tail) which shine without perception, and that they see nothing, proving without a formal trial ('sans comparance') that a lover must have his eyes at mercy through his great desire, is both a pleasant delight and a blindness.' 'Aveulissance' is presumably formed on *aveulir*, 'to make or go blind'. It is not in Gf.

1293   [*en*] Either 'en' as in P6S1 or 'i' as in P7W is required both for sense and metre.

Laisse xxxv

1306   *ouvrage* The comparison is with a building from footing to ridge ('combles' I 1309. 'Outrage' in P must be a scribal error.

1319-20 'And for this, that is in order to be turned to great good, a small ill must not be driven out and rejected.'
        The variants 'qui puet' etc. for 'que por' in I 1320 may be an attempt to modernize the text, cf. I 1236 where P7 has 'K'il puist' for 'Que por' and also I 1335-6.

1322-23 This extension of the description of the peacock spreading its tail and looking about presumably pleased with himself is a vivid little scene which contrasts with I 1324 where the poor creature is brought down to earth. This is lost in the other mss. which omit these lines.

1326-28 'When he realizes that he is enamoured of the best lady, one by whom no man can be loved or gladdened (i.e. whose love all men are incapable of achieving) for anything they can do even ('et') by loving for ever.'
        The change from the singular to the plural in I 1328 is curious and the line may have dropped from the other tradition because of this. However, the line makes the passage more meaningful and could quite well be genuine.

1334-36 'And if he has rushed into great honours ('los') in arms (i.e. has swiftly sought great honour in arms) and sees that he is defeated in this matter, namely to have such fame, he is as a result ('en') quite humiliated.'(?)
        The variant reading of line I 1335 seems to be the *lectio facilior* which fails to connect meaningfully with the following line.

1338   [doit] 'tous' in P may be a scribal error and I have inserted 'doit' from the other manuscripts. It makes sense and I have placed it after 'estre' as in Q1 as the line in that manuscript seems better rhythmically.

1339   [chi] The moving of 'chi' is necessary for the metre and this entails the altering of 'Ciex' to 'Cis'. The latter seems to be the better reading in any case as the opposition between the golden peacock before their eyes and the one that was eaten ('celui' in I 1340) is underlined.

1343   'For this reason I lay the obligation on him, the delay is of little significance, who...
        Edea's reasoning seems to be that as Porus had killed the peacock upon which the ceremonial vows were taken it was his place to be first to make an offering.

1347   *marié(es)* 'Marié' as in P6P7Q1 in apposition to the five names preceding seems preferable to 'mariees.' The past participles in lines I 1348, 1349, 1350 and cascun in I 1351 must refer to a masculine antecedent so that if 'mariees' in P is right the subject of 'ont' in I 1348 must be the brides and bridegrooms.

This is clumsy unless 'Et' is supplied in I 1347. 'Et no' for 'nostre' would be metrically sound but was not used and presumably was not intended.

If we accept 'marié' in I 1347 then the order is first Porus, then the four other bridegrooms, the other knights who had made vows and lastly Alexander. This is confirmed in I 1393-98 where it will be seen that the ladies are in the fourth rank with Alexander.

1348-51   'Now Love has served them in such a way that it rewards them and has at once presented them (lit. served) with that for which Danger had enslaved them ('asservis'). For Love has made each one find what he sought.' See note on *Dangier* I 175.

Laisse xxxvi

1364-74   This passage no doubt reflects the feelings of a jongleur or minstrel whose professional activities, and consequently whose reward, have been curtailed by the speech-making and other non-musical pursuits of this feast. According to the programme outlined by Alexander (I 1156-76) there were to be five days of feasting (confirmed I 1183) followed by five days of full court interspersed with five days of feasting and merrymaking. Presumably the musicians were more in demand on the feast days than on the days of full court such as the thirteenth and fourteenth days. They would therefore look forward to the fifteenth day, Edea's day of feasting, as being the last chance for a rich reward. But in the midst of this feast Edea begins her long speech describing the peacock (I 1202-54). It is therefore only just that she should make good the harm she has done in reducing their reward (I 1370-71) by reintroducing the custom of choosing a treasurer from amongst them who will take charge of the takings and share them out equally.

pas This reading of P in I 1372 seems preferable to the variant 'fors'. The complaint of the musicians was, following P, 'because there was not heard merrymaking at (the ceremony of) the peacock'. The other reading, 'there was heard nothing save merrymaking ... ' gives the musicians no grounds for complaint.

clachonnier in I 1373, literally 'porte-clefs', perhaps in this context 'keepers (of the takings)'. The replacement of 'de' by 'que' seems necessary in I 1374 and is well supported.

1408,1411 *esligier* In 1408 'obtain'; in 1411 'redeem'.

1409   Marcien's gift does not represent a vow as he was not present in Epheson at the time the vows were made. The significance of the sparrow-hawk he offered is not clear although it is interesting to note that he later compares this bird unfavourably with an eagle when asked to suggest a prize for the best vow (II 1108-10, II 1135-40).

1417   *auquel* refers to 'l'estandart' I 1415.

1422   *saudoiier* This usually means a mercenary and it is curious that Aristé should offer an image of one to represent himself. Perhaps it was to humiliate himself because a knight would not normally agree to stay in a city when glory could be won outside. As Alexander says in the *Voeux* (W 5959):

    Le commun de Phezon en la cyté lairés.

Brisebare seems to have been mistaken about Aristé's vow (I 1425-30 and II 607) for he merely vowed to serve Fesonas and right her wrongs but not to remain in Epheson during the battle. The passage in the *Voeux* reads as follows (W 3972-78):

> 'Sachiés que je promech et veu a ceste fois
> Qu'en la grosse bataille servirai Phezonnois
> Et Phezone la bele, qui porte les crins blois,
> 3975   Au poing et a l'espee d'or fin arrabïois
> Si ne m'en partirai ne des ans ne des mois,
> Si seront apaisié encontre les Yndois
> S'a force ne m'en trait Alixandres li rois!'

The words 'ne m'en partirai' in line 3976 must mean that he will not depart from his vow, not that he will not leave the city. Indeed, when Alexander arranges the battle order he sends Aristé to fight with Cassamus in the fifth battalion: 'Aristez avoec vos' (*Voeux* ms. W 5955).

1424   This description of Aristés offering is omitted in the other mss.

1428   *paassier* I have not found this word in the dictionaries.
It may be a form of *paisier* 'to be reconciled with' or it is possibly a scribal misspelling of *apaisier* cf. 'apaisié' in line 3977 of the *Voeux* quoted in the note to line I 1422.

1430, 1432-3, 1435 These lines occur only in P and P6 but they seem to be genuine.

1436   Betis' offering, like that of Marcien (I 1409) does not symbolize a vow as Brisebare says in I 1437. At the time of the vowing Betis was a prisoner of the Indians but he was returned to Epheson in time for the battle and accompanied Perdicas on foot at Alexander's command.

1438   *baivier* This word in not in Gf. nor in T-L. It may mean Bavarian deriving from *Baiuwari (Pope § 636) and Brisebare obviously means it to describe an infantryman of some kind. The variants suggest that the word puzzled the scribes also and as Betis did not make a vow in the *Voeux* we cannot seek aid in that poem. Perdicas's vow to fight on foot was expressed thus (*Voeux* W 3994-5):

> Qu'adont descenderai enmi la praërie
> Avoecques les sergans, si leur ferai aiie.

In the *Restor* Perdicas is said to have fought on foot '*a guise de bourgois*' (II 609).

1443,1445   These lines are omitted in the other mss and are difficult to defend. The identical word at the rhyme in I 1444 and 1445 may indicate that the latter is corrupt.

1454   *apairier* Paired rings were sometimes made to fit together to form a single ring.

1457   This line is omitted in the other mss. except P6, perhaps because of its obscurity. It would be improved by substituting *relenquier* for 'prolongier' as in II 896 where Ydorus's vow is recalled.

1459   *l[ar]gement* This reading of the other mss. seems better than 'longement' as in P.
bringier I have not found this word. Gf. gives only *briguier* 'to quarrel' and *briguer* '*rechercher en se servant de brigues*'. T-L gives only the substantive *brigue* '*Streit*'. It may be that the scribe of P transposed the letters gu reading the latter as an n. The variants 'dangier' of N6Q1S1W and 'targier' of P7 are probably revisions.

1466   Articles of clothing were frequently given to jongleurs and one of the tasks of the king's almoner was to prevent the king from giving too many robes away. See Fleta II ed. H.G. Richardson and G.O. Sayles, Selden Society LXXII, (London 1955), p. 130.

1469   [aver] This seems a necessary correction.
'And base misers let them be eaten by moths and worms through their overweening pride, for they prefer wealth with their ill-fame to the good-liking of good folk which can do (one) a lot of good. (lit. advance one much)'. cf. a similar passage in the *Voeux* (W 8649-51):

> Cil qui ont gentil cuer sa robe a desnuee
> Et pour faire s'onnour a aucun l'a donnee,
> Mais li chaitis avers convoitex l'a gardee.

1473-84   These lines are omitted by the other mss except P6 which has omitted only I 1475 and 1478-80 but has four extra lines at the end. It seems to be a question of editing as the lines occur again at the end of the poem (II 1243-1249 except that I 1475, 1479-80 and 1484 have no equivalent there) and the extra lines of P6 (I 1483 a-d) follow them (II 1250-1254). The lines may have been appended to Part I to bring it to a satisfactory conclusion

Notes for Part I, Lassie xxxvi, continued

independently of Part II but they are not necessary here in an edition which contains both parts of the poem.

Part II describes the end of the same feast as that of Part I cf. II 1313 'a son quinzime jor' and II 1315' L'endemain Alexandres ses hommes assembla'. It appears therefore that all the debating, the finding of an eagle and the memorial service for Cassamus in Part II take place on Edea's day in addition to the description, praise and adoration of the peacock in Part I.

NOTES ON THE TEXT: PART II

Laisse i

5-6   *offrande* This is apparently a collective noun with 'faite', feminine singular, agreeing. The plural 'samblables', II 6, indicates that the gifts are being considered individually. P7Q1S7 show that attempts have been made to make II 5 conform with the plural in II 6 but the different variants for 'faite' and the fact that group Yb have 'faire' instead of this word show that the singular was probably in the archetype.

        veus The variant 'diex' of Ya shows that the scribe of the archetype of this group had not understood II 6, that is that the offerings were intended to recall the vow of each person.

        repetation I have not found this form elsewhere and it may be an eccentric spelling of *repetition*, that is, the offerings were a symbolic repetition of the idea of the corresponding vow. Gf. quotes S6 'repentacion' and N2 'repectation' glossing them as *'repentir'* and *'considération', 'égard'* respectively, however the idea of 'repetition' suits the context better.

12   Alexander calls only those who did not make vows to debate the merits of each vow.

13   *a bas ton* The variant 'abandon', which does not suit the context, sets the rest of the manuscripts against PP6W and possibly P7 which has 'son sermon'.

16   *la fin c'est le coron* The oblique case is guaranteed by the rhyme but it is difficult to explain 'c'est'. P6P7S7 resolve the problem with 'et' for 'c'est'. Perhaps 'c'est' has the force of *id est* and 'le coron' should be considered in apposition to 'la fin'.

22   *frachon* 'faint-heartedness'(?) I have not found the word in this form but it could be the Picard for *fraction* < L. L. *fractionem* with shift to tʃ. Gf. glosses *fraction* as *'action de briser', 'infraction', 'bruit'* and T-L. as *'Brechen', 'Bruch', 'Bruchteil'* which are not appropriate. Perhaps the noun suggests 'weakness' or 'discouragement' here as it is linked with 'hide', cf. C. L. *frangi* 'to be discouraged'. Cicero for example says in a letter to Atticus 'quod me audis fractiorem esse animo' which is translated by the editor as 'You say you have heard that I am rather down in the mouth'. See *Cicero to Atticus*, edited by D.R. Shackleton Bailey (Cambridge, 1966), V, Book XI: 12,4. An example is found also in Tacitus. Cicero was criticized 'a Bruto autem, ut ipsius verbis utar, tamquam "fractum atque elumbem" ', 'and by Brutus, to use his own expression, as "feeble and emasculate" ', Tacitus, *Dialogus de Oratoribus*, translated by Sir W. Petersen (London, 1946), 18. The noun *fractio* is in the *Glossary of Later Latin* glossed as 'weariness of spirit'.

        The many variants indicate perhaps that *frachon* was either obsolescent or unknown to the scribes.

25   *biau[s] fais* The plural seems preferable here to the singular of N6Q1W.

27-32   P makes little sense with 'hautement vouer' and by substituting *hardement voé* which is well-supported, and the past participle *achievé* in II 28 we have, with 'science' in II 32, a repetition of the triad 'proece-hardement-science' in II 21 which is expanded in II 22-24. These are the three qualities needed in undertaking an enterprise and the idea is applied to the present circumstances (II 25-26). *Hardement* and *proeche* have played their part (II 27-28). It only remains to evaluate the deeds by calling on *science* in the shape of the 'menestreus de non' (II 29-32).

36-37   Cf. the proverb 'Communement on dit que qui a le prouffit a la guerre il en a l'honneur', Le Roux de Lincy, Vol. II, 350. Unlike the proverb, Brisebare

227

Notes for Part II, Laisse i, continued

appears to be separating the material benefits, 'le proufit' in II 37 and 'biens' in II 38, which the small man desires, from the honour without which the noble baron would perish.

45-46   'and therefore let it (the honour) be given in such a way that there may be neither blame nor reproach in the matter.'

Laisse ii

56   *en partie* 'aside' or 'some of them'(?) Gf. does not help here but T-L. gives both *'zum Teil'* and *'beiseite'* both of which make sense in the context. Some of the musicians must have been left in the great hall to play for the dancing while Alexander and his company were debating the merits of the vows in the Chamber of Venus.

65-68   'Each one of us, however little wealth he may have, must do, according to what we have arranged, the same as the King of Ermenie. You are in this ('i') as good as a king and I am worth no more than his followers.' Alexander himself may be the King of Ermenie as his grandfather was so called in *RAlix* Br. I, 150, 'Olimpias ot non, fille au. roy d'Ermenie'. The place perhaps owes its name to Armenia.

69   *en une riulle onnie* 'in an equal row' i.e. with no one taking precedence.

70-71   It is clear that the egalitarian spirit is to last only as long as the debate. Afterwards each will receive the honour due to his rank.

72   'Let us go forward to the point (lit. to the living quick) in the matter which is arranged'.

80   *Mesire(s)* I have bracketed the s as it may be scribal. Although the form *sires* with analogical s is used for the nominative singular in all cases except II 933 where it occurs at the rhyme, it cannot with certainty be ascribed to Brisebare as it does not affect the metre. The form *sire* is used regularly in direct address in P. The form *Mesires* does affect the metre in II 80 unless one admits the elision of e followed by s, not normally found in careful poets. As Brisebare's prosody is generally meticulous it seems not unreasonable to assume that the original form was *Mesire*.

Only P6Q1 support P in this line, but it is the best reading, 'He is my lord and you (are) his', and is reinforced by II 83-84.

85-86   'He is such a one (wherefore there is no need that he should be reproved for it) as to stake ('metre') heart and body, land and fief and life.'

90   Obviously Alexander is the 'roi de Mazonie' but it is not clear what land is referred to. See I 67, note, on Clarus le Mazonois.

94-96   P is obscure here but the other readings are no better. Perhaps, ' "Fair one," said the mighty king, "you have defeated my intention. Your own aim is set at so high a good (i.e. is so worthy) that I dare not sing your praises further lest I speak wrong of you" '. The idea behind 'que ne mesdie' seems to be that the speaker fears that his very praise may be so unworthy of its object as to amount to abuse.

The variants 'presser', 'prier' for 'prisier' in II 96 are no improvement.

99   *puirie* 'offered'. An uncommon word found only in N2PP6W. The other scribes have found less good substitutes, perhaps seeking to eliminate an obsolescent word.

100   'refused by each and feared by the majority' ('du plus').

105-21   In this passage Alexander describes the role of a herald rather than that of a minstrel, although their functions must have overlapped in many cases. The idea is that the one who watches a battle is better able to judge the merits of the contestants than those taking part. In P,W the question is treated in a general way: (II 107) 'When a knight...'' The rest have made it particular: 'When I...' This weakens the text for Brisebare is clearly setting off the detached view of the Chief Minstrel against the diminished power of judgement of any man in the thick of the battle, not only of Alexander.

112   *arramie* 'pitched battle'. The word is used in the *Voeux* e.g. W 3992: 'Se li roys se combat a bataille arramie'. The word was obsolescent by the

fourteenth century which perhaps explains the substitutes of the other tradition.

114 'When he receives a fine blow how he returns it.'

119 'It is well that he who sees it forget it not.'

122-23 'for he who plays chess vacillates more easily than he who watches the game and does not take part.' (*s'esbanie* lit. 'enjoys himself')

Brisebare rounds off the laisse with the proverb on which Alexander has based his argument. It seems to be a variant of 'The onlooker see most of the game' but I have not found the proverb recorded in French collections. The idea it contains must have been expressed in some form in French. The earliest example quoted in the *Oxford Dictionary of English Proverbs* is dated 1578 but corresponds quite closely to the idea in *Restor* II 122-23: 'As at Cheastes, though skylfull players play,/Skyllesse vewers may see what they omyt'.

Laisse iii

125 This line describing Alexander in apposition to II 124 seems to have misled the scribes. Q1W omit it and still make sense. N1N6OQS1 keep it but omit II 126 thus making the description in II 128-34 apply to Alexander instead of to the 'roi des menestreus'. These mss then alter 'li varlés' to '.i. vallés in II 144-45.

126 *Li rois des menestreus* E. Faral discusses the position of minstrels and heralds in *Les Jongleurs en France,* (Paris 1910), pp. 268-69. The title of *Roy* was given either as an honour to one who excelled in a contest e.g. *le Roy du Chapelet* who was the winner in the *Course du Chapelet* or the *Roy des Poètes,* the one whose poems were considered best at a court; or it described a function, for instance in the household of Philippe de Bel in 1288 were a *Roy des joueurs de flûte*, a *Roy des Ribauds*, a *Roy des Hérauts.*

In the *Restor* the 'rois des menestreus' or 'rois des hiraus' as he is called in II 146 must have been very versatile. In II 126-29 he appears to be an elderly residential chief minstrel. From II 130-33 it seems that he sometimes usurps the role of the privileged court fool. He also shows some knowledge of the work of a herald or King of Arms in II 136-8 and II 576.

les autres aquite He speaks on behalf of the other minstrels.

131 *habite* This has caused difficulty as the variants indicate, and as so often, W and Q1 omit a difficult line. Apart from the usual meanings such as 'to dwell' *habiter* could also mean 'to approach' cf. Beroul *Tristan* 490 'Ne l'un de vos l'autre abiter'. Could this be the meaning in II 131? The man would put on his act of a crippled dwarf in order to go up to the valiant knights and abuse them with impunity so perhaps a possible rendering is: 'and like a hunch-backed dwarf and as if crippled he will approach and call the brave men cowards...'

Of the variants for 'habite', 'abisse' does not rhyme and 'herite' is required for the next line. Only N2 offers a possible solution: 'He lives there like a hunch-backed lame dwarf'. But this may be a revision as it omits 'com' before 'contrais' which is found in P7 and N5S5S6S7 as well as in P.

According to E. Welsford (*The Fool* (New York, 1961), pp.113 ff.) the vogue for the court fool was increasing during the fourteenth and fifteenth centuries and reached its height in the sixteenth century. The first authentic reference to a royal French fool found by Welsford is in 1316 when 12s. was paid 'pour une robe de 3 garnemenz, pour mestre Geffroy le fol' (Douet d'Arcq, *Comptes de l'Argenterie*, (Paris 1851), p. 9). Some fools had valets, others had keepers, but on the whole they were kindly treated, received visits from relatives and were honourably buried. Some were mad, some probably suffered from epilepsy and sometimes a sane fool would pretend to be insane. Presumably it was by doing so that he could get away with insults such as those expressed in the *Restor* II 132.

139 [*guerre mortel*] The singular is necessary here because of *est...confite* in this

line and 'elle est...descrite' in II 142.

145   'May I be blamed as you wish. I never ask to take an arbitrator concerning it.' i.e. I will abide by your decision.

arbite I have not found this spelling in the dictionaries. Most of the other manuscripts have the spelling *arbitre* and P7 has rewritten the line, perhaps to avoid the problem. Nyrop I § 361, 2° quotes the O.F. form *traïte* besides *traître* but it is not clear whether the form without *r* occurred in neglected speech or was accepted in literary works.

Laisses iv to xxv are taken up with a discussion of the merits of each vow except that of Cassamus who was killed in the battle of Epheson. There are eleven protagonists and each speaker is allowed to make a speech on behalf of his or her hero. This defence is then attacked by the next speaker who proceeds to speak on behalf of his own hero and so on. After eleven speeches each protagonist, in the same order, makes a second speech defending the person of his choice. The following is the order of procedure:-

The Chief Minstrel	of Epheson	for Gadifer	of Epheson
Cliton	Greek	for The Baudrain	Indian
Marcien	Indian	for Floridas	Greek
Tholomer	Greek	for Edeas	of Epheson
Antigonus	Greek	for Aristé	Greek
Alexander	Greek	for Porus	Indian
Emenidus	Greek	for Perdicas	Greek
Filotas	Greek	for Ydorus	of Epheson
Festion	Greek	for Caulus	Greek
Licanor	Greek	for Lyone	Greek
Elyot	of Epheson	for Fesonas	of Epheson

In the *Restor*, instead of having one man defend a thesis against all comers, as in a mediaeval university disputation, we have eleven people defending eleven different vows. And although each speaker attacks the previous speaker and is in turn attacked by the following one, there is no retort, no rapid exchange between the debaters as in a master's disputation. Nor do they speak in syllogisms although Brisebare does have a fondness for the triad, e.g. II 150-53, II 155-57, II 587-89. In fact the form suggests rather the formal arguments of a jury at a Puy where the relative merits of poems were debated and a prize, usually a crown of flowers, awarded.

Laisse iv

147   *guerre[s] morteus* There is a false concord in P and N2. Both the singular and the plural have support in the other mss and I have added s to 'guerre' as this is the simplest change, but with some hesitation as the line is a reprise of II 139-42 where I introduced the singular to suit the context.

149   P is alone with this line although it has a genuine ring. *li souverain* 'the highest, noblest'.

151-52   These lines, omitted in all but PP6P7Q1W are necessary as there can be no 'moien' (II 153) without an end as well as a beginning.

firent The plural is difficult to account for in II 151 as the line stands, and the variants for 'voloir', namely 'valoir' in Q1W and 'valeur' in P6P7 do not solve the difficulty. It may be that 'de' replaces an original 'et' for the line would then balance the previous line with a double subject.

157,159   Omitted in all the other mss these lines appear to be asides to the audience for the thread of the narrative goes from 156 to 158 and then to 160. Lines 157 and 159 may have been omitted in the archetype of the other mss. because of the difficulty of fitting them in; but a skilled jongleur could easily speak the asides in such a way that the thread of the sentence was not lost. The two lines together with II 156 add up to three points in Gadifer's favour and this triad, a favourite device of Brisebare's, is lost in the other mss.

	Of course, the lines may have been added by a redactor but if so it seems odd to insert them in the middle of a sentence in this way.
157	'and of fine quality that he can look at this matter'(?) Or perhaps, reading 'se' reflexive for 'ce' 'that he can think of going...'
161	Only in P and perhaps W with 'prieus'. The revisions of the other mss may be due to a misunderstanding of or a wish to avoid the Picard *prius* for *perils,* cf. I 558 where all but PP6 have 'peril' for 'pril' and omit 'que' (except Q1) to correct the metre. However, in I 561 N6S1W have 'Prius' as P although P6Q1 have 'Peril', and P itself has 'peril' in I 593 and II 852.
164	Hypometric in P but not in the other mss. I retain it as it is more vivid and has the play on *cors*, 'horseback charge' and *son cors* II 165, 'himself'.

Gadifer vowed last in the *Voeux* (W 4278-84), and Brisebare may have got the idea of a charge from the lines, 'Et je veu et promec et voel que vous sachiés/Qu'a l'estandart Clarus ert mon frain adreciés', (W 4279-80).

171-72	*voel* in II 171 seems to have two meanings and to govern two constructions, one with the infinitive and one with the subjunctive: "Nevertheless I do not intend to criticize the knight for anything nor do I claim that anyone can rise higher through valour..."
174	*relever* Gf. *'élever à un grand honneur'* This occurs only in PP6Q1U but it it seems a better reading than the variant 'reveler'.
176-80	Cliton is building up a picture of Alexander's valour in order to enhance the Baudrain's merit in taking his sword.
177	A reference to Alexander's conquests and to his aerial flight and his descent into the sea. See I 16 and I 20, notes.
179-80	'that in him one can see one's reflection where prowess is concerned and all other virtues if one examines the matter carefully'. i.e. one can measure one's prowess and other virtues by his: they are a standard to which we should aspire even though we cannot reach it.
181	Q1,W have 'puis' for 'pour' i.e. "With good reason can I consider his vow as unique". In P 'Par raison' refers back to 'a bien examiner' in the previous line i.e. 'And with good reason (sc. should one examine the matter carefully) in order to uphold his (the Baudrain's) vow as unique'.

singuler Gf. quotes this line in S6, treating the word as a verb and glossing it as *'garder', 'exécuter en détail'.* I think this is mistaken as it is based on the S6 reading 'et singuler'. All the mss except Yb have 'a s.', cf. 'singulers' in II 355 where it is also used adjectivally.

| 182-84 | 'Since fortune and the gods wish to treat him (Alexander) in such a way (i.e. as described in 176-80) and he (the Baudrain) has brought them (the gods) so low despite their power as to come and take his (Alexander's) sword from him in the midst of his people.' |

The Baudrain's vow to take Alexander's sword 'ou milieu de sa gent' is recorded in *Voeux* ms. W 4090-95.

189	*anui* This word in the sense of 'harm, distress' as in I 38 'peines et anois' is a better reading than S7W 'ami'. P7S1S6 with 'anemi' have a hypermetric line.
190	*veulent* I have left this as it is supported. The variant 'doivent' may be right but it sounds like the *lectio facilior.*
195-97	Yet has our king courage to look a noble man in the face, the will to attack and strength to kill him, and so by so much was the vow harder to fulfil.
198-205	Cliton points out that he is hampered in putting his case by Alexander's presence. If he were not there he could praise him unreservedly thus increasing the Baudrain's merit.
205	'So ('se'=*si*) one must set aside and annul the case' (as made out for Gadifer).
209	'One can well learn to speak from your words' (i.e. I can answer you out of your own mouth).

Marcien is going to build up his case for Floridas on the basis of Cliton's defence of the Baudrain. If the latter is as great as he is said to be then the one who took him prisoner is even greater.

For Floridas's vow to take the Baudrain prisoner see the *Voeux* ms. W 4204-16.

| 213 | 'By the greatness of the deed (of the Baudrain) can one prove the other (that of Floridas)' |

Laisse v

224 'That I shall not dare to run away even if I am defeated.' i.e. I shall have to stand my ground even in a hopeless situation.
This seems to be an answer to Cliton (II 195-96) rather than to Marcien's general praise.

225-27 'My lord,' said Marcien, 'there is nothing wrong in that (in taking flight?). I should have staked little on what a braggart said. And so I have come back to my view:...'

228 *fu* in P is better than the variant 'fust'. Marcien is not casting doubt on the Baudrain's prowess. Indeed, the braver he was the better, for it increases Floridas's glory.

230 P6 'iel uic a' is perhaps a misreading of *le livra*.

232-33 The passage is obscure as it is difficult to interpret 'porte' meaningfully. Perhaps: 'He (the conqueror) must hold sway and be placed above him by as much as the enterprise to which he is committed has import.'

234 [*pris*] This is well supported and seems to be the better reading. 'fais' may have been copied in error from the previous line.

235 'For my part I give it to him no matter by whom it (my decision?) may be blamed (*laidis* 'abused').

237-54 Marcien sets the vow of Cassamus above all the others. The latter does in fact get the prize of honour in the end through some mysterious trick (II 1072-1074).

240 Cassamus had vowed to set Clarus on a horse again if he found him dismounted in the battle. (*Voeux* W 3953-3959) See II 1139, note.

241 [*S'a*] P's reading of 'Se' would be defensible if 'meschief' were nominative. In view of the unanimity of the other mss. it seems preferable to alter 'Se' to 'S'a' rather than to change the case of 'meschief'. In *Voeux* W 3954 Cassamus says, 'Et je truis au dessous le riche roy Clarus'. The variant 'a meschief' for 'au dessous' occurs in N1P1P4S1S2 and this may be the source of 'a meschief' in the *Restor*.

246 *Es[t] es* < *ecce* is normally followed by the oblique case e.g. I 973 'es .i. vallet'. The variants 'Et' and 'Est' may be scribal attempts at emendation but 'Est' is well supported and seems to be the most intelligent reading.

247-50 This passage has a proverbial ring although I have not found an exact equivalent. Brisebare is apparently comparing Cassamus's vow to set his enemy on horseback again in the battle with the action of a man who gives back his winnings to his rival at gaming in order to be able to go on playing. He all too often finds himself the loser in the end. Perhaps the nearest to this idea is Morawski *Prov.* 2347 'Teus cuide gaingnier qui pert'. A similar idea is expressed in *Erec* 5874-5 'Tex cuide avoir/le geu joé, qui puis le pert'.

253 'And seeing that this brave man is dead' (lit. 'come to the end of this earthly life').

258 *chi estes ses amis* 'You are his friend in this' recalls the proverb 'Louange d'amy n'a nul crédit, ny mépris d'un ennemy.' Le Roux de Lincy Vol. II p. 257.

266 'Let mine be the crown, yours the dispute'(?) It is not clear what Alexander means here as he too took part in the debate. Perhaps he is rebuking Tholomer for taking the arguments too seriously as in his outburst in lines II 258-60. When he says 'This is surely an occasion for laughter' (II 261) and 'I can't pay as much attention as all that to what he means/to the way he is judging the matter' (II 265) he is clearly intent on taking the heat out of the debate. He seems to be content to hear everyone's praises sung but sees no reason for them to come to blows about the finer points of the arguments. *sens* is difficult to translate both here and in II 279 and 281. In II 265 Alexander could be referring to the sense of Marcien's arguments or perhaps simply to the discourse itself; but when Tholomer takes up this point in II 279 'Tout li sens sont seüt' he uses the plural and is perhaps referring to Marcien's ways of looking at or judging his subject (see II 210-34).
Line II 264, omitted in the other mss., may be another performer's aside, perhaps to draw attention to his own need for refreshment. It would be unnecessary in a copy intended for private reading and may account for the omission of the line in the other mss.

271 'When they had drunk they took up the discussion again'. The plural 'ont' is

supported by N2P7Yb. The rest have 'a' of which the subject must be
Tholomers in II 272. In P the main verb of which Tholomers is the subject is
found in II 274 but this line is omitted in all the other mss so that those which
have 'ont' in II 271 are incomplete.

Laisse vi

278   'But I do not wish because of this to acquiesce in all he says.'

279-81   The passage is difficult chiefly because 'sens' in II 279 and 281 is ambiguous,
see II 266, note. It seems that the passage makes sense only if we accept the
gloss 'way of judging' for *sens* (Gf. Supplement gives *'manière de juger, de
comprendre'*). Thus, 'All those ways of judging (that is those used by Marcien)
are known, but if some, through learning, are perfect in one respect in another
they are less so. Well then, no one can know and understand all the ways of
judging ...'

In II 625 also the only really acceptable meaning for 'sens' is 'way of
thinking, or of judging'. In other instances in this text *sens* is used without the
definite article and means 'good sense', e.g. I 4, II 936.

Marcien's method of defending Floridas is to prove the greatness of his feat
by demonstrating the greatness of his opponent (II 213). He therefore agrees
with the previous speaker, Cliton, that the Baudrain was a brave fighter and
infers from this that Floridas who took his prisoner was greater (II 210-12).
He then praises the Baudrain even more by stressing the might of his adversary
Alexander (II 215-20) so as to lend even more weight to his argument that
Floridas was the greatest (II 227-30). Marcien then concedes that there was one
greater vow, that of Cassamus, but as he is dead the prize must go to the
second best, to Floridas (II 237-57). It is difficult to cap this argument as no
one conquered Floridas in the battle and it is probably for this reason that
Tholomer attacks Marcien's method in this passage.

285-90   These lines recall Edea's vow in *Voeux* (ms. W. 4076-80):

> Et je veu au paön que restorés sera
> Du plus fin or d'Arrabe que on trouver porra:
> Sor .i. piler d'or fin li ouvriers le metra.
> Ce será le restor, et si en souvendra
> A celui et a cele qui le paön verra!

285   *engendre* It would be more accurate to say that the original peacock slain by
Porus 'engendered' the vows but perhaps Tholomer's argument is that the sight
of the golden peacock will revive the memory of the other vows and they will
live again.

286   *colians que calendre* 'making neck movements like a lark'(?). The peacock must
have had an articulated head; or perhaps light glinting on the jewels and
polished surfaces gave an impression of movement.

For *calendre* Gf. has *'grande alouette d'Europe'*, presumably the crested lark.
Aloe in I 365, 698 is probably the skylark *(alauda arvensis)*.
colians This does not seem to be particularly appropriate to these birds and
Brisebare may have had in mind the medieval bird lore of the bestiaries,
e.g. *Li livres dou tresor* of Brunetto Latini which describes the *calendre* (Book
I, 155) as turning its head away from a sick man who is to die and staring
fixedly at one who will live.

Laisse vii

303-15   In the *Voeux* Aristé merely vowed to serve Phezone and the Phezonnois, see
I 1422, note. Cassamus and his fifth battalion had help in the end from Aristé
who came up 'avoec ceus de Phezon' (*Voeux* W 6460) which may have misled
Brisebare. This conflicts with Antigonus's arguments in the *Restor* that Aristé
gave up any hope of glory on the battlefield.

305   [*nul*] In P 'ma' must refer to the speaker, Antigonus, and this does not make sense. There is no reason why Aristé should come to succour him more than anyone else. It is possible that 'ma' conceals the original version, perhaps 'sa' referring to Aristé, i.e. he would not leave Epheson for his own business, namely securing honour in the field. However, 'nul besoing' has the support of all the mss. and I have accepted it as being feasible.

       besoigne The 'ne' at the end of this word in P may be a case of dittography as 'ne' follows. P has the following forms of the word: 'besoigne' I 458,619 (obl.) I 657 (nom.); 'besoins' I 678, II 695 (nom.); 'besoig' I 1062, 'besoing' II 1320 (obl.).

312   *seroit grief* Unless we read this as impersonal 'it would be more grievous to him if one ...' there is a non-agreement in all the mss. except Q1 which has 'feroit mal' and P6 with 's. griés'. However, 'cil qui' in II 314 needs a personal subject to balance it in 312 unless Brisebare changed the construction in the middle of the sentence either intentionally or by negligence. The matter could perhaps best be rectified by changing 'seroit' to 'feroit'.

318   [*a toute*] This order is well-supported and it is difficult to account for 'toute a'. It may be a scribal error.

319   *voel que le pris sien soit* 'I wish the prize to be for his (sc. vow)'. Or, reading 'siens' as in P6P7Q1W 'I wish the prize to be his'.

       P has a rare *le* for *li* here.

324   Alexander takes up Antigonus' words in 320-21: 'There is one born who could well do it (i.e. oppose your view) without being in error (sans pechiet)'.

Laisse viii

325   *eut* One syllable in Picard, Pope § 549 and § 1029.

327   This flattering description of Alexander's speech has dropped out of the other mss, but it could well be genuine.

332-33   These lines recall the 'aurea mediocritas' of Horace (*Odes* II, 10,5) according to whom a middle condition was a guarantee of peace and tranquillity and preferable to all others. Cf. Le Roux de Lincy, Vol. II, 248, 'Le milieu est le meilleur' and ibid. p. 333 'Vertu gist au milieu'.

338-39   There seems to be a pun *avalois-outremontans*. It is clear that the Avalois were considered less good fighters than the Outremontans but it is not certain what people are intended. For *avalois* Gf. gives *'habitant d'Austrasie'* and quotes the *Restor* in S6. The Avalois have also been identified with the inhabitants of the Low Countries, particularly of the Lower Rhineland. For *outremontans* (Gf. suggests *'celui qui habite au delà des monts'* and quotes the *Restor* in N2 and S6. Outremons was also the land of Gos a friend of Porus in *RAlix* Br. III, 1910. It may even be an adjective formed on *monter* meaning 'an exceptional person'.

340-43   In the *Voeux* it was love for Fesonas which made Porus seek to double his vow (W 4039-41). His actual vow is in *Voeux* W 4047-51.

340   *doublés et plus qu'en trois* It seems that Porus's vow to win the battle and to take Emenidus's horse was so great that it could be considered as more than a double vow. In fact Porus did not win the day, nor even one skirmish. He did take Ferrant from Emenidus but lost him again and broke his thigh in falling. It was apparently the outrageousness of the vow that counted and the valiant attempt to carry it out. Alexander discusses this point in his second speech (II 811-15).

341   *archadanois* i.e. Emenidus of Archade. See I 239, note on Arcade.

343   Emenidus is compared to the standard perhaps because it was a rallying point in battle.

Laisse ix

351   This line, omitted in the other mss, appears to be a parenthesis. It may also be corrupt. 'Of all good qualities he was the chief' (?)

352-53   'you are indeed skilled enough to extol Porus if you were followed in the matter.' i.e. if we all agreed with you. The implication is that Emenidus does not agree for he goes on to refute part of Alexander's argument, that concerning himself (II 362-68).

354   *se* Probably adversative here, 'And yet ... ' for Emenidus is going to concede part of Alexander's argument (II 354-61).

358   *rouegniés* I have found only meanings such as 'cut, tonsured, beheaded' for this word. 'I place none beside him however high-tonsured he be'(?) i.e. however great he may be. There may be an archetypal error here common to all the manuscripts.

360   *es[t,]* Both P and P6 have 'es' here but as the nominative case follows I have substituted *est* which is well supported, cf. II 245-46.

361   *[seroit]*, *bi[en]* Both these corrections seem necessary and are well supported.

362   *taisi[é]s* This correction is necessary for the rhyme. Four palaeographical lapses in three lines is unusual in P.

373-78   Only P has 'dont' in II 373. The other mss. have more straightforward readings one of which may be correct but I prefer that of P. 'It is the rule, wherefore indeed it cannot be changed. The boaster always thinks he is but little exalted and the brave man, the more his brave deed is told, the more he fears that he is being jeered at and mocked. For the merit of others is so firmly fixed in his heart that he always wishes to count himself among those of least reputation.' *umilité* (II 370) seems to represent the virtue of modesty and self-deprecation. In II 817 en lui humiliant refers to this same trait in Emenidus. Again, in II 1196 humiliant describes a humble, modest attitude. Elsewhere in the *Restor* the adjective *humle* I 118, II 776, the adverb *humelment* I 1230 and the noun *humilité* I 963 seem to describe a courtly virtue, a blend of courtesy, modesty and affability. Alexander's 'humility' is referred to in this sense in *RAlix* Branch III 2236-37 when Porus says to Alexander after the latter has conquered him and refused to take his riches:

> Humilités te vaint et fait rendre ton gage
> Onques si larges hom ne fu de nul parage.

380-83   In *Voeux* W 3990-98 Perdicas vowed to go dismounted on to the battlefield and fight 'avoecques les sergans' (W 3995).
        (en) Line 380 is hypermetric, I therefore omit en as do Q1S7W.

384-86   'To be on foot is more difficult for a nobleman and to be mounted for a villein, unless he knows how through long experience ('de viés), than to fight with ten bolted doors.'
        N2P6W with '.x. huis verilliés' are more intelligible than P. Presumably the idea behind this is the difficulty of fighting one's way through the barred gates of a fortress. The variant 'bresilliés', 'burned down' is odd and 'milliers' is an imperfect rhyme. It may be that an original *dis huis* has been transcribed as .xviii. as in N5S7 and this has been misread as .xiiii. in S5.

389   Omitted in the other mss this line seems genuine enough. It may perhaps have been added by a performer, possible Brisebare himself, to soothe an audience likely to take offence at the suggestion that a nobleman cannot remain standing for long (II 388).

391   *loiiés*, 'hired'(?) This reading is possible, *loier* being a by-form of *louer* < *locare*: 'for each man is worth what he is hired for'. However, P stands alone with 'loiiés' and 'tailliés' in the other mss may be the better reading here: 'for each man is worth what he is cut out for'. This suits the comparison in II 384-86 between a nobleman fighting on foot and a villein on horseback, each trying to do what he is not cut out for.

392   Only N2P6W have this line as in P. If 'a cheval' is taken to mean 'on horseback' then a verb is missing, but if 'a' is the verb the sentence is clumsy; 'When someone has a horse and it is knocked down'. P7 has avoided the difficulty with what appears to be a revision and N5S5S7 with 'ist' have a hypermetric line.

Laisse x

402	*Tudiele* Tudela in Spain (?). The name occurs also in *RAlex* Br. II 263.
410-12	For Ydorus's vow see *Voeux* W 4124-31. She vowed to love Betis *'loyalment de vrai cuer sans faintise' Voeux* 4131.
414-17	This passage on loyalty and valour is omitted in most of the other mss. only N2P6Q1 besides P having it in its entirety. There seems to be no reason to reject it as Filotas is building up his case to prove that loyalty is greater than valour.
419-20	An obscure passage and, judging from the variants, it has caused difficulty to the scribes. The comparison of a wicked man (uns mauvés) with a willow switch ('harcele') is odd, but it is difficult to extract any other meaning from the text. Filotas's argument is that too much credit has been given for mere prowess for even a wicked man can show valour in the field but valour without goodness is worthless. I suggest therefore: 'A certain wicked man may well be extremely brave, lashing like a scourge, but valour without goodness is not worth a spark'. *chinglans* T-L. gives *cingler* < *cingulare* 'to strike' 'to whip'. It appears to be used mainly in connection with *verges* and T-L quotes for example: *'verges... Molt agues et ciunglans'.*
420	*estincele* Only in P, the rest having 'cenele', 'rose hip'. Both are objects of small value but as a spark better represents the idea of the glory due to valour being extinguished because goodness is lacking I retain 'estincele'.
421-23	'We are judging as one does a ewe in lamb what we see externally; but within the chamber of the heart is loyalty which heaps up good.' Filotas argues that the virtue of Ydorus's vow is not apparent like that of the others for it consists of the true love hidden in her heart. The comparison with the ewe is odd, but apparently one cannot tell from the external appearance whether a ewe is in lamb.
425	*turiele* Only in PP6. The variant 'tourterelle' may be a *lectio facilior.* Reading 'turiele', Ydorus was 'filled with loyalty like a little tower', i.e. she was a tower of loyalty.
426-27	' ... that fellow is tormenting himself for nothing. It seems that her heart is jumping for joy.' In other words her vow was not too difficult as she was only too happy to remain true to Betis.

Laisse xi

435-37	Caulus's vow is recorded in *Voeux* W 4096-4106.
443	Hypermetric in all except P7. I have altered the order of the words to restore the metre.
449-52	Caulus is the subject of 'avroit' II 449 and of 'avoit' II 451; the Baudrain is the subject of 'avoit' II 450 and of 'averoit' II 452. 449 and 452 express Caulus's intention to take the Baudrain's helmet or cut off his head and 450-51 express two conditions that might prevent him, either that the Baudrain had his helmet glued on or that Caulus's own arm was put out of action. See *Voeux* W 4098-99, 'Que j'avrai vostre hiaume s'il ne tient a cyment/Ou la teste en vendra se braz ne brise ne fent!'.

Laisse xii

467	[*des*] This has the support of the other mss and must be right for reasons of metre and meaning. Clarus and his sons were not Lyone's 'souverains'. For Lyone's vow see *Voeux* W 4156-59 and II 971-81 note below. The joust was inconclusive as both were unhorsed and Lyone was carried back into Epheson, but he was considered to have fulfilled his vow to joust with Canaan.
473	*trecule* Under *treculer* Gf. refers to *traculer* in the Supplement but I cannot trace the word there. The variant 'recule' makes good sense but in view of P6 'trescule' which supports P it must be considered as a possible *lectio facilior. au daarrains* Adverbial phrase meaning 'finally, in the end' in opposition to 'adiés' II 472: 'The brave man would always wish to be among the foremost whereas the coward falls back(?) in the end'. The variant reading 'aus derrains' in opposition to 'des premerains' in the previous line is also possible: 'falls back among the hindmost'.

475   *mostrer ses caukains* 'to show his heels'. Licanor cannot mean that Lyone was keen to run away as in the Mod. Fr. *montrer ses talons.* Presumably he was keen to gallop away to meet his opponent, thus showing his heels, but I have not found other examples of this use of the expression. Only P6W support P; P7 has 'cointains' which may be connected with cointement 'ornament', and the rest have 'lorains' 'ornamented straps on bridle and saddle'.

476   *premerains* This is supported by P7 only. 'Fezonains' is an attractive alternative as it avoids the repetition of 'premerains' within five lines, but it may be a revision and I have therefore retained P's reading.

477   *li viellars hermitains* This is Cassamus who would be the host in Epheson. He had been a hermit but took up arms again on behalf of his nephews and niece against Clarus. *Voeux* W 434-39.

> 'Biaus niés,' dist Cassamus, 'de bon cuer le t'otroi
> Tout le cuer me revient quant d'armes parler oi,
> Piecha ne chevauchai ronchin ne palefroi,
> Ne vesti gambison ne portai escu bloi.
> Hermites ai esté en bois et en chaisnoi
> Or m'est venu en gré guerroier a Clarvoi.'

489   Elyot is scornful of a vow whose worst consequences were the need of a hot bath after it.

490   *levains* 'leaven'. The raising agent used to exalt or raise up ('eslevés') Lyone is Licanor's speech which according to Elyot has puffed up Lyone's worth for a rather routine action.
Only P and W have II 488-91.

Laisse xiii

497   'My lord, will you say if it pleases you that I should say more?'
498   *desloie* Perhaps 'free oneself', 'let oneself go', hence 'speak freely'. This is in fact what Elyot does for, after asking demurely for permission to speak, she makes by far the longest speech of the eleven.
501-02   For Fesonas's vow see *Voeux* W 4005-12. She expresses her gratitude to Alexander for coming to the aid of Epheson by giving him the right to choose her husband: 'Que ja n'avrai ami ne mari haut ne bas/Se de par lui ne l'ai' (W 4010-11).

506   *soie* This must be the possessive adjective here. 'If I were a knight or his lady'(?) A *demoisele* could be the wife of a squire ('Gattin eines escuier') according to T-L. who quotes: *'la danselle que je cuidoie avoir et faire damoiselle et joir de s'amor'.*

509-53   The abstract nouns in this passage reflecting the medieval idea of courtly love have been regarded as allegorical personifications and given capital letters although they are not written thus in the manuscript.

514-15   *i envoie* The word may have a different meaning in each line, i.e. 'sends' 514 and 'invites' 515, but the repetition may be due to a scribal error. The other mss have 'le convoie' 'escorts her' in 515.

524   'For Love would be bringing this about and not I' i.e. I would not be responsible for my action.
526   *escondit i otroie* 'grants excuse for it' seems preferable to the reading of the other mss which read 'et' for 'i'.
529   *si de mi le faisoie* 'If I did it of myself' i.e. of my own accord and not compelled by the power of love.
540-52   Elyot argues that if one is already in love (and Fesonas was in love with Porus) one is vowing against Love and consequently against Right and Fortune if one vows to take a husband chosen by another person. 'If Fortune and Love were not in accord' (II 545) i.e. if the man chosen were not the one I loved 'I might very well have him from Love Lose-all' ('Amors qui tout pert').
The reading 'puet' for 'pert' in II 544 weakens the argument for if Alexander

Notes for Part II, Laisse xiii, continued

<table>
<tr><td></td><td>did not choose the man she loved then Love could not be said to be all-powerful; or if it were all-powerful then there would have been no danger to Fesonas in making the vow she did. Indeed in II 546-7 Elyot seems to weaken her own argument for if, as she says, Fortune can do only what Love consents to then Alexander could choose only Porus as Fesonas's husband.</td></tr>
<tr><td>551-52</td><td>'Indeed, and so unconditionally ('nuement') that I would not exclude my lover or anyone else to whom I gave myself.' Or reading *anui* for 'ami' 'I would not exclude harm to myself nor to another to whom I were given.'</td></tr>
</table>

essentiroie This seems to be the same verb as *essenter* perhaps with change of conjugation.

nuement 'without condition', 'simply'. 'Meïment' in P6 a contraction of 'meïsmement', 'above all' is also a possible reading. 'me vient' of Ya is no doubt a scribal misreading of this.

Q1, which frequently omits difficult lines, has omitted II 551-52 and has instead the following which is a simple explanation of the position, perhaps by a redactor who thought the matter needed clarifying:

550a	Se Alexandres vausist aler une autre voie
b	Qu'il eust donné .i. autre a Fezone la coie
c	Que Porrus son ami en qui bien multeploie
d	Dites, que feïst elle, par amours vous en proie?
e	'Je n'ai pas,' deïst elle, 'lasse ce que cuidoie!'

553	'He who wages war on Love has to fight hard.'
554-1043	In this section (laisses xiv to xxv) each speaker again and in the same order defends the claim of his hero to the prize.

Laisse xiv

564	*au desrengier* 'at the breaking of ranks'. A term used of a knight who rides forward ahead of his rank to challenge the enemy.
569	*assigier* In Gf. *assegier, assigier* are glossed as 'to besiege' 'establish,' 'dispose', but the variant 'esligier' of the other mss meaning 'obtain' is better as a pendant to 'achater' and 'bargennier' in II 568. The word in P may be the result of an erroneous reading of s for l in *asligier*, possibly a dialectal variant of *esligier*.
571-73	'And when it comes to giving a verdict and declaring the right you do not know how to speak about it, rather do you try to help yourselves out with some confused opinion ('trouble semblant') compounded of hoping and thinking'(?)
574-75	'You are like the heralds, to balance the good (i.e. to apportion it equally), who do not know how to act and so want to talk about it.

contremoiier 'to counterbalance'. Gf. quotes the *Restor* in S6 as the only example of the phrase *au bien c.* and suggests *'à parler proprement'*. This ignores the idea of counterbalancing or dividing in halves contained in *contremoiier* and the Chief Minstrel is particularly stressing the antithesis: what one likes the other dislikes and what one can do the other cannot do. He develops this in II 576-77 where he claims to have some talent for describing feats of arms but has no liking for the fight whereas the knights love the fight but have no skill in talking about it'.

578-84	'But he who wishes to love jousting and tourneying has indeed need of all this: thought, speech and action; a man that is who wishes to know the whole trade of arms: to think, meditate on and desire a noble deed, to act in order to set in motion and complete this great action, to speak to give true judgement of warlike acts, for it is a great wrong to judge a fighter unjustly.'
593	'In some way you must come to an agreement/be reconciled.

Laisse xv

602	[*se vanta*] I have substituted this for 's'avancha' because of the syntax, for in **P** there is no antecedent for 'qu'a' in II 604. 'Se vanta' is well supported.

610   [*Lyones*] It was Lyone who jousted with Clarus's son. The error in P is presumably scribal.

614   *A ame(r)* The infinitive in P and also in N5P6P7S6S7 implies some verb such as *voua* which is lacking.

625   *a rebois* Perhaps an alteration for the rhyme of *a rebors*. 'With your way of judging you would assign the prize perversely (or wrongly)'.

Laisse xvi

630-31   These lines could be omitted as II 632 follows logically on 629. W does omit them but they have the support of most of the mss.
     Only P has 'resclaire' II 630, 'shines forth' and 'par' II 631. The variant 'repaire', 'dwells' occurs in the other mss, as does 'a' for 'par'. The variant 'a' is preferable grammatically and may well be the correct reading.

634-37   'For if the god who is mightiest in dignity wished to recreate his valour from all brave men and put it in a single vassal to bring him to perfect merit and to make a mirror and example to all brave men ...'
     Only P has 'refaire' in II 635. The variant 'retraire' with 'la' or 'lor' for 'sa' is perhaps a better reading: '... to take from every brave man his deed of valour ...'
     This idea of concentrating the valour of many brave men into one is expressed in a different way in the *Voeux* when Floridas lauds Porus and says his prowess could be divided into ten and make ten brave men (W 4035-37):

> Tant par estes poissans et de hardi penser
> Que, qui poroit proesce en .x. pars desmembrer,
> 4036a   On en feroit .x. preus pour grant painne endurer
> De la haute proesce que Diex vous vot donner.

644-45   'There is not one who if he allowed to be taken from him (the king) the price of a miniver skin would not for that reason ('por tant') let himself be torn to pieces.'

647   'beside this man's vow no other may please'.

649   This line has caused difficulty as the variants indicate but I think P has the best reading.
     paire 3rd person singular Present Subjunctive of *pareir?* 'however little it may appear by my words' i.e. however inadequate my advocacy of him may seem (?)

650   Another end of laisse line omitted in the other mss. It can be included in Marcien's speech or be considered a personal comment by the author.

Laisse xvii

660   *nareus* This word and the variant 'vareus' seem to be equally unknown. See I 61, note.

663-64   Only in PP6P7. WYa combine the two lines but only W makes sense. Although 663 without 664 makes sense N2Yb have 664 without 663 which does not. Both lines are supported to a certain extent by the mss which combine them so they could be genuine, although it must be admitted that from PP6P7 Edea appears to be running about too much. W has skilfully eliminated this frantic movement and produced a duller version: the others have made nonsense.

666   *a piteus* 'pitiably'. Not in Gf. but T-L. gives *'jammervoll', 'kläglich'*.

671   *jueus* 'playful'(?), or perhaps 'blithe', cf. *jocunde: jueusement (Gloss. de Douai)* quoted in Gf. Supplement under *joios.*

679   *desireus* The variant 'diseteus' of P6P7W may be right although 'desireus' is supported by the rest. Both readings seem to be examples of litotes: 'I am not at all desirous ... ' meaning 'I am very desirous', and 'I am not lacking (sc. in ability) ... ' meaning 'I am very capable'.

Laisse xviii

681   For *n'estra* P has the support of W only. For *ester* lit. 'to stand' T-L gives
'*Bestand haben*', '*gelten*' so perhaps a possible rendering is '(it is clear) that
none of these vows will have value save only in itself'. Tholomer is then going to
point out that Edea's vow is enhanced by being both a mirror and a reminder of
the other vows.

       The variant 'ne sert' may have arisen through the misreading of a titulus, or
the reading of P W may also have so arisen. The variants 'n'afiert' and 'ne fet' are
perhaps misreadings of 'ne sert'.

690   'And many a great good happens with little impulse' i.e. with little to set it in
motion.

693   [*Et*] This following 'verront' in II 691 is probably better sense than 'En' and is
well supported.

695   [*les*] This is necessary following the plural in the previous line. The idea seems
to be that if necessity takes them by surprise, i.e. if they are hard-pressed in
battle, the memory of the peacock will spur them on to great feats.

700-04   Tholomer is answering Antigonus's criticism in II 297-99.

703   *aviutissement* 'dishonour' occurs only in P. It gives a satisfactory reading and
there seems to be no need to replace it with one of the variants.

705-08   Brisebare, or his authority, seems to be refuting the proverb 'Tant vault la chose
comme elle peut estre vendue', Morawski *Prov.* 2303. He may also have had in
mind: 'Chose donnee doit estre louee', ibid. 389.

710   [*Nous*] This is supported by the other mss and it could be that 'Que' crept into
P in error from the next two lines.

717   [*moult*] The line in P makes little sense and *moult* is well supported.

720   *desmesureement Desmesure* seems to be treated as a virtue here and 'mesure' is
rejected as a luke-warm quality which inhibits a man's progress to honour (II
721-29). 'Proëche', 'hardement', 'vigeurs' which lead swiftly to honour are
opposed to 'mesure', 'cremeur', 'atievissement' which prevent one attaining to
honour.

725   *atievissement* 'a cooling off', 'lukewarmness'(?) Neither Gf. nor T-L. have this
noun, but under *atiedir*, '*lau werden*', '*lau machen*' T-L. notes the past
participle *ateviz* a form which supports the conjecture that *atievissement* is a
cognate noun. Gf. notes *atainisement* in N2 commenting that it is a 'mot
douteux exprimant l'idée de tempérament'. Neither this nor the other
variants suit the context as well as 'lukewarmness' for the argument is that this
attribute makes one pursue honour so slowly that hardly anyone attains it who
undertakes an enterprise by its side, in company with 'mesure' and 'cremeur'.

       This argument against *mesure* is contrary to popular wisdom which
generally teaches moderation, e.g. 'Quanque l'en fet par mesure si profite et dure,
quanque l'en fet sans razon vait a perdicion'. Morawski, *Prov.,* 1730.

       P is alone with 'leur lés' in II 727, but I think it is better than 'leur los'
which most of the other mss have. After all, if *mesure* and *cremeur* gave their
consent to a deed or counselled it, it is odd to argue that they impede it (II 728).

729   *le(s)* This seems to be a scribal error although W also has 'les'. The scribe may
have been misled by 'mesure et cremeurs' in the preceding line, but the pronoun
must refer back to 'hounor' in II 726.

732   *sert* In spite of the variants 'ert', 'si iert' etc. I think that 'sert' is the better
reading as, unlike the others, it will do for 'tans present' and 'tans a venir' as
well as for 'tans passé'.

740   Only in P, the line must be a comment of the author rather than of Antigonus,
for the latter does not refer to 'li escris' to make his case.

Laisse xix

745   *latine et ebrieue* Brisebare may mean Latin and Hebrew speaking, i.e. learned,
or perhaps eloquent here. Aristotle taught Alexander these languages in *RAlix*
Br. I, 335-36, 'Il li moustre escripture, et li vaslés l'entent,/Grieu, ebrieu et
caldieu et latin ensement'.

750   [*que il*] The line is hypometric in P and I have introduced the reading of
P7S5S6S7W.

761   *Chiere* In Gf. Supplement *'accueil', 'traitement'*. So 'The treatment one metes out to him is much worse than to a man one hates without mercy or respite'. This is a better reading than the variant 'Guerre' for Aristé is being commiserated with not because he has to endure fierce fighting but because he had to miss it.

771   [*i*] The line is hypometric in P and has caused trouble to the other scribes. P6 has five minims after 'plus de jus' which I take to be 'i jiue' and this seems to be the best reading.

774   'In my view there is no one who can shift me from this opinion.' Only in P.

Laisse xx

793-94   'So when I go examining justice carefully I can only give the prize to the best fighter.

802   'It is a vow having two sides (or aspects) and strengthened by being doubled.'

803   *por le mains soffissant* 'on account of the least important' (?) Perhaps Alexander means the lesser of the two aspects of his vow mentioned in the previous line.

809-10   Porus is described as doing better than the proverb: 'Le bon commencement atrait la bonne fin 'Morawski *Prov.* 1058.

814-15   'And the good intention which was his unceasingly must be counted as a work (i.e. a fulfilled aim) in my opinion (lit. with the consent of my opinion)'

819   *N'a proëche sor lui* Perhaps, 'is not an act of bravery over him', meaning that Emenidus is easy to overcome. The variants do not help.

820   *Abilant* Some oriental city or land. I have not found it in *RAlix* but the name Abilance occurs in Br. II, 1042, where Betis de Gadres spurs his horse 'qui fu nes d'Abilance.

824   *fissent* Possibly a scribal error for *fussent*.

828   *leonant* Perhaps an invented form to give a rhyme in -ant and meaning 'leonine'.

833   *passés vous en atant* 'Have done now'(?) Emenidus uses almost the same words at the end of Alexander's first speech (II 348).

836   'You could well build up an image of a brave man by talking'(?) Only in P.

Laisse xxi

839   *nus ne m'aidera* P is alone with 'm'aidera'. P6S1 make sense with 'm'adira' i.e. 'no one will convince me that there is any greater vow ...' 'me dira' of the other mss. is probably a revision of this. In spite of its difficulty I have left P unchanged as there is some support in W. This ms. has 'ma' only and then leaves the line unfinished. It may be that the scribe paused for consultation over a difficulty and forgot or was unable to complete the word. There would have been no need to hesitate over *m'adira* which is straightforward so P may conceal the original reading.

851-67   The comparison between the relative dangers of fighting on foot and on horseback is interesting. The cavalry were supreme in the field at this time but the situation was soon to be changed by the tactics of the Swiss infantry, and of the English bowmen during the Hundred Years War.

861   Only in P. The two previous lines tell of the advantage in battle given by the horse which bears the weight not only of the rider but also of all his protective armour. In II 861 the weapons are added to the list. I do not think it is possible to determine whether the line is Brisebare's or not. *quanques* This form seems to be peculiar to the scribe of P.

878   *trubers* This word probably derives from the Germanic proper name Trudbert and in this context is obviously derogatory. Gf. La Curne and von Wartburg all suggest the gloss *'homme débauché'* but this is unsuitable here. Filotas is arguing that Perdicas cannot win the prize 'par voie de droit' (II 875) and that if the company do award it to him they will be mocked and called 'trubers et ignorans'. A scoundrelly character named Trubert did exist in folk literature and he was above all a deceiver and cheat. In the farce by Douin de Lavesne (ed. J. Ulrich, Dresden, 1904) the eponymous hero says:

> 827 Sire dus, je ai non Trubert:
> Bien vos puis tenir por fobert (dupe).

But this fellow was so successful in his deceptions and so ruthless that he could hardly be mocked.

Another Trubert is perhaps nearer the mark. He is a Me. Pathelin type of advocate in *La farce de Me. Trubert et d'Antrongnart* by Eustache Deschamps (in *Oevres complètes* ed. G. Raynaud, Paris 1891) and he does indeed intend to deceive:

> 118 'Ta cause sera soustenue
> Si fort et de si bon endroit
> Que je te feray de tort droit.'

However, his attempt to cheat his own client at gaming is foiled and he is mocked. He laments:

> 470 'Trubers doy je estre appellez bien:
> On m'a fait un beau jugement!'

Brisebare could not of course have derived his knowledge of the word from Deschamps (1346-1406) but line 470 of the farce quoted above indicates that the word was already known as a derogatory noun or adjective and in view of the character of Trubert the idea expressed is that of the deceiver deceived or the dishonest but foolish advocate. This interpretation is more meaningful in the context in the *Restor* than *'débauché'*, 'scoundrel' or even 'deceiver' as it accounts for Filotas's fear that they will be mocked in their attempt to award the prize wrongly.

879 This line is obscure and has been much revised in the other manuscripts.
esta Gf. under the head *esta(t)* gives *'arrêt'*, *'fête'*, *'audience judiciaire'*, all of which fit the context: the decision that Filotas is afraid will be made to give the prize to Perdicas, the festivity that is taking place, or the formal hearing of the cases for all the vows. But 'bien' causes a difficulty for Filotas seems to be saying the opposite of what he means. Is he, I wonder, indulging in heavy sarcasm when he tells his audience what will happen if the prize is given to Perdicas? He says: 'Each of these good people will rightly call us dishonest and ignorant advocates for it and will mock us for making such a wise decision if he wins without more ado.' I think in this case that the meaning *'arrêt'* is better than *'fête'* or *'audience judiciaire'*. If on the other hand Filotas is not being sarcastic but is being straightforward, and 'bien' has no overtones a possible rendering is: '(they) will mock at us in order to make a good decision/festivity/ formal hearing'.
sans plus This usually means 'alone' in O.F. but this does not suit the context here, nor in II 911. In both these cases the version 'without more being done' or 'without more ado' makes sense but I have not found this meaning recorded elsewhere.

Laisse xxii

881 'By a well-ordered speech whether false or true'(?).
883 *faire assais* 'to make tests or trials' i.e. to find out where honour etc. originate.
cf. *assaiant* for *essaiant* I 672.
888 [*Qui nous maine*] I have supplied this from the other mss. as the reading of P seems to make no sense and may have arisen through scribal confusion.
899 Only in P the line is simply an extension of the description of Betis.
901 *compaignie verde* For *vert*, feminine *verde*, Gf. gives *'vif, énergique'*. Filotas is comparing Ydorus who fulfilled her vow through her enduring love with those who achieved their aim through physical prowess on the battlefield.
The line occurs only in P and the whole passage seems to have caused difficulty considering the number of lines omitted: W II 900-04, 0 901-04, Yb 901,

903-04, the rest 901; but only in 901 is there a masculine antecedent, 'on', for 'armés', 'agregis' and 'irais' in II 903. In the mss. which have II 903 but omit 901 these adjectives can only qualify 'Boine Amors' in II 900 which is feminine. Indeed P7 has attempted to remedy this by writing 'Armee' and 'agregie'.

904   *le cuir, l'achier, les ais* These may refer to the leather of jerkins or harness, to the steel of armour and to the boards which formed the base of the shield. It is perhaps more likely that all three refer to the shield: the wooden boards, the leather covering and the steel strengthening.

905-16   This comparison between the relative merits of love and prowess is not easy to follow. Filotas begins with his statement that 'The essence of love is loving without ceasing'. He then makes three further statements about love's functions namely that love is the flower (of loving?), that prowess is its refuge and that a lady's love is the ray or full measure(?) of mercy (II 906-07). By this he may mean that love brings its own embellishment ('la flors') such as that described in II 909, that love willingly takes up its abode in a noble and brave man, and that a lady in love will show mercy, presumably to her despairing suitor.

Then, taking himself as a hypothetical case, he shows that he too can demonstrate these attributes; but if he does appear pleasant and gay and eager to take up arms this proves that love has come to him (II 909-11). The idea 'Amors est a moi trais' is perhaps intended as an example of 'proeche' being 'li retrais' of love expressed in II 906. The third attribute, that of mercy, is also within his capability and anyone showing mercy without an ill intent represents love without fault or falseness (II 912-13). This being so there is nothing wrong in the pursuit of arms, indeed a handsome man (or 'brave' reading 'bons' for 'biaus') is embellished and strengthened through it (II 914-15). Nevertheless, the greater is worth more than the lesser. (II 916).

What he means, I think, is that all these are superficial manifestations of love, they represent love, (II 913) but they are not really true love ('Boine Amors' II 900 whose essence is 'amors sans relais' (II 905) and whose rule Ydorus followed.

916   *li eskais* This word seems to be of unknown origin. Gf. Vol. III p. 474, col. 3 quotes this line from the *Restor* and suggests the meaning *'petit'* for *eskais* . In the same volume p. 350 col. 3 under *escait* is the tentative gloss *'petit morceau, éclat de bois'*.

Two different solutions are offered in the variants. One group N1N5S5S7 has 'estrois', S6 'estrais' thus comparing the thick with the narrow, and P7 compares the seed ('grains' for 'gros') with the twig ('esclais' for 'eskais').

As *li gros* can be a heavy coin I have searched for a coin of smaller value but have been unable to find one with a name remotely resembling *eskais*.

I have left the line as in P as it has some support and its general meaning is clear.

920-23   ' ... you are living and feeding on a very great wonder, never before was such a one, by extolling her deeds; but with very little effort (*frais* lit. damage caused by breaking) you will be able to see that you do not please us in this matter.' Line 921, omitted in the other mss, seems to be necessary. A possible rendering of the other tradition would be: '...you are feasting by extolling her i.e. you are relishing it, enjoying it. This can then be opposed to the final comment 'but it does not please us.'

Laisse xxiii

924   *plest* The preterite *plot* as in most of the other mss is preferable grammatically but I retain 'plest' as there is partial support for it in S1 with its hesitant 'plost'.

928   *descrire* 'delineate, explain'. Festion is making the point that the arguments of the others ('raisons' II 927) are easy to convey whereas no-one can describe properly what Caulus achieved (II 932-3). The variant 'desdire' seems to be a *lectio facilior* for the point of Festion's argument would be lost if the others were easy to contradict.

929 P7 ends here. Probably the last seven folios of the quire have been lost.

936 *en qui sens je me mire* 'In whose wisdom I reflect myself' i.e. whose wisdom I imitate.

938-43 This passage is obscure and may be corrupt. Festion has just said that Caulus should not be deprived of the prize simply because he, Festion, is not such a convincing speaker (II 935-37). He then continues: 'And if you do give it to him, whoever may think the worst about it I shall never thank you on his behalf, however much he may urge me to, nor will I say 'May God reward you for it'; but let Love have the thanks who inspires in his heart desires to be so worthy that he chooses such a vow, namely to seize the helmet from the best man in the army'.

The difficulty is that Caulus was one knight who seems to have had no lady in mind so there seems no reason to say 'Mais grace en ait Amors' (II 941). However there is no major disagreement among the manuscripts over this passage. It may be that Caulus made his vow through love for Alexander for in the *Voeux* he is extremely angry at the Baudrain's vow to take Alexander's sword and immediately vows to take the Baudrain's helmet in revenge *Voeux* W 4096-4106).

939 *detire* Analogical present subjunctive. The verb *detirer* usually means 'to pull,, tug, wring' and in the examples quoted by Gf. and T-L. the object is generally *cheveux, barbe, mains.* However T-L. gives cases where the object is a person and the gloss is *'jem. drängen, bittend nötigen'* which seems more fitting here, i.e. 'to press urgently'.

940 Is this line a negative form of the formula:
Molt grant mercis et Dex le vos mire?

943 *empire* 'Army' seems preferable to 'empire' here. The word is used with this meaning in *RAlix* e.g. Br. II, 126-29, 'Et a dit as Grigois, 'Chevalchiés sagement: Ves l'empire de Gadres qui nos vient au devant' '.

945 *gire* This must be the infinitive following 'fist'. 'He forced him to lie over his saddle-bows.' For the possible development of *gire* from *iacere* see E. Spalinger, *Absterben von IACERE im Galloromanischen* (Bern, 1955), p. 55.

946-47 [*des*] *puing*[*s*] The plural is necessary because of 'fuissent' in II 947. All the mss save S7 have the plural in 946. 'He took from his hands, whoever may have ceased from laughter over it, his sword as quickly as if they (sc. the hands) were of wax.' W and O have the singular 'fust' for 'fuissent' with a feminine subject in 947 so that the sword is like wax. The other reading is better.

The formula 'qui qu'en laissast le rire' may express astonishment and awe at the thought that it was the great Alexander who was being overpowered in this way.

948 [*Caulus*] This must be right here as Caulus took the Baudrain's helmet.

952-53 'One could not go on praising all day long without ceasing for one injures (or condemns) no brave man by it', i.e. it would be a waste of time.

N2 with 'Le' for 'Ne' has perhaps a better reading, 'One could go on praising him ... ', i.e. it does not matter to me because you cannot harm my candidate by it. P6S1W also have 'Le' for 'Ne' but the nominative 'nus boins' in these mss makes a less good line. The rest support P with 'Ne' so I leave it although it is not really satisfactory.

954 *lire* 'recite, proclaim'. Taking 'lire' in this sense the line is meaningful and P has the support of P6S1W. The variant 'dire' is probably a *lectio facilior.*

955 This line, omitted in the other mss, is another end of laisse line which may be a direct comment by the author to his audience, but I include it in Licanor's speech as it is equally suitable there, 'For of all things it (sc. telling of a better man) makes one choose the best man'.

Laisse xxiv

961 *ç'avant* This is difficult to account for and the variant 'qu'il vaut' of the three other manuscripts having this line may be correct, 'Each one must be retained (or received, reading with W 'receüs') for what he is worth'. This does however imply a certain order of merit whereas Licanor seems to be arguing that they are

all equally good. As he says in II 959-60 each of them performed his brave deed so well that he would not be willing to oppose a single one of them. It may be then that P contains or conceals the original reading. If ç'avant' is accepted as an abbreviation of *ça avant*, 'further', then the line can be read as expressing a second consequence of II 959 'Cascuns le fist si bien', the first being in II 960. Hence, 'Each one for this reason ('por tant') further must be retained'. It is as if he is compiling a short list of excellent candidates and all the contestants can be on it provided Lyones is not excluded (II 963-64).

962   *haïne et amor jus* 'love and hate apart' (for they would affect one's judgement). cf. Morawski *Diz* XXXIX:

> Homs qui veult jugier loyaument
> Doit garder au commencement
> Qu'il ne soit trop d'amours sourpris
> Ne de grant haïne entrepris.

963   [*Lyones*] This must be right here. The mistake was probably caused by a confusion of L with the symbol for *et*.

966   *qui estoit crueus* refers to Clarus not Canaam. The other mss have tried to improve the syntax by inserting epithets suitable to Canaam in II 966 and adding 966A to describe Clarus. Canaus was one of the four sons of Clarus. All save Porus were killed by Alexander at the battle of Epheson and Clarus was killed by Cassamus.

969   *deust* See I 740, note.

970   *palus* The flat marshy ground or lush meadows (cf. 'pres herbus' II 971) of the encampment? Or the word may be a deformation for the rhyme of *palis*, 'palissade', perhaps set up round the camp.

971   *Et* This makes sense and is well supported. 'Ains' may have crept in from the previous line.

971-81   The herald whom Lyone uses as a messenger is not mentioned in Licanor's first speech from which it seems that Lyone goes himself to Clarus's tent to ask for the joust 'a jointes mains' (II 481-82). This corresponds to the vow in *Voeux* W 4156-58.

> Je veu et si promec et bien ert acomplis
> Qu'aprés mangier irai devant le tref Clarvis
> Pour demander la jouste a l'ainsné de ses fils!

When the actual performance of the vow is described (*Voeux* W 4474-82) Lyone sends '.i. garçon qui estoit a escus' to Clarvus and it is presumably on this passage that Brisebare bases Licanor's second speech in the *Restor*.

979   Only in P; the line could be genuine as Lyone must have thought it necessary to explain to Clarus why he is asking for a joust just before the battle.

998   *Dyanus* Probably a rhyme variant for *Dyane* which occurs in II 1257. The form 'Dyanus' occurs again at the rhyme in II 1267 where it is clear that the body of Cassamus is lying in the 'temple Dyanus', but from II 1236-37 we learn that Betis will place the prize awarded to his uncle 'el temple de Marcus/Ou on aloit servir Dyane et Cupidus'. It seems then that the *temple Dyanus* and the *temple de Marcus* are one and the same and that Dyane and Dyanus are the same deity.

1000   Another end of laisse line only in P. It seems to belong to Eliot's speech rather than to be a comment of the author or redactor.

Laisse xxv

1004   *anuie* 'annoy'(?) The variant 'amuse' meaning 'deceive', 'mislead' may be better here. Eliot is arguing that they are all allowing themselves to be confused and misled by presumption ('Cuidiers') without submitting their assumptions to examination by clear reason ('Raisons', II 1003). But if they have indeed been upholding their opinions by stratagems designed to deceive ('par ruze', II 1002) it has all been a waste of breath (II 1005).

1006	I have not found the proverb in French collections but some such proverb or saw must have existed. At a later date Shakespeare, or a contemporary of his, was to use the same idea: 'An idiot holds his bauble for a god'. (Titus Andronicus, V.l. 79).
1006-11	Eliot flatters the judges, as did the candidates at the literary contests held in the *Puys.*
1008	*parvenue* The variant 'pourveüe' of the other mss is tempting, but 'parvenue' agreeing with 'ounor' is a possible reading and I therefore retain it: 'men of worth and of perfect honour'.
1013-14	'For if your deed (i.e. the one you are upholding) pleases us and someone else abuses you for it, if one will look more clearly this will be (sc. seen to be) a great want of judgement.' Eliot is arguing here that the very differences of opinion expressed show a blameworthy lack of judgement. If they had all sought the truth by the *'juste voie'* (II 1012) instead of arguing *'par ruze'* (II 1002) they would all have reached the same conclusion. As she points out later (II 1022-23) each one has upheld his opinion but it would have been better to have sustained it well. There is only one truth, one 'vraie issue' (II 1024) and that is that Fesonas should have the prize.
1017	This is inexact as Porus did not win the battle.
1019-21	*estre doit Gadifer ... Et celui ... Ou le preu Floridas* 'it must be Gadifer's ... or his ... or brave Floridas's.
1034	*guerre esmue* See note on hiatus, p. 43, and Phonology note iii, p. 45
1036	*rendue* 'made known' or 'repaid'. Both meanings are given in Gf. The vow was of course known already but Eliot's argument may be that the details which made it more serious e.g. her love for Porus should be made known.
1041	*assentue* This and assentus in I 1167 are probably forms used for the rhyme. Gf. gives examples of both *assentus* and *assentis*.

Laisse xxvi

1047	*auditeurs* The judges at literary contests held in the *Puys* were called *entendeurs*. According to T-L. persons called to hear witnesses at a judicial hearing were called *auditeurs*.
1055	*feront* Only in P, the rest having the second plural 'ferons' or 'feron'. The actions described in this line take place before the lots are drawn as it is clear from II 1056-59 that the company were to pray that the lot should come out fairly, and after that Alexander would draw out one name. In II 1067 also 'fisent le sort' describes what was done before the lots were drawn. Could *un sort* be the collection of slips of parchment forming the lottery? Elyot was to have these slips hidden in her hands (II 1054) and they (i.e. 'les brievés reading P) would then form the lottery. 'Ferons', 'we will make' is less good for Elyot already has the names in her hands. In II 1067 again 'les brievés' is a more logical subject of 'fisent' than 'they', i.e. the company in general. *sortis* In view of the foregoing this seems not to mean 'drawn' or 'obtained by lot', for which 'saquerai' is used in II 1059 and 'pris' in II 1070, but rather 'formed' or 'provided'; but I have found no support for this in the dictionaries.
	The manuscripts which omit II 1048-58, N1N6OQU, are incomprehensible when they take up the narrative in II 1059.
1062	*ja n'en serai desdis* 'I shall never go back on my word', or, reading the variant 'sera', 'It (the name you draw) will never be opposed'.
1064-65	It is odd that this vivid picture of the company putting the names together and mixing them up should be omitted in all the other mss.
	[les ont] This seems to be a necessary correction and is merely a question of substituting l for s. The mistake arose perhaps because of the letters *le* at the end of 'ensemble'.
1069	*[ouvré]* The line is hypermetric with 'aouré' which has three syllables in this text, cf. I 213,1295, also 'aourer' I 374, 'aouree' I 1209. I therefore substitute 'ouvré' from N2S1W.
1078	*Jovis* A different deity from Jupiter in the next line? The only other reference

to either of them is in I 125 where 'Jupiter et Venis' are designated as gods of the Greeks.

1083   Gadifer was the elder son of Gadifer du Laris (I 208 'Gadifer l'ainsné') and one would therefore expect the king to have made him the recipient of his uncle's prize. The choice of Betis may have been due to the exigencies of prosody.

1088   *Persis* Perhaps a rhyme variant of *Perse, Perssie,* or the province of Persis on the Persian Gulf. In I 193 Marcien is 'de Perssie' and in I 209 'de Persse'.

1088a   Omitted from P. A blank was left for the line, perhaps because the scribe could not read his copy, and the words 'que c'est fais d'aidier ses anemis' are written in the lower margin (181r). The rubricator has filled the blank with the rubric, 'Comment Elios parla sagement'. This belongs to the next laisse and is one of many misplaced rubrics.

Laisse xxvii

1092a   This line although present in all the other mss is not in P. As it is not essential to the sense I have not included it in the body of the text.

1106   *(samble),* [*soit*] The line is hypermetric in P and the reading of the other mss. (except P6) has been accepted: 'be your words true or false'.

1108-40   In this speech Marcien first suggests two possible prizes: a sparrow-hawk and a chaplet of flowers. Each one is rejected, the sparrow-hawk in II 1108-10 and the chaplet in II 1111-25. He then suggests a golden crown (II 1126-34) and an eagle (II 1135-40) — a double prize for a double vow.
haute volee Only P has this expression in II 1108, the rest having 'grant renommee'. I have retained P's reading as it provides a point of comparison with the eagle, the bird 'de plus haute volee' (II 1136).
comparee (II 1110) It may be that something has dropped out here in the archetype as the sparrow-hawk is finished with in three lines and is not compared with anything else. As the text stands one can only suggest: 'its condition is not of such high quality as to be employed for or compared with such a prize'. But if it is to be used as or to represent the honour won by Cassamus can it also be compared with it? One would expect after II 1110 a line such as *'Avoec l'aigle qui est de plus haute volee'* and this if followed immediately by II 1137-38 would give a satisfactory point to Marcien's argument. But the eagle is not introduced until II 1135 when Marcien offers it as his suggestion for the prize. What does follow after II 1110 is Marcien's next suggestion, the *chapiel.* His argument here is followed through logically. The qualities of the circlet of flowers are described and he uses the symbolism of the perfect circle to exalt it (II 1111-15). Then follows the reason for rejecting it namely that the flowers quickly fade and this detracts from its perfection (II 1116-25). The golden crown is then extolled and suggested as the prize (II 1126-31) and finally Marcien argues (II 1132-40) that because of the surpassing quality of this vow both the eagle and the gold crown should be given. As we have already noted the first mention of the eagle is in II 1135 and there is only a summary account of its qualities in II 1136-37.
    The idea of giving a crown to the winner was probably taken from the Puys where the main prize was the title of *roi* accompanied by a crown, usually of silver. Other contestants were given crowns of leaves.

1112-13   'For the circumference into which the circle is closed demonstrates perfection for it is not measured.'
cierne The gender is guaranteed feminine by the rhyme but the word, deriving from *circinum,* is considered to be masculine in all the dictionaries.
    The idea of these lines seems to be that the circumference of a circle having neither beginning nor end cannot really be measured. One can only take its measure by selecting an arbitrary point of departure.

1116-17   'But the flower which adorns the twig has by no means arrived at perfection.'
1119-20   This appears to be a parenthesis in which Marcien moderates his condemnation of the flowers as a worthy prize. They may not be perfect but they are nevertheless worthy of honour even when heaped into a barn.

1121   *Ensi est* I think this refers forward to II 1123 and not back to what has just been said i.e. 'With prowess it's like this: through the perfect end we praise the fine beginning', (unlike the chaplet of flowers which dies in the end).

1132-35   'Seeing that this deed of valour surpasses all others – no one knows anything but good of it, that is proven truth – and the vow is so noble that no one aspires higher, I advise that the eagle crowned with a golden crown be given as the prize.'

1139   *double* Only Porus made a double vow, that is to perform two separate feats. Cassamus vowed only to aid his enemy Clarus should he find him unhorsed in battle, see II 238-52. Perhaps this was considered to be double in power or valour, as Marcien says (II 245-46), 'Aidier les anemis en morteus fereïs/ Est fais deseure fais hardis outre hardis'. Or perhaps by remounting his enemy he had to fight twice, see II 240, 241, notes.

1147   *otroiie(t)* The feminine form (-iata > -ie in Picard) makes better sense than the masculine, both 'otroiie' and 'acceptee' agreeing with 'sa parole' in the previous line.

1152   *(Et)* Perhaps introduced in error from the previous line. Only P has both 'Et' and '.i.' but each word has some support in the other mss. As the line is hypermetric with both I have dropped 'Et'.

1154-55   Only in P. Although 1154 could be dispensed with I think 1155 is necessary.

Laisse xxviii

N2 has four lines of summary in red preceding this laisse at the top of 158r. as follows: 'Comment li roys Alixandres trouva que Cassamus qui/estoit trapassez avoit l'ounour de la bataille/Et le donna a Betis son neveu et comment Betis fist couronner l'aigle-'. The first three lines refer to laisse .xxvi., II 1070-87.

The dancing, parading and presenting of the eagle described in this laisse are performed with typical courtly ceremony. The *carole,* a chain-dance, could be danced in a ring or opened out at any point to form a line, the dancer in front becoming the new leader. This appears to be what happened. The king, his followers and musicians enter in a line (the eagle borne by 'li sergant le roi', II 1151) and make their way through the revellers 'a force et a viertu' (II 1159-61). The ring opens out with Elyot now the leader and the dancers go to meet the king and his retinue. She takes the eagle and parades it flanked by Emenidus and Marcien (II 1162-68). Elyot leads the singing of a *roondet de carole*, the others responding with the chorus (II 1169-75). She then, with great ceremony offers the eagle to and withdraws it from the eleven people who had made vows (II 1183-97). Finally she offers it to Betis who receives it formally in the name of his uncle and gives thanks to the gods and to the king (II 1198-1226). He continues to parade the eagle in the next laisse while Elyot and the King rejoin the other festivities (II 1227-31).

1162   *ataignant* The variant 'achaignant' in Q1W seems less good and may have arisen through a palaeographic c/t confusion. If this reading is correct then either the dancers spread out to encircle the king's procession or the procession encircled the dancers. In either case it would be difficult for Elyot to go 'par dedevant' in order to carry out her intricate manoevres with the eagle.

1164   *paraument* Not in Gf. but T-L. gives *'gleichmässig',* i.e. 'equally', 'similarly', 'symmetrically'. Perhaps 'balancing it well' or 'steadily' are possible renderings, a notion reinforced by the following four lines which relate how Emenidus and Marcien, one on each side, supported her in her task. The variant 'parement' in N2Q1 taken in the sense of 'parade', 'ceremony' is a possible alternative, i.e. 'in high ceremony'.

1167   *qui ... l'aloient adestrant* The plural verb no doubt refers to both Emenidus and Marcien although Yb have the singular 'aloit'. The meaning of 'right hand' had clearly faded from *adestrant* and the knights would lead Elyot, one on each side and each supporting an elbow. A miniature in P (181vo. col. II) shows Elyot and the knights in this position. There is a similar miniature in W.

1170-73   These four lines contain a *rondeau* or *roondet de carole* with a six-syllable line which has been written out in *pas alexandrins.* The music for the song is given in P only and has two lines of melody, 1 and 2, which are repeated as shown in the right-hand column below. The solo lines would be sung by Elyot and the refrain by the rest of the company (II 1174-75).

			Melody
Ensi va qui amours	A ⎫	Refrain	1
Demaine a son commant	B ⎭		2
A qui que soit dolours	a	Solo	1
Ensi va qui amours	A	Refrain	1
As mauvais est langours	a ⎫	Solo	1
Nos biens mais nonporquant	b ⎭		2
Ensi va qui amours	A ⎫	Refrain	1
Demaine a son commant	B ⎭		2

The song would be either unaccompanied or accompanied only by the less strident instruments cf. II 1169 'Les trompes font taisir'.

Fr. Gennrich published this song in 'Rondeaux, Virelais und Balladen', *Gesellschaft für romanische Literatur*, 43 (1921), p. 287. He was unable to discover who composed the music and it seems that P contains thé only known record of it.

The *cantilena rotunda* or *rotundellus* was popular in the north of France. Johannes de Grocheo, a lecturer at Paris, wrote *c.* 1300 of *rondeaux*: 'Et huius modo cantilena versus occidentem puta in Normannia solet decantari a puellis et juvenibus in festis et magnis conviviis ad eorum decorationem'. *(New Oxford History of Music,* edited by A. Hughes (Oxford, 1954), II. p. 245, footnote 1.).

It seems likely that Brisebare included only the refrain in the *Restor* i.e. line II 1170, for the writing-in of the whole song has resulted in a false rhyme in II 1171. In addition some manuscripts have a different version of the song so that the various redactors have presumably added the words they knew.

N2 and W are as P except that N2 has 'talent' for 'commant' in II 1170. In W staves are ruled for the musical notation but the notes have never been written in. In N2 the words of the song are underlined in red. The other versions are as follows:

P6   Ensi va qui amours
      Demaine a son commant
      A qui que soit dolours
      Ensi va qui amours
      A nous est grant douçours
      Solais et fieste grant
      Ensi va qui amours
      Demaine a son commant.

S1   Ensi va qui amours
      Demaine a son talent
      Et qui sont si sougis
      Et font tuit si comant
      En joie sont tout jours
      Baut, lié et joiant.

P6 has the same false rhyme as P in line II 1171 but S1 avoids it. S1 does not repeat the refrain and the rhyme sequence is eccentric so that it cannot be considered a true *rondeau.* Both these versions are more light-hearted than the rather melancholy song in P.

S6S7 omit II 1171 but otherwise have a version very similar to that of P. However they have 'maine' for 'demaine' in the refrain which gives a hypometric line. It is possible that this results from a recollection of another rondeau which has a seven syllable line and occurs in the *Lai d'Aristote* by Henri d'Andeli (early thirteenth century). It is sung to humiliate Aristotle by a lady who is riding round her garden on his back and is published by Gennrich (op. cit. p. 14):

> C'est la jus la fontaine
> Ainsi va qui amors maine
> Bele Doe i ghee laine ('washes wool')
> Ainsi va qui amors maine
> Et ainsi qui les maintient.

In spite of the similarity of the refrain this is clearly a different song altogether with a different metre but it may have been better known than the courtly version of P and may have influenced those scribes who wrote 'maine' for 'demaine'. These are, in addition to S6S7 already mentioned, those of the group N1N6OQU plus Q1. Apart from S6S7 they have only line II 1170 and omit the rest of the song.

The remaining two manuscripts N5S5 also have only the refrain of line II 1171 but they have 'demaine' as in P.

The meaning of the song is a little obscure and I suggest the following as a possible rendering of it: 'Thus goes he whom Love governs at his command. To whomsoever it may bring pain thus goes he whom Love etc. To ill-natured people lassitude of spirit is our good (i.e. the benefit we derive from Love), but nevertheless thus goes he whom Love governs at his command.'

1178   *ciex qui* Perhaps not 'the one who' but rather 'anyone who' so that all those who knew about the vows would be telling the others why Elyot was parading the eagle.

1179-81   These lines, omitted in the other mss, merely expand the content of II 1178 but they give a lively picture of those in the know busily informing the people around them and I see no reason to reject them.

1183a   This extra line in Ya is another indication that the archetype of the group misunderstood the idea of a live eagle crowned with gold. In II 1209-10 Elyot instructs Betis to keep the eagle alive and this group includes these lines but they probably did not associate the live eagle with the golden one that had been introduced into their version.

1185   *dariant* 'mocking', 'teasing'(?) This may be a northern form of *deriant* but it is not in Gf. or T-L. Other examples in P of unstressed e being represented by a are 'assaiant' I 672, 'assais' II 883, 'manace' II 801.

1189   [*Lyone*] Ydorus appears in II 1188 so this must be Lyone who would otherwise be omitted. The same mistake occurs in Ya.

1198   *alet ourdiant* or *alé tourdiant*(?) T-L. gives *'umherschweifen'* for *ordier* which perhaps better conveys the idea of Elyot's movements than *tordre*, present participle *tordant*.

1204   [*frere*] A necessary alteration. Betis was the son of Cassamus's brother Gadifer du Laris.

1221-23   'And blessed be our king whom I see so mindful that because of him ('en s'occoison') they (the gods) do not diminish any good; rather does he (Alexander) set it on its way to the right port when he sees it drifting.' Betis is presumably arguing from Alexander's speech (II 1075-87) made after he drew Cassamus's name from the lottery. Cassamus had clearly been chosen by the gods and Alexander was not going to deprive him of the honour. His claim to it was perhaps considered 'waucrant' (II 1223) and 'afoibli' (II 1224) simply because he was dead, but Alexander had declared, 'Je ne li retaurai tout ne soit il pas vis' (II 1077).

1225-26   [*fust*], [*Se*] These changes are necessary and are well supported. Betis is no doubt referring to the prize ('ceste hounor'), represented by the eagle that he was holding, which would not have existed ('dont il ne fust noiant') if the king had not suggested it, ('remise avant').

Laisse xxix

1234   Following this line YaYb have a passage describing the peacock. I give the version of S5.

	a	Des l'eure que fet l'ot le prist a conmencier
	b	Moult richement a faire de moult tres bon or mier
	c	Tout de fin or massis la queue par derier
	d	Semencie de pierres qui moult font a prisier
	e	Rubis et esmeraudes et dyamans moult chier
	f	Et les elles telles comme a eulz il affiert
	g	A esmaus ellevees moult firent a prisier
	h	Et les yex de la teste .ii. escarboucles chier
	i	Qui grant clarté jetoient au point de l'annuitier
=1234	j	Par deseure le dois fist .i. pillier drecier
	k	De fin argent massis et tel le fist forgier.

Variants
a   N5S1 D. ore, S6 Et d. lors, S7 De l'e.; N5S1 l'ont; S1 l. pris, N6OQU l'enprist, N1 l'anprint; N1 a mancier.
b   N1N6OQU f. d'un; N1N6OQ om. 'tres'; N1N6OQU b. ouvrier.
c   N1N6OQU m. a q.
d   N1N6OQU Et s'., N5 Semenciee, S6 Tout s., S7 Semences; N1 fet.
da   N1N6QU Qu'estoient (N6U Qui erent) precieuses de bon bericle cher. O Estoient precieuses diamés et phaphirs cher.
e   O om., N5 om. e, f, g.; Q Tubis; N6 esmerade; S7 et escarboucles c.; N6 et diapre m.
f   N1N6QU e. estoient t. c. il a., O l. helles estoient tout ainsi qu'il a.; S1 e. ytelles; S1 om. 'il'.
g   O om.
h   U E. es; N6Q escarboucle, N1 escarble.
i   OQ Que; N6 j. a p.; O d. la menuyt.
j   S1 P. desouz; OU d. les d.; N1 l. dos; S1 .i. biau p., OQU .i. palais, N1 .i. peles, N6 .i. paille; S7 Dessus le piler fist le paon atachier.
k   S7 Qui ert d. f. a. ytel l.; N1N6OQU m. itel l.

This description of the peacock was a necessary addition to a redaction of Part II only. N6S1 which have Part I do not need it but they presumably copied a Ya redaction for Part II. N2 lacks this passage as well as Part I.

1245   *gagier* Only in PP6W the word may convey the idea of keeping a pledge thus implying that Edea was trustworthy and kept her word. She was in fact about to pay her goldsmiths. In a similar passage at the end of Part I Edea is described as 'a qui n'ot qu'enseigner' (I 1476) and it will be noted that 'qu'enseignier' is a variant of 'que gagier' in II 1245, whereas in I 1476 P6 has 'que gaigier' for 'qu'enseignier'.

1252-53   Edea leaves the way open for them to return and therefore wishes them 'God be with you' but not 'goodbye'. See I 1473-84, note.

Laisse xxx

1254   W has 'Oues' for 'Lues' here and in II 325. The guide letter l in the margin with its very large loop probably misled the illuminator.

1265   *qui que miex* Only P has this form of the phrase, P6 having 'q. mius puet', the rest the more usual 'q. miex miex'. I have not found the phrase in P elsewhere but the meaning is clear.

1267   See II 998, note.

1271-82   Brisebare has mingled Christian and ancient rites in this office of the dead with its promise of salvation, sacrifices to the gods and the 'Te Deum laudamus'.

1272   *langhes* 'tongues'(?) An example of synecdoche perhaps, i.e. tongues to sing. It may also be a Picard form for *lances*. Gossen § 42 found the graphy gh+ e or i generally represented hard g in Picard, but in the same paragraph he also noted that *langhe* stood for *lanche*. In P g alone is often soft, e.g. 'juga' I 815,

251

'jugons' II 421. The variant 'lor gent' could be right but I prefer to leave P unchanged.

1274   *les cierges* This must be nominative plural following *'furent alumet'* and presumably *cierge* is feminine in P, cf. 'cierne' II 1112 which is also feminine. W is hypometric with 'li cierge'.

1275   *Philosophe poethe* I retain the singular although many of the mss have the plural. The philosopher poet may have been a kind of *vates*, a bard divinely inspired or a pagan priest. Le Roux de Lincy discusses them in *Le Livre des Proverbes français* (Paris, 1842), I, xxxii to xxxvi. The title *Philosophe* was apparently given in the Middle Ages to certain persons of antiquity. Guyot de Provins in his *Bible* (before 1250) talks of *'philosophes'* 'Qui furent ainz les chrestiens'. Collections of sayings attributed to them were used in the schools and exist in several manuscripts of the thirteenth and early fourteenth centuries.

1280-81   P is confused here and the variant 'a l'aigle atachier cantoient' makes sense. *portraioit* in 1281 perhaps means that the verse represented the *te deum* in the language of the singers. The variants 'porte avoit', 'se disoit' and 'avoit non' look like revisions.

1286   Emenidus is the subject of 'dona' and therefore the host at the dinner although Epheson was the stronghold of Gadifer, Betis and Fezonas.

1292   *estraignes et testus* Only PW have 'testus' although Q1 with 'crestus' gives some support. The variant 'menus' of the other mss seems to be a revision. One would expect both words to be either nouns or adjectives. If 'estraignes' is an adjective meaning 'marvellous' then 'testus' would presumably also be an adjective but I have found only meanings such as *'têtu'* or *'qui a une (grosse) tête'*. If both words are nouns then 'testus' may be the chub, which as a dish is said to be not very delectable, and the only gloss I have found for 'estraignes' is 'entrails' which would be even less delectable. Or is it perhaps a *hapax legomenon* formed on *testee*, 'whim' and meaning 'whimsical', 'fantastical'?

Laisse xxxi

1316-18   P is confused here. It appears that the scribe copied 'ses hommes' (II 1316) in error from the previous line. I therefore substitute Marcien from the other mss. I then replace Marciien (II 1317) with 'Betis et' and this completes the tally of five bridegrooms. Line II 1318 is lacking a verb such as *presenta*, I therefore substitute 'et si lor presenta' in II 1317 for 'nul n'en i oublia', an obvious line filler.

1324   This anticipates the plot of Antipater and Divinus Pater in *RAlix*, end of Br. III and beginning of Br. IV, see I 270-71, note. In P the *Siege of Defur*, the *Voeux, Restor* and *Voyage to Paradise* are all inserted into the *Roman* between Br. III and Br. IV.

1327-28   Only in P; they could be an editorial addition, but they sound genuine.

1330-31   Refers to the author of the *Roman.*

1333   *Celui* Jacques de Longuyon, the author of the *Voeux*. Brisebare seems not to have known his name. It occurs only in W at the end of the extended version of the *Voeux.*

1334-35   Brisebare is naturally referring to himself.

1340-43   This explicit occurs complete only in PP6 but the passage could be genuine and Brisebare was perhaps pleased to end as he had begun with a proverb.

INDEX OF PROPER NAMES

Abilant — Oriental city II 820.

Alemaigne — In the *RAlix* land acquired by Philip as part of Olimpias' dowry I 24.

Alier — Geographical location of unknown origin I 1100, 1397. II 8.
Var. Alir S1 I 1100.

Alixandre — *The Romance of Alexander* I 9.

Alixandre(s) — Alexander the Great I 12, 52, 92, 226, 233, 240, 253, 276, 278, 383, 387, 406, 423, 430, 434, 439, 447, 452, 454, 460, 489, 510, 650, 856, 857, 874, 885, 893, 981, 1010, 1017, 1037, 1046, 1067, 1094, 1100, 1143, 1145, 1182, 1191, 1354, 1397, 1405, 1429, 1452, 1460. II 8, 14, 306, 322, 326, 780, 1315, 1323, 1331.

Amazone — Country of the Amazons I 27.
Var. Mazone S1W; Anthioce P7

Antigonus — One of Alexander's twelve peers I 268. II 294, 323, 325, 700, 735, 742, 777, 779.
Var. Antigonne O II 700 ; Antiocus P7 I 268; Ainthiconus S1 I 268; Anticonus P7 II 294, 323, Q II 700, 735, N6 II 735, S1 II 742; Antiquonus N6 II 323, S1 II 325, 700, 735; Anchiconus N6 II 742; Antichonus P7 II 742; Enticonus Q II 742.

Anthiocon, -ton — Anthiocus, one of Alexander's twelve peers I 268, II 10.
Var. Anticonum P7 I 268 ; Ethiocon P6 I 268; Antigonon P6Q1 II 10;

Antipater — Alexander's liege man and murderer I 271.

Archade, -cade — Arcadia, given by Alexander to Emenidus I 239, 896, 903, 907, 1402. II 828
Var. Arcage S1 I 1402, N1N6OQ II 828.

archadonois — adj. Arcadian II 341.
Var. arcadiois P6P7W; acardonnois N2N6U; ahardonois QOS1; au cardonnois N1; de Cardonnois S7; acardiois Q1.

Aristé(s), Arr- — One of Alexander's twelve peers I 193, 209, 266, 1043, 1178, 1422. II 303, 316, 606, 739, 744, 749, 775, 1190.

Arrabe — Arabia I 155, 474.
Var. Arrable S1 I 155, 474.

arrabians — adj. Arabian I 1095.

arrabiois — adj. Arabian II 611.

Arrabis (obl. pl) — Arabs II 241.

Aspremont — Land of Blaton, Emenidus's father. Probably an imaginary country. I 341.

Aufricois — Africans I 24.

Aumarie — Vague oriental place perhaps owing its name to Almeria I 197, 477. II 59.
Var. Surie P7 I 477 ; Almarie P6 II 59 ; Amarie N6O II 59.

avalois — adj. Of Avalterre in the lower Rhineland (?) II 338. See note.
Var. avielois P6.

Aymes,-mon — See Emenidus.

Euuagille (Saint)	The Gospels I 324. Var. Ewangile P7; Euangilles P6.
Faus s'i fie	Nickname of the magician employed by Alexander I 489.
Femenie	The land of the Amazons I 28.
Ferrant	Emenidus's horse II 605, 789.
Fesonas, Fez-, Ph-; Fezone, Phezonus (all .n. and obl.); -ois (obl.)	Daughter of Gadifer du Laris, sister of Betis and young Gadifer I 194, 941, 1049, 1076, 1099, 1146, 1425, 1447. II 26, 54, 304, 501, 510, 535, 555, 607, 615, 751, 1025, 1033, 1186. Phezonus I 1171. II 1287. Phesonois I 49. Var. Phezon P6 I 1049; Fezonie Q1 II 26; Pheonnois W 149.
Phezonois (obl.)	People of Epheson II 602.
Festion(s)	Alexander's liege man and friend I 269, 1044. II 11, 426, 431, 920, 925. Var. Fesonus(?) N1 II 11; Phezom S1 II 11.
Filippon	See Phelippes.
Filotas,-tes	One of Alexander's twelve peers I 269. II 398, 430, 873. Filotes II 401, 882, 924. Var. Philote S5S6 II 882, OU II 924; Philotain N1 II 924.
Floridas (nom. & (obl.),-dant (obl.)	Brother of Dauris, taken by Alexander at the siege of Defur I 262, 1044, 1444. II 214, 229, 234, 256, 600, 649, 655, 675, 1021. Floridant II 1189.
Franchois	The French I 27.
Frize	Friesland I 1124. Var. Frisse S1.
Gadifer(s) du Laris	Egyptian prince, brother of Cassamus and father of young Gadifer, Betis and Fesonas I 35, 46, 47, 901, II 357.
Gadifer(s), -fier	Son of Gadifer du Laris and elder brother of Betis and Fesonas I 49, 157, 166, 208, 217, 228, 260, 291, 904 916, 949, 1016, 1027, 1042, 1125, 1126, 1148, 1174, 1345, 1412, II 155, 186, 558, 617, 621, 629, 1019, 1190, 1258, 1287, 1317, 1339. Gadifier II 585. Var. Gardifer S1 I 1042.
Gadres	Gaza, scene of the *Fuerre de Gadres* I 1133, 1137.
Gadrois	Men of Gadres I 34. II 595.
Galois (Terre des)	Wales I 1130. Var. Gabois S1.
Graciiens	A Chaldaean of Tyre, allied to Alexander and cousin of Sanson I 264, 1045.
Gregois, Grig-,Grej-	Greeks. Nom. pl. Gregois II 1089. Obl.pl. Grigois II 336, Grejois II 603.
gregois	adj. Greek I 50.
Gresce,-sse	Greece I 25, 268, 474. II 1096.
Griu,Grius, Grieu, Griex, Gris	Greeks. Nom.pl. Griu I 53. II 1141, 1176. Grieu I 1202. Gris I 1355. Obl.pl. Grius I 112, 114. II 439, 616, 1092. Griex I 36, 125, 1201. II 125, 192, 349, 640, 776, 833, 837, 1096. Gris II 220.
griue	adj.f. Greek II 742.
Hollande	Holland I 1124. Var. Hillande S1.
Inde	India I 258. Inde Major I 25, 1096. Var. Inde Menour P6 I 1096.
Indois	Indian(s) I 47, 1039, 1202, 1393.

Jhesus,-on,-u   Jesus I 326, 374, 1386.

Josaphat,   Valley near Jerusalem, scene of the *Fuerre de Gadres* I 30.
    Vaus de   Var. Josaphas P6N6Q1S1.

Jovis   Jove II 1078 (Apparently a different deity from Jupiter II 1079).

Jupiter   Jupiter I 125. II 1079.

Karles,-lon   See Charlemaine.

Kenelius   The Canaanites I 114.
    Var. Arabieus P6P7.

Laris   Land of Gadifer and Cassamus, in Egypt I 46.

Licanor(nom. &   One of Alexander's Twelve peers I 267. II 11, 462, 952, 956. Licanors II
    obl.),-ors   459.
    (nom.)   Var. Lincanor P6P7 throughout; Canor N1 1267.
[Lydone],   Niece or cousin of Emenidus and sister of Pirus de Monflor I [1131], [1174].
    [-nus]   Lydonus I [1148].
    Var. Lidoine N6Q1S1W I 1131, Q1 W I 1174; Lindoine P6 I 1131, 1174;
    Lindonus N6 I 1148; Lindeüs P6 I 1148.

Lÿone(s),   One of Alexander's twelve peers I 267, 1178, 1439. II 466, 474, 485, [610],
    Lÿon   [963], 969, 983, 987, [1189]. Lyon I 1042.
    Var. Lyoine N5 II 466, Q1 II 474, N2P6S1 WYb II 1189; Lioyne N6P6
    QU II 963, Lyoines Q1 II 466, N2N5 II 485; N2, WII 963; Liainne N1
    II 474; Liaine N1N6OS1 II 485; li leone P6 II 969; Loinne S7 II 466.
    Loinne S7 II 466.

Macedone   Macedonia I 380.
    Var. Macedoine Q1.

Macedonois   Macedonians I 114, 1355. II 1776.

macedonois,   adj. Macedonian I 12. II 347, 597.
    -nus, mach-   macedonus I 69, 1154.

Marciien(s),   Nephew of Clarus. King of Persia I 193; cousin of Porus I 1008.
    -tiien(s),   I 84, 193, 209, 260, 956, 958, 1041, 1107, 1109, 1115, 1122, 1147, 1346,
    -tïens   1409. II 10, 87, 97, 208, 215, 222, 225, 276, 495, 648, 651, 1088, 1101,
    -cïens,-tïon,   1103, 1142, 1146, 1166, 1317, 1337. Martïon I 290. Marcïus I 1173.
    -cïus,   Matiien II 61.
    Matiien   Var. Marcias P6 I 1008, 1115; Marci N1, Marssi Q II 10; Mercie N1N6OQ
    II 61; Mercien O, Merquien N6S1, Marquen N1 II 495; Marcoen S6 II 61;
    Marcille N6OQS1, Marceille N1U II 97; Marsillon N1N6QU II 1166.

Marcus,-chus   God of the Baudrain, Edea, Emenidus and Alexander, also of Marcien I 90,
    (nom. and   160, 777, 1062, 1160. II 956, 1256.
    obl.),   Var. Martus, P7 I 1160.
    Marcon(obl.)

Mars   Roman god of battles II 1079. Perhaps the same as the preceding.
    Var. Marcus P6; Marc S1.

Mazonie   A kingdom of Alexander's, perhaps the same as Amazone II 90.
    Var. Mahonnie N1.

Mazonois   Name given to Clarus of India I 67.
    Var. Maionois N6S1.

Mercurus,-is   The god Mercury II 1078. Mercuris II 1057.

Monflor   Fortress of Pirus, brother of Lydone I 270, 1136.

Nicolas   King of Caesarea, killed by Alexander I 23.
    Var. Nychalas Q1.

Nicole   Country or city of Nicolas I 23.

Nicholois   Followers of Nicolas I 23.

Norewegue	Norway I 1102. Var. Norvede N6S1; Norvege W; Morenge P7.
Olimpias, -pis	Olympias, mother of Alexander I 1100. Olimpis II 1076. Var. Olimpe N1 II 1076.
outremontans	adj. Of Outremons, the kingdom of Gos(?) II 339. Var. contremontans S1.
Perdicas	One of Alexander's twelve peers I 267, 1042, 1431, 1437. II 380, 390, 608, 840, 1191. Var. Perducas P6 throughout; Perdican N1 II 608.
Persant,-ans	Persian I 24. II 10, 1166. Var. Persie Q1 I 24.
Perssie,-sie, -sse	Persia I 193, 209, 474, II 61.
Persis	Persia or Persis(?) II 1088.
Phelippes,- -ippon, Phil-,Fil-, [Philippe]	Philip of Macedon, father of Alexander I [381], 422, 437, 453, 858. II 124, 1076. Var. Philippe W I 381.
Phezonas, Phes-	See Fesonas.
Pirus,Pieron	Pirus de Monflor, brother of Lydone and nephew of Emenidus I 270, 1136. Var. Pyrron Q1W I 270, Q1 I 1136; Pieres N6S1, Porrus P6 I 1136.
Poron(obl.)	King Porus of India I 258.
Porus(nom. & obl.)-on (obl.)	Porus, son of Clarus and nephew of the preceding I 259. Cousin or uncle of the Baudrain I 54. Cousin of Marcien, see I 1008. I 58, 77, 85, 90, 1003, 1007, 1039, 1047, 1054, 1066, 1093, 1099, 1145, 1170, 1342, 1393, 1400. II 1, 26, 335, 345, 353, 359, 602, 714, 785, 787, 810, 817, 1017, 1034, 1040, 1189, 1316.
Prians	Priam, king of Troy I 1074.
Rommains	The Romans I 27.
Rosenés	Roxana, wife of Alexander, daughter of the Caliph of Baghdad I 652, 667, 726, 770, 816. Var. Resones W I 652; Rosette P6 I 652, P6P7 I 667, P7 I 770; Rosenne W I 726, 770; Rosones P6 I 770.
Salemon	King Solomon, son of David I 319.
Sanson	Cousin of Graciien of Tyre and Alexander's liege man I [267], 1045.
Surie	Syria I 24. II 110.
Tholomer(s)	Ptolomy, one of the twelve peers and cousin of Danclins I 257. II 11, 258, 268, 272, 275, 293, 678, 680, 736, 741. Var. Tholome S7 II 268; Tholomes P7 II 258.
Tir,Tyr	Tyre in Phoenicia I 29, 1045.
Tudiele	Tudela in Spain II 402. Var. Trudelle N2; Rudelle S6S7; Turielle P6.
Venus,-is	The goddess Venus I 549, 943. II 974. Venis I 125. II 1079. la Cambre Venus. A room in the castle of Epheson I 76, 234, II 57, 1308.
Veus du Paon	Poem by Jacques de Longuyon I 280.
Ydorus,-rie	Lady at the court of Epheson, sister of Edea I 942, 1104, 1146, 1172, 1453. II 54, 410, 424, 613, 874, 894, 917, 1188. Ydorie I 194.
Yrlande	Ireland I 1097. Var. Illande N6S1.

GLOSSARY

aaisiés	p.p.adj. able II 399
abandoner	v.a. bestow on II 302; v.refl. *se va sor aus abandonnant* she keeps on going up to them II 1193.
abanois	s.m. amusements I 99.
abaubis	adj. out of countenance I 1333; tongue-tied II 273; astonished II 1071.
abusion	s.f.*sa grant a.* the great devastation he had suffered I 358.
acheree	p.p.adj. sharp I 574.
achier	s.m. steel I 505, II 904.
acoillir	v.a. *ot sa voie acoillie* had set out on his way I 461.
aconsiue	pr.subj.3 (aconsivir)v.a. imitate II 750.
adite	p.p.adj. thrown into confusion II 140.
adrechiés,-ie	p.p.adj. fine, noble II 74, 360; well-formed I 514.
aé	s.f. age I 384; life-time I 990.
aësius,assiue	adj. easy I 110, II 748.
afaire	s.m. importance I 551; dignity II 634.
affremer	v.a. reinforce II 7; v.n.(pr.p.afrumant) affirm II 821.
aherdre	v.a. (hunting term) to start up, or seize(?) I 696. See note.
ais	s.m. wooden boards II 904. See note.
alieue,aliue	pr.ind.3 (aloer) v.a. guide I 1273; employ II 743.
aloier	v.a. bind II 513; v.refl. commit oneself II 316.
alois	s.m. alloy(?), bonds(?) I 18. See note.
amblure	s.f. *va l'a.* (of horse) walks at an amble I 931.
amender	v.a. pardon I 313; v.n. atone for I 219,1021; *g'i sai a a.* I can improve on that II 170; s.m. merit I 1118.
amer	adj. painful II 769; s.m. arduous task I 1299.
amesnier	v. refl. become reconciled II 593.
amortis	p.p.adj. dejected I 1324; defeated I 1335; reduced to nothing II 1306.
amoustrer	v.refl. reveal one's mind II 431.
anguelet	s.m. corner II 1114.
aniel, obl.pl. aniaus	s.m. ring I 1447, 1454.
anïeus	adj. annoyed II 677.
anois,anui	s.m. harm I 38, 648, II 189; cause for anger II 605.
aouvrir	v.a. to open I 700.
apartenir	v.n. be appropriate I 1312, 1332.

aport	s.m. offerings I 1368, 1374.
aporter	v.a. allege I 2. See note.
aprochier	v.a. accuse I 811; attack II 356.
archons	s.m. saddle-bows II 945.
ariue,aroie	pr.ind.3(*areer*) v.refl. align oneself II 537, 778.
arrengier	v.refl. line up I 1390.
arriere	adv. *a.mis* rejected I 1319.
asorté	p.p.adj. paired off I 959, 977.
asprement	adv. energetically II 729.
assaier	v.a. to sound, i.e. question in an indirect manner I 672.
assais	s.m. *faire a.* to examine II 883.
assenee	adj. endowed with wisdom II 1099.
assener	v.a. to award II 31, 36, 154, 206, 257 and passim; to allot I 1160; v.n. succeed I 734.
assigier	v.a. obtain(?) II 569. See note.
assiue	see aësius.
atachier,ataquier	v.refl. commit oneself II 589; join II 1228; v.a. to attach II 1235, 1280.
ataindre	v.a. prove guilty I 1021; arrive at II 465; catch up with, meet II 1162.
atievissement	s.m. lukewarmness II 725. See note.
atirer	v.a. *mes raisons . . . n'atire* I do not dispose my arguments II 935.
atrais	s.m. lures II 889.
aveulissance	s.f. blindness I 1291.
avis	s.m. opinion II 236, 254, 334 and passim; *ce m'est avis* I think II 175; *sans avis* haphazard II 869, 1059; action of looking around I 1323; adv. almost I 692.
avisee,-és	adj. well-considered I 591, 952; showing forethought I 1080, 1189, II 898.
aviser	v.refl. think I 744, 822, 837, II 868, 873; v.a. inform I 295; catch sight of I 809; II 157 see note.
aviutissement	s.m. dishonour II 703.
awarder	v.a. await I 1187.
baivier	s.m. Bavarian(?) I 1438. See note.
beanche	s.f. aspiration I 1266.
beer	v.n. aspire I 554, II 1134.
biois	s.m. form of *biais*(?) *un cuir de b.* a skin stretched on the bias I 20.
braderie	s.f. junk-shop I 463.
bringier	v.n. to quarrel, intrigue(?) I 1459. See note.
brisier	v.a. make an end II 592; *prison brisie* interrupted imprisonment I 203. See note.
broie	s.f. hesitation I 175. See note.
buschier	v.n. to bang II 1237.
buske	s.f. *a la b.* by drawing straws (game of chance) II 444.
cachier	v.a. drive away I 1319; order out I 1429; pursue II 719.
caieler	v.a. to lead II 414.
calendre	s.f. lark II 286.

camion	s.m. small pin I 294. See note.
camp	s.m. field, *avoir c.ne voie* to have freedom of movement(?) I 165.
caplison	s.f. slaughter I 263.
cargier,kierkier	v.a. entrust to I 396, 500, 731; *de ses armes cargiés* weighed down by his arms II 384.
caroler	v.n. perform a chain-dance I 1142, 1380, II 48.
carpite	s.f. small carpet II 127.
castiier,-oier	v.a. instruct II 517; reprove II 85. See note.
cauchie	s.f. causeway I 496, 513.
cauchiés	p.p.adj. dressed (lit. with foot and leg gear on) II 1260.
caukains	s.m. heels II 475. See note.
cauper	v.a. cut off I 582.
caus	adj. hot II 332.
ceans	(on *cheoir*)*bien c.* lucky I 1227.
chers	s.m. venison I 189; stags I 703, 706.
chiere	s.f. face I 195, 501, 571, II 88, 749; treatment II 761. See note.
clos	adj. lame I 495.
cois,coie	adj. silent I 5, II 624; calm II 327, 496.
cois,kius	s.m. choice I 13, 106, II 330, 615.
coisir	v.a. see I 120, 933; notice I 492; choose II 658.
coloier	v.n. to look about one I 1323, II 286; be on the look-out I 765.
comprendre	v.a. invade II 1160.
confort	s.m. help II 217, 862, 1318.
conforter	v.a. support II 825, 927.
confusion	s.f. destruction I 337; embarrassment II 40.
contenanche	s.f. behaviour I 1293.
contregagier	v.a. redeem I 1407.
contremander	s.m. refusal to appear (legal term) II 162.
contremoiier	v.a. counterbalance II 574. See note.
contrepeser	v.a. set in the balance II 619.
con-,couvenant	s.m. condition I 657; circumstance II 813, 1214; pl. assent I 1090.
conversation	s.f. way of life I 336, II 20.
converser	v.n. to live I 1230, II 1217.
corliue	adj. *gens c.* messenger II 770.
cortement	adv. briefly(?), quickly(?) I 65. See note.
coupe	s.f. blame II 1288.
courre	v.n. run I 564, 703.
cousteus,-ant	adj. arduous II 656, 819.
creanter	v.a. agree to I 917; *le vous creant* I grant you that II 834.
cruchon	s.f. increase I 288. See note.
cuidier	s.m. expectation I 1262, II 516; thinking II 573; presumption II 588, 846, 1004.
dangier	s.m. resistance I 175, 1350, see notes; *a poi de d.* readily, i.e. with little

resistance II 554.

dariant	pr.p. of *derire* v.a. to mock, tease(?) II 1185. See note.
debrisier	v.a. and n. to break I 1285, 1415; v.refl. bow gracefully while walking II 1231.
decachier	v.a. pursue II 856.
decaïr	v.n. fall I 1271.
decauper	v.a. cut down II 158
declaration	s.f. exposition II 24; declarison I 308, not in the dictionaries, is probably a form of the same word.
defalance	s.f. weakness I 1270.
deffois	s.m. delay I 45, II 601.
defoukier	v.refl. go separate ways, i.e. disagree II 586.
desfroër	v.a. break II 186, 451.
delüer	v.a. confuse II 1004.
demanevet	adj. lost I 794.
denonchier	v.a. declare II 571, 1178.
descanlé	pp.adj. separate, not paired off I 958.
descendre	v.n. acquiesce II 278.
desclaver	v.a. detach II 443.
descogneüe	s.f. want of judgement II 1014.
deslaiier	v.refl. hold oneself back I 1460.
desliue	pr.ind.3 *desloër* v.a. displace II 744, 774.
desloiier,-liier	v.a. disclose II 73; set free II 531; v.refl. speak freely II 498. See note.
despechier	v.a. extricate(?), break into(?) I 507. See note.
despicier	v.a. (for *despecier*?) divide up I 1369.
despis	adj. contemptible I 1302.
despoillier	v.a. take off (garments) I 1466.
desraisnier,-resner	v.a. defend I 1426, II 607.
desrengier	s.m. breaking of ranks II 564. See note.
desriue	adj.(on *desreer*) impetuous II 749.
desrois	s.m. harm I 39; blameworthy action II 596.
destinee	s.f. intention I 530; *a boine d.* appropriately II 1094.
destrois	s.m. narrow passes, or perhaps 'straits' here as Tyre was an island fortress I 29. adj. in distress I 21, [434].
desvoiier	v.n. err (by playing a wrong note) I 1383; deviate II 560; go astray II 587; v.a. push aside II 538.
detirer	v.a. to urge(?) II 939. See note.
dois	s.m. dais I 57, II 1234.
dois,doit	s.m. finger I 55, 322.
droimons	s.m. swift ships I 17.
droit	s.m. right of admission I 198; *le d.de lor usage* user right I 232; *saus tous d.* saving all rights II 282; truth II 413.
droiture	s.f. justice II 1032.
duel	s.m. cause for vexation I 413.

effort	s.m. armed force II 1318.
embatement	s.m. (variant of *esbatement*) amusement II 715.
empains	p.p. impelled II 466.
empire	s.m. empire II 457; army II 943. See note.
enbuissie	p.p. hidden II 116.
encapeler	v.a. to crown II 424.
enconvenenchie	p.p. promised I 458.
encor	adv. *e.anuit* this very night I 477.
enfance	s.f. childish folly I 1273.
en-,esforchiement	adv. with all one's might I 441, 1380.
enforchier,-cier	v.a. dismiss from II 306; strengthen II 395.
enfourchiés	p.p. astride II 110.
enfruns	adj. morose I 173.
engignier	v.a. get the better of II 567.
engramis	adj. full of fury I 696, II 1049.
enkierkier	v.a. take on (a duty, task) I 869.
enquenus or enqueuus(?)	p.p. of *enquëoir*, Pic. form of *enchëoir* v.n. to fall, suffer the loss of I 875. See note.
enteser	v.a. strive for I 389; raise (a weapon) to strike I 566.
entierver	v.a. to question I 609.
entremetans	adj. bold I 1079.
entreprendans	adj. venturesome I 1219.
envois	s.m. natural endowment (lit. 'sent', sc. from God?) I 7.
escavie	adj. slender I 190.
escliche	s.f. flexible shoot cut from tree II 1116.
esclois	s.m. urine I 41.
escondit	s.m. refusal I 1315; excuse II 526.
esconse	s.f. a precious stone I 1238. See note.
escu	s.m. shield I 870, II 408, 566, 869; a semée of escutcheons II 972; protection I 97.
eskais	s.m. something small II 916. See note.
eskiever	v.a. avoid II 760.
esligier	v.a. obtain I 1408; redeem I 1411.
eslongier	v.a. thrust aside I 147; prolong II 1253.
esmovoir	v.a. rouse, set in motion I 862, II 1034.
esmüer	(p.p.Pic.esmue) v.n. to rise II 1030.
esnüer	v.a. expose II 1031.
espantee	adj. frightened I 536.
espargner	v.a. take notice of I 354.
espeus	s.m. bridegroom I 1184.
esprivier	s.m. sparrow-hawk I 688, 1049, II 1108.
essenter	v.a. select(?) I 1121.
essentir	v.a. exclude II 551. See note.

esseuté	prep. except II 357.
esta	s.m. decision, festivity, judicial hearing(?) II 879. See note.
estierkir	v.a. make taut, i.e. puff out I 699.
estrais,-te	p.p.adj. begotten II 884; worn out II 895.
estrois	s.m. press (of battle) I 36.
esvertuer	v.a. strengthen II 1027.
euereus	adj. fortunate II 673.
eul	see *oel*.
fachon,fai-	s.f. appearance I 1049; construction I 781, 1035; *remetre en f.* to repair I 316.
fais	s.m. burden II 389, 860, 888; difficult enterprise II 695.
fait,fais	s.m. exploit I 89, 249, 276, 306 and passim; *de fais* full of deeds, active I 1231.
falis	adj. cowardly II 242, 473.
faus	adj. mad I 653.
fer	s.m. chain I 56.
figaration	s.f. *par f.* metaphorically, through supposition(?) I 323. See note.
figureement	adv. symbolically II 685.
folie	s.f. lust I 528.
foliier	v.n. indulge in licentious behaviour I 553.
forchiue	adj. mighty II 763.
forcourre	v.a. overtake II 1303; v.n. go astray II 1043.
forgier	s.m. large box I 717. See note.
forjugier	v.a. judge unjustly II 397, 584.
formener	v.a. ill-treat II 968.
fortraire	v.a. take from fraudulently II 919.
fourfais	s.m. transgressions II 893.
fourmeüs	p.p.adj. incensed I 863.
frachon	s.f. faint-heartedness(?) II 22. See note.
furnir	v.a. accomplish I 151.
gagier	v.a. to refuse I 920; *en qui n'ot que g.* in whom was nothing but keeping pledges, i.e. who always kept her word(?) II 1245. See note.
garde	s.f. cause for fear, *nus g.ne s'en donna* no one worried about it I 613.
gieron	s.m. skirt of tunic I 755; *li sont au g.* (who) are round his skirts, i.e. close by him(?) I 1038.
gire	v.n. to lie II 945.
gliue	s.f. limed twig II 752.
gravais	s.m. hooks I 505.
habiter	v.n. approach(?) II 131. See note.
harnas	s.m. equipment, i.e. tools of the trade I 156.
hengance	s.f. perhaps a biform of *henguison* eagerness I 1278.
herluser	v.a. beguile I 801.
hinguer	v.n. turn towards I 554.
hiretee	p.p.adj. entitled by descent II 1137.

horneskiue	adj. implacably hostile II 766.
hourder	v.a. protect by encircling II 192.
huee	s.f. renown II 255; shout of acclaim II 1111.
huer	v.a. abuse II 1013.
huerie	s.f. shouting I 518.
hus.	s.m. shouts of acclaim II 1280.
iex,yex	see *oel*.
indignation	s.f. unworthiness I 328. See note.
infers	s.m. hell I 708.
ius	see *oel*.
joielet	s.m. gift II 1098.
joiiel, joiaus	s.m. gift I 670, 760, 838.
joint	adj. swift II 565
joli	adj. splendid I 136, 1301, 1322; merry I 988; ardent I 1325, II 909.
joquerie	s.f. *sans faire j.* without stopping I 490.
joquier	v.n. to remain II 765.
jouvent	s.m. youth II 405; gaiety II 713, 885.
jüer, giuer	v.a. play (a game) II 122, 247, 249, 771; v.refl. to jest II 1007.
jüeus	adj. playful, blithe(?) II 671. See note.
keute	s.f. elbow II 1168
kiegnon	s.m. little dog I 330.
kierka,-kie	see *cargier*.
kius	see *cois*.
langues	s.f. Pic. form of *lances* or *langues* II 1272. See note.
lapidier	s.m. jeweler I 795, 800.
las	s.m. snares I 1113; toils II 988.
leus	s.m. wolf I 495.
liue	s.f. time required to cover a league, i.e. a limited time II 772
liuer	v.refl. engage oneself II 765.
loiier	v.a. bind I 1446, II 387.
loiier	v.a. to hire II 391; s.m. reward I 1465, II 34, 291, 792.
lois	s.f. oaths I 63; law, custom II 333 (form with s for the rhyme?)
los	s.m. praise I 1313; honour I 1334, 1336; consent II 815, 960; lot II 1205.
lus	s.m. pike I 1180.
machue	s.f. fool's bauble II 1006.
malasiue	adj. bad II 761.
maleïchon	s.f. wickedness I 338.
manandie	s.f. wealth II 65.
maniier	v.a. administer I 1368.
marcais	s.m. marsh II 902.
maree	s.f. great quantity II 1153.
marés,-ois	s.m. marshland I 30, 32.

maris	s.m. the afflicted I 1294.
marit	s.m. husband II 1026.
mars	s.m. (*marc*) denomination of weight for gold and silver usually regarded as the equivalent of eight ounces Troy I 182, 1411.
martire	s.m. havoc II 948.
mauvés,-vais	s.m. coward I 274; wicked man II 419, 967; ill-natured people II 1172.
melliue	adj. warrior-like II 747.
menchoinne	s.f. untruth II 429.
mendier	v.n. be lacking in II 63.
mesdire	v. n. speak wrong of someone II 96 s.m. poor speaking II 937.
mestrais	s.m. trickery II 913.
miel,mius	s.m. honey I 119, II 1145.
migne	s.f. clothes-moth I 1470.
mignier	v.a. Pic.form of *mangier* I 1469.
mirer	v.refl. see one's reflection II 179, 936. See notes.
mistere	s.m. inherent power I 1249.
miue	Pic.form of possessive adj.fem. mine II 773.
mius	adj.used substantivally: the best I 345. sm see *miel*.
mouvans	adj. lively II 746.
mouvoir	v.n. depart I 421, 927; *meüs, mus* affected by emotion I 878, 1307.
muanche	s.f. inconstancy I 1287.
müer	v.a. to change I 336, II 287; *ne puet m.ne rie* he cannot help laughing II 87.
murmurant	adj. quarrelsome II 1212.
murmure	s.f. quarrel I 1242.
nareus,-ois	adj. foolhardy(?) I 61, II 660. See notes.
nation	s.f. lineage I 357; homeland I 788.
nature	s.f. inherent quality I 373, II 157; human qualities(?) II 1057.
nervee	adj. reinforced with sinews, hence, strong I 575.
nes	s.m. nose I 641. pp.adj. born II 324. adv. not even, *n.que* no more than II 562.
niier,noiier	v.a. deny II 539, 590.
nois	s.f. nut II 617. s.m. denial(?) Used in phrase *ce n'est nus n.* there's no denying it(?) I 22, II 335, 606. See I 22, note.
nonchier	v.a. denounce I 51, 802; proclaim II 202, 448, 982; relate II 1179.
nonne	s.f. none I 484.
norois	adj. superb; Norwegian(?) I 62, 930.
norrir	v.n. grow I 148, 350; v.a. bring up I 498; feed I 1273.
nuement	adv. unconditionally II 551, 1039.
nus,nue	adj. devoid of II 1270; completely revealed II 1040.
o,oie	adv. yes I 1055; yes(I have) I 755.
occoison	s.f. circumstance I 277; cause I 1237, 1296, II 715, 1304; *en s'o.* because of it/him I 287, II 1222; *par s'o.* through its means II 4.
och	pret. 1 of *avoir* I 832; pr.ind.1 of *oïr* II 169.

oel,eul,iex,yex, ius — s.m. eye I 1012, 1084, 1281, 1288, 1290, II 1194, 1300; *a l'oel* with one's own eyes II 289; *uns iex* glances I 1113.

oelletés — p.p.adj. decorated with eyes I 135.

oes — s.m. use I 1159.

oevre — s.f. deed I 598, II 581, 1036; work of art I 951, 953; workmanship I 1206, 1480; matter II 72; feat II 815.

ondoier — v.n. brim over II 499.

onnie — adj. equal II 69.

ordenance — s.f. *par droit o.* disposed in regular order I 1281.

ordener — v.a. to marshall II 563; v.n. decree I 622; *ordenee* predestined I 539.

orgene — s.m. or f. portative organ I 1377.

orgoel, orguius — s.m. arrogance I 117, II 1270.

ostius — s.m. tools I 116.

ostoir — s.m. hawk I 365.

oumage — s.m. power to give as a fief I 240.

ourdier — v.n. step hither and thither II 1198. See note.

ourdir — v.a. devise II 66.

outrecuidier — v.refl. be over presumptuous I 653; s.m. overweening pride I 1470; outrecuidans I 1080, outrecuidiés II 390 arrogant.

ouvrer — v.a. to carry out I 953, II 210; embroider I 954; s.m. fashioning I 725; v.n. to act II 575, 579, 582.

paiage — s.m. toll for entry to a place I 244.

pailleus — s.m. cob-walls II 663.

paire — s.f. his equal II 639. Also pr.subj.3 of *pareir* v.n. to appear II 649.

palus — s.m. or f. marsh, or palissade(?) II 970. See note.

par — Used for *part* in *de p.moi* for my part II 396 and *de p.le roi* by order of the king II 616.

parant — adj. of high quality II 1182.

paraument — adv. steadily, well-balanced(?) II 1164. See note.

partie — s.f. share I 478; *en p.* aside(?), some of them(?) II 56. See note. *sans faire p.* without jousting, i.e. without fighting over it I 201.

pas — s.m. *en cel meismes p.* forthwith I 1103.

pechiet — s.m. error II 321, 324; wrong II 584.

peniu,-ius,-iue — adj. arduous I 61, II 505, 759, 763.

peril,pril,prius — s.m. perilous situation, danger I 558, 561, 593, II 161, 852.

peser — v.a. esteem II 203 ; *ce poise nous* we regret this I 418.

pietiier — v.n. step to and fro (in a dance) I 1378, II 1174; tap lightly with the foot (to attract attention?) II 89.

piteus — adj. compassionate II 672; *a p.* pitiably II 666.

pius,piue — adj. compassionate I 118, II 776.

plenier — adj. violent I 1406, II 570; princely II 1240; *mes p.* main courses II 1293 ; *court p.* plenary court I 1165.

plet,plais — s.m. discussion I 739, II 882; judicial assembly II 238.

plois — s.m. episode, incident I 9, 65; *villains p.* unseemly behaviour II 614.

plus — *sans p.* without more ado(?) II 879, 911, 977. See II 879, note.

pois	s.m. measure I 6, II 339; *outre mon/son p.* against my/his will II 328, 600.
porfaisant	adj. successful II 1197.
porporter	v.a. offer here and there II 99.
portraire	v.a. depict I 707, II 908; represent I 1337, II 1281. See note.
porveüs	p.p.adj. prepared, ready I 1161, 1I 1290: provided with II 983 ;endowed with II 987.
presse	s.f. thick of battle II 900.
preu	s.m. and adj. brave(man) I 52, 107, 1218 and passim. profit II 36, 657; advantage II 688; adv. very II 363.
preuc,pruec	prep. *aler p.* to go to fetch I 225, 903.
pril,prius	see *peril.*
puchier	Pic.form of *puisier* v.a. draw from II 379.
puirier	v.a. to offer II 99.
pule	s.m. people I 320, 444.
pumier	s.m. apple-wood I 370, 1439.
quasser	v.a. break open I 402; suppress I 1139.
quatis	p.p. hidden I 691, II 1054; stealthy I 494.
ques	Pic. form of *queles* I 287.
quis	s.m. the dead(?) I 1217. See note.
racointier	s.m. settlement of accounts II 1249. Cf. *recouvrier* I 1483.
rais	s.m. ray(?), full measure(?) = *res II* 907.
raliance	s.f. rallying-point I 1212.
ramenee	s.f. vigour, impetus II 1121.
rapieler	v.a. revoke, retract I 1129, II 413.
rebrois, rebois	s.m. resistance I 42; a *rebois*(for *a rebors*?) the wrong way, or contrary to your wishes(?) II 625.
recoper	v.a. diminish, cut short II 1105.
recouvrier	s.m. payment I 1483. Cf. *racointier.*
refaire	v.a. do in one's turn I 170; recreate II 635;
refais	adj. refreshed II 915.
refus	s.m. refusal II 1258 *avoec le r.* among the rejected II 963.
rekierkier	Pic.form of *rechargier* v.a. impose as a duty II 102.
relais	s.m. *sans r.* unremittingly II 905.
remanant	s.m. remainder. Here, a woman who has belonged to another man I 651; *de r.* unceasingly II 814.
remirement	s.m. respectful contemplation II 688.
renvier	v.a. give back II 114.
repetation	s.f. symbolic repetition or reproduction(?) II 6. See note.
repetement	s.m. The same as *repetation*(?) II 730.
reprouver	v.a. recommend to one's attention I 560; discredit II 1124.
reprou-,-provier	s.m. shameful conduct II 594; reproach II 1233; ill-fame I 1471.
requerre	v.a. seek II 550; attack II 111, 141.
rescreer	v.a. to delight I 715.

rescrier	v.a. entertain I 1143, see note, I 1182.
resner	v.n. hold sway II 232; reign II 485.
resprendre	v.a. excite II 289.
retraire	v.refl. go away/back I 788 ;v.a. relate II 892.
retrais	s.m. refuge II 906.
reuber	v.a. carry off I 522.
reuberes	s.m. robber I 607.
reue	s.f. wheel *est en se r.mis* has spread his tail I 1321.
reveler	v.n. rejoice II 405.
reverser	v.a. exchange I 587.
reviaus	s.m. joy II 150; entertainments II 885.
riés	s.m. pasture II 383.
riulle	s.f. row II 69; method, order II 1059.
riules	s.m. rule(principle) II 532, 908, 918; (that which is normally the case) II 373.
roi-,royauté	s.f. kingdom I 380, II 457.
rois	s.f. net I 693.
rois	adj. steadfast I 43.
rouegniés	adj. tonsured(?) II 358. See note.
saingler	s.m. boar I 704.
sains	s.m. saints II 485; adj. whole I 317; prep. = sans I 284.
samblant	s.m. thought I 677; opinion II 573, 779, 815.
sanna	Pic.form of *saigna* I 643.
saus	s.m. leaps *si grans s.li donra* it will give such great leaps for him, i.e. it will gallop so hard II 858; *faire les s.menus* trot (of horse) II 1262.
semenchie	p.p.adj. besprinkled, refers here to an heraldic semée II 972.
servage	s.m. bond-service I 896.
siecle	s.m. earthly life II 253.
simulation	s.f. intent to deceive I 307, II 31.
singuler	adj. unique, exceptional II 181, 355.
siuc	pr. ind.l of *sivir* II 648.
siue	pr.subj.3 of *sivir* II 769; adj. his II 775.
soffrans	adj. long-suffering I 1243.
soffrir	v.n. wait patiently I 1244, II 328, 1119.
sort,sortis, sortir	II 1055, 1058, 1067. See note to II 1055.
sos	s.m. fool II 1006.
sos-,sousprendre	v.a. lure away II 292 ;take unawares II 447,695; take away by sleight of hand II 1065.
souffissance	s.f. contentment I 1263.
souffissant	adj. important II 803, 950.
souples	adj. down-cast, or suppliant(?) I 448. See note.
sous-,sos-, souspechon	s.m. doubt I 300; fear I 780, 1060.

sousplanter	s.m. wrongful deprivation II 44.
sousploier	v.refl. submit I 176; v.n. bow II 831, 1187;
soustais	adj. rhyme variant of *soutis* clever(?) II 898.
sus	adv. thereon I 576, 1389; *en s.* away II 1300; *s.et j.* up and down I 876; *je li met s.* I lay the obligation on him I 1343.
tais	s.m. muddy places II 900.
tes	Pic.form of *tels* such I 1090, II 1041.
testus	.s.m. chub(?) or adj. fantastical (on *testee* a whim)? II 1292. See note.
toueillier	v.a. shake, mix up II 1065.
tour	s.m. circumstance I 429 ,skill, trick I 503; means I 1111.
trache	s.f. track II 894.
trais	s.m. traces II 894.
travers	s.m. transit toll I 244.
treculer	v.n. = *reculer*(?) fall back II 473. See note.
trestorné	s.m. hindrance I 394.
triiés	p.p.adj. tested, well-tried II 355.
triue	s.f. respite II 762.
tronchon	s.m. spear-shaft I 370.
trubers	s.m. dishonest and foolish advocate(?) II 878. See note.
turiele	s.f. small tower II 425.
uiseuse	s.f. idleness I 3.
vains	adj. weak II 474.
vair	adj. bright I 527, II 898 ;miniver II 645.
varier	v.n. vacillate II 122, 782.
vautie	adj. curved II 108.
vergondans	s.m. timid person I 1237.
veulie	s.f. perhaps=*folie*, or a rhyme variant on *veul* s.m. wish I 516.
vienois	adj. of Vienne(?) II 599.
vierilliés	adj. bolted II 386. See note.
viuté	s.f. dishonour I 413.
voirre	s.m. glass I 18.
voirrois	adj. of glass I 16.
vois	s.f. authority I 14, II 616; word, speech II 75, 325.
vuidier	v.a. *pied v.* to abandon I 1427.
waucrant	adj. adrift II 1223.
wihot	s.m. cuckold II 132.

APPENDIX

Proverbs in the *Restor*

Brisebare uses proverbs to introduce and to close his work and also to support his arguments. It is not surprising therefore that they are more numerous in Part II, the debate. I give the line references in the *Restor* followed by a corresponding proverb as recorded in the collections of Morawski and Le Roux de Lincy. These are in three lists: List A contains proverbs expressing the same idea as Brisebare's, B those which are called to mind by Brisebare's words, although not necessarily enunciated by him as proverbs, and C those expressing a different view from Brisebare's.

A

I 3	Multam enim malitiam docuit otiositas. Ecclus. 33. 29. This seems to be the origin of the proverb which Le Roux de Lincy, II, 353, quotes from the *Restor*.
I 5	Qui le bien set dire le doit. Le Roux de Lincy II, 300.
I 143	Ce que l'ung ne scet l'autre scet. Mor. *Prov.*, 328. See note.
I 180	Endementres que li geus est biaus le fait bon laissier. Mor. *Prov.* 646.
I 184	Bien est li avoirs emploiez/Qui pour les bons est desploiez. Mor. *Diz*, Quatrains Apocryphes CLXIX.
I 624	On fait bien mal pour pis abattre. Le Roux de Lincy, II, 273.
I 1262, II 690	De peu de chose vient grand' chose. Le Roux de Lincy, II, 213.
II 104	Qui mielz set mieulz doit dire. Mor. *Prov.*, 1997.
II 173	N'est si fort ne truisse son per. Mor. *Prov.*, 1380.
II 201	L'on ne doit ja home loer devant luy. Mor. *Prov.*, 1484.
II 289-90	Je ne croy pas ce que je oy dire maiz ce que je voy. Mor. *Prov.*, 982.
II 309	C'avient en un jour qui n'avient en cent ans. Mor. *Prov.*, 315.
II 332-33	Le milieu est le meilleur. Vertu gist au milieu. Le Roux de Lincy, II, 248, 333. See note.
II 420	Biautés ne vaut rien sans bonté. Le Roux de Lincy, II, 178.
II 453	An adverty en vaut deux. Le Roux de Lincy, II, 330.
II 538	Qui boute l'ung il frappe l'autre. Le Roux de Lincy, II, 293.
II 853	Aise vait a pié qui son cheval maine en destre. Mor. *Prov.*, 41.

II 1123	La fin loe l'oevre. Mor. *Prov.*, 1002.
II 1216	Amy pour aultre veille. Mor. *Prov.*, 81.
II 1219	Les bontez ne sunt pas boinnes qui vont toutes d'une part. Mor. *Prov.* 1049.
II 1342	Du bien le bien doit chacun dire. Le Roux de Lincy, II, 216.

The following have a proverbial ring but are not recorded in the collections:

I 4	Also in *Le Romans de Baudouin de Sebourc* quoted by T-L. under *enfouois*. It recalls two parables, the Talents (Matt. 25. 14-30) and hiding one's light under a bushel (Marc. 4. 21-25).

I 316-17, I 965, II 34, II 122-23 (see note), II 1006 (see note).

B

I 1251-52	Tel samblent estre bon par dehors qui sont mauvais par dedens. Mor. *Prov.*, 2323.
II 17-18 and II 809-10	Le bon commencement atrait la bonne fin. Mor. *Prov.*, 1058. See II 809-10, note.
II 247-50	Teus cuide gaignier qui pert. Mor. *Prov.* 2347. See note.
II 258	Louange d'amy n'a nul credit, ny mepris d'un ennemy. Le Roux de Lincy, II, 257.
II 300-03	Mieus vaut amis en voie que argent ne or mier. Mor. *Prov.*, 1241.
II 421-22	A l'aigneler verra on lesquelles sont prains. Le Roux de Lincy, I, 37. See note.
II 553	Amor veint tute rien. Mor. Prov., 89.
II 792	A tel sergant tel loiier. Mor. Prov., 166.

C

The following examples in which Brisebare expresses a different view from the folk-wisdom of the proverbs are all discussed in the notes on the text: I 142, I 303-04, II 36-37, II 705-08, II 724-27.

BIBLIOGRAPHY

Dictionaries

Du Cange	*Glossarium mediae et infimae latinitatis* (Paris, 1840-50, Niort, 1883-87), 10 vols.
Godefroy, F.	*Dictionnaire de l'ancienne langue française* (Paris, 1880-1902), 10 vols.
Grandsaignes d'Hauterive	*Dictionnaire d'ancien français* (Paris, 1947)
La Curne de Sainte-Palaye	*Dictionnaire de l'ancien langage français* (Paris 1875-81), 10 vols.
Littré, E.	*Dictionnaire de la langue française* (Paris, 1873-74), 4 vols.
Murray, J.A.H.	*A new English Dictionary* (Oxford, 1888-1928), 10 vols.
Souter, A.	*Glossary of Later Latin to 600 A.D.* (Oxford, 1949)
Tobler, A. and E. Lommatsch	*Altfranzösisches Wörterbuch* (Berlin 1925-
Wartburg, W. von	*Französisches Etymologisches Wörterbuch* (Bonn and Basel, 1928-68), 20 vols.

Linguistic Works

Foulet, L.	*Petite syntaxe de l'ancien français* (Paris, 1930)
Gossen, C.T.	*Petite grammaire de l'ancien picard* (Paris, 1951)
Nyrop, K.R.	*Grammaire historique de la langue français* (Copenhagen, 1899-1930), 6 vols.
Pope, M.K.	*From Latin to Modern French* (Manchester, 1952)

Miscellaneous Works referred to

Barron, W.R.J.	'Luf-daungere' in *Medieval Miscellany presented to Eugene Vinaver* (Manchester, 1965), pp.1-18.
Bordier, H.L. and L. Brièle	*Les archives hospitalières de Paris* (Paris, 1877)
Gary, G.	*The Mediaeval Alexander* ed. D.J.A. Ross, (Cambridge, 1956)
Donkin, Enid	'Le plagiat de Jean Brisebare' *Romania*, 86 (Paris, 1965), 395-404.
Faral, E.	1. *Les arts poétiques du XIIe. et du XIIIe. siècle* (Paris, 1924)
	2. *Les jongleurs en France au moyen âge* (Paris, 1910)
Gennrich, F. (ed.)	*Rondeaux, Virelais und Balladen aus dem Ende des XII., dem XIII. u. dem ersten Drittel des XIV. Jahrhunderts mit*

	den überlieferten Melodien, Gesellschaft für romanische Literatur 43 (Dresden, 1921)
Guy, H.	*Adan de le Hale* (Paris, 1898)
Hughes, A. (ed.)	*New Oxford History of Music* Vol. II (Oxford, 1954)
Latini, Brunetto	*Li Livres dou tresor* ed. F.J. Carmody, University of California publications in modern philology, 22 (California, 1948)
Le Roux de Lincy	*Le Livre des proverbes français et recherches historiques* (Paris, 1842), 2 vols.
Lewis. C.S.	*The Allegory of Love* (Oxford, 1936)
Lote, G.	*Histoire du vers français* (Paris, 1949-55), 3 vols.
Migne, J.-P.	*Patrologia Latina* Vol. 171, (Paris 1844-90), 221 vols.
Morawski, J.	1. *Les diz et proverbes des sages* (Paris, 1924)
	2. *Proverbes français antérieurs au XVe. siècle* (Paris, 1925)
Pannier, L.	*Les lapidaires français du moyen âge des XIIe., XIIIe. et XIVe. siècles* (Paris, 1882)
Paris, G.	1. *Deux rédactions du roman des Sept Sages de Rome* (Paris, 1876)
	2. Review: *'Trois poèmes de Jean Brisebarre le Court, de Douai* ed. A. Salmon, Mâcon, 1896', *Romania* 26 (Paris, 1896), 104-05
Richardson, H.G. and G.O. Sayles	*Fleta II*, Selden Society 72 (London, 1955)
Ross, D.J.A.	1. *Alexander Historiatus* (London, 1963)
	2. 'A new manuscript of the Latin *Fuerre de Gadres* and the text of *Roman d'Alixandre* Branch II', *Journal of the Warburg and Courtauld Institutes*, 22 (1959), 211-253
	3. 'Nectanebus in his palace', *Journal of the Warburg and Courtauld Institutes*, 15 (1952), 67-87
	4. Review : *'Jean le Court dit Brisebare. Le Restor du Paon* edited by R.J. Carey', *Medium Aevum*, 37, no.1 (1968), 80-84
Salmon, A.	'Trois poèmes de Jean Brisebarre le Court, de Douai', *Mélanges de Philologie romane dédiés à Carl Wahlund* (Mâcon, 1896), pp. 213-224
Smith, W.G.	*Oxford Dictionary of English Proverbs*, 2nd ed. revised by Sir Paul Harvey (Oxford, 1966)
Spalinger, E.	*Absterben von IACERE im Galloromanischen* (Berne, 1955)
Studer, P and Evans, J.	*Anglo-Norman Lapidaries* (Paris, 1924)
Thomas, A.	*Histoire littéraire de la France* Vol. 36 (Paris, 1927)
Tobler, A.	*Vom französischen Versbau*, (Leipzig, 1903)
Webb, J. (ed.)	*A roll of the household expenses of Richard de Swinfield bishop of Hereford during part of the years 1289 and 1290*, Camden Society Old Series, 59 and 62 (London, 1854 and 1855)
Welsford, E.	*The Fool* (New York, 1961)

274

Literary Texts Cited

Atticum   Epistolae ad T. Pomponium Cicero, edited by D.R. Shackleton Bailey
(Cambridge, 1966), V, Book XI: 12, 4.
Biblia Sacra Vulgatae Editionis Desclée Lefebvre (Tournai, 1885)
Buik of Alexander John Barbour, edited by R.L.G. Ritchie. See *Voeux du Paon*
Dialogus de Oratoribus Tacitus, edited by Sir W. Petersen (London, 1946)
Erec et Enide Chrestien de Troyes, edited by Mario Roques (Paris, 1955)
Karel ende Elegast edited by R. Roemans and H. van Asche, 4th ed. (Amsterdam,
1959)
Karl und Elegast Der Mitteldeutsche edited by J. Quint (Bonn, 1927)
Karlamagnus Saga ok Kappa hans edited by C.R. Unger (Christiania, 1859)
Le Parfait du Paon Jehan de le Mote, edited by V. Hands, unpublished thesis for
Ph.D., London University, 1957
Another edition by R.J. Carey, Studies in Language and
Literature 118, University of North Carolina, 1972
La Prise de Defur and Le Voyage d'Alexandre au Paradis Terrestre edited by L.P.G.
Peckham and M.S. La Du, Elliott Monographs 35 (Princeton,
1935)
Renaud de Montauban edited by H. Michelant (Stuttgart, 1862)
Restor du Paon Jean Brisebare, edited by R.J. Carey under the title *Jean le Court
dit Brisebare: Le Restor du Paon* (Geneva, 1966)
A fragment corresponding to lines I 250-905 of the *Restor*
was published by G. Bonnier under the title *Une histoire de
brigands, Otia Merseiana*, 3 (1903), 23-45
Roman d'Alixandre Published under the general title *The Medieval French 'Roman
d'Alexandre'* at Princeton in the Elliott Monograph series as
follows:
I   *Text of the Arsenal and Venice Versions* M. S. La Du,
E. M. 36, 1937
II   *Version of Alexandre de Paris: Text* E. C. Armstrong,
D. L. Buffum, B. Edwards and L. F. H. Lowe, E.M.
37, 1937
III   *Version of Alexandre de Paris: Variants and Notes to
Branch I* A. Foulet, E. M. 38, 1942
IV   *Le Roman du Fuerre de Gadres. Texte d'Eustache*
E. C. Armstrong and A. Foulet, E. M. 39, 1942
V   *Version of Alexandre de Paris. Variants and Notes to
Branch II* F. B. Agard, E. M. 40, 1942
VI   *Version of Alexandre de Paris. Introduction and Notes
to Branch III* A. Foulet, E. M. 42, 1976
VII   *Version of Alexandre de Paris. Variants and Notes to
Branch IV* A. Foulet and B. Edwards, E. M. 41, 1955
Tristran   The Romance of Beroul, edited by A. Ewert (Oxford, 1953)
Trubert Douin de Lavesne, edited by Jakob Ulrich, *Gesellschaft für Romanische
Literatur*, 4, (Dresden, 1904)
Trubert et d'Antrongnart La Farce de Me. Eustache Deschamps, *Oevres Complètes*
Vol. VII, edited by G. Raynaud (Paris, 1891), 155-74
Le Vengement Alixandre Gui de Cambrai, edited by B. Edwards, E.M. 23 (Prince-
ton, 1928)

La Venjance Alixandre Jehan le Nevelon, edited by E.B. Ham, E.M. 27
(Princeton, 1931)

Les Voeux de Paon Jacques de Longuyon, edited by R.L.G. Ritchie in *The Buik of Alexander:* John Barbour, Scottish Text Society, New Series, 4 vols. (Edinburgh and London, 1921-29). Volume I contains the *Fuerre de Gadres,* Volume II part one of the *Voeux* and volumes III and IV part two of the *Voeux,* all based on ms.W

An edition by Brother Camillus Casey entitled '*Les Voeux du Paon* by Jacques de Longuyon: an edition of the mss of the P redaction' (unpublished Ph.D. thesis, University of Columbia, 1956) is available from University Microfilms, Ann Arbor, Michigan, Pubn. No. 17,046

The Wife of Bath's Prologue and Tale The Complete Works of Geoffrey Chaucer, edited by F.N. Robinson, 2nd ed., (Oxford, 1957), pp.76-88.